CHANGED FOREVER
Volume 1

SUNY series, Native Traces

Jace Weaver and Scott Richard Lyons, editors

Changed Forever

Volume I

American Indian Boarding-School Literature

Arnold Krupat

On the cover: Apache students on their arrival at Carlisle Indian School in 1886 and three years after, both photographs taken by John N. Choate. Courtesy of the National Anthropological Archives.

Published by State University of New York Press, Albany

© 2018 State University of New York

For information, contact State University of New York Press, Albany, NY
www.sunypress.edu

Library of Congress Cataloging-in-Publication Data

Names: Krupat, Arnold, author.
Title: Changed forever : American Indian boarding school literature. Volume
    I / Arnold Krupat. Other titles: American Indian boarding school literature
Description: Albany, NY : State University of New York Press, [2018] |
    Series: SUNY series, Native traces | Includes bibliographical references and
    index.
Identifiers: LCCN 2017022009 (print) | LCCN 2018005523 (ebook) |
    ISBN 9781438469164 (e-book) | ISBN 9781438469157 (hardcover : alk.
    paper) | ISBN 9781438469140 (paperback : alk. paper)
Subjects: LCSH: Off-reservation boarding schools—United States—
    Biography. | Boarding school students—United States—Biography.
    | Indian students—United States—Biography. | Hopi Indians—
    Biography. | Navajo Indians—Biography. | Apache Indians—Biography. |
    Autobiographies—Indian authors.
Classification: LCC E97.5 (ebook) | LCC E97.5.K78 2018 (print) | DDC
    371.829/97—dc23
LC record available at https://lccn.loc.gov/2017022009

10 9 8 7 6 5 4 3 2 1

For Julian Rice

"*What has become of the thousands of Indian voices who spoke the breath of boarding-school life?*"

—K. Tsianina Lomawaima

"*We still know relatively little about how Indian school children themselves saw things.*"

—Michael Coleman

"*Boarding-school narratives have a significant place in the American Indian literary tradition.*"

—Amelia Katanski

CONTENTS

ILLUSTRATIONS

ACKNOWLEDGMENTS

MANY PEOPLE HAVE ENCOURAGED AND HELPED ME THROUGHOUT MY WORK on this book, and it is a pleasure to thank them. Professors Scott Lyons and Jace Weaver, editors of the Native Traces Series at the SUNY Press, supported this project from its earliest stages and offered useful suggestions until the latest stages, and I thank them both. Scott invited me to participate in two seminars at the University of Michigan for which I am grateful, and my gratitude extends to his students and colleagues for their responses. Dr. Peter Whiteley of the American Museum of Natural History read early drafts of a couple of the Hopi sections of this book, corrected many errors large and small, and generously offered the benefits of his enormous erudition on all things Hopi. Occasional email exchanges with Professor Paul John Eakin and Dr. Julian Rice were consistently illuminating and encouraging, and I thank both of them. Geoff Danisher of the Sarah Lawrence College Library obtained a great many interlibrary-loan materials for me. I would, in this as in former projects, have been lost without his help. Mika Kennedy of the University of Michigan provided valuable information regarding illustrations, and Jean Hofheimer Bennett enhanced my meager computer skills. Two anonymous readers for the SUNY Press offered useful suggestions for revision for which I am grateful, and I am grateful, too, for the work of my editor, Amanda Lanne-Camilli. An earlier version of the study of Edmund Nequatewa's *Born a Chief* appeared in the journal, *a/b:autobiography studies*, and I thank the editors for permission to reprint.

INTRODUCTION

FROM THE FIRST MOMENTS THEY SET FOOT ON THESE SHORES, THE European invader-settlers of America confronted an "Indian problem." This consisted of the simple fact that Indians occupied lands the newcomers wanted for themselves. To be sure, this was not the case for the Spanish invaders of the Southeast and Southwest in the mid-sixteenth century, whose intent for the most part was to find treasure and to convert and missionize the tribal peoples they encountered. But in the Northeast, the English, from the early seventeenth century, and then the Americans, as they made their way across the continent, came to understand that, broadly speaking, America's Indian problem permitted of only two solutions, extermination or education. Extermination was costly, sometimes dangerous, and, too, it also seemed increasingly *wrong*.

In time, it began to appear wiser, as the title of Robert Trennert's "Introduction" to a study of the Phoenix Indian School put the matter, for policymakers to proceed according to the assumption that "The Sword Will Give Way to the Spelling Book" (1988, 3), thus offering, again to cite Trennert, an "Alternative to Extinction" (1975). Educating Native peoples—teaching them to speak, read, and write English, to convert to one or another version of Christianity, and to accept an individualism destructive of communal tribalism, ethnocide rather than genocide—was a strategy that might more efficiently free up Native landholdings and transform the American Indian into an Indian-American, inhabiting, if not quite melted into, the broad pot of the American mainstream.

In a fine 1969 study, Brewton Berry remarked that so far as the choice between "coercion" and "persuasion" (23) was concerned, "Formal education has been regarded as the most effective means of bringing about assimilation" (22). Robert Trennert writes that when the Phoenix Indian School was founded in 1891, it was "for the specific purpose of preparing Native American children for assimilation.... to remove Indian youngsters from their traditional environment, obliterate their cultural heritage, and replace that... with the values of white middle-class America." Complicating the

matter, he adds, was the fact that "the definition of assimilation was repeatedly revised between 1890 and 1930" (1988, xi). Further complicating the
matter well into the 1960s was the fact that "white middle-class America"
was generally not willing to accommodate persons of color regardless of
whether they shared its values or not.

In the *Annual Report of the Commissioner of Indian Affairs* for 1890, the
"Rules for Indian Schools" stated clearly that the government, in "organizing
this system of schools," intended for them to "be preparatory and temporary;
that eventually they will become unnecessary, and a full and free entrance
be obtained for Indians into the public school system of the country. It is
to this end," the "Rules" continued, that "all officers and employees of the
Indian school service should work" (in Bremner, vol. ii, 1,354). Although
a "full and free entrance" to all public schools in the United States was legally
available to Native Americans—as it was not to African Americans—on
those occasions when they availed themselves of the right to attend, they
were not especially welcomed or well served. Indeed, as Wilbert Ahern has
written, "The local public schools to which 53% of Indian children went
in 1925, were even less responsive to Indian communities than the BIA
schools" (1996, 88).

In her study of the St. Joseph's boarding school in Kashena, Wisconsin,
Sarah Shillinger affirms that "Assimilation was an important, if not a more
important goal than education to the supporters of the boarding-school
movement" (95). Her conclusion, however, is that the boarding schools'
"results were closer to an integration of both cultural systems [Indian and
white] than . . . to assimilation into Euro-American society" (115). This
seems to me accurate, and I will quote other writers on the subject who state
roughly similar conclusions in different ways. But the degree to which any
single individual could successfully integrate "both cultural systems" varied
a good deal. As we will see, some boarding-school students had little trouble
"living in two worlds," as the metaphor is often given—a metaphor that is
usually unexamined and one I will interrogate a bit further on. Others found
the two "cultural systems," Native and settler, to be in conflict in greater
or lesser degree, so that "bridging the gap"—another largely unquestioned
metaphor—was painful and difficult. Further complicating the matter is
the fact that one of the "cultural systems" was backed by the overwhelming
power of the colonial state.

Around the turn of the twentieth century, as Adams wrote, "Those responsible for the formulation of Indian policy were sure of one thing, the Indian could not continue to exist as an Indian." Indian people, therefore, "had to choose ... between civilization or extinction" (1995b, 28), and to become civilized, Indians needed to be educated. "By the early 1890s," according to Wilbert Ahern, "Thomas Jefferson Morgan, commissioner of Indian affairs, had designed the means to extinguish American Indian cultures by going after the children, pulling them from their homes, and indoctrinating them with 'American civilization'" (1996, 88). To cite Adams once more, "The boarding school, whether on or off the reservation, was the institutional manifestation of the government's determination to completely restructure the Indians' minds and personalities" (1995a, 97), to change them forever.

Although the aim may have been to provide the boarding-school students with—I cite the title of Adams's important book—an "education *for* extinction," (my emphasis) cultural extinction or ethnocide, that phrase does not adequately describe the reality of what went on at many of the schools. For example, as Joel Pfister wrote in his study of Richard Henry Pratt and his Carlisle Indian School—see just below—"Education for extinction does not appear to convey comprehensively what Carlisle was set up to do either during or after Pratt's rule" (2004, 94) from 1879 to 1904, and until its closing in 1918. Further, although federal education policies for Indians assuredly were designed, as K. Tsianina Lomawaima and Teresa McCarty state, "to erase and replace" Indian languages, cultures, and religions, eventually, they note, the schools did allow for "teaching Native arts and technologies," and also engaged in the "production of bilingual primers, for use in bilingual classrooms in the 1940s" (xxii). This is only to say that any approximately accurate account of the Indian schools, as I will have occasion to say many times, cannot be based on reductive generalizations.

જીજી

In the seventeenth century, the Reverend John Elliot had founded fourteen towns of "praying Indians" in the Massachusetts Bay Colony to separate his Indian converts from tribal members who had refused Christianity, providing lessons in "Latin and Greek for those he hoped would become teachers and missionaries" (Berry, 12). Indeed, two Wampanoag men, Caleb

Cheashahteamuck and Joel Hiacoomes both attended Harvard in the 1660s, and the College of William and Mary had about twenty Indian students by 1712. But we have no record of what any of these students thought of the educational experiences they underwent. In the eighteenth century, the Reverend Eleazar Wheelock established the Moors Charity School for Indians to train Native people to missionize among their brethren, and some of the letters written by "Wheelock's Indians," along with diaries and other writings by the Reverend Samson Occom and Joseph Johnson, Wheelock's star pupils, have been preserved. In the early nineteenth century, we find a number of mission schools among the Cherokees, and, after the Civil War, under President Grant's "peace policy," several Protestant denominations were permitted by the government to operate reservation schools. But it was only in 1879 that the bright light and pre-eminent model of the boarding-school movement, the off-reservation Carlisle Indian Industrial School (see figure 1), was founded by Captain Richard Henry Pratt.

Pratt was a complicated man and much has been written about him. The nearly hagiographic biography by Elaine Goodale Eastman named him "the Red Man's Moses" (1935), a description first applied to him, she noted, in a 1900 commencement address given by Indian Commissioner Merrill Gates (219). More recently, there is Ward Churchill's revisionist

1 Captain Richard Pratt with Navajos from New Mexico newly arrived at Carlisle Indian School. Photograph by John N. Choate. Courtesy of the National Anthropological Archives, NAA INV 02292400.

account of Pratt as founder of a genocidal policy (2004). Pratt also wrote his own story.[1] Dr. Martin Luther King is said to have remarked that the white South loves individual black people but hates the race, while it is the reverse in the North. Pratt would seem to have had the South's view of Indians. He got along well with a great many individual Indians, at first some of the Kiowa, Cheyenne, and Apache prisoners of war he oversaw at Fort Marion, Florida, where in the 1870s he was in charge, and over the years he showed affection for a considerable number of his Indian students, many of whom clearly reciprocated that affection.

But Pratt detested Indian cultures, so far as he knew them. His often-quoted motto was, "Kill the Indian and save the man!"[2] For all the violent determination of the slogan, in hindsight, it was a vain and naive oxymoron. Students took half a day of very basic instruction, mostly in literacy and simple arithmetic, along with half a day of manual instruction for the young men, and some form of "domestic science" for the women.[3] Thus, although the celebrated Carlisle football team, with its star, Jim Thorpe, was, for the most part, made up of college-age men, and Carlisle competed against—and sometimes beat—some of the best American college teams, Carlisle was in no way a college, offering no more than an eighth-grade education. (Many of the boarding schools did not go past the sixth grade.) Moreover, it was "Not until 1889," ten years after Carlisle's founding, that Pratt awarded "any diplomas, and even then only 14 students graduated out of the 178 leaving for home!" (Adams 1995a, 290).

Pratt had been a soldier and he ran the school like a military academy; students marched, saluted, drilled, wore uniforms, and were punished for disciplinary infractions.[4] This regimentation was a major part of the program to transform Native people, and it was not until the 1930s that the reformist commissioner of Indian affairs, John Collier, "ended the military system for all Indian boarding schools" (Gram, xiv). Along with basic instruction in gardening or farming, in handling cows, horses, and pigs, Carlisle's industrial programs instructed Indian boys in carpentry, blacksmithing, and harness-making—even as it was becoming clear that automobiles would soon replace the horse—and provided instruction in tinsmithing at a time when mass-produced metal products were coming widely into use even on the reservations.[5] Worse yet, as the Indian school superintendent Leo Crane wrote as late as 1917, once the Indian student returned home, "He was in the ludicrous position of being a blacksmith where there were no forges, a carpenter where lumber was scarce, a tailor where flour-sacks were used for clothes, a shoemaker where moccasins were worn, and a painter where there was nothing to paint" (in Adams 1995b, 42).

The training young Indian women received at Carlisle, as at the other boarding schools, consisted in such things as how to set a table and how to use stoves, irons, and washing machines—all of which were sure to be absent or rare once they returned home. And, too, once these students returned home having slept in what Polingaysi Qoyawayma's chronicler, Vada Carlson, called a "real bed" (*No Turning Back*, 59), and once they had indeed worn tailored clothing (the shoes, not so much), had sat on chairs and eaten at tables made by skilled carpenters, how would they respond to the living conditions they found on their return home?

The general unavailability on the reservations of the white man's cultural innovations, or indeed, the disapproval of them by relatives and friends when they were available, often led former students to "return to the blanket," in the disparaging phrase of the boarding-school proponents. This referred to the fact that, in greater or lesser degree, some returned students reverted to speaking their Native languages rather than English, abandoned the Christianity on which the schools insisted, and even actively opposed government efforts to "civilize" Native peoples by means of boarding-school education—an education they had themselves experienced. Indeed, as Wilbert Ahern concluded, returned students often became "defenders of community interests" (in Reyhner and Eder, 202) rather than proponents of boarding-school education. In the great majority of cases, the situation of returned students was often a complex and difficult matter.

Important to Pratt's program at Carlisle was what he called the "placing-out," or, simply, the "outing" system, something he had begun to develop at his prior posting at Hampton Institute under General Samuel Armstrong.[6] Pratt's outing program at Carlisle sent a number of young Indian men and women to live for a time with local white families, to whom they provided labor or domestic service in return for their board and some very modest pay. This was not compulsory; students had to request or agree to an outing assignment, although it is not clear that they understood they had a choice in the matter. Most of the families to which Native students were "outed" were farm families. The theory was to expand these young people's experience of white ways beyond the school grounds and to make them appreciate the jingle of a couple of quarters in their trouser or apron pockets. In practice, for the most part, the outing system provided cheap labor for the host families with lessons primarily in subservience for the guest Indians. Although it soon became clear that the outing system was above all "a way for white families to obtain cheap servants" (Reyhner and Eder, 139) and that it "did more than any other [boarding-school practice] to reinforce the concept of the suitability of Indians for menial labor," (Child, 81–82), it nonetheless was practiced by those off-reservation boarding schools whose location made it feasible.

By 1902, there were twenty-five off-reservation boarding schools (see figure 2). These were meant to be, as David Adams (among others) has termed them with reference to Erving Goffman, "total institutions" (1995a, 101) engaged in the surveillance and control of their students, who were treated in some measure as inmates.[7] Nonetheless, as we know both theoretically and from a great many empirical studies, even "total institutions" rarely achieve total control; for the boarding schools, the documentation is overwhelming that students in a variety of ways escaped the totality. Still, there is no question that, as John Fire/Lame Deer said, for many of the students, "The boarding schools leave a scar. We enter them confused and bewildered and we leave them the same way" (35). And, too, a fair number did not survive, as the school cemeteries make all too clear. This must be fully acknowledged, for all that it is not the whole story.

2 The boys' dormitory at the Albuquerque Indian School sometime between 1880 and 1890. Photograph by Ben Wittick. Courtesy of Palace of the Governors Photo Archives, Santa Fe, NM, #086869.

Pratt was dismissed from Carlisle in 1904 and the school closed for good in 1918, near the end of the World War I. Ten years later, the 1928 government survey, *The Problem of*

Indian Administration, generally known as the Meriam Report, was intensely critical of the boarding schools, and under John Collier's tenure as commissioner of Indian affairs (1933–45) some of them were closed while others were substantially altered. For example, under Collier's direction, the military system was abandoned, religious observances for students were no longer compulsory, and the curriculum, as I have noted, might include elements of Native culture and history and, on occasion, Native languages; some of the boarding schools became public high schools. Looking back some forty years, Brewton Berry would conclude that "the feeling is general" that the schools had failed "to meet the Indians' needs," and had failed to prepare the students "to participate effectively in American society" (41). A great many subsequent studies have confirmed Berry's assessment. Worse yet, having failed to prepare the students "to participate effectively in American society," the schools in many cases, as I have noted, succeeded in making it difficult for returned students "to participate effectively" in the Native societies to which they returned.

It was not until the 1990s, however, that some of the darkest aspects of the boarding schools would be brought to light. That the schools often provided inadequate nutrition, hygiene, and health care had been clear for some time and abundantly evidenced in the Meriam Report. But even that extremely critical 1928 account did not plumb the depths of some of the extreme corporal punishment meted out, nor did it look into the matter of sexual abuse at the schools. I won't attempt to offer anything like whatever might be the "whole story," but simply present a few examples. Others will appear as we consider individual narratives.

As noted, Pratt ran Carlisle as a military institution, and, to his credit, from the first insisted that if his students were to behave like soldiers, both young men and young women "should have the same food allowance as soldiers" (Reyner and Eder, 137). The degree to which this was carried out at Carlisle is unclear—and at any rate, as we will see further, even when food was adequate or approximately so, a good deal of it was strange and unpalatable to Indian students. A great many letters and interviews (e.g., in Child, Cobb, T. Lomawaima, Shillinger, Vuckovic) and a great many boarding-school autobiographers (cited in Coleman, B. Johnson, and in this volume) testified to the fact that students were often hungry.[8] In that students frequently shared bath water and towels, there were many cases of trachoma, tuberculosis, measles, pneumonia, and influenza, some of which proved fatal.[9] The availability of chamber pots, privies, and, later, flush toilets varied considerably. Berenice Levchuk has poignantly described her late-twentieth-century visit to the cemetery at the Carlisle Barracks, then home to the U.S. Army War College and Military History Institute, and Jacqueline Fear-Segal has written about it as well (231ff). Myriam Vuckovic has given an account of the cemetery at Haskell (21, 33), and Clifford Trafzer and Jean Keller have published on the cemetery at the Sherman Indian School in Riverside, California. At the time I am writing (2016), members of the Native American Boarding School Healing Coalition—more on the Coalition below—have just been to Washington to discuss the return of the remains of thirteen children buried in the Carlisle cemetery.

In his 1989 autobiography of more than 250 pages, *Indian School Days*, Basil Johnston mentioned no molestation or sexual abuse at St. Peter Clavier's Indian Residential School in Canada, which he attended. It was only in 2007, in an extraordinarily moving foreword to Sam McKegney's *Magic Weapons*, that Johnston told of having suffered these things. Tomson Highway's autobiographical novel, *Kiss of the Fur Queen*, is very explicit about the sexual abuse of young boys by teaching brothers at the Catholic Residential School in Canada that he and his brother attended. Berenice Levchuk's recollections of her own boarding-school experiences in the United States include the memory of "a nine-year old girl [who] was raped in her dormitory bed during the night" and "a certain male teacher who stalked and molested girls" (184). Sarah Shillinger writes that "In July, 1993, former students at the Mount Pleasant Indian School in Mount Pleasant, Michigan, publicly accused teaching sisters at the school of sexually molesting them while they were students" (8). She also states that there was no evidence of such abuse at the St. Joseph's school, the subject of her study. Clyde Ellis found that two female teachers at the Rainy Mountain School left after admitting to having kept the company of male students at night (110). They claimed that the nature of their relationship was strictly friendship. Johnston also noted that older boys sexually abused younger boys. How common forced sexual relations between students and staff at the boarding schools might have been is almost surely beyond exact determination.

Sarah Shillinger discovered from her interviews with former boarding-school students that "A theme that runs through the students' remembrances is physical abuse" (14). That this occurred widely and well past the middle of the twentieth century is indisputable. It is a matter that will appear frequently in the narratives I will examine, and it is worth considering here. In his 1903 attacks on Keam's Canyon School[10] superintendent Charles Burton, Charles Lummis wrote that "'corporal punishment' and 'cruel or degrading measures' are absolutely prohibited by the rules and regulations of the Indian Service" (18). He makes reference to the 1900 edition of the Indian Service rules in which he quotes Rule 249 as stating that "In no case shall the school employees resort to corporal punishment" (75). I haven't been able to find the Indian Service Rules for the year Lummis cites. But in the 1890 "Rules for Indian Schools," Rule 53 reads: "Corporal punishment must be resorted to only in cases of grave violations of rules, and in no instances shall any person inflict it except under the direction of the superintendent, to whom all serious questions of discipline must be referred"[11] (in Bremner, vol. ii, 1,355–56). The same language appears in the 1892 "Rules for Indian Schools." Nonetheless, Burton used a rawhide whip at Keam's Canyon School, and Herman Kampmeier, principal teacher at the Orayvi Day School, "a man of violent and uncontrolled temper," according to Lummis, "had been guilty of repeated and intolerable brutalities" (76), as was his successor, John Ballenger. (Kampmeier and Ballenger were indeed dismissed from the Indian Service as unfit.) Margaret Jacobs's recent research cites an affidavit submitted in 1903 by Laura Dandridge, "a matron at Keams Canyon [School] between 1899 and 1902," alleging that two teachers there "'each carried a club . . . when marching Hopi children to the school-room.'" For any misstep or trivial offense, Dandridge testified, "'the offending boy or girl in the company would receive a whack from the club'" (in Jacobs 2004, 40). Ms. Dandridge also reported a third teacher engaging in brutal practices. It seems doubtful that the 1890 and 1892 Rules were so radically changed as to permit these things some ten years later. But clearly the rules regulating corporal punishment were flouted on a daily basis, and I will cite the testimony of many students who endured it.[12]

Trennert says of the Phoenix Indian School that although it had a "jail as early as 1893, . . . and although the demand for strict discipline was constant, there was little overt brutality" (1989, 598). But he also observes that this changed "around 1917, soon after John B. Brown became superintendent" (1989, 599). Many schools used their jails as a substitute for corporal punishment, but "overt brutality" was nonetheless sufficiently widespread to have been noted in the Meriam Report. Shortly after its publication in 1928,

Indian Commissioner Burke "issued circular #2526 . . . forbidding corporal punishment altogether at Indian schools" (Trennert 1989, 603). This was not, however, before the Phoenix School's disciplinarian, Jacob Duran, along with his assistants, had been accused of "periodically whipping, beating, and abusing Indian students" (Trennert 1989, 605), accusations that had been made against many disciplinarians and teachers employed by the Indian Service.

Anna Moore Shaw, a To'hono Akimel (Pima) woman who attended the Phoenix Indian School from 1908 to 1918, describes a matron who "was strict and frequently used her strap" (134) on the girls, in particular "strapping" them while they "were still on [their] hands and knees" (136) scrubbing floors. Scott Riney remarks the violent abuse of students by several women teachers at the Rapid City Indian School (147–48), some of whom frequently administered "a very good strapping" (160). As Riney observed, there were clearly instances where the "line between acceptable [physical] punishment and outright abuse was . . . crossed" (160), even by the standards of the period. Other boarding-school autobiographers have reported acts of sadism (e.g., Fred Kabotie: Mr. Buchanan's "razor strop—it was leather, with a metal hook on the end" [12]) and demented savagery (e.g., Peter Razor's knee cap was broken by a female teacher wielding a hammer (62).

Although government rules prescribed a careful regulation of corporal punishment, there is no question that it frequently occurred. Bad enough in itself, its infliction on Indian children, it has frequently been written, was made worse by the fact that Native American parents did not physically discipline their children. Not to mitigate the undeniable brutality of some of the punishments meted out at the schools, it must be said that this latter statement is an idealized overgeneralization. Although I have found no study surveying the disciplinary practices of any given tribal nation during any particular time period, my almost forty years of reading do indeed confirm that Native parents for the most part did *not* use physical means to discipline unruly children.[13] Nonetheless, Hopi parents might call in a mother's brother, the family authority figure, to give a child a swat, or they might pour water over them if they misbehaved.[14] There are also anecdotal accounts of Native parents briefly holding an unruly child close to a smoky fire that would sting the eyes and nose.

It is also the case that the ritual whipping administered to Hopi boys and girls during their initiation into the Katsina society was partly to make them mind their elders. This is something that might be alluded to by the *katsinam* (kachinas) themselves or by the godfathers of the initiates. Occasionally, as would be the case with Don Talayesva (see below), a child might receive more than the usual four strokes because they were "naughty." Edward Curtis, at Walpi on First Mesa in 1921, reported one of the whipper *katsinam* saying, "We have come to whip the children that are bad" (170), and Julian Steward's later (1927) account of an initiation, also on First Mesa, includes a *katsina* saying that part of the rationale for the whipping is that the children "do not obey their mothers and fathers"; thus the *katsinam* "are going to help you old people so that they will mind you" (64). Nonetheless, unlike what occurred at the boarding schools, there was indeed no systematic corporal punishment meted out to unruly children by adults in Native nations.

In regard to some of the more brutal boarding-school practices, Andrea Smith, in a chapter called "Boarding School Abuses and the Case for Reparations," claims that on occasion or often the boarding schools went so far as to "violate […] a number of human rights legal standards" (42). She has made the case for government reparations to boarding-school students and their descendants. A lengthy article in the *New York Times* for June 3, 2015, had the headline, "Report Details 'Cultural Genocide' at Schools for Aboriginal Canadians" (A7). "That is the conclusion reached by the country's Truth and Reconciliation Commission after six years of extensive research" (A7). It notes for the Canadian schools, more often under religious auspices than was the case in the United States, many of the same abuses I have described in the American schools, along with some far worse. The article states that although the "Canadian Government apologized to former students in a landmark 2008 court settlement," Justice Murray Sinclair, "an Ojibwa" who led the Commission, made the important point that more than an apology was needed, the Commission having found that "all too often, policies and programs are still based on faded notions of assimilation" (A7).

It is nonetheless important to acknowledge that the history of the Indian boarding schools is not exclusively a narrative of victimization and enforced suffering. Nor is it the case that all tribal nations were opposed to the schools. Clyde Ellis writes that when the Kiowas signed the Medicine Lodge Treaty of 1867, they asked that it include the requirement for the government to build schools for their children. By the end of the 1880s, when no schools had yet been built, the "tribe petitioned for a school of their own" (54). The Rainy Mountain School finally opened in 1893; when plans to close it were announced after World War I, the tribe again protested. The Kiowas' petition to the Indian Office begins, "To discontinue the institution would mean the removal of the very backbone of the tribe" (in Ellis, 183). As we will see below, the 1868 Treaty between the Navajo nation and the U.S. government included the government's promise to build schools and the Navajos' promise to send children between the ages of six and sixteen.

The Bloomfield Academy for Chickasaw Females, with "a curriculum equal to a junior college education" (Cobb 94) and controlled by the Chickasaw tribe (with federal government involvement) from 1865 to 1907, was not a typical boarding school, but it was one valued by its students and their families. This is true as well of the Cherokee Seminary for young women run by the Cherokee Nation and the federal government. Its curriculum was modeled on that of Mount Holyoke College, and it trained its young, affluent students "to become homemakers and teachers" (Mihesuah, 98) on a model "nearly identical to Victorian society's white women" (Mihesuah, 3). No Cherokee language, culture, or history was taught at the Seminary. K. Tsianina Lomawaima, acutely critical of the boarding schools, nonetheless found that in the twentieth century, "In the Indian Territory, education was by and large a desired commodity" (36).

In an 1885–86 petition, Hopis from First and Second Mesa wrote to Washington that

"We are also greatly concerned for our children. We pray that they may follow in their fathers' footsteps and grow up—good of heart and pure of breath. Yet we can see that things are changing around us.... We would like our children to learn the Americans' tongue and their ways of work. We pray you to assist in causing a school to be opened in our country, and we will gladly send our children to the on-reservation boarding school that opened at Keam's Canyon in 1887."[15]

There were no signatories from Orayvi on Third Mesa, where, as we will see further, opposition to the Americans was much stronger. Of course these thoughtful and concerned Native parents could not know whether it would indeed be possible for their children to "follow in their fathers' footsteps" once they had learned "the Americans' tongue and their ways of work," nor could they know the conditions their children would encounter at the schools. There is no question that even those parents who favored the schools wanted their children, as Brenda Child has written, to be "involved in the life of the family and the tribal community" (47). There is also no question that the boarding schools systematically attempted to thwart such continued involvement.

Some of the Hopi children who attended Keam's Canyon School went on to the Sherman Institute in Riverside, California, and, as Diana Meyers Bahr has observed, "Even alumni whose memories are depressing or ambivalently fond and regretful retain an undeniable attachment to the school" (2014, 3). Miriam Vuckovic noted that Haskell's "indigenous students' reactions ranged from complete rejection to enthusiasm, and most felt ambivalent about their boarding school years" (2). It was also the case, as Ellis noted of the Rainy Mountain School—and this is true for other of the boarding schools—that "In times of family crisis," the school "became a child provider of last resort for Indian parents" (37). These few examples—there are many others—"compel [...] us," as he concludes, "to recognize the full complexity of the history of the Indian boarding schools."[16]

Although a great many students found the schools destructive, more than a few, as we have seen and will see further, did not. John Gram, for example, has written that in spite of Pratt's well-known slogan, "no Indian was killed at AIS [the Albuquerque Indian School]. Indeed, one may conclude that AIS was a happy and nurturing place. This is the pervading sentiment of its alumni" (xvi). If that is an exaggeration on the sunny side, it is nonetheless based on wide consultation with alumni. As Superintendent Cora Dunn of the Rainy Mountain School said in 1899, " 'Our purpose is to change them forever' " (in Ellis, xiii), and I have adapted her words as the title for this book. But, as Clyde Ellis, who quoted Dunn, states, "The seeming incongruity of going to boarding school and staying Indian was not so much a conundrum as a fact of life" (196). That the schools in one degree or another "changed" their Indian students is indisputable. But "killing the Indian" by the process of cultural erasure and replacement was not easy to do—at least not if the man or the woman were actually to survive.

Just as many Native parents wanted schooling for their children, so, too, many students were grateful to the boarding schools for the education they received, appreciating what they had learned about Euro-American ways of living, while feeling their Indianness intensified, either in terms of an enhanced awareness of their national identities (Hopi, Chickasaw, Kiowa, Navajo, Apache, and so on), of the possibilities of pan-Indian identities,[17] or both. As Amanda Cobb put it, "What U.S. policymakers had not counted upon was the ability of Indian nations to adopt white ways without losing their own tribal identities"[18] (32). I think her statement is supported by the evidence, but it must once more be noted that this "ability" was more pronounced on the part of some individuals than others, and, too, that all those who "adopted white ways" while also retaining their "tribal identities," integrating the two, did so very differently from one another.

In her interviews with former Chilocco Indian School students, K. Tsianina Lomawaima asked them about a Miss McCormick, a particularly harsh head matron. What she found was that "The range and disparity within student responses to this one individual indicate the difficulty of making generalizations about key facets of boarding-school life" (48). This is the conclusion one would draw as well from Kim Brumley's recent compilation of the recollections of twenty-nine Chilocco students from the class of 1933 to the class of 1980. Similarly, Scott Lyons has written that his Ojibwe grandfather, Aubrey Lyons, whipped at the Flandreau School in South Dakota, ran away four times, while his Dakota wife, Leona, loved Flandreau (23). Anna Moore Shaw, whom I quoted earlier, wrote that "we can never go back to the old ways of life. The white man and his cities surround us—we must embrace those of his ways which are good while keeping our pride in being Indian . . . a blending of the two" (7–8). A great many of the Navajo people who provided accounts of their lives for Broderick Johnson's book voiced similar opinions (e.g., Mrs. Bob Martin: "Fort Lewis was a wonderful school, and I learned a lot there" (132), and many other boarding-school autobiographers have done so as well. David Adams, author of *Education for Extinction*, has more recently published "Beyond Bleakness: The Brighter Side of Boarding Schools, 1870–1940."

This, let me repeat, is in no way to justify the ethnocidal boarding-school policies, their often cruel and truly savage practices, and some of the dire consequences to Indian students who experienced them. "Too few of the lessons [Indian students] learned," Ahern writes, "were empowering; too many were destructive" (1996, 88). The National Native American Boarding School Healing Commission still has much work to do. Yet, as K. Tsianina Lomawaima put it, the "moral" of the Chilocco Indian School "falls somewhere between the depiction of boarding schools as irredeemably destructive institutions"[19] and the opinion of one of the former students she interviewed that Chilocco "'really was a marvelous school'" (164). After examining a very great number of Indian boarding-school autobiographies,

Michael Coleman concluded that "No Hopi or Navajo or Sioux response to the schools emerged" (194). Myriam Vuckovic's attention to Haskell "students' responses to their schooling [revealed]... there was no single boarding-school experience." Instead, she found that the students' "reactions ranged from complete rejection to enthusiasm, and most felt ambivalent about their boarding-school years" (2).

Of course students who "completely rejected" their boarding-school experience were not likely to memorialize it in writing. As Jeffrey Ostler has written, "Only the most resilient children later wrote"—or, for that matter, chose to discuss—"their experiences, whereas those who suffered deeper damage did not" (154). There is no question that although the record of boarding-school narratives is rich, those who have spoken or written of their experiences represent only a very small percentage of boarding-school students. Ruth Spack confirms that "The dearth of accounts reveals that the overwhelming majority of students remained silent" (109). We do not have the words of those who sickened and died at the schools, nor did any who succeeded in running away from the schools care to elaborate on what they had rejected. This is true as well of those who may have remained in school for several years only to turn their backs on their education on their return home. Even those more "resilient children" who did provide accounts, as we will see, presented a wide range of responses, all with at least a measure of "ambivalence," as I have noted.

The boarding-school movement has, to date, received a considerable amount of scholarly attention.[20] The earliest studies worked largely from the perspective of the government—although many involved in teaching at or administering the schools were themselves extremely critical of that perspective. More recently, K. Tsianina Lomawaima, Brenda Child, Clyde Ellis, Clifford Trafzer, Myriam Vuckovic, and others have offered studies based on letters from and interviews with a great many boarding-school students themselves. In the third edition (1999) of her 1974 book, *Education and the American Indian*, Margaret Connell Szasz, writes that "Between the late 1970s and the late 1990s [she has] been moving away from an earlier focus on policy to a more recent focus on the Indian community itself" (xi). This is as well the orientation of this book in which the testimony of the boarding-school students themselves is central.

Coleman's study, as some earlier studies had done, arranged the material by topics: curriculum, health, resistance, rebellion, identity, and so on;

Coleman quotes from a wide range of Native boarding-school autobiographers who addressed these matters. Ruth Spack, who examined all "of the one hundred autobiographies... Coleman found for his book" (109), read them specifically to determine how the students responded to the requirement that they learn English, what Spack calls in her title, *America's Second Tongue*. Spack, like Coleman, Szasz, and others, is looking, as I have said, to balance a scale that had been weighted heavily toward the government and administrators' accounts. But although the material they cite allows the reader to know what each autobiographer thought of one or another of the matters referenced, it gives no feel for any individual author's boarding-school experience beyond these matters, no sense of his or her experience as even an approximate whole. This is not meant as a criticism of these fine books, all of which are histories.

But I am a literary worker in cultural studies, so this volume will, generally speaking, reverse the historians' procedure. As I have quoted Coleman, "We still know relatively little about how Indian school children themselves saw things" (194), and one way to learn more about how the students "themselves saw things" is to look closely at what they themselves had to say in a range of autobiographical texts. It is in these texts that we may hear, as I have also quoted Tsianina Lomawaima, many of "the thousands of Indian voices who spoke the breath of boarding school life" (xii), and I will quote them at some length. As Lomawaima noted of the more than fifty former boarding-school students she interviewed for her study of the Chilocco Indian School, "for each of them, boarding school is only part of the story. For most of them, it is an important part" (159). And insofar as the texts exist, these student voices may still be heard.

Their voices speak of a range of experiences, yet they regularly reference what I will call a number of *scenes of initiation* or *initiatory loci*, and also a number of *topoi* (frequently the same "topics" the historians of the boarding schools had remarked) as they are encountered by one or another boarding-school autobiographer. Thus, for example, I consider the Dining Room to be an initiatory locus—new and strange things happen in this place— while Food—its kind and quality or lack thereof—is a topos. Discipline, frequently in the form of corporal punishment, is a topos, but one that has no particular locus in that it might be administered in the classroom, in a teacher's office, in the dining room, or almost any other place—perhaps a jail—at a given school. The topos, Clock Time, or what Myriam Vuckovic has termed, "Living by the Bell" (59), is also encountered everywhere: the dormitory, the dining room, the classroom, or the parade ground. In each of these loci students in the boarding schools woke, ate, studied, or marched according to the clock, its time signaled by the bell or bugle or whistle. Naming—that is, the de-individuating bestowal of Tom, Dick, Harry, and Sally to replace the highly distinctive names all students brought with them—is a topos,[21] along with what I will call the Cleanup, the scrubbing and, in particular, the hair-cutting that took place almost immediately upon each student's arrival. The Dormitory is the locus for the students' nightly rest and also on occasion for the topos, Sex. But sexual relations among the students (or with others at the schools, when it occurred) are certainly not limited to the dormitory. The topos Outing Labor might have a family farm as locus—that was its rationale, based on the substantial farming community around Carlisle—but Native student workers might be housed in tents or otherwise transient, makeshift quarters. Identity is an important and complex topos, but what one can say about it for any particular student depends on shifting loci of home, family, school, and other matters, all of these varying over time. Not a single one of the many boarding-school students we will consider ever entirely abandoned a sense of being a Hopi, a Navajo, or an Apache, although each understood his or her tribal identity or, on occasion, a more nearly pan-Indian identity in a variety of ways.

Along with this introduction, *Changed Forever* consists of two parts and three appendices. Part I examines six book-length Hopi autobiographies that deal extensively with their subjects' boarding-school experiences. All of these Hopi boarding-school students lived through a climactic event in Hopi history, the 1906 Orayvi Split, an event that was very much bound up with the government's insistence that Hopi children attend the schools. Part II examines four full-length Navajo autobiographies and a collection of briefer Navajo life-history accounts, all of which treat the boarding-school experience of their subjects in greater or lesser detail. The two parts of the book are followed by three appendices of differing lengths. Appendix A discusses the Orayvi Split in 1906 on the Hopi Third Mesa in more historical and cultural detail than seemed appropriate for inclusion in the studies of—or the endnotes to—the individual autobiographies. Appendix B briefly describes what might be called the genre of Navajo life histories, including fictionalized ones and ones that do not include boarding-school experience. Because I know of only three Apache life histories that discuss their subjects' boarding-school experience,[22] and because only two of them offer many details, I discuss them in appendix C, rather than in what could have been a third part of the book.

This first volume of *Changed Forever* pays attention exclusively to the Southwest for the simple reason that there are more Hopi and Navajo (along with a couple of Apache) autobiographical texts representing their subjects' boarding-school experience in detail than there are from any other tribal nations. A second volume will consider Lakota boarding-school autobiographies and a range of boarding-school texts from various regions, along with the legacy of the boarding schools in Native American literature.

∽

I'll close this introduction with a few words about methodology. *Changed Forever*, as the table of contents indicates, is divided into sections dealing with individual texts. As will soon be clear, the readings I offer for those texts proceed in something of a summary fashion; I quote and describe boarding-school materials from each book, providing cultural and historical background along with analytical and critical commentary. Both anonymous readers of my initial draft of this book expressed concerns about this procedure, noting the absence of what one called a "driving argument of the study." I want briefly to address these concerns.

First, it is likely that almost no reader of this book will have read all or even many of the boarding-school texts studied here. Most of them are little known, and many are out of print; I very much hope the attention given them here will remedy that, but such a remedy is for the future. The texts, then, have not received much scholarly or critical attention, and virtually none from literary scholars. Amelia Katanski's study of boarding-school writing, for example, mentions a few of them and offers a reading of none of them. This is not the usual case with the texts considered in most academic studies. To be sure, these texts are not "as good as" Shakespeare—or Silko or Vizenor, Welch or Erdrich. But I have found them interesting in all sorts of ways and I believe they deserve a contemporary audience. Thus, it seemed important to offer prospective readers of these books the historical and cultural materials needed to read them as fully as possible, and my discussions offer something like annotated critical editions of these autobiographies. Frank Mitchell's *Navajo Blessingway Singer* already has full and fine annotations by the editors, and Leo Simmons, editor of Don Talayesva's

Sun Chief, included a great deal of contextual information in that book. Both of those books are available in recent editions. But the others, those that are still in print and those that are not, have no such information. I do summarize—often more than I would like—but I also provide a great deal of historical and cultural context and critical commentary of a specifically literary kind. And, again, the summaries are all constructed from the words spoken or written by their boarding-school authors.

Second, it is true that there is no "driving argument" in this book, an absence that would constitute a near-fatal flaw for some academic studies, but not, I think, for this one. In a recent monograph I posited the genre of "Native American elegy."[23] The two volumes projected for this study posit the genre of "American Indian boarding-school literature." For the first study, I found a common thread in my examples of the genre that did allow for something like a "driving argument." It seemed to me that all the performances and texts constituting the genre of Native elegy were marked by a sense—very different from that in Western elegy—of personal and individual loss as importantly social and communal loss. Elegiac performance or text was not so much "to praise famous men" as to console the people for their loss and thereby enable their "survivance," to use a now-familiar term taken from Gerald Vizenor's work. Each did this differently, and often in ways that were not immediately apparent, but each performance or text was guided by this principle whether or not the performer or writer was consciously aware of it.[24]

The common thread in the texts that make up the genre of American Indian boarding-school literature is that every single one of them testifies to its subject's retention of an ongoing Indian identity. But unlike the Native elegists all of whose performances or texts were—consciously or not—guided or undergirded by the principle of sustaining the ongoing communal life and health of the People, neither the Native boarding-school autobiographers nor their editors set out to show how Indian identities were retained. Instead, they had any number of purposes, sometimes no purpose other than to accommodate someone who had suggested that a record of their experience would be valuable.

Some of the boarding-school students went to the schools willingly and some by compulsion. Experiencing the topoi of the Cleanup, in particular the cutting of their hair, some were pleased with their new appearance while others were horrified by it. After the Naming, some liked their new names, some found them of little concern, and more than a few were outraged at losing an important part of their identity. Among those who endured Corporal Punishment, many were deeply upset by their suffering, but some simply were not—or so they say. In the same way, while several Resisted or attempted to Run Away, others stayed long after the time for which they'd enrolled—or left and then returned. All of these experiences—and many more—went into the making of whatever sense of Indian identity these students retained, identities, as I have said, that were rich, complex, and variegated. But it simply is not the case that the texts constituting the genre of American Indian boarding-school literature are all guided by the principle of retaining Indian identity. Although their subjects, in one way or another, did retain a strong sense of Indian identity, describing how this came about is not what motivates the various accounts. And this is why this study does not have a "driving argument."[25] Instead, I've taken seriously Tsianina Lomawaima's question: "What has become of the thousands of Indian voices who spoke the breath of boarding-school life?" (xii) and tried to present some of those voices as fully as I could, consistent with a critical study, to anyone wishing to listen.

PART I

Hopi Boarding-School Autobiographies

IN A REVIEW OF EDMUND NEQUATEWA'S AUTOBIOGRAPHY, *Born a Chief: The Nineteenth-Century Hopi Boyhood of Edmund Nequatewa* (1993), Peter Whiteley refers to the "canonical corpus" of "Hopi autobiography" (1994, 478), a canon to which he would add Nequatewa's book. However "canonical" this "corpus" may be, it nonetheless remains a body of work little known to most students of American autobiography. The Hopi autobiographical canon consists of the following texts: Don Talayesva's *Sun Chief: The Autobiography of a Hopi Indian* (1942), Polingaysi Qoyawayma's (Elizabeth Q. White's) *No Turning Back: A Hopi Indian Woman's Struggle to Bridge the Gap between the World of Her People and the World of the White Man* (1964), Helen Sekaquaptewa's *Me and Mine: The Life Story of Helen Sekaquaptewa* (1969), Fred Kabotie's *Fred Kabotie: Hopi Indian Artist* (1977), Albert Yava's *Big Falling Snow: A Tewa-Hopi Indian's Life and Times and the History and Traditions of His People* (1978), and Edmund Nequatewa's *Born a Chief: The Nineteenth-Century Hopi Boyhood of Edmund Nequatewa* (1993).[1] All the texts of the Hopi autobiographical canon belong to the genre of American Indian boarding-school literature; each subject describes his or her experience of school at some length. This is unusual for the life-history texts of any given Native people, and a major reason for beginning this study with the Hopi canon.

I'd like to thank Peter Runge and the Special Collections staff at the Cline Library of Northern Arizona University for their generous help. Dr. Peter Whiteley of the American Museum of Natural History read an earlier version of this essay, provided a great deal of valuable information, and corrected several errors I had made. Any errors that remain are solely my responsibility. An earlier version of this chapter appeared in *a/b: autobiography studies*.

1

I have arranged the titles of the books making up the Hopi canon according to their dates of publication, although Nequatewa, whose book was published last, was born earlier than the others, in "around 1880" (xv), according to P. David Seaman, his editor. Kabotie, the youngest of these autobiographers, was born in 1900, and the others were born between those two dates. All of the Hopi texts—like most of the others I will consider— are what, many years ago, I called "Indian autobiographies."[2] That is to say they are bicultural composites in which the named Native subject's story has been transcribed, arranged, edited, or otherwise constructed by a white collaborator or collaborators. In one instance (Talayesva), the editor was a sociologist (Leo Simmons); in another (Yava), the editor was a folklorist, a novelist, and ethnomusicologist (Harold Courlander). Three worked with enthusiasts of the West: Kabotie with Bill Belknap, Qoyawayma with Vada Carlson, and Sekaquaptewa with Louise Udall. Unlike the subjects of a great many earlier Indian autobiographies, all of these Native people spoke and read and wrote English so that each had substantial say as to the final text.

Boarding-school experience played a significant part in the life of each of these Hopi autobiographers, who all went to school at a time when Hopi social and ceremonial life underwent critical change. For the Hopis, as we will see, the central date is 1906.

1

Edmund Nequatewa's
Born a Chief

EDMUND NEQUATEWA WAS BORN IN THE VILLAGE OF SHIPAULOVI, ON THE
Second Mesa of the Hopi reservation, in "around 1880" (Seaman, xv),
as I noted. In 1942, he asked Alfred Whiting, an ethnobotanist whom
he knew from the Museum of Northern Arizona where both were for
a time employed, to write his life story. Nequatewa, Whiting, and Sterling
Macintosh, a "local student" (Seaman, xxiv), collaborated during May and
June of that year to produce a manuscript that Whiting worked on sporadically for almost twenty years without presenting it for publication. P. David
Seaman, an anthropological linguist, came into possession of Whiting's
papers after his death in 1978—Nequatewa had died in 1969—the several
typescripts of the autobiography among them, and it was Seaman who produced the final version of *Born a Chief* (1993).

The Alfred F. Whiting Collection in the Cline Library at Northern
Arizona University includes three bound volumes of typed manuscripts in
which are to be found several earlier versions of Nequatewa's autobiography. Each of the volumes is titled *I, Edmund: The Hopi Boyhood of Edmund
Nequatewa*, and all are dated 1961, the last time Whiting and Nequatewa
worked together. Despite the 1961 date, volumes 2 and 3 are made up of
materials from May and June of 1942, when Whiting and Nequatewa first
worked together. Volume 1 contains Whiting's final collation and revision
of all of these texts following his last meeting with Nequatewa. The Cline
Library also houses the P. David Seaman collection, volume 8 of which lists
among its contents:

3

I, Edmund: The Story of a Hopi Boyhood
As told by Edmund Nequatewa to Alfred F. Whiting
Carbon copy of original collated by P. David Seaman
24 December, 1977,

a year, that is, before Whiting's death. That carbon copy, is, unfortunately, missing from the volume, and only the title page testifies to its having existed. The "Contents" page of the 1977 collation is there, however, and, since it reproduces almost exactly the "Contents" page of Whiting's final 1961 revision, it seems likely that the missing carbon copy would also closely reproduce that final revision. But those "Contents" pages—Whiting's last one from 1961 and Seaman's from his 1977 collation—differ from the "Contents" page of the book that was published in 1993 as *Born a Chief.* Those differences can only be the result of Seaman's revisions, and I'll discuss a number of them in what follows.

In 1887, the federal government had established a boarding school at Keam's Canyon, about thirty-five miles from Nequatewa's village on the Hopi reservation. The government required all Hopi children to attend. At Orayvi on Third Mesa, the largest and oldest Hopi town, there was general opposition to the schools and many parents hid their children from the government agents and Indian police lest they be taken by force. Some Second Mesa Hopis also opposed the schools, but here the majority favored them and encouraged their children to attend.[1] This difference of opinion, blandly to call it that, added to longstanding disagreements among important Hopi leaders, and led to the Orayvi Split of September, 1906, a major development in Hopi history. Whiteley writes, "In 1906, Orayvi, the largest and longest-occupied Hopi settlement, divided roughly in half: the 'Hostile' faction led by the Spider and Fire Clans, was forced out by the 'Friendlies,' led by the Bear Clan.... The Hostiles founded two new villages, Hotvela and Paaqavi, six miles to the northwest"[2] (2003, 152).

James Gallagher wrote that he "opened the [Keam's Canyon] School October 1, 1887 with an attendance of 52 pupils. After... about 2 weeks, there was a general stampede for the mesas" (in Coleman, 166). Those students who did not run off were nonetheless close enough to their home villages to receive visits and food packages from relatives, or even to be whisked away sporadically for various ceremonial occasions—as would be the case with Nequatewa. Thus the Keam's Canyon School could never quite become the sort of total institution that might threaten Indian identities in the way the off-reservation boarding schools attempted to do.

Nequatewa, as a boy, had been shot in the knee by an arrow (45).[3] His family treated the wound by traditional means; it healed, and for a time did not trouble him. Then, when he was about fifteen, he began to feel severe pain in the area of his knee, and developed life-threatening infections that incapacitated him for weeks. Two medicine men were called on to diagnose and treat the problem, the second of whom identified the cause of the illness as the machinations of a female witch, someone who did not want Nequatewa to become chief of the One-Horn Society.[4] To help save the sick young man, Nequatewa's paternal grandfather, a man who will influence his life profoundly, tells the medicine man that "He will never become a chief of this fraternity. From now on he is mine.... I am going to be here from now on to care for him, and if he gets well, nobody shall ever take him away from me. I will teach him and tell him of the course of life that I want him to take" (70). Grandfather announces that although the young man "is my son's son, ... from now on he is my own. From now on I am not going to call him Grandson; I am just going to call him Son" (70). The young man gets well, although there is permanent damage to his leg.

"The course of life" the grandfather wants his "son" to take involves going to school, and at several places in the book grandfather elaborates the reasons for his commitment to the white man's education. Grandfather had already sent his biological son, Kachina,[5] to the boarding school at Keam's Canyon, and Nequatewa refers to him as "uncle" (85). But a father's brother would not be called "uncle" by Hopis, who reserve that title for a mother's brother, an authority figure with whom one would not anticipate having "fun."[6] It is likely that Whiting, Seaman, or both referred to him as "uncle" rather than "father" so as not to confuse a non-Hopi audience.

Nequatewa is about fifteen years old when he begins school, and his uncle, as Whiting's typescripts indicate, is only a little older.[7] This should remind us that while the boarding schools most certainly enrolled young children, it was also common for them to have teenagers and even older men and women in, say, the first to third or fourth grades. In response to grandfather's decree, Nequatewa says he thought "it would be great fun to go away with my uncle, and I would always be looking forward to that day when we will leave home for school" (85). Here, as in other places, Nequatewa's diction diverges slightly from standard English, because, as Seaman states, in order "to follow Whiting's wishes" (xxv), "The Hopi narrative style used by Edmund has been left largely unedited" (xxiv). I'd question whether Nequatewa's (only slightly) nonstandard English has anything to do with "Hopi narrative style." (I will also question the practice of anthropologists or amanuenses who refer to their consultants by first name only.)

When the great day comes, Nequatewa, his grandfather, and his uncle make the long ride to school on burros. Soon after their arrival, he participates in several of the *initiation scenes* at specific *initiatory loci* of boarding-school literature, for example, "The Dining Room," "The Clean-Up," and "The Dormitory," and engages with a number of the topoi of boarding-school literature, e.g., "Clock Time," "Food" (which I will refer to sometimes as "the Mush"), "Sex," "Religion," "Resistance," "Outing Labor," "Running Away," and "Identity." Most of these scenes and topics appear throughout the Hopi autobiographical canon as well as in a great many other boarding-school autobiographies.

Nequatewa first encounters the Dining Room. "That evening," he says, "we went to dinner with the rest of the boys and grandfather went with us" (87). Here he is served what I will call the Mush. This is to say that in view of the large quantity of oatmeal of widely varying quality and preparation they were served, some of the students gave the generic name "Mush" to all the strange and often unpleasant foods they encountered[8] (12). Nequatewa and his grandfather are served "light bread" rather than *piki*, the thin corn bread he is used to, along with tea into which "they had poured some milk or cream" (86–87). The tea is warm, and he "never had drank anything warm before" (87). "All the supper didn't taste very good to me," Nequatewa says, "and what I had took down all wanted to come up" (87). When his grandfather gets up to leave, he follows him, and, "as soon as [he] got out of the door" (87) he threw up.

He then asks his grandfather for some familiar food and is given watermelon and *piki*. Soon "somebody came along, one of the school boys, and said that it was time for us to go to bed" (87–88). He is now initiated into the Dormitory. Here, he encounters "some strange looking things," which his uncle Kachina tells him "were the beds on which we have to sleep" (88). He shares a bed with his uncle, and, after finally getting to sleep, falls off and lands on the floor: "Then I just can't go back to sleep again for fear I might fall off" (88). I have earlier mentioned Basil Johnston's account of smaller boys being sexually abused by bigger boys in the dormitory, Johnston and

Highway's accounts of boys being molested by priests, Sarah Shillinger's discovery of girls abused by nuns at Catholic boarding schools, and accounts of lay teachers' inappropriate behavior elsewhere. Edmund Nequatewa's narrative, however, has no mention whatever of sexual abuse by fellow students, faculty, or staff. It may be that Nequatewa and Whiting chose not to record such matters. But of course it also may be that such matters are not recorded because nothing of this sort occurred.

The boys are awakened by a bell. Many boarding-school students have commented on how strange they found the strict regimentation of each day, marked either by the sound of a bell or, on the military model, a bugle. Clock Time, the Western rationalization of the life-world, so that one eats at a certain time, whether one is hungry or not, performs certain tasks at certain times whether they are necessary then or not, is one of the consistent topoi of boarding-school literature. Before going to breakfast, however, Nequatewa finds that he must accompany the other boys to wash up. He notes that "There was only three towels on a roller, on which everybody wiped their hands and faces" (88). Something like this was the situation at the boarding schools generally and it led to widespread epidemics of trachoma, tuberculosis, smallpox, and other diseases. (Although, as we will see, an outbreak of smallpox on the Hopi reservation did not reach the school.)

Breakfast consists of "oatmeal, coffee, bread, and fried potatoes" (89) that "don't look like food to me" (89), Nequatewa remarks. But before sitting down to this unappealing meal, he observes that "everybody stood at the table behind their chairs. On the first bell, everybody bowed their heads, and I don't know what they said. It must be the grace that they had repeated"(88). The observance of various Christian practices, Religion, is another of the topoi of boarding-school literature. Here, in that "everybody" said "the grace" according to Nequatewa's observation, one would think that all the students could speak English. But whether they could, or how well they could is very much in question. Thus, Fred Kabotie has remarked, in regard to required hymn singing at boarding school, "[W]e'd sing Hopi words to 'Jesus loves me, this I know' that sounded like the English but had funny meanings. Miss Beaman [the visiting religionist] never caught on" (11). Polingaysi Qoyawayma illustrates this when she describes her classmates singing, "Deso lasmi, desi no." English translation: "Jesus loves me, this I know." Hopi translation: "The San Juan people are bringing burros"[9] (*No Turning Back*, 14).

Breakfast is followed by something more than a casual wash. I have called it the Cleanup, an initiatory scene that every boarding-school student endured. An important part of the Cleanup was the cutting of the Indian boy or girl's long hair. This was done for two reasons: it was intended to prevent the spread of lice, and it was intended as a de-Indianizing gesture, one that would differentiate the newly shorn child from his or her age-mates who had avoided or escaped the schools. For many Native peoples, long hair would be roughly cut short as a sign of mourning. For Hopi males, the cutting of the hair was emasculating "because long hair was highly valued as a ritual mark of manhood entitled by *Wuwtsim* initiation" (Whiteley 1988, 94–95), the tribal initiation that almost all males underwent sometime between adolescence and marriage. (See below.) Indeed, Charles Burton, who had arrived at Keam's Canyon School as superintendent and reservation agent in 1899, as I noted, used hair-cutting as punishment for antigovernment behavior on the part of adult Hopi males, "a matter," as Whiteley writes, "of great and long remembered resentment"[10] (1988b, 94).

This does not, however, seem to be the case with Edmund Nequatewa. He remembers that a man came with "a pair of scissors, and I remember a pair of clippers, too. He sat me on a chair and he went to work and cut my hair off, just like taking my scalp. Took it all off, down to the skin!" (89). Hopis were strongly opposed to killing, but in the past Hopis had indeed taken the scalps of vanquished foes. Although Nequatewa compares what was done to him to the "taking of his scalp," a horrible experience, he does not comment further. Next in the Cleanup is a bath with heated water and "hard brown laundry soap" instead of "toilet soap" (89), as Nequatewa makes the distinction. After this, he and his uncle dress in "a new outfit of clothes" (89). (But uncle Kachina must have been through all this before.)

A further aspect of the Dormitory at Keam's Canyon School, that the windows are barred and the boys locked in at night with no toilet facilities available, leads to acts of Resistance, another topos of boarding-school literature. To protest the situation, a number of the bigger boys (and Nequatewa is himself at least fifteen) "decided that they will just crap all over the floor, which they did" (91). Confronted by the disciplinarian—every boarding school had one or more disciplinarians—who demands to know who is responsible for the mess, a number of "big husky boys" step forward and announce that unless the padlock is removed, the school staff "will find the mess every morning" (91). The disciplinarian makes the point that the

padlock can't be removed "because you boys get out and run away" (91)—
a telling statement. But after a discussion with the superintendent, "he gave
us buckets every night" (92). Corporal Punishment was a common topic of
boarding-school life. But Nequatewa's account of his time at Keam's Canyon
School does not include any physical discipline being meted out by the disciplinarian or—as in other schools—by any of the teachers. Immediately
following this scene of Resistance, Nequatewa introduces the subject of "love"
(92). It is the boarding-school topos that is better covered by the term Sex.

Nequatewa states that a number of the boys "would call on their girls
at night," as "was *customary* with the Hopi" (92, my emphasis) immediately
contradicting himself with the statement that he "was too young to know
what was going on" (92). At fifteen he certainly did know "what was going
on" and that it was the "customary" Hopi, male cultural behavior called
dumaiya in which, as Mischa Titiev wrote, teenage boys who now sleep
mostly in their respective kivas,[11] free from parental supervision, "go to call
on the girl of their choice, sometimes by pre-arrangement, and sometimes
on the mere chance of getting a favorable reception" (1944, 31). Although
the dormitory windows are barred by "pipes" (92), these are not unassail-
able. Nequatewa notes that two boys "would pull on the bars while two
got out." Those "two would then pull on the bars from the outside to let
the rest of them out" (92). Seeming to know pretty well "what was going
on," Nequatewa explains further that "These things must have always been
planned ahead," because when the boys got "to the girls dormitory, the girls
had hung down their sheets to pull up the boys" (92). It would seem likely
that a number of pregnancies resulted from these nocturnal encounters, as
it would also seem likely that both the boys and the girls would be punished
for these behaviors, but Nequatewa says nothing further on this matter.

It is indeed the case, as Peter Whiteley has observed, that Nequatewa's
book is "signally lacking in the sexual preoccupations that drew such attention to *Sun Chief* [the autobiography of Don Talayesva]" (1994, 478). In
that *Sun Chief* was published in 1942, the year in which Nequatewa asked
Whiting to record his autobiography, I can only wonder whether it was that
publication, by a Third Mesa Hopi man some ten years Nequatewa's junior,
that prompted him to do so—and, perhaps, in regard to matters of sex, to
handle matters differently.[12] It's also the case, as Mischa Titiev had noted,
that Hopis by this time had "developed a tacit understanding" of "the white
man's professed standard of morality" (1944, 30), and had learned to be

circumspect in these regards. Nequatewa himself, as we will see, had also for long been a Christian when he told his story, and had thus perhaps internalized these standards, for all that he doesn't falsify youthful Hopi sexual practice. These dormitory scenes can serve as an illustration of Tsianina Lomawaima's observation that "Much of student life was unobserved by and unknown to school staff or administrators" (29).

The usual stay at Keam's Canyon School was four years—the length of time Native parents agreed to allow their children to attend the schools varied—and, Nequatewa notes, "How much a child will learn depends on how much they want to learn in four years. On the average, they reach the third grade. They hardly learn to speak English" (94–95). This may in part have been because the school at Keam's Canyon, as Edmund Nequatewa tells it—other accounts have strongly differed—did not prohibit the students speaking their native language. Nequatewa states that "Everybody spoke Hopi on the grounds, and the teachers all spoke English. The students would be able to speak some English, but they won't be able to speak enough to understand much of anything" (95). Speaking Hopi for the most part, and engaging in "customary" courting behaviors, receiving visits from relatives who bring food packages (see just below), the Hopi students at Keam's Canyon were in no danger of losing their Indian Identity, another of the topoi of the boarding-school experience.

Grandfather returns to visit his sons "two months after he had left [Nequatewa] there" (93). He has brought familiar food from home that Nequatewa stores away for a later time. The visit begins on a Friday and Nequatewa and his uncle, Kachina, tell grandfather that they don't go to class on Saturdays, but, rather, work hauling wood and water and cleaning up the grounds (95). This is something they also do during the school week, when "All the boys would be chopping wood or tending their gardens" (95). The academic curriculum at most of the boarding schools was subordinate to industrial programs that taught a variety of trades ostensibly aimed at giving the (male) students skills that might allow them to assimilate into the mainstream society. (The young women, as noted, were taught "domestic sciences.") Nequatewa says nothing of the academics at Keam's Canyon School. He does say that the school had "an industrial teacher" (95), although it "didn't have any shops"; he does not mention learning any particular trade or skills from this teacher.

After supper, Nequatewa says, grandfather "took us"—him and his uncle Kachina—"up on the hill" (95), one of a number of scenes in the book in which grandfather, from a hilltop, shares seriously considered speculation as to what the coming of the white man means for Hopi people. The thoughts he offers—to categorize them broadly—have to do with knowledge and with ethical behavior (e.g., 96), with the "traditions" of the Hopi, and how they relate to the People's current situation. These are matters he has discussed with many others (96), and the tentative conclusions he has reached explain his strong commitment to schooling for his sons and for Hopi children more generally.

It is grandfather's belief that "the time will come when every [Hopi] family's child will be going to school" (97), and that time is not far away. The young people need to "go to school and learn to speak and write the English language," so that they may "become our leaders" and "be able to compete with the white man" (96). To that end, he tells Nequatewa and his uncle Kachina—they are only in their first and second year at the Keam's Canyon School—"When your [four-year] time is up, you might see you have to go to school some more, which is what I want you to do, because I want you boys to learn something" (97). But there is an even more important reason for his sons to go to the white man's schools, a reason that derives from Hopi prophecy that long predates the arrival of the United States Americans. What grandfather ultimately hopes his sons and other Hopi children will learn at the schools is whether or not these white men do or do not possess the knowledge and the wisdom that would mark them as the *pahaana* whose return for the benefit of the Hopis has long been prophesied.[13]

Pahaana was the legendary elder white brother of the Hopi who long, long ago, when the world was still young, went off to the east with the promise that he would one day come back with wisdom and knowledge beneficial to the Hopi. A great deal has been written about this. On the one hand, the legend is considered to be very ancient; on the other, Mischa Titiev believed that it probably arose when the Hopis first encountered the Spanish invaders in the mid-sixteenth century (1944, 71), a long time ago nonetheless. Whiteley notes that the first written mention of *pahaana* dates from the mid-nineteenth century (1988b, 329n8). Earlier, it had become clear that the Spanish, in view of their actions, could hardly have been the true *pahaanam* (plural). But in the last decades of the nineteenth century there was considerable debate about this subject among Hopi thinkers regarding the Americans. In particular was the question, as grandfather raises it, of whether the Bible they brought was indeed "the book of knowledge which holds the truth" (111).

As I noted, Nequatewa had earlier worked with Mary-Russell Ferrell Colton to publish *Truth of a Hopi: Stories Relating to the Origin, Myths and Clan Histories of the Hopi* (1936). Colton's notes to that book refer to the Hopis' belief in the return of the *pahaana* "as one of the general '*theories*' of the people" (131, second emphasis mine), and Nequatewa, narrating in English, also uses that term. Back-translating, Colton wrote that "The Hopi word for a 'theory' is *tutavo*" (131). Somewhat more recently Voegelin and Voegelin spoke of Hopi people being bound by "sets of *didactic ethics* (called *titavo* ...)" (53, my emphasis), a term the *Hopi Dictionary* defines simply as "advice, instruction, counsel" (676). Whiteley has glossed this as *Hopinavoti*, "a sort of Hopi hermeneutics" (1988b, 255). (The *Hopi Dictionary* defines *navoti* as "teachings, traditions, body of knowledge, cultural beliefs" [309]). Thus different Hopi "theories" are interpretations of Hopi prophecy that bear on a range of matters, such as What is the present state of Hopi religion? Should Hopi people send their children to the white man's schools? Has *pahaana* returned? These interpretative-hermeneutical questions had and continue to have serious material consequences.

Grandfather tells his son about what Nequatewa calls "the Hopi traditions, all the *theories* about what is going to come to pass" (*Born a Chief*, 107, my emphasis). In his hope that his sons will find out more about these things by attending school, grandfather would have been one of those called the "Friendlies," "progressives" roughly speaking, and sympathetic to schooling, who were in conflict with the "Hostiles," "traditionalists," again roughly speaking, opposed to the schools. If learning "to compete" with the white man was an important reason to go to school, discovering the true nature of the white man—could he possibly be the *pahaana*?—was an even more important reason. Grandfather will have a good deal more to say about these matters very soon.[14]

That year, Nequatewa's grandfather visited his sons "oftener ... until cold weather set in," and soon after, "it was near Christmas" (97). This is Nequatewa's "first Christmas," and it is an occasion so new and strange that he "didn't really know what was going to happen" (97). Many things "happen"—I won't take the space to summarize the three-page description

Nequatewa gives of this first Christmas at boarding school—but nowhere is there any reference to the religious nature of the holiday or what it means to Christians. While he would have learned from early in his time at school that what the students at Keam's Canyon were doing before meals was saying *grace*, it's not clear whether his observation that the "schoolhouse was just one building, sort of like a *chapel*," and that the Christmas songs were "old-fashioned Christmas *hymns*" (98, my emphases) derive from that time or from later experience. Nequatewa describes no religious instruction or practice at Keam's, although other accounts (e.g., that of Don Talayesva) make clear that these existed. (He also says nothing about the military organization of the Keam's Canyon School.)

During his fourth year at school, 1898–99, there is a smallpox outbreak on the Hopi reservation, and grandfather uses what David Seaman calls "the smallpox scare" to persuade the administrators at Keam's Canyon to let him take his son "for the special baptism he had arranged for him" (103), what grandfather will call his "Kachina ceremony"[15] (112). Baptism, of course, is a Christian practice, but it has a Hopi ceremonial equivalent: hair-washing in yucca suds, and the ethnographic literature uses "baptism" for that Hopi practice. Peter Whiteley quotes Yukiwma, leader of the Orayvi Hostiles, in an interview with the Reverend H. R. Voth in 1905, referring to "our elder brother," the *pahaana*, as "the one who has not had his head washed," which Whiteley glosses as "[i.e., is not a Christian]" (1988b, 270), one who has not been baptized. Grandfather describes the washing of his son's head in the "Kachina ceremony" a second time as a "baptism" (106), and Nequatewa himself refers to it that way twice (106, 107). Both are quite clear about the difference—as Yukiwma obviously was—between the hair-washing/baptism that makes one a Christian and the hair-washing/baptism that is part of the ceremonialism that makes Hopis Hopis.

It is odd that grandfather calls this a "Kachina ceremony," especially because the book has already given us Nequatewa's participation in two *katsina* ceremonies prior to his time at boarding school. The very first chapter of the book is called "Kachina," and in it Nequatewa tells of the coming of the *katsinam* when he was about six years old. For the most part, Nequatewa recalls the occasion as a sort of Hopi Christmas, a time when good children get more presents than do naughty children. But he remarks the necessity of having his hair washed—twice, in that he petulantly dirtied up his hair after its first washing in yucca suds. And he also—something about which

I'll have more to say just below—represents the occasion as "the first time [he] got any *suspicious* ideas"—because of the way he "could see the light clear across the eyes through the *mask*" (12, my emphases) and because he thought it would be difficult to eat with "only [the] little bit of mouth" they had—that the *katsinam* might not be the supernatural beings he had always believed them to be.

Chapter 4 is called "Initiation at Shipaulovi," and it tells of Nequatewa's actual initiation into the *Katsina* society. He does not describe having his hair washed, but notes what seems unusual, that at "about ten years old" (31), he was the "youngest" of the initiates. (Many accounts indicate that the initiates are usually eight to ten, although on some occasions the "youngest" might be no more than six.) An unidentified man who will be his god-father, carries Nequatewa piggyback into the kiva where there is "a big sand painting" on which he stands. Two *katsinam* come into the kiva with "cholla cactus whips in both hands," which they discard, taking up instead "a big bunch of yucca" with which they will whip the children to be initiated (30). Nequatewa's godfather offers to take the first two blows himself, and "whack, whack, right across his back, and his back just raised up with these welts" (31). Nequatewa says that because he "was born chief," he "must be respected," so that he "kept [his] blanket on, and . . . got one whack on the back," with his godfather turning "right around under those two Kachina, and he got the rest of it"[16] (31). Three days later, after a period of fasting, his godfather again carries him to the kiva, and "After a while the Kachina came: The first one came in. I looked up. No masks; I recognize everyone [*sic*] of them! Of course I was then surprised . . . and before that time I was afraid of the Kachina. . . . Then when everything is over, that is the time they tell you that you mustn't talk about it or tell anyone about it. If you do, a whole bunch of Kachina . . . will come and put you to death" (32).

Describing this aspect of the Katsina initiation at Walpi on First Mesa in 1911, Edward Curtis wrote that "On Totokya night [the night of the seventh day of the ceremony] in the kivas the novices for the first time see the kachinas unmasked, and learn that these are only men, not supernatu-rals" (172). He notes that "the novices are sternly warned not to reveal this to young children" (172). Dorothy Eggan some time ago called this aspect of the ceremony, when, "at initiation the child learned that the *katsinas* were not *real gods* but merely representatives of them" (372), the "disenchantment," and Sam Gill has more recently adopted the term for a "performance" study of *katsina* initiation. In any case, Hopis do not actually regard the *katsinam* as "*gods*" but rather as "spirit beings who, upon the prayers and right living of the Hopi, come to the villages during the growing season with their beneficence and sage advice" (Glowacka, D. Washburn, and Richland, 551). Nequatewa's discovery that he could "recognize everyone" (32) of the men impersonating the *katsinam* comes as something of a surprise (although, as noted, he had had suspicions); he does not, however, treat the revelation as something especially profound or life-altering.[17]

Although grandfather, as I have said, calls it his "*Kachina* ceremony" (112, my emphasis), what takes place is very different from the *katsina* initiation Nequatewa had already experienced. Here, the ceremony takes place in a "house," not in the ritual space of the kiva; there are no *katsinam*, no ritual whipping, and no moment of disenchantment. Although his grandfather will later state that "We told you that the Kachinas are supernatural beings, but they're not," adding—casually, it would seem, although this is an important issue—"all the ceremonies are like that. In a way every ceremony is devious" (112). This latter observation further conveys grandfather's "friendly" thinking on these matters, in that *pahaana*'s return was prophesied to "coincide with a stage when the Hopi way of life has become corrupt and decadent" (Whiteley, 1988b, 271) or, as he says, "devious."

In grandfather's ceremony, Nequatewa's hair is washed in "soapweed" (104), first by a man who uses an ear of white corn that he dips in the suds (104–5), and then by other men who use only their hands. When this is complete, the man who had first washed his hair "took a handful of fine cornmeal and rubbed it on [his] face" (105). He then takes up another ear of corn and rubs it on Nequatewa's breast, saying, "'From now on your name is such and such,' and he explained what the name meant" (105). Nequatewa does not tell us his new name or "what the name meant"; he would also have received a new name at his actual initiation years earlier, although he does not report that either. Whiteley explains that for males, "new names are conferred by an initiating 'godfather' and his close female relatives" (1998, 109). Here, grandfather is the initiate's "sponsor," and because the "godfather must be of a clan other than his [the boy's] own or his father's" (Whiteley 1988b, 60) it is the godfather who "baptizes the boy and gives him a new name deriving from his (the godfather's) clan" (Whiteley 1988b, 61). These initiation names, Whiteley writes, are used "principally in ritual" contexts (1998, 110). Because grandfather takes him back to school the following morning where such a name would never be used, and despite the fact that Nequatewa later indicates participation in various ritual activities (see below), he states that he "never was called by this new name" (107)—a name, again, which is not provided.[18]

Before sending Nequatewa back to school, grandfather explains the "reason that you are being baptized here this night" (106). He and his friends "have been wondering for a long time who to select for our purpose" (105), the purpose of finding out whether or when the true *pahaana* will come, what to make of Christianity and its singular book, and how to understand Hopi prophecy in light of current events. Nequatewa's grandfather, articulating some of the thoughts and concerns of any number of Hopi thinkers at the end of the nineteenth century, hopes his adopted son will gain insight into these matters by continuing his schooling. He states that, on the one hand, Hopi wisdom handed down "from our elders" affirms that "the Hopi and the bahana are not friends." And yet, on the other, "They are brothers and are supposed to be on an equal basis in life" (106). "We have been wishing, all of us, and hoping . . . that we could see the true bahana come" (106), because when he does come, the prophecies say that he will bring new knowledge, destroy the corrupt, and make things fresh and beautiful. To "find out who is right and what the truth is in this world" is the mission entrusted to this newly baptized/ initiated young man. "After that time," Nequatewa says, "grandfather would be coming into Keams Canyon about twice a month . . . telling [him] about the Hopi traditions, all the theories about what is going to come to pass" (107).

Nequatewa returns to the school, which is soon quarantined from the Hopi villages to the west to prevent the spread of smallpox. For this reason, his grandfather could not visit from December until near the end of April when the quarantine is lifted. Nequatewa then has an opportunity to return home, where he discovers that his parents, who had survived the epidemic, show very few pockmarks; others, he notes, are severely scarred, and, of course, many have died. His parents have again moved, and his visit is a short one. Almost immediately on his return to Keam's Canyon, "a lady came up from the boarding school at Phoenix," to which "about sixteen of the children thought they would like to go" (110). When asked if he wants to go, he says he doesn't know. Told that his "grandfather says you are going," he responds, "He said I am going, and if he says so, I'll go" (111).

It is once more a visit from his grandfather, one in which he and his son sit on a rock on a hilltop, that serves as a prelude to the departure for Phoenix. Nequatewa is once more urged to find out all he can about the white man's "book of knowledge which holds the truth of what I have been telling" (111) in the four years he will now spend at the off-reservation boarding school. "The book that holds the truth is a black book," grandfather says, "and it is about that thick" (111). Curiously, despite Christian attempts to convert Hopi people—Baptists had been involved in the founding of the Keam's Canyon School in 1887, H. R. Voth had established a Mennonite Mission at Oraibi in 1893, and Mormons had been in Hopi country at least since the mid-nineteenth century with a base at Tuba City from the 1870s—it is nonetheless grandfather's understanding that "the white people keep [this book] at the bottom of the pile where Hopis cannot see it," because if they could "ever learn the truth of this book," they could "compete with the white man" (111). He talks of having gone to the Baptist mission at Mishongnovi the other day, where he was told "that it was the true knowledge that they had brought to us," a knowledge that would save the Hopis from going to hell, a place roughly comparable to Maski, the Hopi land of the dead. (See below.) Grandfather had "wanted to go further into it that [he] might understand and find out the truth" (111) for himself, but he does not read nor does he understand English.

For that reason, he charges his newly-baptized and newly-selected son to "be sure to choose this book and find out all you can about the truth," warning him, however, that "one thing you must never do: don't ever get baptized into this thing until you bring me back the truth" (111). Once grandfather is convinced that what the Christians say in their black book "is the truth . . . you and I will then be baptized" (112). After reminding Nequatewa that he must not "forget what [grandfather] is sending [him] down there for," he reiterates, "if that book really contains the truth," he must "come back someday and study the people here," his own Hopi people, to determine, it would seem, what, if any relationship, might be established between Hopi beliefs and those of the Christians.

လ

Founded in 1891, the Phoenix Indian Industrial School operated for almost a hundred years; it closed in 1990, having become a high school in 1935.

On May 1, 1899, Nequatewa and six Hopi girls traveled by wagon about 70 miles south to the town of Holbrook, where they board a train for the Phoenix school 186 miles to the southwest. It is his first time on a train. Although other boarding-school autobiographers traveling on trains for the first time to one distant school or another may also have faced this problem, only Nequatewa (once more) mentions bodily functions. At one point, when the train makes a stop, he gets off to urinate (116), only to learn, on his return, that the train has facilities onboard for such needs.

If the problem of how to sleep on a bed presented itself on Nequatewa's first encounter with the Keam's Canyon dormitory, the Phoenix dormitory presented the problem of how to deal with heat much greater than any Nequatewa had known in Hopi country, as well as "a lot of mosquitoes" (116). Sleeping only fitfully, he is awakened early "by the sound of the bugle, which [he] will never forget" (116). He notes with amazement that he "Never saw so many boys and girls" (116) (see figure 3). This is no wonder in that, by June of 1899, shortly after Edmund Nequatewa arrived, the Phoenix

3 Little girls praying beside their beds at the Phoenix Indian School in 1900. It's been suggested that the little girl turning toward the camera was told to do so by the photographer. For more on this photo see Margolis and Rowe. Courtesy of the National Archives and Records Administration, NARA 75-EXP-2B.

Indian School had more than 700 students (Trennert 1988, 64). The boys and girls line up to go to breakfast, but not before, as Nequatewa says, he "heard the band play *The Star Spangled Banner*"[19](117). He says then that "we *marched* up to the dining room" (117, my emphasis). Although Nequatewa does not further remark on this, the Phoenix Indian School was indeed run on a strict military model; both girls and boys marched everywhere, and "practiced army drill routines whenever possible" (Trennert 1988, 48). But Keam's Canyon boarding school had also been run on military terms, and, as I'd said, Nequatewa made no mention of that fact.

When he gets to the dining room, Nequatewa wants to sit down and get something to eat. But of course, as he observes with a measure of ethnographic distance, "*they* have to go through a ceremony of saying grace before eating or sitting down" (117, my emphasis). In his review of *Born a Chief*, Peter Whiteley had observed that Nequatewa was already "a seasoned ethnographic interpreter, well-versed in relativizing his cultural identity . . . as well as simply a Hopi man of his generation" (1994, 479) when he dictated his autobiography. This is to say that like all the Hopi autobiographers—indeed, like all Native people who worked with anthropologists—Edmund Nequatewa was both a "typical" or "representative" Hopi person of his time, but also, in some degree, "atypical," not strictly "representative," with distinctive personal or "individual" traits, among which, to be sure, was the willingness or desire to narrate an autobiographical narrative.

Nequatewa is thirsty, but he finds the Phoenix water too salty, and "coffee . . . was still worse" (117), as bad as his first warm tea at Keam's Canyon. During breakfast, Nequatewa remarks that he was with his "uncle then—Edwin" (117). Of course the reader had not known that he had an uncle named Edwin at the Phoenix School. But uncle Edwin turns out to be none other than uncle Kachina—who will occasionally be referred to by that name. The male students are officially grouped into military companies (121), but they are unofficially grouped into gangs. On his third Sunday at Phoenix—if Nequatewa has attended religious services on the previous Sundays, this is not mentioned—uncle "Edwin took his gang down to the canal"; for "the boys," Nequatewa discovers, "were kind of organized in different gangs" (118). There, he is initiated into the manly art of chewing tobacco, something that makes him ill, although he is persuaded of the necessity of mastering the practice. The authorities, aware of the tobacco use, make fruitless efforts to eradicate it, although it is not clear whether they have any awareness of the "gang" organization—perhaps another instance of student life that evades surveillance and control, what Amelia Katanski has called "the formation of a complex multivalent student culture" (44).

At age nineteen or a little older, the tobacco-chewing Edmund Nequatewa is put into a second-grade classroom (119) that might also have had students as young as seven or eight years old. Although he is unhappy about this—he had been in the third grade at Keam's Canyon—he admits that he still cannot speak English very well (121). Phoenix, similar in this regard to all the off-reservation boarding schools (and very likely to the Keam's Canyon School as well, contrary to Nequatewa's testimony), does not permit the students to speak their own languages. Insofar as the majority of the students were not Hopi but, rather, Pimas, Papagos, and Maricopas, English is the language in which the young men can best communicate—although it is entirely possible that most of them did not speak better English than Nequatewa himself.[20]

The academic programs at most of the boarding schools, as noted, were not strong and this is true for the Phoenix Indian School as well (Trennert 1988, 46). Indeed, Nequatewa says almost nothing about the few hours a day he spends in class during his first year. And, from Nequatewa's description, the Phoenix School's "outing" program, insofar as it existed, operated in what seems a thoroughly casual manner. During summer vacation, when most of the students from nearby tribes have gone home, Nequatewa—despite the heat, which he once more remarks—joins his uncle Edwin to work away from the school pumping irrigation water for local farmers. The two are each paid two dollars a day for eight hours of work (120). This is not, of course, work that required any of the vocational or industrial skills the Phoenix School taught.

During this time, Nequatewa says, "Edwin had been going to a special session of a Bible class," and, "All of a sudden [he] remember[s] that [he] was supposed to study that big book that [his] grandfather had mentioned" (121). It is something of a surprise that he has forgotten this in that grandfather had not merely "mentioned" it but stated and repeated its importance again and again. Nequatewa participates in the Bible class for about a year and a half, discovering that he "wasn't speaking English well enough to understand what this was all about" (121). When both the school superintendent and the Bible teacher are transferred, "For a while [they] didn't have any Bible study" (121). Once the new superintendent arrives, however, he doubles down on Bible study, requiring the students to go into the class-rooms on Sunday afternoon where "each teacher had to take up the Bible" (122). So onerous was this instruction that many of the students, we are told, "used to go off some place Sunday afternoons to keep away from it" (122). Nequatewa follows their practice. When "they made everybody go into the Bible class every afternoon, I didn't pay much attention to it," he says, once more forgetful of his grandfather's instructions. Rather, he "got so [he] was caring more about pitching hay or picking melons someplace" (125) to raise the price of train fare back home for the next vacation period.

"After school started again," Nequatewa tells us, he "found out that [he] had been promoted and was in the same class with [his] uncle" (125). It is in this class that his behavior leads to another important topos of boarding-school literature, Corporal Punishment. I've noted that there was indeed a disciplinarian at the Keam's Canyon School, although Nequatewa described no physical punishment meted out to misbehaving students. At Phoenix, however, Nequatewa is viciously assaulted by a teacher in a manner that exceeds acceptable practice—and this judgment is not merely the projection of a contemporary perspective onto that of an earlier period. The assault is once more precipitated by Nequatewa's excretory needs, no show of resistance intended.

One day, he says, he "got sick right in the school building," where he "knew that there wasn't any restrooms for the students." He is not merely "in the school building" at his time of need, but in the classroom, "so sick... [he] knew [he] would have to get outside" (125). To this end, he "got up from his desk and handed a note to the teacher saying that [he] was sick." One may remark with admiration that, given the urgency of the occasion, he did not depart immediately, and, too, that he felt his ability to write English sufficient to produce a communication the teacher would understand. He relieves himself, and, feeling better, "walked back over to the classroom" (125). He "had hardly sat down when the principal teacher," Miss Flora Harvey, as David Seaman's note identifies her, "stuck her head in the door and said, 'Ed, will you come to my office. I would like to see you'" (126). As he enters her office, Miss Harvey strikes him across his face with a ruler! He is able to take the ruler from her and break it on a table. She exclaims, "'How dare you!'" in response to what is now very much an act of resis-tance. She then locks the door and grabs another ruler with which to strike him. He picks up a chair to defend himself, accidentally breaking a window behind him as he raises it. He "jumped out that same window," and, as the principal teacher is phoning the disciplinarian, Nequatewa heads directly to the school superintendent's office.[21] Resistance to discipline is also a topos of boarding-school literature; how that resistance is dealt with varies enormously, depending on the ethos of any particular school and, even more, the inclinations of different members of the staff.

The superintendent—this would be Samuel McCowan, who had arrived in 1897—seems welcoming. He asks Nequatewa the problem, and, when he has shown him "the red lines on [his] face," and explained the situation, the superintendent, also by telephone, calls the principal teacher to his office. By the time she gets there, the disciplinarian has arrived as well. Both receive a stern reprimand about hitting students, especially hitting "them across their faces with a ruler like that." The superintendent concludes, "from now on both of you understand to keep your hands off the pupils" (127). I will admit that having read a great deal about physical punishment at the boarding schools, these words came as a surprise. Perhaps because the superintendent had sided with him in this matter, "Ever since then," Nequatewa says, he "never could make up with the principal teacher, and [he] was always thinking of how [he] could get away from that school" (127). The chapter in which Nequatewa is struck by the principal teacher, leading to his determination to "get away from that school" is called "The Runaways." Running Away is also a topos of boarding-school narratives.

With a clear purpose now in mind, Nequatewa "paid more attention to geography lessons, because it is the only way [he] can find [his] way out" (127). The distance from Phoenix to Hopi country is about 250 miles, and Nequatewa "didn't attempt to make a start until after New Years' [*sic*]" (128). As it happens, "one of the Hopi boys, named Paul, knew that [he] was going to try to get away, and he said that he wanted to go [along]" (128). Nequatewa advises Paul to stay, but the young man is determined to accompany him, even borrowing money from a relative of his whose name just happens to be Edwin. The trip, mostly on foot and full of all sorts of adventures, occupies some thirty pages of the book. Paul, as Seaman's *Born a Chief* portrays him, may be the only Hopi wimp in recorded literature.[22] Hartman Lomawaima, who "knew Edmund Nequatewa during his senior years" (1,330), wrote that this part of the story "reads like a script for a Bob Hope and Bing Crosby *Road* picture" (1,330), or, to stay within that time frame, an Abbott and Costello movie, with Paul the hapless Costello.[23]

Both Hartman Lomawaima and Peter Whiteley note the anticlimactic quality, after a very eventful journey, of Nequatewa's arrival home (Whiteley 1994, 479; H. Lomawaima, 1,330) Nequatewa discovers that his parents have once more moved, and, when he finds them, says only that "They were surprised to see [him]" (155). But the authorities are determined that Nequatewa and Paul return to Phoenix, and, when they announce themselves unwilling to do so, they are told they would be put in chains and brought back by force. Nequatewa initially makes the point that if he is taken back to Phoenix, he will run off again at the first opportunity. Finally, however, accepting the word of the reservation agent and superintendent, Charles Burton, that he would be treated better this time, he agrees to go. At this, Paul—as Seaman represents him in the book—begins to cry (161).

The journey back to Phoenix is not described. Once there, however, Nequatewa finds his old bed—he says he doesn't know what happened to Paul (161)—and resumes his old routine. Nequatewa then says, "Oh, yes, something important I forgot to mention. My grandfather had died about the first of the year in 1902. I got a letter about two weeks after his death, in January. That is why I did not expect to see my grandfather when I ran away from school" (162). Given the role Nequatewa's grandfather had played in determining the course of his life thus far, his death would indeed seem to be "something important," although its importance is undercut by the fact that it is presented as just "something... [Nequatewa] forgot to mention." But this manner of presenting grandfather's death is entirely David Seaman's. In volume 3 of the Alfred Whiting Collection, the earliest draft of the autobiography, May-June, 1942, there are two pages titled "OUTLINE OF EVENTS HOPI AUTOBIOGRAPHY" (8–9). The list of events under the title "THE ESCAPE" begins with "Grandfather is dead!" (9). And in volume 1, Whiting's final version of the autobiography from 1961, Nequatewa says, "In January of 1902 I had a letter from home saying that my grandfather had died two weeks before" (185), and it is only after noting grandfather's death that he tells the story of leaving school with Paul, returning home, and agreeing to go back to Phoenix. This is to say, Edmund Nequatewa did not "forget" to "mention" his grandfather's death, "something important," but, rather, noted it in his story at the time he learned of it. The way we have it is the result of David Seaman's editing.

Back at school, Nequatewa says that during his stay at home his father had reminded him of some of the things grandfather had told him, and he engages in "another Bible study" (162). And then, abruptly, his board-ing-school education comes to an end, its last two years represented in two short paragraphs. He arrives home "about the twenty-eighth of June, 1904"[24] (163). The final chapter of the autobiography is called "The Boy Becomes a Man." Why it is called that is not clear until the last sentence of that chap-ter, which is the last sentence of the book. The twelve pages of this brief final chapter are strongly marked by grandfather's concerns.

Nequatewa's mother, who had begun attending church, asks him whether "the dead really go to heaven" (164) and whether, as the new mis-sionary, a Miss McClean, has taught, "the bad people will go down into the underworld and have their punishment" (165). She thinks he "might have learned something about all these things, because Grandfather has sent [him] to school to learn the truth" (165). He responds skeptically to his mother's questions, does not attend church services, and soon finds himself in a direct confrontation with Miss McLean. He tells her in no uncertain terms that "The only thing [she has] done for these people whom [she has] supposedly converted is to take them out of one superstition and take them into another" (166).

Although Hopi religious belief and practice are characterized here as no more than another "superstition," Nequatewa states that "At the same time" as he was opposing the missionary, he "was listening and looking around very carefully, because [he] wanted to study [his] own people's side. From then on [he] was in all the ceremonies and had been initiated into most of them ... following what [his] grandfather had asked [him] to do. For, as he said, it was the only way to find the truth" (167).

Meanwhile, he notes, by the time he got back home, "Father had begun to believe in God," and, despite having "visions from God" (168), "He also practiced as a medicine man"[25] (167). For all his belief and visions, father tells a nephew of his named Roscoe that the missionaries "are just hypo-crites," and that "There is no such thing as Sunday. Sunday is just like any other day" (168). Father also affirms to Nequatewa that his "father, who is your grandfather, really did know and has told us the truth. All the Hopi ceremonies are wrong" (169). Whether the Hopi ceremonies "are wrong," and whether Hopi ceremonialism should come to an end is, around this time—the fall of 1904—a matter of intense controversy on Second Mesa, Nequatewa's home, and even more intensely on Third Mesa, at Orayvi. Father, like grandfather before him, would seem to be a Friendly, in the majority at Second Mesa, as I have noted, where Hostiles "were not so numerous as at Oraibi"[26] (Whiteley 1988b, 103).

Nequatewa recalls that "Grandfather had said that we would be in the midst of this trouble, that the end will come when every soul is drunk with fear. I believe that something is going to happen. The world will come to an end. And on that day the wicked will be done away with as my grandfather had stated" (167). As for his own belief as to how this will come about, the only thing he says is that "Whoever will do away with the wicked will not be the Bahana that we are seeing today. I do believe now that he whom the Hopi call Bahana is the heavenly God" (167). In volume 3 of the Whiting Collection, Whiting observed that although this "heavenly God" "can be confused with the Christian God in Heaven" (298), it is indeed the Hopi "Heavenly God," called "Sotukeunangwi," whom Nequatewa "equates to Bahana"[27] (306).

These important matters are temporarily dropped as Nequatewa's aid is solicited by a Shipaulovi chief who believes he is entitled to land currently belonging to Shongopovi. Complications arise and Nequatewa responds to them by leaving "the Hopi towns and [going] out to Navajo country" (171), where he remains for about a year. The Shipaulovi chief sends people to look for him, one of whom, a "fellow who was supposed to be [his] uncle" (172), threatens him before begging him to return (173). The two argue. "Most of the argument," Nequatewa says, "was on the clan house and that [he] should go back to the clan house and take up the fraternity chief-tainship and try to do all [he] could for the benefit of [his] people" (173). Nequatewa informs this "uncle" that he "never would do that," and although he "asked [him] why several times," Nequatewa tells us that he didn't respond because he "did not want to expose [himself] yet, nor [his] grandfather's theory" (173). Nequatewa does tell this uncle that *he* could "take posses-sion of the clan house and give himself the authority to be the chief of the One Horned Fraternity, and that [he, Edmund] was through with that fraternity"[28] (174).

Nequatewa returns to Navajo country, and, "Within a year's time . . . was speaking pretty good Navajo" (174). But he then abruptly leaves "to go to the snake dance" (174) among the Hopi. He attends a corn roast, meets a young woman (unnamed), and they marry. The last sentence of the book is: "You might say that evening [of his marriage] my childhood was over" (176). (See figure 4.)

4 Edmund Nequatewa and his wife, June, in 1934. Courtesy of the Museum of Northern Arizona. E100C(1934).047.

In that the subtitle of the autobiography is "The Nineteenth Century Hopi Boyhood of Edward Nequatewa," and the last sentence announces, or at least suggests, that Edward Nequatewa's boyhood—"childhood"—"might" be over in the early twentieth century, the boy having become a married man, it is tempting, from a Western perspective, to place the book in the familiar category, structurally and thematically, of a bildungsroman or developmental narrative. But the book is not constructed that way at all.[29] The autobiography's important experiences and events—I have singled out reservation boarding-school and off-reservation boarding-school experiences in particular—are not treated as steps along a way that at last becomes clear, apparently disparate parts of childhood that now, retrospectively, may be seen as forming at least a tentative whole. Very much to the contrary.

Nequatewa's grandfather, the only (more or less) developed character in the book, again and again prescribed a path for his adopted son to follow, and the autobiography might have been structured as a journey to carry out—or, indeed, to reject—grandfather's wishes. As I noted, Whiting, back in 1942, thought that *Born a Chief* "sort of falls short"; he'd thought that a title referencing grandfather and his concerns about the "black book" would be preferable. Nequatewa may or may not have been aware of Whiting's feelings on this matter, and Seaman, who would have had to have been aware of them as he assembled drafts of the autobiography in 1988, chose not to act on them. Indeed, he countered them by presenting grandfather's death, as I've noted, as no more than "something [Nequatewa] forgot to mention." In much the same way, although grandfather's serious concerns and his hopes for his son's schooling are recalled and revisited in this final chapter they are not sorted out (something Western novels and life-writing at least *used to do*) but left, as it were, in a tangle, all a muddle. The concluding sentence simply deflects attention away from them, offering only the boy-has-become-a-man observation.

I suspect that was probably the way Edmund Nequatewa wanted to leave things and if so, Seaman's editing respected his wishes. Although he did not live to see the published text, we nonetheless have an ironically critical reflection on the ending from Alfred Whiting himself. Volume 3 of the Alfred Whiting Collection, the earliest version of the autobiography (1942), contains a detailed "OUTLINE OF EVENTS" to which I have already referred. Its penultimate section is called "ANTICLIMAX." Nequatewa

> Works at the Agency
> Chief of Shipaulovi calles [*sic*] him back.
> Gets into trouble with the chief.
> Spends a year living with the Navajo.
> He renounces his right to the Clan house and
> the Chieftanship [*sic*].
> He is married and settles down to a life of
> henpecked duplicity. (9)

Unwilling, it would seem, to allow this bleak "ANTICLIMAX" to serve as his last word on Nequatewa's life history, Whiting added an "EPILOG" offering information not in the autobiography itself. The "EPILOG":

> He discovers the formula, by which Hopi
> beliefs and Christianity can be merged
> Jehova's [*sic*] Witnesses. (9)

I cannot say whether or to what degree this "EPILOG" influenced Seaman's editing.

What is clear is that Seaman (1) removed the dates and ages that Whiting had included, (2) excised a great many names that Nequatewa had provided, and (3) undercut the importance of grandfather's death by making it something Nequatewa had merely "forgot to mention." Of course, it may be that the general flattening out of detail and emotion that Seaman produced is valuable in providing Nequatewa's own sense of these matters, which is not a Western sense at all—although it leaves the book, from a Western perspective, without the high points or dramatic moments of self-fashioning that readers of autobiography have become used to. This is an issue translators and editors must face when translating not merely from one language to another but from one culture to another, what the editor of a life-story may encounter when trying to mediate between the sense of self and eventfulness of a non-Western subject and her usual assumptions about these matters. Although *Born a Chief* is little known, it has an important place in the canon of Hopi autobiography. The detailed account it provides of one Hopi man's experience of the boarding schools of the American Southwest around the turn of the twentieth century makes it as well a notable example of American Indian boarding-school literature.

2

Albert Yava's
Big Falling Snow

ALBERT YAVA WAS BORN IN 1888 ON FIRST MESA IN A TOWN KNOWN AS TEWA Village to Tewa people, but called Hano by Hopis. (See figure 5.) Yava's father was Hopi and his mother Tewa, and because both peoples reckon descent from the mother, he was, strictly speaking, Tewa.[1] In that his Tewa people had lived on First Mesa among the Hopis for some 250 or 300 years, speaking both Tewa and Hopi, Yava thought of himself, as the subtitle of his autobiography has it, as a Tewa-Hopi Indian. In the 1970s he worked with the anthropologist, folklorist, musicologist, and novelist Harold Courlander to produce *Big Falling Snow*.[2] Albert Yava died at the age of ninety-two in 1980.

5 Tewa Village or Hano on First Mesa, 1905. Courtesy of the Cline Library, Northern Arizona University. Item # 408.

Courlander's introduction to *Big Falling Snow* gives a detailed account of how the book came into being. Courlander writes that his "first recording sessions with Yava were in 1969, and they continued thereafter from year to year whenever [they] could manage to get together at First Mesa" (xiii). Yava narrated in English. By 1975, Courlander wrote, "it seemed to [him and Yava] that what [Yava] had voiced on tape might be sorted out and set down as a book of recollections" (xiv). That led to "the process of transcribing many hours of recordings and notes and of bringing all the pieces together into their appropriate context" (xiv). Courlander was guided in this "process" by his strong sense of Yava's modesty "about putting himself forward" (xiv), and his concern that his recollections be taken primarily as a contribution to the understanding of his people's culture and history. Although Courlander had interviewed Don Talayesva and knew his autobiography, *Sun Chief*—we will examine it in the next section—he understood that Yava, who had been at the Keam's Canyon School with Talayesva, was extremely critical of the highly personal revelations in that book.

Courlander writes that "Once the transcribed material was structured, a continuing correspondence between Author and Editor helped fill gaps in the narration" (xiv). Despite Courlander's passive-voice assertion that the "transcribed material was structured," I suspect it was Courlander who did most of the structuring, and, unlike Alfred Whiting and P. David Seaman working with Edmund Nequatewa, he did not choose to arrange the material in strict chronological order. Courlander was by far the most accomplished of the editors of Hopi boarding-school autobiographies in terms of literary skill, and he had also had substantial experience recording oral narratives and songs. I believe he chose to structure Yava's life story as he did the better to convey the meandering feel and the ebb and flow of oral narration. Nonetheless, the discussion that follows does treat the life-history materials in mostly chronological order.

Continuing his account of the making of the book, Courlander writes that "In 1975, Dewey Healing, Mr. Yava's son-in-law" visited with him, and, over a period of "several days," recorded "further comments and explanations. Mr. Yava received the resulting draft of the manuscript in early 1977 for corrections, deletions, additions and whatever second thoughts he might have"[3] (xiv). One of the deletions, as Courlander would later note, consisted of "a brief description of the Kachina Society initiation" (148n47). In keeping with traditional views of ritual knowledge, as I have noted at some length above, Yava "deleted it for reasons of propriety. Inasmuch as he himself was not a member of the Kachina kiva group, he felt that the information was not his to dispense" (148n47). In a meeting in July of 1977, Courlander says that Yava "reviewed the manuscript page by page and recorded further comments" (xiv), and that "As nearly as possible, Mr. Yava's own words are retained throughout the final text ... [;] even where editing was required, the substance remains faithful to his intentions and meanings" (xiv). *Big Falling Snow*, first published in 1978, is a fascinating text.

Yava's experiences at school began when he "was five or six," and "first went to the day school below the mesa at Polacca," which was called the Polacca school (9). Yava does not offer a scene of Naming at the school, having described how he came to be called Albert Yava earlier, as part of some general recollections. "The name that was given to [him] when he was born," he had said, "was Nuvayoiyava, meaning Big Falling Snow." He "received this name because [his] father belonged to the Raincloud, or Water Clan," and "Snow is an aspect of rain"[4] (3). In traditional fashion, he was named by his "aunts on the father's side ... , and they usually selected a name that revealed the father's clan affiliations" (3). He then gives three further examples of the way a child's name reveals its father's clan, one of which is especially worth noting.

Yava says that "If a man's name is Chucka, meaning mud, you know that his father was Sand Clan, because earth and sand together cover the breast of mother earth" (3). As we will see in the following section, Don Talayesva, a man whom Yava knew, and who had published his autobiography, *Sun Chief*, more than thirty years before Yava's, had been given the name Chuka as a child.[5] Yava does not mention Talayesva here, but in offering his thoughts about the Western form of autobiography as it relates to Hopi cultural understanding, he surely had him in mind.

Yava makes clear his feeling that "If I seem to say a lot about myself, it is really my times that I am thinking about. I am merely the person who happened to be there at a particular time. It is hard to put down something with myself as a center of interest—that is, to say I did this or that. It makes me out as important which isn't the way I see it. We Tewas and Hopis don't think of ourselves that way" (4).

As we will see further, Talayesva's editor Leo Simmons most certainly pressed him to "put down" a great many things "with [himself] as a center of interest," repeatedly urging that he "think of [himself]" in what was very much a *ka-Hopi*, a not-Hopi (or Tewa) way. Yava again addresses this later in his narration when he specifically refers to "a personal narrative by Don Talayesva, called *Sun Chief*" (81). He acknowledges that he "knew Don when [they] were boys at Keam's Canyon School," and that Talayesva "told a lot of things in his book that were true of his experience among the Oraibis." But, says Yava, "If there's any fault to find with the book it's that he talked about a lot of personal things, like his adventures with women, that most Indians wouldn't want to drag out in public" (81). It's Yava's sense that "those editors at Yale who worked with him on the book must have pushed him into it," as surely was the case. "Maybe I am too old-fashioned," Yava reflects, "but I find these things kind of embarrassing and not very illuminating" (81).

Although "Nuvayoiyava was the only name [he] had till [he] went to school," because his "teachers couldn't pronounce it very well they shortened it to Yava" (3). Expressing a measure of exasperation, Yava says that shortening his name "wasn't enough for them. They didn't like it that the children had no family names. So they sort of turned our individual names into family names and then gave us personal names like John, Mary, Henry, Peter and so on" (3). Although the teachers and staff at the boarding schools were probably not fully aware of it, the Hopis and Tewas were matrilineal societies, so the names they brought with them weren't at all the names of their fathers, and thus apparently available to serve as surnames—although, as noted, those names did reference paternal clan affiliations. And the forenames assigned represented a substantial de-individuation of each child, for although there are many Johns, Marys, Henrys, and Peters, whose names convey nothing whatever about the persons who bear them or of their families, there would be, except on very rare occasions, only one Nequatewa, Nuvayoiyava, or Talayesva. And, as Yava had made clear, those names provide a good deal of information about the person who bears them. "One teacher," Yava says, "wanted to call [him] Oliver, but another one who took a personal interest in [him] said, 'No, I like the name Albert, and that's what we're going to call him.' This explains how [he] came to be called Albert Yava" (3). Of course the teacher's "personal interest" is merely an arbitrary expression of what that teacher "likes"; Albert is no more meaningful to its bearer and his community than Oliver.

Yava's attendance at the Polacca Day School involves no Cleanup, doubtless because this is indeed a day school and the children go home in the evening to eat and sleep. Yava does say that "On [his] first day at school, they gave [him and the other children] all new clothes, white man's style" (9). He doesn't say anything about what that "style" might be, but, unlike what will be reported by some Hopi girls—Polingaysi Qoyawayma and Helen Sekaquaptewa, as we will see—Yava makes clear that the children— he means the Hopi boys—"didn't like those clothes very much because they made [them] feel ridiculous," so much so that when "the teacher sent [them] outside for recess [they] took off the clothes and hid them under some bushes, then [they] ran naked back to the village up on the mesa" (9). This very early instance of Running Away invites the attention of "the truant officer," who happens to be a "Hopi uncle" of Yava's named Chakwaiena. He "had to chase [the runaways] all through the village and over the roofs to catch [them]. When he did, he took [them] down to the school and [they] had to put those clothes on again and listen to the teacher, a tall white man named Mr. Spink, trying to teach [them] things in English" (10). Yava had earlier said that "Altogether [the students] felt pretty strange, getting edu- cated in a language [they] didn't understand" (9), and, along with the odd clothing they had to wear, it's no surprise that they "ran away several times before [they] gave up" (10).

Yava recalls that "One of the things Mr. Spink taught... was how to count... but [the children] couldn't get it because [they] didn't know what he was talking about," so they "just sat there dumb" (10). As it happens, his Hopi uncle, the truant officer, was in the classroom one day, and "he jumped up and said, in Hopi of course, 'What's the matter with you kids? Don't you understand anything? Just say like I do, 'One and two and hai hai hai!'" (10). That makes the children laugh, and "Even later, remembering made [them] laugh" (10). When a new day school opens and the students are transferred to it, they encounter "a teacher named Miss Cunningham," but find "It was still hard... to understand English and to pronounce English words" (10).

On returning home, the children solicit their parents' advice on learning the white man's language. The mothers, Yava says, suggest they " 'Watch [the] teacher's tongue, then you'll know how to say the words'" (10). Yava "had a girl cousin in that class, and she went home and told her mother, 'Oh, that teacher's tongue is so loose! She says, "A-atah, o-cha-tah "'" (10). His cousin, he imagines, "must have thought that was English" (10). Despite the very real difficulties Yava and the other students encountered, as Edward Dozier observed in *Hano*, "the necessity of learning a new language is not a strange phenomenon" (59) to Tewa children who early in their lives must master a second language, Hopi, one very different from their own.[6] (Hopi and Tewa belong to different linguistic groups, Uto-Aztecan for Hopi, Tanoan for Tewa.)

Looking back on these early years at school from the vantage point of the present—this would have been around the mid-1970s—Yava offers shrewd historical perspective. "You have to remember," he says, "that this school business was new not only to the children but also to most of the people in the villages" (10). He points out that "There had been a big commotion when the Government gave the order that all the children would have to attend school," and that "There was a lot of resistance," even more "on the other mesas . . . than on First Mesa" (10), his home. The "conservatives—you can call them that or Hostiles" (10), already "felt very strongly that the white man was cramming his ways down [the] throats" of the people. At the time he began attending school, "at the age of five or six, around 1893–94," Yava says, "the problem had not yet been settled" (11). He remarks that "Many people felt that the Government was trying to obliterate [Hopi] culture by making the children attend school"—which is, of course, exactly what the government at that time was trying to do. He offers the reasonable assessment that "the schooling the children have been getting over the past seventy-five or eighty years has educated them to the white man's ways but made them less knowledgeable about the traditional ways of their own people," concluding, "Something important is being gained, but something important is being lost" (10). He then offers some observations concerning the 1906 Orayvi split; he will have more to say about the split later on.[7] The "Tewas," he says, "were mostly on the progressive side;" indeed, "One of [the] most prominent Tewas, Tom Polaccaca (the Hopis called him Polacca), was very determined that the children should have a modern education" (11), and, indeed, the day school at the foot of First Mesa had been named for him. Yava notes that "with all the pushing and pulling, it took quite a while for the struggle" between the conservative Hostiles and the progressive Friendlies "to be resolved" (11). In that it was literally a "pushing" match that decided the "struggle," Yava's verb choices imply a good deal more than most readers would know. "When the split came in Oraibi in 1906," he says, "the conservative bunch, led by the Fire Clan and the Water Coyotes, established the village of Hotevilla, and once they arrived there they refused to let their children go to school" (11). (See appendix A.)

It wasn't until 1911, Yava recalls, that "the Government sent in troops to round up the Hotevilla children and take them to boarding school by force" (11). By that time, he "was working for the Bureau of Indian Affairs in Keam's Canyon" and he "was sent with a team and wagon to Hotevilla to pick up a load of children." The children were brought "to the Oraibi day school and kept ... there overnight." The next day, he says "we took them to Keam's Canyon and settled them at boarding school" (11). This recollection serves as a transition back to his own time at the Keam's Canyon School.

Yava states that he was transferred to the Keam's Canyon School "In 1896," when he "was eight years old"[8] (12). He gives the distance from First Mesa to the school as "about ten miles," noting that it was "quite a bit further from the other mesas" (12). "The boarding school," he says, "was in what they later called the 'old plant' because a new building was opened in 1903, and that one was called 'the new plant'" (12). At Keam's Canyon, he encounters both the Cleanup and the Hair Cutting. He recalls that "When we kids arrived on the first day of school, the first thing they did was to give us baths and cut our Hopi-style hair and make it white man's style" (12). "Our families," he states, "didn't like our hair being cut." He then offers a commentary I have found in none of the other Hopi boarding-school accounts. "Our traditional hairstyle," he says, "was meaningful. The long hair we boys wore on the sides symbolized rain, you might say fertility, and it seemed to our parents that the whites were pretty high-handed and insensitive, as well as being ignorant of our ways" (12).

Although it is run by white government employees, Yava finds Hopis and other Indians also working at the Keam's Canyon School. Tom Polaccaca is there along with a half-Cherokee school carpenter and his part-Cherokee wife who is the cook (12). Here, too, there are runaways: "If some kid ran away from school to go back to his village, which happened once in awhile, one of the teachers named Frank Ewing"—Yava often supplies the names of teachers, staff, and others he encounters—"got on his roan horse and went after him" (12).

"The new school building that opened in 1903 was pretty modern for those times," Yava recalls (he also often gives exact dates). "It had an electric power plant, electric lights, and steam heat from coal-fueled boilers"[9] (12). Nonetheless, he remembers that "some of the kids ... would rather have been anywhere but in that school, at least at the beginning." Still, "a lot of us liked it and were glad to have a chance to learn the white man's ways so that we'd know how to cope in later years." As for himself, he "was always glad to learn or experience something new" (12), very much the stance of a Tewa progressive. Rather than the Dining Room and the Mush, Yava recalls "a gardener at the school, a man named Bennet Hill who was a Civil War veteran. Eating the vegetables he raised was [his] first experience eating white man's crops" (12). He does not say whether that experience was positive, although his generally open and progressive outlook would suggest that it probably was. Like Edmund Nequatewa, he mentions neither the military organization of the school nor any required religious observance. Nor are any punishments mentioned.

As had Edmund Nequatewa, Yava speaks of "the smallpox epidemic [that] hit the villages in 1898. [He] was ten years old and at the old plant school at Keam's Canyon" (13). Although "Oraibi wasn't affected much,... on First Mesa and Second Mesa quite a few persons died." Yava "was very lucky because [his] family weathered it" (13) as had been the case with Nequatewa's family. When he "was in the eighth grade [he] began to wonder what [he] was going to do with [himself] when [he] was through at the Keam's Canyon School" (14). He says that "At that time, the children were detailed to work half a day and to attend classes half a day," pretty much the practice at the Indian boarding schools generally. "Once when [he] was working in the kitchen with Mrs. James [the part-Cherokee cook] she said to [him], 'Albert, wouldn't you like to go away to school after you are finished here?'" (14). He asks her where she has in mind and she tells him that she and her husband "have been transferred back to Oklahoma [at that time, about 1905, it was still Indian Territory, not yet Oklahoma]. There's a big government school there at Chilocco. The students are from different tribes" (14). He replies that because "There isn't really anything for [him] on the reservation," he would "like to go further in school and learn something useful." He then asks Mrs. James how he "should go about it" (14). She advises him to "talk to the superintendent. Maybe he can get you enrolled" (14).

Yava goes to see the superintendent, whom he describes as "an elderly man with a long beard. His name was Lemon" (14). This is Theodore Lemmon who had succeeded Charles Burton in 1904 and would remain at the Keam's Canyon School until 1906. Yava finds Lemmon sympathetic; he offers to "write to the people in charge over there and see if they can pay for [his] transportation"; he will also "make out the [necessary] papers" (15).

The problem, as it would be for other of the Hopi autobiographers, is that, as the superintendent explains, "somebody has to sign for [him]. If [his] father and mother are alive, they have to approve" (15). Students not only are not forced to go to any off-reservation school by this time, but parental permission—as we will see again—is required. But when Yava voices his desire to attend Chilocco, his stepfather "didn't say anything," and his "mother said, 'No, I want you to stay here.'"[10] (15). He tells his mother that he wants to improve his English, but "She just kept saying she didn't want [him] to go away" (15).

At some point, his "father heard about what was going on and he came to the house." He, too, says, "No, you can't go," adding that he would "fight the superintendent on it" (15). Yava explains that "the superintendent hasn't anything to do with it," and that he is "the one who wants to go to that school." But "All [his] father would say was 'no.'" This only makes him "more and more determined." He understands that his parents "believed [he'd] be better off staying in the village," because "most people were not very comfortable about letting their children go away to school" (15), even the progressive people of Tewa Village. But Yava is aware that "there were a number of young people who were going to Phoenix or Haskell and other places like that for schooling, and some were going to the Indian School at Riverside, California," (15) And he is set on going to Chilocco.

Yava has a friend named Claude who is facing the same problem; Claude wants to go away to school but his "mother and father won't let [him] go" (15). Once the two young men have "made up [their] minds," they leave the village, walking the ten miles to the school and talking "all the way back to Keam's Canyon about how [they] were going to manage it" (15). The plan is to "get in the wagon with" Mr. and Mrs. James "when it came time for [them] to leave" (15). Fortunately, his uncles—mother's brothers—come to Yava's aid. An uncle of his named Irving Pawbinele is "employed at the school as a watchman" (15), and, having "been at the Phoenix Indian School," he "knew what schooling could do to help a person."[11] Pawbinele encourages Yava "to keep trying and said he would help if he could" (15). But because he did not sign the necessary papers, Yava "still didn't have an okay" to go. Fortunately, that comes from another uncle, "a policeman... in Keam's, Nelson Oyaping." This uncle, Yava explains to superintendent Lemmon, is, "In the Hopi-Tewa way,... responsible for [his] welfare," and he is willing to sign the papers. Lemmon agrees to this (16). As it happens,

Yava's friend Claude has also managed to get someone other than his parents to sign for him, and "Finally the day came for [them] to take off" (16).

The Dining Room at Keam's Canyon School is mentioned for the first and only time as the place where a team and wagon pulled up and all the students "who were going to Chilocco piled in." Yava notes that "We were all boys except for one Navaho girl" (16). They get to Indian Wells, about thirty-five miles south, "the first day, and stayed overnight at the trading post," arriving the next day "at Holbrook after sunset" (16). It is there that they will take a train east to Indian Territory. Although both Yava and Claude had indeed obtained the adult permission of a relative to go to Chilocco, both are wary that "some of [their] people might be following [them] to take [them] home, since [their] parents had not given their approval" (16). For this reason in part, "Mr. and Mrs. James thought it would be good to try a night train" (16). Mr. James tells Yava that the "little canvas satchel" filled with prunes he is carrying is unnecessary because "We'll get our food along the way." Yava is "embarrassed . . . because it showed [he] didn't know anything about travelling the white man's way" (16)—not that there is any way he might have known about that. Yava says that they traveled "all night to Albuquerque"—a distance of some 235 miles from Holbrook—where they "had to change for a different train." The group have "breakfast at the station and [get] on another train going east" (16).

As other Hopi boarding-school autobiographers would also note, dealing with food on the trains could be something of an adventure. "About ten o'clock or so, a man came through the cars with a tray of fruits. He was saying, 'California fruits, California fruits'" (16); perhaps California had been the train's point of departure. Hopi people, Yava observes, always offer visitors "something to eat as hospitality," and, imagining that "it must be the same way here," he "grabbed a little basket of plums and started eating them instead of the prunes [he'd] left behind" (16–17). While the man waits, looking at him, his "brother Hugh"—this is a cousin of his also headed to Chilocco—explains that this is not "just hospitality," and that he "had to give the man money" (17). Fortunately, his uncle Irving had given him two dollars (16) and he uses one of the dollars to pay for the fruit, receiving "change, of course" (17).

The adventure continues when "about noon the man came through the cars again, and this time he had something [Yava] hadn't ever seen before—bananas." Hugh buys two, giving his "brother" one. Yava "took it for granted that you were supposed to eat bananas like pears or peaches, and... went ahead" to discover that the "banana was sweet inside, but the rind was pretty tough" (17). When Hugh asks what he'd done with the peeling, he learns his mistake. Then Hugh showed him "how to take the outside off," and that "was something else [Yava] learned when [he] went out in the world, how to eat a banana" (17). The party has to change trains in Kansas where Yava encounters another problem. In the station restaurant, he "sat on a stool but... kept falling off because [he] felt like [he] was still riding and swaying" with the train's motion. "Everybody thought it was a great joke, how [he] couldn't stay put on the stool," although he thinks "some of the other kids felt that way too" (17).

They "had to wait quite a while for [the] next train," and Yava, ever curious on his initial foray "out in the world," goes to the "shop in the station" where he "wandered around... looking at all the things they were selling." "[T]wo things in particular caught [his] attention—some dark specs and a big box of pencils" (17). He tells us that he had been "always curious about specs, and wondered what you could see through them." So curious had he been that if a "teacher was wearing specs [he] would sort of get around in back of him and try to get a glimpse through them," although he "was never successful at that" (17) at the Keam's Canyon School. He reveals, too, that he had been "always impressed that the teachers carried big bunches of pencils in their pockets," and it seemed to him "that the pencils had a lot to do with being educated." As he has some money left, he "bought a pair of the dark specs and a handful of pencils." He puts the pencils in his jacket pocket but they stick out awkwardly, and the others ask why he has them. He says that he'd "got them for school, because all the teachers wore pencils like that." He says they "poked fun" at him, but he "didn't mind" (17). The "specs," sunglasses surely, are a disappointment in that he "couldn't see anything but the same things [he'd] seen before, it was just that they were darker" (17).

At last the party from Keam's Canyon School gets to Chilocco in Indian Territory (it would enter the Union in 1907 as the state of Oklahoma), a journey of just over 900 miles. The Chilocco Indian Agricultural School was one of five nonreservation boarding schools authorized by Congress in 1882. It opened its doors in 1884 with 150 students, all from Plains nations. Modeled after Richard Pratt's Carlisle, it operated, until the 1930s (the school did not close until 1980), according to a strict military regime, with some former students reporting no fewer than twenty-two bugle calls a day. Like Carlisle, it offered half a day of academic classes and half a day of practical or vocational training to both its male and female students. Its first graduating class in 1894 was made up of six boys and nine girls. Of some 18,000 Indian students in attendance over Chilocco's long history, only about 5,500 graduated; the last graduating class of 1980 comprised no more than twenty-four students. Although Chilocco was an Indian agricultural school, it would seem that very few of those who attended became farmers (Bess, 98).

After the train pulls in to the station, the students from Arizona drive "to the school in surreys" (17), and on their arrival are taken "right to [the] dormitory buildings, one for girls, the other for boys"[12] (17). Yava and his dorm-mates are put in the charge of "a Sioux Indian, Asa Little Crow" (17–18). It is late at night, and dark, but when the light is turned on, Yava is surprised to find that "Most of the boys who were there were real light skinned" (18). He exclaims to Hugh, "this is a white school!" "Here and there," he says, "you could see a boy dark-skinned like [them], but most of them even had light hair" (18). He later learns that "they were Indians, all right, but they were Cherokees and other tribes." This was the first time he "ever knew that Indians came in different colors" (18). Having spent many nights in the Keam's Canyon School's dormitory, he notes nothing further of interest on his first night at Chilocco.

"The next morning," however, they "were awakened by a bugle call, and somebody shouted, 'Roll out! Roll out!'" (18). As noted, the Keam's Canyon School, like the other off-reservation boarding schools, was organized on a military model, although Yava, like Edmund Nequatewa, had said nothing about this. But there is no avoiding Chilocco's military organization. Once awake, the boys "made their beds first, then went down to wash up." Yava notes that "The adjutant, as they called him—his name was Amos Dugan—marched [them] around like soldiers. Everywhere [they] went [they] marched, until [they] were dismissed." Yava affirms what he had already made clear, that "This place was run like the army, like a military training school. Everything was done according to military discipline" (18). In that "Only one Hopi had been at that school before," the Hopi students are "a curiosity" (18).

Yava, like other students at government boarding schools a great distance from the reservation, is homesick at first, even thinking that he had made a mistake by coming to Chilocco (18). But "some of the older boys talked to [him] and encouraged [him], and after that [he] began to feel okay" (18). A problem, however, is that although he "had completed the eighth grade at Keam's Canyon," here he is "put back in the fourth grade" "for some reason he never understood" (18). Edmund Nequatewa had also been put back at the Phoenix Indian School to which he'd come from Keam's Canyon. In Yava's case, it is not that Chilocco is more advanced than the Keam's Canyon School had been, for, as he discovers, "They were teaching stuff in [his] class that [he] had had long ago. The books they were using were the same fourth grade books [he'd] had back at Keam's." Thus he finds himself "bored and discouraged … and just sat and drew pictures on paper most of the time" (18). Although he has to complete the school year in fourth grade, his teacher, a Mrs. Richards, "figured out what the matter was, and at the end of the year she had [him] skip two grades," putting him "back nearer to where [he] should have been, but not all the way." Despite his less-than-ideal situation, Yava "started to really study." He also "got into athletics … running, junior football, baseball and things like that" (18). Sports were important at the boarding schools, and, although he notes his participation, he says nothing further about what his engagement in these sports was like, an aspect, perhaps, of his disinclination to elaborate upon his personal experiences.

Similar to the other Indian boarding schools, "Chilocco had a trade school program for the boys … [who] would work at a trade half a day and go to … classes the other half." "They were trying to teach us something practical," Yava understands, "carpentry, blacksmithing, making harnesses and shoes, and so on" (18). (He says nothing of the girls' training in "domestic sciences.") Because he was "always interested in leather," he "asked to get in the shoe- and harness-making program," eventually receiving "a harness-maker's certificate" (18). When summer comes, the Hopi students who are very far from home are not the only Indians to remain at school. "During the summer vacations," Yava says, "about three hundred of us went over to Colorado to thin beets." He "also did other things during … summer vacations." He "worked with a pipe-laying gang, and once … worked on the Otoe Reservation baling hay" (18–19). This latter work quite clearly—and probably the other work as well—could hardly be considered to fulfill the aims of any "outing" program; rather, the Indian students provide cheap labor.

Although Yava and his friend Claude from Tewa Village "had signed up for three years" at the Chilocco Indian School, "at the end of that time

[they] were not prepared to go home because [they] didn't see what [they] could do for a living on the Reservation" (19). As we will see further, many boarding-school students came to feel this way. For all his success at learning shoemaking and harness-making, these trades (and whatever trades Claude had learned) apparently will not—as Leo Crane had lamented earlier regarding Indian carpenters and blacksmiths—permit the two young men to earn "a living on the Reservation." Thus, they "stayed on" at school, with Yava graduating "in 1910." Reflecting on this time, Yava "can't say [he] was well educated, but [he] did learn some things that have been useful... all [his] life, and [he] is grateful that the government made it possible" (19).

Perhaps as a consequence of his explicitly stated Hopi-Tewa distaste for offering personal observations or putting himself at the center of things, Yava says nothing about student interaction in the dormitories, dining rooms, or elsewhere at Chilocco. (He also says nothing about the quality and quantity of the food, an important topic for most of the boarding-school students.) Apart from the brief mention of the leather work in which he engaged and the sports in which he participated, he offers no details about his experiences, nor does he describe the academic curriculum at Chilocco (with the exception of that boring fourth grade). Although he notes the military organization, the marching, and the ranking among students (e.g., Amos Dugan, the adjutant), he does not reveal any rank he may have been assigned or attained. Nor is there a single word—as for his time at the Keam's Canyon School—about any punishments for student infractions of the rules. If there were, as there must have been, instances of Resistance or Running Away, these, too, are not mentioned—although he had told of the latter at the Polacca Day School. The largest omission perhaps has to do with the Christian practices and observances imposed on the Indian students both at Keam's Canyon and Chilocco. We know from his powerful testimony later in the book that Albert Yava did not become a Christian (see below), but he certainly would have been made to say grace at meals, attend church services, and even engage in some Bible study.

Yava was consistently reticent about personal matters, but one may surmise that another reason he did not speak of these boarding-school matters was that ultimately, they had little or no effect on his Hopi identity. After acknowledging his gratitude to the government for enabling him to learn some useful thing, he says, "looking back from where I am now," a man in his mid-eighties, "I think my life really began when I returned to the Hopi

Reservation. That was when I had to meet my problems face to face" (19). The "problems" he is recalling are the problems of a Hopi-Tewa returned student. "Going back to the time when I returned from Chilocco," Yava says, "I think I was pretty discouraged by what I found on the Reservation." This is a sense that many returned students had on first coming home. He observes that there didn't "seem to be any opportunities to earn money" (19), a necessity, since his People by then were, to a greater or lesser degree, enmeshed in a cash economy. Nor, once home, did he "see any way of using that learning [he] had gotten at school," a very common complaint of returned students. Although he'd gone back to "helping his stepfather with his work," cultivating fields for him and herding sheep, it is hard work and water was a constant concern (19). He manages to do "little jobs here and there," getting "work of one kind or another at the Indian Agency in Keam's Canyon" (20), and doing the best he could. Then, there "weren't any jobs available for some time," he says. Eventually he obtains employment once more at the Keam's Canyon Agency, where "they gave [him] a job taking care of the horses" (21). This was work for which he was well qualified because, fortunately, he'd somehow "learned a lot about horses and mules when [he] was at Chilocco" (21).

It's at this point that Yava notes that the Agency had in its employ several Hopi interpreters, and that "some time later when those men left," the job was given to him. Obviously he'd also learned a lot about English when he was at Chilocco, although Courlander provided no example of just what Yava's spoken or written English was actually like. Whenever the Agency needed him to interpret, he says, "they called [him]." For this work he "earned twenty dollars a month, which made [him] feel rich" (21), although he continued to do "other work as well" (21). His position as Agency interpreter will lead to more than material enrichment.

For, as Yava will later explain, "If it hadn't been for [his] work as an interpreter at the Keam's Canyon Agency [he] might never have become a member of the Kwakwanteu or One Horn Society" (72). His decision to do so comes from his recognition that his job as interpreter "was not only to translate words but to translate culture" (72). If his boarding-school education had prepared him to do the former, only further immersion in Hopi ceremonial life could enable him to do the latter. He had realized, for example, that there had been times when Hopis would come to the Agency and he would interpret "for them and the Agency people" (72), all the while sensing "that some of the village or clan spokesmen were holding back a little, not saying everything on their minds." They didn't trust him "to interpret faithfully for them," he suspects, not so much because he had been away at school, but rather "because [he] didn't belong to one of the important kiva groups" (72). Only those "who had been initiated into the kiva groups, particularly the four main fraternities were the 'real' Hopis," he understands, while "the rest of us were unfulfilled, like unripened corn" (72). Yava speaks to one of the Hopi men at the Agency who confirms this to him "confidentially" (72).

Until this point, Yava had said nothing about his participation in any aspect of Hopi or Tewa ceremonial life. In his introduction, as I noted, Courlander had made the point that Yava had "originally had a brief description of the Kachina Society initiation" in his story, "but deleted it for reasons of propriety" (148n47). That he could describe the *katsina* initiation strongly suggests that he had taken part in it. But he deleted it, Yava had told Courlander, because he "himself was not a member of the Kachina kiva group," therefore "the information was not his to dispense" (148n47). It's not clear what he meant by this—perhaps that he was not a member of the Katsina Clan? What is important to recognize is Yava's adherence to the belief that ritual and religious knowledge are not everyone's to know or disseminate.

Subsequent to their *katsina* initiation, as Edward Dozier wrote of First Mesa Tewas, "about the time a boy or girl has reached the age of fourteen or fifteen... [an] important event awaits them. For the boy the event is membership in the Hano Winter Solstice Association, and the initiation is generally simple but of great significance"[13] (61). Although a majority of adolescent Tewa boys and girls participated in this initiation, Yava does not seem to have done so; at least there is no mention of it. The Winter Solstice Ceremony of the Tewas at Hano parallels the Hopi *Soyalangw*, and, although, as I have noted, there is Curtis's record of Yava's Hopi father's involvement with that latter ceremony, it does not seem that Sitaiema, when his son was fourteen or fifteen, pressed him to participate. Nor does it appear that Yava's Tewa uncles urged him to participate in the Hano Winter Solstice initiations either. It's possible, of course, that Yava was away at school in December when he was the appropriate age for initiation. Nonetheless, when Yava was "still going to school in Keam's Canyon" (73) in his early teens, his father, Sitaiema, did want him "to be initiated into... the One Horn

Fraternity" (72), even picking out the required sponsor for his son (74). His father is proposing that Yava participate in the Hopi Wuwtsimt, which Yava calls "the New Fire Ceremony"[14] (74).

It's curious that his father suggested this to him when Yava was so young, for it is more usually men in their late teens, "Soon after adolescence, but usually before marriage," as I had quoted Mischa Titiev, who participate in the Wuwtsimt, their initiation representing "the transition from boyhood to adulthood" (Titiev 1944, 130). It is on the occasion of the New Fire Ceremony in November that a young man, as Yava explains, may be initiated into one of "the four important societies:" "the Kwakwanteu, usually called the One Horn ... ; the Aalteu ... usually called Two Horn to distinguish it from the One Horn ... the Wuwuchimteu and the Tataukyameu."[15] (74). Either because he was still only in his early teens or for some other reason, Yava is not sure that he wishes to accede to his father's desire. He raises the matter with his mother and stepfather; his mother speaks to her brothers, and the Tewa uncles, "who have a lot of authority in such things" (74), say, no, "Let him just be a Tewa" (73), and Yava is not then initiated.

Yava feels very differently, however, once he has returned from Chilocco, spent some time as Agency interpreter, and understood the importance of belonging "to one of the important kiva groups" (72). Therefore, when the sponsor formerly chosen by his father approaches him again, Yava agrees to be initiated. (He is also older at this time, more nearly the typical age.) He "decided to go ahead with it despite the opposition of [his] uncles" (74), because he now "realized that as a translator for the Keam's Canyon Agency [he] had to know much more about the inner workings of Hopi life, how the people were ceremonially related, who were the moving forces" (74). To be a good translator on the Hopi reservation, he understands, requires knowledge the boarding schools could not provide—knowledge, indeed, the boarding schools would rather he did not possess.

Working, as a man in his eighties, with Harold Courlander, having long ago become a member of the Kwan society, Yava clearly believed that he could relate some of the details of his initiation without violating propriety, and he does so at some length (74–79). Although the new name he is given on his initiation, Eutawisa, does not "stick," as Yava had told us earlier (3), he elaborates here on the range of its meanings. The name, as he had noted before, literally translates to "Close in the Antelopes," and it does indeed derive from his sponsor's membership in "the Deer Clan, related to the

Antelope" (78). But after his initiation, Yava learned from his sponsor—his name is Nitioma and he is a Tewa, but one who "belong[ed] to the Walpi fraternities" (Curtis 107)—that it also has a very particular Tewa meaning, for the name refers "'to how the [Tewas] were barred [from the Hopi villages] when [they] first arrived at First Mesa'" (79). Yava, as he has many times said, is a Hopi, to be sure, but very much a Tewa as well.

It's at this point in his life, after his Wuwutsimt initiation into the One Horn fraternity, that Yava is ready to marry, although Courlander had placed some brief commentary about his marriage much earlier in the narrative. He becomes interested in "a Tewa girl working at the trading post [in Keam's Canyon] by the name of Ida Haupove" (21). For reasons that are not given, her family does not approve Yava's seeing her. But the girl herself is intent on marriage, telling Yava that if "we can't get married the Indian way we can get married white man's style. We can go to the Agency for a license." Once they have their license, they go "to the Keam's Canyon Baptist Church to be married" (22). Yava is not happy about this not only, it would seem, because he is no Christian but because "all of Ida's folks were down on us." When, later, his "own people arranged an Indian wedding for [them]," "That made everything better" (22). Again, his Tewa-Hopi identity is very much intact.

Yava's marriage is a happy one and three girls are born to him and his wife. But his wife is killed when the "brakes in her car failed and the car went over" the "cliffside mesa road" (23). He is then "about twenty-four years old . . . and for quite a while . . . felt lost and restless." In what follows, he narrates with the sort of detail unusual for him—a full four pages, pages 22–25—how he came to marry his second wife, a Hopi woman. She is a married woman with three children of her own but estranged from her husband, and Yava describes a good deal of interaction among relatives and friends of the couple before they are married in Keam's Canyon "by a missionary over there" (25). But this marriage, too, does not last. His third wife, Yava tells us, "was Virginia Scott, a Navajo woman from Leupp." She, too, has been married before, although her husband has left her. Yava makes clear that the two "had a legal marriage"—he does not specify whether it was an "Indian wedding" or not—because he "didn't want to live with someone he couldn't call his wife" (25). Although the couple has five children together, his third wife, he says, also leaves him "and the children after we moved down to the Colorado River Reservation." At this point he breaks off, observing, "I think I've said more than enough about my personal life" (25). It is only later that we learn the family did not move to the Colorado River Reservation until 1952, after Yava's retirement from his "job at Keam's Canyon" (128), so that while it is indeed the case that "his wife abandoned him and the children" (128), she did so only after no fewer than thirty-five years of marriage, something one could not possibly guess from his earlier account.

Although he admits that he doesn't take some things literally in Hopi religious belief (108), Yava is not, as I've noted, a Christian. He has gone to many church services, and had a great deal of experience with missionaries of several denominations (136), but he has "not heard anything yet to persuade [him] that what they have is superior to what [the] Tewas and Hopis have" (136). One may assume that this includes his religious experiences at the boarding schools, for all that they were not mentioned. As he repeats a few sentences later, he doesn't "believe any of the Christian denominations has something valuable that [Hopis] don't already have" (136). (See figure 6.) Just as Albert Yava had comfortably navigated the differences between being a Tewa and a Hopi, so, too, did he navigate successfully the considerably greater differences between the societies in to which he was born and the dominant American society.

6　Albert Yava, undated photograph. NARA 210-G-K371.

3

Don Talayesva's
Sun Chief

IN THE "AUTOBIOGRAPHY OF AN ACOMA INDIAN," PUBLISHED IN 1943, THE anthropologist Leslie White wrote that "The autobiography of a Pueblo Indian is about as personal as the life story of an automobile tire" (327). "They are not individualists," he explained; "they are not given to reflective introspection and analysis." He admits that although he had "tried numerous times to secure autobiographies," he had not had "much success"[1] (326). Although White had been to Orayvi in 1932 and met Don Talayesva, perhaps he had not yet read Leo Simmons's *Sun Chief: The Autobiography of a Hopi Indian*, published the preceding year.[2] For in that book, Simmons, a Yale sociologist, had managed to do exactly what White despaired of, eliciting from Talayesva all sorts of "personal" details—in particular, details of Talayesva's very active sex life. If Talayesva's autobiography offered little that might qualify as "analysis," it most certainly contained a great deal of "reflective introspection." *Sun Chief* attracted immediate and broad attention, with many reviews, including ones by Clyde Kluckhohn and other prominent anthropologists; its French translation, *Soleil Hopi* (Hopi Sun), was graced with a preface by none other than Claude Lévi-Strauss. In 1951, David Aberle published "The Psychosocial Analysis of a Hopi Life-History," a study of *Sun Chief* that ran to 133 pages. Finally, I'll mention that when I first read *Sun Chief* in 1976, it was already in its sixteenth printing (paperback price: $4.95). Many more printings were to follow, and a new second edition has recently (2013) appeared, with a forward by Matthew Sakiestewa Gilbert. All page references are to this second edition, whose pagination differs from the many printings of the first edition.

In an introduction titled "The Project and the Procedure," Simmons wrote of meeting Talayesva "in June, 1938, as a result of correspondence with Dr. Mischa Titiev of the Department of Anthropology at the University of Michigan" (4). Titiev, as the reader learns from *Sun Chief*, had rented a room in Talayesva's house in 1933, and the two became friendly. Through Titiev's intercession, Simmons, five years later, also rented a room from Talayesva and began working with him on what he (Simmons) initially described to him as a "cultural study projected to fill in the gaps in the data of the Hopi literature" (4). Talayesva was paid "thirty-five cents an hour ... [for] formal interviewing" (4). Simmons was particularly interested in the interplay of culture and personality, and, "from the start," he writes, when Talayesva "described an item in the customary cultural pattern, he was asked specifically what his own experience had been" (4), Simmons now assuring him "that his own story was of much greater interest ... than a general description of his culture" (4). The work was facilitated by the fact that at the end of July, Chief Tawakwaptiwa, who had been at the Sherman Institute in Riverside, California, with Talayesva after the events of September, 1906 (see below), adopted Simmons as his "son," with Talayesva adopting him as his "brother" (4).

In the interest of elaborating his personal experience—something that, as Albert Yava had observed, is a thoroughly *ka-Hopi* or un-Hopi practice— Talayesva "was taught" (5), Simmons writes, how to report daily events "together with his mental and physical reactions to them," and to record them in a diary, which he would continue to fill after Simmons's departure. He was to "receive seven cents a page" (5) for any writing he did. When Simmons returned to Orayvi in 1940, "about 350 hours had been spent in interviewing, and Don had written about 3000 pages of diary in longhand"[3] (6). In March, 1941, Talayesva came east to visit Simmons, spending two weeks with him in New Haven. He had by that time "written about 8000 pages of his diary in longhand" (7). Simmons reduced this enormous amount of material to a narrative, which, as he notes, was still "more extensive ... than here published" (8) as *Sun Chief*. This narrative "was read to Don slowly," so that he could make corrections or add comments. Simmons concludes his introduction by emphasizing that the "material is offered at the present time in the hope that experts in the various approaches to the study of individual behavior in social and cultural perspective will see fit to criticize and cooperate in the formulation of hypotheses, the testing of theories, and the extraction of principles that may have more general application" (9).

Toward these ends, Simmons added to Talayesva's story a section called "Concerning the Analysis of Life Histories," and four appendices: "An Example of Situational Analysis," "Legends and Myths of the Hopi," "A Guide to Hopi Kinship and the Identification of Don's Relatives," and "A Sample of Don's Composition," the first three of these specifically directed to fellow social scientists.

The fourth, however, allows both social scientists and students of literature to see that although Simmons claimed "Don was exceptionally fluent" in English "for a Hopi of his age"—and, to be sure, of his educational background—there is nonetheless some distance between "Don's Composition" sample and the actual prose of the book.[4] Of course, the distance between the content and structure of the book as we have it, and the raw materials from which it was assembled—texts of the formal interviews, the 8,000 pages of diary material, and Talayesva's adjustments to all of these—would surely be far greater. But I can't provide any evidence for this judgment on my part. This is to say that if these materials still exist, I have not been able to find them.[5] Yale University's Beinecke Library possesses two boxes of Simmons's papers cataloged as "A Life History: the Autobiography of a Hopi Indian, Don C. Talayesva drafts of an autobiography" (WA MSS S-2206). They are dated "ca. 1942," 1942 also being the date of *Sun Chief*'s first publication. Both boxes are made up of folders containing a typescript draft of each of *Sun Chief*'s chapters, with one exception, which I'll note below. The typescripts in Box 1 are very heavily marked up, with, occasionally, text written on the backs of pages. Simmons must have done an enormous amount of work to get from the raw materials, as I've called them, to these versions, but, again, I can't provide an account of that work.[6] My focus here is on Talayesva's experiences at on- and off-reservation boarding schools and the impact those experiences had on his subsequent life.

∽

Don Talayesva was born in 1890 at Orayvi, the largest and oldest Hopi village on Third Mesa. The first three chapters of his story offer a very full account of growing up Hopi around the turn of the twentieth century, with portraits of a range of kin and of participation in ceremonial activities, in particular, his own painful *katsina* initiation.[7] Chapter V, "School on the Reservation," begins, "I grew up believing that Whites are wicked, deceitful people.... they were proud and domineering—and needed to be reminded daily to tell the truth. I was taught to mistrust them and to give warning whenever I saw one coming" (93). Talayesva notes the dissension between the Friendly and Hostile factions, the latter in the majority at Orayvi, and the majority Hostiles' unwillingness to send their children to the boarding school at Keam's Canyon.

But on the opening of the Oraibi Day School "at the foot of the Mesa" (94) in 1892, he observes that "Some parents were permitted to send their children to this school" (94), his Hostile parents among them.[8] His older sister attends first, experiencing the topoi of the Cleanup and the Naming: "the teacher cut her hair, burned all her clothes, and gave her a new outfit and a new name, Nellie" (94). "Nellie" doesn't like school, and stops attending, only to be "compelled" to return about a year later. The teacher having forgotten her name, Nellie now becomes "Gladys" (95). Talayesva's older brother avoids the school until 1900, when, on his arrival, he, too, has his hair cut, his clothes burned, and the name "Ira" bestowed upon him (95).

A year earlier it had been "decided that [Talayesva] should go to school" (95). Unwilling to have his "shirt taken from [his] back and burned," he heads down to the school wrapped in a Navajo blanket. He enters "a room where boys had bathed in tubs of dirty water" (95), and, apparently knowing the drill from Nellie/Gladys, Ira, or other day students (but unaware of the dangers of dirty bathwater), he steps into a tub and begins washing himself, only to have a white woman enter and exclaim loudly enough so that he jumps out of the tub, darts through the door, and runs naked up the mesa. He is caught, brought back, and told that the woman had only meant to praise him "for coming to school without a policeman" (95). This woman then administers the Cleanup and the Naming: she scrubs him, cuts his hair, dresses him in "very baggy overalls" (but he is also "measured ... for a better-fitting suit") (95), and bestows on him the name "Max," a name he does not like (95). Talayesva briefly describes two Christmas celebrations, "one in the school and another in the Mission Church" (96), but all in all, he says, he "learned little at school the first year" (96).

In January, Talayesva "danced for the first time as a real Kachina"[9] (96). Because of the smallpox outbreak that had moved from First Mesa to Second

Mesa and now threatens Orayvi, he also gets vaccinated. "The old people said that the vaccinations were all nonsense," and that it was the prayers of the Hopi that "had persuaded the spirits to banish the disease" (97)—which, as Edmund Nequatewa had also noted, disappears in the spring. Talayesva briefly describes seeing what he believes to be the torch of the deity Maasaw, and Maasaw will play a significant role in his later life.[10] "In October [he] returned to day school and continued until the following spring," but "did not learn much" (98) in that time either. It is in the autumn "that some of the people took their children to Keams Canyon to attend the boarding school" (99), and he, too, goes, accompanied by his mother and father. He is taken in by the school matron, Mrs. Weans, who "gave [him] a bath, clipped [his] hair, and dressed [him] in clean clothes" (99).

Talayesva's experience of the Dormitory is positive. He sleeps on a bed for the first time, "something new," and finds that it "felt pretty good" (99). Apparently he did not fall off as Edmund Nequatewa had. He says nothing about submission to Clock Time, although he would have awakened when everyone else awakened, dressed and washed when everyone else did, and gone to breakfast with the other children, all at the same hour. Nor is there any mention, at this point, of the students saying grace. Talayesva also says nothing about the military organization of the Keam's Canyon School, just as Edmund Nequatewa and Albert Yava had not. In the morning, he encounters the Mush. "For breakfast," he says, "we had coffee, oatmeal, fried bacon, fried potatoes, and syrup"—(100) pretty much what Nequatewa had described. He finds the "bacon... too salty and the oatmeal too sloppy" (100). His parents have spent the night and after "breakfast we were all told to go to the office and see the superintendent of the Reservation, Mr. Burton" (100). This is Charles Burton, whom we have met earlier, the man who, despite the derogatory reports about him, Edmund Nequatewa had trusted, returning to the Phoenix Indian School on Burton's promise that he would be treated better than he had been.

Before Talayesva's parents leave for home, his father advises him, "don't ever try to run away from here. You are not a good runner, and you might get lost and starve to death. We would not know where to find you, and the coyotes would eat you" (100). Running Away is a frequent boarding-school topos, but considering this possible fate should he run away, Talayesva says he "promised" (100) not to make the attempt. He cries with homesickness but is comforted by a boy named Nash, who assures him that his parents will surely come visit and bring him some familiar food, just as Edmund Nequatewa's grandfather had done for him.

At noon, the students return to the dining room for lunch. Talayesva this time does observe that "At the table somebody spoke a few words to God, but failed to offer him any food" (100), an omission from his Hopi perspective. He finds the lunch food "very good."[11] He spends the afternoon with Nash "cleaning up the trash in the yard" (100), the sort of task boarding-school students were often assigned. Their work completed, the boys take a "walk up the southeast mesa to the highest point," and stay so long that as they "climbed down the mesa, [they] heard the supper bell ringing." They run, but "arrived late" (101), and are immediately met by the disciplinarian who "struck Nash twice on the buttocks" (101), for not properly observing the dinner hour. As a new boy, Talayesva is this time spared corporal punishment; he will not be spared next time. Nequatewa and Yava, at Keam's Canyon at about the same time, had not described any physical punishment being meted out.

The boys are allowed into the dining room where Talayesva comments on "a thing called hash, which [he] did not like. It contained different kinds of food mixed together; some were good and some were bad, but the bad outdid the good." Talayesva is sure he "would never like hash" (101). Along with prunes and rice, he also encounters tea for the first time. His reaction replicates Edmund Nequatewa's: "The smell of it made me feel so sick," he says, "that I thought I would vomit" (101). He also notes a problem with "defecating," for, although "Little houses called privies were provided— one for boys and another for girls," when he "went into one of them [he] was afraid to sit down [lest] something ... seize [him] or push [him] from below"; he was "uneasy about this for several days" (101). When it is time for bed, a matron takes him "to the small boys' dormitory, where she made us undress except for our underwear, kneel, and put our elbows on the bed. She taught us to ask Jesus to watch over us while we slept." Talayesva notes that formerly he "had tried praying to Jesus for oranges and candy without success, but [he] tried it again anyway" (101).

He begins his education "at the very bottom in the kindergarten," despite the time he had spent at day school, and despite the fact that he is "the biggest boy in the class" (102). But Edmund Nequatewa and Albert Yava had also been put back. The teacher asks Talayesva his name but, since he does not like the name Max he had been given, he does not respond. His silence leads to another Naming; now he is called Don (102), a name to which he does not object, for all that it is as meaningless to him as Max. He describes some lessons, and "Soon we were reading long sentences like 'A rat, a rat, cried Mae'" (102). This progress notwithstanding, Talayesva "grew tired of school and thought of running away," although he had been warned against it. A nephew of his father's at the school cures his despondency and homesickness by the curious means of teaching him to ride pigs, hitherto unknown animals that he finds "horrible with their little eyes, sharp mouths, and dirty faces" (102). Riding them, however, is sufficiently amusing that he "thought to [himself] that if my home-sickness returned I would ride a pig again" (102). This dimension of schoolboy ingenuity and invention does not seem to have come to the attention of the disciplinarian or the teaching staff.

Although neither Edmund Nequatewa nor Albert Yava had described required church attendance at Keam's Canyon, Talayesva says that "Every Sunday we were taken to the chapel, where we sang, prayed, and had a lesson about Jesus Christ" (102). In February he is promoted to the first grade and manages to send a message to his father asking for a visit and some Hopi food. As Edmund Nequatewa's grandfather had done, Talayesva's father arrives "bringing some watermelons" (103). "A few weeks later," Talayesva writes, "we had some excitement at school." This involves Sex. Talayesva informs us that the "assistant disciplinarian, an Oraibi man named Edwin[!], ... climbed through a window into the girls' dormitory one night to sleep with his sweetheart. ... Soon some of the larger boys tried this with other girls" (103), engaging in *dumaiya*, the "customary" Hopi behavior Nequatewa had described. But this is not, of course, behavior acceptable to the whites. One of the boys is caught and pressured into providing "a long list of names" (103) of boys who had been similarly engaged.

The following day is a Sunday, and "As we lined up to go to breakfast," Talayesva says, the superintendent, Mr. Burton, "came with a paper in his hand" (103). He begins by calling out Edwin's name, and then some thirty more names. The remaining boys are told to continue on to breakfast where they notice "that many of the girls were absent too." "Mr. Boss, the disciplinarian, said grace quickly," and after "breakfast, Sunday school was called off" (103). From the yard, Talayesva observes the boys and girls receiving "a long, stiff talk. Then they were taken to a room upstairs," where soon he "heard strapping. Each boy received from fifteen to thirty lashes with a rawhide, depending on his age. They were whipped in the presence of the girls, but no boy cried out. Then the girls were taken to another room and paddled, but not before the boys. Some of them cried. After giving the boys another lecture, Mr. Burton marched them through the yard to the toilet, where every boy seemed anxious to go. They were then taken back to the room and locked in again" (104).

Talayesva and his fellows go to lunch, but those who had been disciplined are not fed. At the end of the day, he says, they received "bread and water" for supper "and were then released" (104). Edmund Nequatewa had described no consequences for the "customary" sexual adventures of his dormitory mates, and Don Talayesva, despite the detailed account, offers no comment whatever on what seems extreme corporal punishment—fifteen to thirty lashes with a rawhide.

Just two paragraphs later he notes his father arriving to take him home from school, at the end of the semester, in June. Reflecting on the school year past, he offers a list of what he had learned: "I had learned many English words and could recite part of the Ten Commandments. I knew how to sleep on a bed, pray to Jesus, comb my hair, eat with a knife and fork, and use a toilet. I had learned that the world is round instead of flat, that it is indecent to go naked in the presence of girls, and to eat the testes of sheep or goats. I had also learned that a person thinks with his head instead of his heart" (104). Regardless of whether such knowledge would enable him to find a place in mainstream American society, or aid him on his return to the reservation, it has provided him with a critical perspective on Hopi society. "By the end of the summer," Talayesva says, "I had had enough of hoeing weeds and tending sheep. Helping my father was hard work and I thought it better to be educated" (105). His "grandfather agreed that it was useful to know something of the white man's ways," but, unlike Nequatewa's grandfather, he makes clear that he "feared [his grandson] might neglect the Hopi rules which were more important" (105) than anything the whites might teach.

As it happens, Talayesva doesn't have the opportunity to return to school voluntarily, because, "on the tenth of September the police came to Oraibi and surrounded the village, with the intention of capturing the children of the Hostile families and taking them to school by force" (106). He is taken and "put with the others," his family seemingly recognized as among the Hostiles despite the fact that Talayesva and two of his siblings had voluntarily attended the schools. (And, too, that he had earlier described "little wars" (64) with Hostile children.) This among many other incidents and events makes clear that one cannot always know the actual beliefs or particular behaviors of those called Hostiles or Friendlies at any given time. Once again Superintendent Burton appears, wonders what Talayesva is doing with the captured children, and is pleased to learn that he "was glad to go with him" (106) back to the school. Talayesva arrives while the "children already at the school were eating their supper" (107). Along with a loaf of bread, he is offered hash, which he refuses. He then "went to the dormitory and rested," and, in the morning, has a bath, has his hair clipped, and puts on new clothes, a "schoolboy [...] again" (107).

He is now put "in the dormitory with the big boys," given "some long khaki pants, and promoted ... to the second grade." At twelve, he "felt like a man" (107). He is enough of a "man" to remark that the second grade teacher is "a good-looking blond about forty-five, named Mrs. DeVee" (107). She is concerned to get her students to pronounce English words correctly, and Talayesva finds that he "had to work hard to keep up with the class" (107). It's at this point that his classroom behavior results in his being punished twice. The first time is when he retaliates against "a boy who hit [him] first" (108). He is made to "stand in a corner with [his] left arm raised high above [his] head for a full half-hour" (108). He is next punished for talking "too much with a deskmate." For this, Mrs. DeVee made the boys "chew a piece of laundry soap until foam came out of [their] mouths" (108). Otherwise, this second year of boarding school is uneventful and at its conclusion, Talayesva's father again comes to take him home.

The first sexual encounter he reports occurs in July, with a thirteen-year-old named Mae, "one of [his] ceremonial aunts of the Greasewood and Road-Runner Clan" (109). They have intercourse, although Talayesva, in retrospect, and doubtless following Simmons' instructions "to include [...] the smallest details" (5), remarks that he didn't think he "had an ejaculation" (109). Not quite thirteen himself, he "had already begun to feel restless at night and to dream about girls" (109). He would thus seem to have been well prepared for his return to school in September when he had "occasion to see some of the boys masturbate until they ejaculated." He notes that "Sometimes we played a little with each other," but that when one "boy wanted [him] to pretend that [he] was a girl with him," he "did not want to do it" (109). There seems to be no coercion involved, nor do these sexual activities seem to have attracted the notice of the authorities. There is no mention whatever of teachers or staff attempting to engage sexually with the students or of older children abusing the younger ones. I had earlier cited Titiev (1944, 30) to the effect that Hopi people willing to talk about their lives and culture to the whites had learned to edit or omit sexual behaviors offensive to mainstream moral standards. Talayesva does not do this here nor will he throughout his story. To be sure, he is narrating in the later 1930s, when Victorian morals had loosened considerably. But there is no doubt that his volubility in these regards, something that greatly displeased Albert Yava, is, as Yava had guessed, in response to Simmons's prompting.

There does not seem to be any illness at the school; nonetheless, "some of the boys were playing sick so that they could stay in bed and cut classes" (109). Talayesva, who has had eye trouble in the past, decides to play sick by throwing sand in his eyes (109). The doctor very quickly determines the cause of Talayesva's eye problems, and advises, "don't put sand in your eyes again and pretend to be sick or you will really have sore eyes" (109). Although he had told the doctor that he "was tired of school" (109–10), Talayesva still says that he "had lots of fun at school that year. Sometimes [he] played jokes on the teachers.... They never whipped [him], although the disciplinarian paddled [him] once." He does, however, get "paddled ... pretty hard for wrapping himself in a white sheet and pretending to be Jesus" (110). So much for his third year at school.

In the summer he "returned to Oraibi and worked as usual" in the fields, although he also is one of a group of boys and girls who "return to the Agency [at Keam's Canyon] for two or three weeks to care for the buildings and grounds" and to move equipment for "a new school plant" that is being built (110). It is this "new plant" at Keam's Canyon that Albert Yava had mentioned (12). On his way there, Talayesva again sees "a light, apparently in the hands of an unseen human form, moving along two or three feet above the ground." He finds no tracks, and is frightened once more to think "that it might be the fire of Masau'u or of an evil spirit."[12] (111). When he becomes ill that night, he feels sure "that Masau'u had caused [his] sickness" (111). Fortunately, he recovers quickly.

In September he returns to the new school facilities he had helped build. "It was there that [he] first sat on a modern toilet which was like a spring and flushed." Although he was "uneasy at first and expected the bowl to overflow," he "caught on quickly and liked it—although it was a waste of water" (112). That year, he notes, he "really had sore eyes." The medicines offered at the school do no good, and finally he and a clan uncle cut into the flesh around the eye, releasing a discharge; after this, he "felt better" (113). Apart from being disciplined for mistreating a Navajo fellow student, and eventually getting a kitchen job which "gave [him] a chance to eat more" (113), he describes very little.

The next September, 1905, Talayesva returns to school and is "assigned to stable duty for a time," before being transferred "to the blacksmith shop, where [he] learned to weld iron" (114). "In May, 1906," he is sent to "Rockyford, Colorado, with a large group of boys to work on sugar-beet plantations." In that the Keam's Canyon School did not seem to have a formal "outing" program like that of the off-reservation schools, this mass excursion simply provides cheap labor.[13] The boys "worked eleven or twelve hours a day at 15 [cents] an hour" (115). In that they move "from farm to farm, thinning beets during the day and sleeping in tents at night" (115), it is clear that the modest recompense for their labor does not include any opportunities to absorb the mores of white family-farm life, the rationale for the outing program. Work is again complete by the fourth of July, and Talayesva returns to Orayvi to find that "the quarreling was getting worse" between the Hostiles and the Friendlies (115).

ဢ

It needs to be stressed that the Orayvi split, as has sometimes been written, was not caused by the differences among Hopi villages and factions regarding attendance at the American schools, although differing attitudes to the Americans did become both a factor in and a strategy on the part of the two sides, the so-called Friendlies and the Hostiles. Peter Whiteley has pointed to the fact that the "Leaders of the opposing factions in 1882," five years before the Keam's Canyon Boarding School was established and a full ten years before the Oraibi Day School opened, "represented substantially similar positions to those present at the split of 1906" (1988b, 73).

All of the Hopi boarding-school autobiographers considered in Part I of this book lived through the Orayvi Split, from Edmund Nequatewa, who was about twenty-six in 1906, to Fred Kabotie, who was only six years old at the time. Some of them—Don Talayesva, Polingaysi Qoyawayma, Helen Sekaquaptewa, and Fred Kabotie—were in Orayvi at the time, with Talayesva, as I will note further, actually participating in the pushing match that took place. Thus the Split was an important event for all of the Hopi boarding-school autobiographers, and it is not possible adequately to understand their lives without some ethnographic and historical understanding of it. But rather than interrupt this discussion of Don Talayesva's boarding-school experiences with a lengthy account of the Orayvi Split, I am relegating it to an appendix. I hope the reader will consult it at whatever moment she or he thinks best.

Talayesva, not yet back to school on that September day, took part, as I have said, in the pushing match, lining up with the Friendlies and remarking that "some of the Hostiles were surprised that [he] did not join with them" (115–16). This is understandable in that Talayesva states that "Most of [his] father's relatives were Hostile and many of [his] mother's people, too" (115). Of course they would not have been "surprised" if—as he had remarked earlier and much later told Courlander—he had long been associated with the Friendlies. After the events of September 7, Talayesva returns to Keam's Canyon for what promises to be his sixth and final year of school (two years more than what Nequatewa had described as the norm).

He becomes infatuated with a fellow student named Louise, who tells him she often goes hungry—something not unusual at the boarding schools. Talayesva informs Louise that he is "a kitchen boy," that he loves her, and "will get food from the kitchen" for her. One Saturday, after "feeding her, [he] hugged her warmly for the first time, told her that she was a sweet little thing, and that [he] wanted her for [his] wife" (117). They go into the pantry, lock the door, and hurriedly have intercourse—standing up as Talayesva details the event. He says that "It was the first time that I had found and given real pleasure in lovemaking." After that, he "cared more for her than ever" (117). But a problem arises when he learns who her relatives are and that she is his clan daughter. Their families thus "would not like ... [them] to be in love" (117). Nonetheless, like young lovers in other cultures, they decide to stick together. This leads to their approaching various staff members, along with the new school superintendent, Theodore Lemmon, who, after quizzing Talayesva as to his feelings and intentions, approves their union (118). At that point, the emboldened young lover impulsively tells the superintendent "that he ought to feed us better" (118). "From that day on," Talayesva proudly says, "they did give us a little more to eat, but the other children never knew that [he] was responsible" (118).

In November, "forty or fifty" of the children are told that they "were to go to school at Sherman,... in Riverside, California" (118). This is not presented as a choice. Talayesva notes that "Our Chief, Tewaquaptewa, was also to go and learn the white man's ways" (118). Tawakwaptiwa, of the Bear Clan, was chief of the Friendlies who had remained in Orayvi, but the American authorities were not pleased with their having expelled the Hostiles. As Matthew Sakiestewa Gilbert writes, "Shortly after the Oraibi split, the federal government concluded that Tewaquaptewa acted in an un-American fashion when he forced... the 'Hostiles' out," even breaking "federal law" (2005, 3). Given a choice of prison or an off-reservation boarding school, "Tewaquaptewa chose Sherman since officials [had] sent many children of the 'Hostile' families to the Phoenix [Indian] School"[14] (Gilbert 2005, 3).

Talayesva and Louise will join Tawakwaptiwa (along with his wife and daughters) and a great many other Hopis, seventy-one in all (Sakiestewa Gilbert 2005, 2; 2010, 93), on the journey to Sherman—although superintendent Lemmon makes clear "that Louise would have to leave Sherman if she became pregnant" (118). The two lovers go home briefly to Orayvi before heading to Winslow, Arizona, to take the train to Riverside. On the way, Talayesva says that he and Louise dropped behind the others and then stopped "by the side of the road in a quiet place, and had intercourse" (119).

The Perris Indian School, founded in 1892, in Perris, California, was that state's first Indian boarding school. In 1897, Perris's superintendent, Harwood Hall, finding the school in need of a better water supply and more room, applied to Representative Joseph Schoolcraft Sherman of the House Committee on Indian Affairs for funds to move the school. The funds were appropriated and Perris moved some twenty-five miles south to Riverside. The new school's cornerstone was laid in 1901, named for Sherman, and opened in 1903. It had about five hundred Indian students in late 1906 when the Hopis arrived (Sakiestewa Gilbert 2005, 3).

Talayesva notes that he and Louise got to Riverside on Thanksgiving Day (120). He has come from more than five years at the Keam's Canyon boarding school with some English language skills, with the information that one thinks with the head not the heart, and that the world is round not flat. He can sleep comfortably on a bed, and attend to excretory needs using either a privy or a flush toilet. He knows one is to eat meals at appointed times regardless of whether one is hungry or not, and go to bed at a certain time regardless of whether one is tired or not. He finds hash unpalatable, oatmeal often too mushy, and tea nauseating, but some American foods have proved pleasing. He has experienced church services, grace at meals, prayer before bedtime, and Bible study; he has also memorized parts of the Ten Commandments. He has a sense of various Protestant proprieties (boys shouldn't go naked in the presence of girls, and boys and girls shouldn't swim together), although his own sexual mores are decidedly not Christian as he regularly engages in love-making in an entirely "customary" Hopi manner. Having participated in *katsina* dances, worried about sexual relations with a clan daughter, and continuing to fear *Maasaw*, Don Talayesva can hardly be said to have lost his Hopi identity by the time he comes to California. Chapter VI of *Sun Chief* is titled "School Off the Reservation," and in it Talayesva recounts his experiences at Sherman.

Apparently there is no need for any clean-up. Talayesva and Louise are taken "immediately to the dining room for lunch and served large yellow sweet potatoes which [he] had never seen before" (120). He peels them, and adds "gravy, pepper, and salt." This, he finds, renders them inedible; thus he learns that one should eat "sweet potatoes 'straight'." He also learns "to eat tomatoes raw" (120). He knows that he is to remain at Sherman for three years (120). Apart from these new foods, his first day in Riverside brings all sorts of informal experiences of American urban culture. He learns that there is a football game about to be played between Riverside High School and Pomona College "with admission free" (120), and he decides to go. But, then, growing "tired of the rough football game," he walks over to the roller skating rink with a Hopi friend from Moenkopi where he meets a "pretty" Navajo girl named Dezba Johnson. "In shaking hands with [him] she smiled and squeezed [his] fingers, giving [him] a thrill" (121). Louise by this time had been spirited off by a relative who, he suspects, knows and disapproves of their "courtship" (121).

From the roller skating rink, Talayesva and his new friends go to a zoo where he encounters bears and wildcats, animals familiar to him, but also monkeys, which are not. "By and by a male monkey mounted a female" (121), which amuses him and perhaps serves in some measure as inspiration. After buying "two bottles of strawberry pop, a loaf of bread, and some jam" (121), quite like young Americans their age, Talayesva and Dezba go into the park and sit on the grass under a tree. Dezba calls him "honey," "the first time he had ever heard 'honey' used in courtship," and asks, "Could we fall in love?" (121). They will engage in love-making, although Dezba is in fact married, and will leave Sherman in the spring. Talayesva's event-filled first day in Riverside continues with a return to the zoo and the monkey cage and another visit with the bears. Encountering Louise with the relative who had disengaged her from him, Talayesva thinks he "had better drop Louise, because her mother's sister might get [him] into trouble" (122). In that he finds himself "falling in love with Dezba," for the moment at least he feels "lucky." Riverside, California, is not, of course, New York or Paris, but one may wonder if it did not seem so to Don Talayesva in comparison to Orayvi or Keam's Canyon, Arizona. Still, telling of his first day there almost thirty years later, he does not register any of the surprise, anxiety, or sense of wonder I imagine he might have felt at the time. (Had he ever heard of football or seen it played before? What did he make of roller skating? Or zoos?) Nor does he report upon his first Sherman dinner or his first night in the dormitory.

Of course there is also the actual business of schoolwork. A test on the multiplication tables sends Talayesva back "from the sixth into the fourth grade"; his older brother Ira is "put in the second grade and [both] were given part-time jobs in the bakery" (122), not so much to learn the baker's craft as, again, simply to keep the school going. "Besides going regularly to class," Talayesva says, "we joined athletic clubs and debating societies, and attended many socials, including square dances" (122). He does not mention the rigid Clock Time observed at Sherman,[15] and he says nothing of the school's military organization. Diana Bahr writes that "Although the regimentation at Sherman was not as strict as in other boarding schools"— Chilocco, for example, as Albert Yava discovered—"military drills were used to teach order and discipline. Boys and girls were grouped according to age and size in military-style companies that marched to classes, to the dining room, and to the dorms" (25). Edmund Nequatewa, who, like Don Talayesva, had not mentioned the military organization of the Keam's Canyon School, did describe it at the Phoenix Indian School, as Albert Yava had described it at Chilocco. Perhaps Talayesva did not find this aspect of life at Sherman interesting enough to record. Or he may well have written about these things and Simmons chose to omit them.

At some point, Talayesva is "taken into the Y.M.C.A. by two Hopi boys ... who led [him] into a room" where he signed his "name before [he] knew what [he] was getting into." In signing, he says he had "no idea that

[he] was committing [himself] to Christianity" (123). No mention has been made thus far of any religious observances at Sherman, but Talayesva's unwitting commitment at the YMCA turns out to be consequential. He learns the names of all the books of the Bible, and memorizes scripture verses, for which feat he wins a Bible of his own(123). "At the Y.M.C.A. meetings," one is "expected to stand on [his] feet and testify for Jesus" (123). Talayesva even delivers a "little sermon" in which he promises that once he gets "a clear understanding of the Gospel [he will] return home and preach it to [his] people in darkness" (123). This would seem to be very different from his merely pro-forma dealings with religion at Keam's Canyon. Indeed, in retrospect, Talayesva says, "At that time I was half-Christian and half-heathen [*sic*] and often wished that there were some magic that could change my skin into that of a white man" (123), a clear triumph, at least for the moment, of the ethnocidal and assimilationist aims of the boarding schools, and a development inimical to his Hopi identity.

He learns to "preach pretty well, and to cuss too," he says, and, despite receiving a book at the Y.M.C.A. warning that masturbation "ruined a boy's health and caused him to go insane" (123), he notes "the boys doing it right along" in the dormitory. "Half-Christian" as he currently considers himself to be, he "never masturbated much…because [he] did not want to lose his strength" (123). He describes wet dreams, and occasional dreams "of a girl in bed with [him] who always turned out to be a boy" (123).

In the summer he is "outed" to "Fontana, a farm a few miles away," where he works "pitching hay for $2 a day," and becomes involved with a part-Klamath Mexican cook named Olive. They have copious sex, and are once caught by an "old Dutchman" who worked with them. The Dutchman tells Talayesva "dirty" stories which he "stored in [his] mind to retell some day in Oraibi" (125). He returns to school in the fall "well-dressed in citizen's clothes," with "a good suit," "low-top patent-leather shoes, a fancy hat, a velvet shirt, and a silk necktie"; his hair is "cut in the American style" (125). At this time, he once "again wished that there was some way to turn [himself] into a white man" (125). What next occurs, however, makes clear that regardless of this "wish," elegant citizen Talayesva remains through and through a Hopi.

He learns that an older sister has died in childbirth because of a Two-Heart, a witch "who had cast a spell" on her. Although his father had managed to catch the witch-woman, it was too late. In "grief and anger at this news," Talayesva cries out, "That witch might as well kill us all and be done with it. I don't care if she does kill me. I am a single man with no children" (126). The woman who has brought him this news is "frightened" at his outburst and replies, "'Those are careless words that may cause you to get sick.'" Talayesva states simply, "They did" (126). Simmons provides a note indicating that Talayesva regards this "as the most significant event in his life" (125n.).

He is admitted to the school hospital, where, his condition worsening, at the end of a week, he is moved to another floor. After a month passes, he is put "on a ward with very sick boys who were not expected to live." Talayesva is diagnosed with pneumonia and his name put "on the danger list" (126). He continues to deteriorate, experiencing "dreadful" pain in his chest; he "spits blood," and wants "to die and get out of pain" (127). At this low point, he "began to think of the Two-Hearts and to review all that [he] had heard about them" (127). Then, on a Christmas Eve as it happens, he has a powerful vision, but not one that derives from his recent Christian training.

The lengthy vision Talayesva recorded for Leo Simmons sometime between 1938 and 1941 is very similar to one he had earlier narrated to Mischa Titiev in 1932. Titiev noted that although the "narrative contains many conventional ideas taken from the general pattern of Hopi culture," Talayesva "tends to introduce them as if they were parts of a unique personal experience" (1940, 496). On the one hand, in that Talayesva had not yet met Simmons in 1932 when he narrated for Titiev, perhaps he had on his own developed the distinctly *ka-Hopi* trait of emphasizing his "unique personal experience." On the other hand, in that Titiev did not publish the account from which I am citing until 1940, by which time he had aided Simmons in his project with Talayesva and knew its orientation, he may well be reading the 1932 narration through a later perspective. In what follows, I will work from Talayesva's account as it appears in *Sun Chief*, indicating, on occasion, differences from his earlier version and incorporating some of Titiev's observations.

Seriously ill in the hospital at Sherman, Talayesva sees "a tall human being standing by [his] bed in Katcina costume" (127). He had earlier told Titiev that the man carried a blue prayer feather in his left hand, Titiev noting that "Blue is the color symbolic of the west among the Hopi. The path of the dead and the home of the dead are supposed to lie to the northwest of the Hopi pueblos" (1940, 496). The man announces himself as

Talayesva's "Guardian Spirit," and informs him that because he has "been careless" with his words and invited death, he must now "travel to the House of the Dead and learn that life is important." The Guardian Spirit will both "wait here and watch over [his] body," and he will also "protect [him] on [his] journey" (128). Suddenly Talayesva's "pain disappeared and [he] felt well and strong" (128).

Talayesva next describes in detail a lengthy visionary voyage.[16] It begins with his "traveling" home to Orayvi, where he sees his mother, his father, and his grandfather, no one of whom sees him. He also see his grandmother who appears "ugly, naked . . . with drawn face and dry lips," looking "tired, half-starved, and very thirsty" (129). (In Titiev's earlier version, Talayesva first saw a "big lizard crawling under a pile of rocks," and only then does he see his grandmother who tells him, "my father is a lizard and I have two hearts"[17] (1940, 497).) He believes that the one whom he now calls his "Guardian Angel"—Simmons offers a note indicating the probable Christian influence (129); there is no "Angel" in the earlier version recorded by Titiev—"placed her there to teach [him] a lesson and to show [him] that she was a Two-Heart" (129), a witch.[18] She asks to accompany him to the House of the Dead, but he refuses and hurries on alone, encountering other imploring Two-Hearts whom he repels as well. He comes at last to "the foot of Mount Beautiful, the Judgment Seat" (129). This might also appear to be a Christian reference, one that is absent from the 1932 account. Mischa Titiev, who had seen Talayesva's version for Simmons prior to its 1942 publication, characterizes the addition as "phrasing of a somewhat stilted character that was foreign to his style in 1932," adding in a parenthesis that "(Don has never been converted to Christianity)" (1940, 502)—although, as we have seen, he had, about the time of his vision, been very active in the YMCA.[19]

Now, almost floating on air, he ascends a "mighty stairway to the highest point" (129). He hears the ringing of a bell, and sees a man climbing from the west "dressed in a white buckskin, wearing a horn [head-dress], and holding a spear and a bell" (129). The man is a Kwaani'ytaqa, a "member of the Kwan or Warrior society, who watches the kivas during prayers and guards the village to keep out strangers and let in the dead during the Wowochim ceremonies" (129–30). Titiev provides a note explaining that members of the Kwan or Agave Society, which we have encountered earlier as the One Horn society, "claim the god of death (Masau'u) as their patron. Hence they play prominent parts in all stories of the Afterworld" (1940, 498n9).[20]

The Kwaani'ytaqa tells him to look to the west, the direction associated with death, where he sees two roads. Performing his traditional function of directing "the souls of the dead onto their respective path" (Malotki and Gary, 286), the Kwaani'ytaqa orders Talayesva to take the broad one, to the left, not the narrow one to the right. On that narrow road he sees "naked, suffering people struggling along the path with heavy burdens," and threatened by snakes (130). (There is no description of the narrow right-hand path in the 1932 version.)

Moving swiftly along, he sees in the distance "twelve queer-looking striped animals chasing one another" (130). These turn out to be Hopi clowns who have "painted their bodies with black and white stripes and were joking and teasing one another" (130). Their leader is of the Eagle Clan, which is related to Talayesva's Sun Clan. He advises Talayesva to make haste, for although his Guardian Spirit is protecting him, he nonetheless "must hurry back to [his] body"; if he does so, he "may live a long time yet" (131). There is, however, much more in store for him on his journey before he can think of turning back.

The young man sees many other things before arriving at "the Little Colorado River," where, "On the walls across the canyon [the Grand Canyon] were the houses of our ancestors with smoke rising from the chimneys and people sitting out on the roofs" (131). Although a second Kwaani'ytaqa dressed all in white appears, it is the first one who repeats that Talayesva has "been careless and [doesn't] believe in the Skeleton House where ... people go when they die," once more telling him "We shall teach you a lesson on life" (131). He travels to the southwest, following the first Kwaani'ytaqa, and "trailed by the second who kept off evil spirits." They come to a house where he sees two Kwaani'ytaqas, one making "red yucca suds," while another makes "white suds" (131). Asked to choose between having his hair washed in red yucca suds or white, he chooses the white suds and considers himself "lucky" to have done so, for that means, says one of the Kwaani'ytaqas, that he "may journey back along the Hopi trail and return to life" (132). (Titiev: "Whenever a Hopi undergoes an important change in status, the event is accompanied by head washing in yucca suds.... Hence it was fitting for Don to expect to have his head washed when he visited the region of the dead" [1940 499].)

His hair having been washed, Talayesva is again told to hurry, and, traveling now to the southwest, he sees "a great crowd of people watching a fire which came out of the ground. On the very edge of the flaming pit stood four naked people, each of them in front of another individual who wore clothes" (132). A Kwaani'ytaqa informs him that the naked ones in front are Two-Hearts, witches who had killed the clothed people behind them. Talayesva then sees each of the people who had been killed push a naked Two-Heart into the pit, "causing great volumes of smoke to rise" (132). The Kwaani'ytaqa has Talayesva look into the pit where he sees four beetles; these are what the Two-Hearts have become (133).

He then begins traveling "back over the course" he had formerly covered, and comes once more to the canyon "where the people sat on their housetops" (133). Now, the canyon is full of smoke. Peering down, Talayesva sees "a gruesome creature in the shape of a man climbing the cliff... with a club in his hand" (133). "It was big, black, bloody-headed Masau'u, the god of Death, coming to catch [him]." At this climactic moment, one of the Kwaani'ytaqas gives him a push forward, crying out, "'Flee for your life, and don't look back, for if Masau'u catches you, he will make you a prisoner in the House of the Dead'" (133). Talayesva turns and runs eastward, pushed along by the Kwaani'ytaqas "with their wands or spears," so that he "rose about six inches from the ground and flew faster than [he] had ever traveled before" (133).

When he gets to Cole Canyon, he finds the painted clowns waiting for him; they warn him to leap because "Masau'u is gaining" on him. He does, and is told then to look back, at which point he sees Masau'u giving up his pursuit and returning westward (133). (Titiev: "When Masau'u turned back the act meant that Don was not yet destined to die" [1940, 500n17].) The leader of the clowns then speaks to him, saying:

> Now, my nephew, you have learned your lesson. Be careful, wise, and good, and treat everybody fairly. If you do, they will respect you and help you out of trouble. Your Guardian Spirit has punished you so that you may see and understand. Lots of people love you. We are your uncles and will see that no harm comes to you. You have a long time to live yet. Go back to the hospital and to your bed. You will see an ugly person lying there; but don't be afraid. Put your arms around his neck and warm yourself, and you'll soon come to life. But hurry, before the people put your body in a coffin and nail down the lid, for then it will be too late. (133–34)

Talayesva hurries along and arrives at the school hospital, where he finds his "Guardian Spirit and a nurse at [his] bedside." His Guardian Spirit instructs him to slip under the covers alongside his body and to put his "arms around its neck" (134). Talayesva does so, despite the fact that he finds his body "cold and little more than bones." Soon he "became warm, opened [his] eyes, and looked up" (134). Nurses surround the bed; the head nurse holds his hand. Although his journey had been a long one, it is only "Christmas morning and students were marching from building to building singing carols" (134).

He is told that he "passed away last night," but that because his "heart kept beating slowly and [his] pulse moved a little," the staff did not bury him (134). The nurses are pleased that they will get credit for having saved his life, and they exclaim that they "love [him] more than the other boys and girls because [he] is kind-hearted and act[s] like a brother" (134). So Talayesva reports, although why they would say this is not clear. He hears that a coffin had been ordered for him, and he sees the new suit he was to have been buried in; he also finds some gifts from Santa Claus (134)! For these, he says, he felt "grateful but took pity on [him]self and cried, saying in [his] heart, 'I have learned a lesson and from now on … [will] be careful to do what is right" (134–35). At lunch time he has "a good square meal which made [him] feel perfectly well" (135).

"After lunch" he has a visit from the one he now again calls his "Guardian Angel" (135), who, in a lengthy speech, reminds Talayesva that he had indeed spoken rashly, and, although he has apparently learned a lesson, he will nonetheless be carefully watched. If he behaves well, some day he "will be an important man in the ceremonies," at which time he should make a *paho*, a prayer feather, for his guardian. "Many people never see their guide," the spirit tells him, but he has shown himself to Talayesva, "to teach [him] this lesson." Advising him "to be good, be wise" and to "think before [he] act[s]," the guardian spirit disappears (135). In his wake, Talayesva sees "a soft eagle prayer feather rise up from the floor, float through the door into the hall and vanish" (135).

The following morning he receives a visit from Chief Tawakwaptiwa, to whom he tells the story of his "death journey." Tawakwaptiwa "said it was true, for those were the very same things that the old people said they saw when they visited the House of the Dead"[21] (135). It is another month before Talayesva can leave the school hospital, and one may believe he has regained full health in that he soon has his "pleasure" with Ollie Queen, a Hupa Indian from California who has been his nurse, and whom he had "courted" before his illness. As it happens, "she soon found another friend," so that Talayesva "saw no more of her in private" (136).

He "stayed in school until the early spring of 1908," when he and some other students are sent "to Imperial Valley to help harvest cantaloupes." He returns to Sherman in June "for the Commencement exercises," and then goes back to the cantaloupe fields to work until July, after which he is sent "to work on a dairy farm near San Bernardino" (136). This is a situation he does not like, and he makes the trip back to Riverside via "streetcar" (136). From this point forward, he would seem to pick up exactly where he had left off before his illness, with no reference to the powerful vision he had experienced. "I felt more and more like a prosperous man," Talayesva boasts in *ka-Hopi* fashion. "I dressed well, treated the girls at the socials, and carried my money in the concealed pocket of a fancy belt" (136). He lists other possessions of which he is proud, "a secondhand bicycle" (136) not least among them.

He is soon sent back to the farm at Fontana where he takes up again with Olive. In the fall, he returns to school for his final year, and goes "on a trip to Los Angeles, California, and out to Long Beach to see the Pacific Ocean." It is there that he has his "first boatride, and [he] liked it" (137). He is promoted to the sixth grade and takes "an active part in the debating society in [his] classroom." He finds the business of standing on his feet and "giving proof for everything [he] said" very hard, although he says of that, too, that he "liked it" (137). A problem arises, however, when he "was selected to debate in the auditorium before six or eight hundred students" (137). He feels this is "too much . . . and refused to do it." His refusal is taken as insubordination serious enough that the "assistant disciplinarian was called and offered [him] a choice between debating and getting a thrashing." Talayesva chooses the thrashing, which is severe: "about fifteen blows with a rawhide in a heavy hand," causing him to break down and cry (137). He offers no comment about the severity of a punishment, which kept him "sore for several days," noting only that he "was never again asked to debate in the auditorium" (137).

His remaining time at Sherman is full of "American" activities: he plays baseball, avoids football because it is "too rough" (137–38), learns to "razz" other boys, and to use disparaging comic nicknames. In May he goes with his brother Ira, about whom we had not heard for a while, to pitch hay "for board and $2 a day," although on only their second day they are told to go back to Sherman to prepare for their return home to Orayvi (138). So cosmopolitan have the two brothers become that they go "to a Chinese restaurant to get [their] breakfast" (138). Soon the Hopi students, "enough to fill twelve or fifteen wagons," board the train for home. Talayesva had begun seeing a girl named Mettie from Moenkopi on Second Mesa, but she does not sit with him on the train. Instead, he finds himself with "Irene of the Masau'u clan, . . . the granddaughter of old Chief Lolulomai"—he had preceded Tawakwaptiwa as leader of the Orayvi Friendlies—"and a pretty girl" (138). Although he previously "had paid no attention to her in school," he knew "that Sun Clan boys [like himself] often married Fire Clan women"; indeed, his brother, Ira "was already going with a Fire Clan girl"[22] (138). Talayesva jokes with Irene, asking her "if she would think of becoming [his] wife some time" (138). But Mettie is definitely not out of the picture.

As night approaches, the "conductor called all the girls into the forward car to sleep"; the "next morning they came back" (139), and by "about nine o'clock in the morning" all the returned Hopi students get off the train at Winslow, Arizona where they found "their relatives with their wagons to meet [them]" (139). Talayesva is approached by a "man who looked like a Navaho and was dressed 'sporty'"; the man asks for Chuka, the name by which Talayesva is, at that point in his life, known to Hopi people (139). The man, Frank, is "the new husband" of Talayesva's sister, Gladys, and he has come to take him home. They do not set off immediately, however; several matters precede the departure for home, among them Talayesva's purchase of a rifle. He finds Mettie, and later that afternoon, they have sex "among some bushes." Talayesva says that he "was not afraid to do it, because we were back among our own people" (140). Of course he had shown little hesitation engaging in sexual adventures while away.

"After supper," Talayesva goes into town with some others; they go "through the stores that were still open, and then went to a movie" (140). It would be interesting to know what film was showing in Winslow, Arizona, in 1909. (And, too, whether the theater—since it seems to have allowed admission to persons of color—was segregated in its seating.) He returns to spend the night at the Orayvi camp—students and their relations had set up camps according to the Hopi towns from which they came—where he finds "a big bonfire" and the men "dancing their Katchina dances." Having been away for three years, he notes that he "did not know the tunes" (140). He finds Mettie, lies beside her, and specifies having sex with her "twice more during the night" (140). He "could hear others doing the same thing.... All the fellows were with their girls, for [they] were now free from the school officials and back with [their] uncles and fathers" (140). Their uncles, recall, are their mothers' brothers; their fathers are either their biological fathers or their fathers' brothers.

In the morning Talayesva buys food, Frank picks up an Anglo carpenter he had agreed to transport to Hopiland, and they set off for home. It is necessary to camp for one more night, and this sixth chapter, "School off the Reservation," concludes with Talayesva lying on his blanket, reflecting upon his "school days and all that [he] had learned" (141). To the many secular and Christian skills he had earlier listed, he adds (among other things) the ability to name all the states in the union and all the books in the Bible, from which he could "quote a hundred verses of scripture" and "sing more than two dozen Christian hymns." He can also sing patriotic songs, "shout football yells," and "swing [his] partners in square dances"; he confirms what he had suggested earlier, that he can "tell 'dirty' Dutchman stories by the hour" (141).

Commenting on this passage in *Sun Chief* in 1995, David Wallace Adams noted that for all his "education," Don Talayesva, lying out under the stars, makes clear his desire "to become a real Hopi again" (Talayesva, 141; Adams 1995b, 40), and thus, from the perspective of the boarding-school movement, he is "part of what the Indian Office commonly referred to as the 'problem of the returned student'" (40). Adams does not mention that just before stating his desire, in this passage, to "become a real Hopi again, to sing the good old katcina songs, and to feel free to make love without fear of sin or a rawhide" (141), Talayesva references his "death experience," stating unequivocally that it was his vision that "had taught [him] that [he] had a Hopi Spirit Guide whom [he] must follow if [he] wished to live" (141). From the Hopi perspective, as Mischa Titiev noted, "A Hopi is regarded as 'strengthened' after returning from a visit to the Afterworld" (1940, 504n23), and it is very much a Hopi perspective that dominates his return.

I am emphasizing the fact that having twice stated his desire to be a white man, Don Talayesva's wish to "become a real Hopi again" is a direct— if slightly delayed—consequence of his powerful vision. In that regard, he is not entirely a typical "returned student." (Nor will his subsequent decision to work with social scientists be entirely typical of returned students.)

Meanwhile, there is no question that the kind of "real Hopi" Talayesva will be is a different kind of Hopi than his parents or grandparents were, and for that matter a different kind of Hopi than Hopis of his own generation who escaped or attended the schools very little.

The seventh chapter of *Sun Chief* is called "The Return to Hopiland," and in it Talayesva describes his transition back to traditional life. He tells his parents about his time at school and, in particular, about his visionary trip to Maski, the House of the Dead. He does herding and hoeing for Frank, his sister's husband, and he takes on other paid work; he hunts rabbits for food, and takes up again with his lover, Mettie, while also sleeping with (among others) Jane, Eva, and Elsie, who is the first woman ever to fully undress for him. (He reports a number of other erotic details about his love-making with Elsie as well, and it is impossible to determine the degree to which Simmons pressed him for these, or the degree to which he had come to enjoy this sort of reportage.) He also participates actively in Hopi ceremonial life. The eighth chapter of the book—Simmons made it the central chapter of the book, although with what intentionality I cannot say—is called "The Making of a Man" and, in a manner unlike Edmund Nequatewa's, it does not present marriage (an account of Talayesva's marriage will come two chapters later) as marking the movement from boyhood to manhood. Rather, the transition is marked by "initiation into the Wowochim" (165).

Mettie announces her intention to return to Sherman and she asks him to come with her. But, our narrator says, his "father, grandfather, and two great-uncles urged [him] to forget about school and become a man" (165). Further, his "ceremonial father, clan fathers, mother, godmother, clan mothers, and other relations encouraged [him]; and they implied that any boy [he is at least nineteen] who did not seek membership in the Wowochim proved himself to be either incompetent or kahopi [un-Hopi]" (165). In commenting on Edmund Nequatewa's presentation of his marriage as marking the end of his childhood and the beginning of his manhood, I cited Mischa Titiev's observation that the Wuwtsim "Initiation … marks the transition from boyhood to adulthood" (1944, 130). Let me add to this Peter Whiteley's statement that "to become a fully adult Hopi, a man had to be initiated into one of the *Wuwtsim* societies" (1988b, 195).

Whiteley writes that the Hopi "ritual cycle is coordinated with the natural cycle, which dictates parallel cycles of secular human activities. Wuwtsimt and Soyalangw [see just below] serve as master ceremonies that bring together many religious concerns, renewing and reorienting the world and human society's position within it" (1988b, 59). Wuwtsimt may be said to begin the ritual year in October or November, and Talayesva provides a detailed, day-by-day description of the elaborate ceremonial activities that mark his initiation. It is on the fifth day of the ceremony that he gets his new name, Talayesva, which means "Sitting Tassel," a name indicating "the Greasewood and the Bamboo clans" to which his sponsoring godfather belonged. He observes that "The Greasewood has a tassel and so does the Bamboo" (167)—thus his new, ceremonial name. On the sixth day, before sunrise, the newly initiated young men are "led to the east edge of the mesa to pray and report [their] new names to the Sun god," for, as Talayesva says, "we were no longer boys... this established our manhood and fixed our names forever; and that for anyone to use our childish names again"—he had, as noted earlier, been called Chuka—"would be like a slap in the face"[23] (168).

After Wuwtsimt, Talayesva participates in Soyalangw, the winter solstice ceremony, in which the participants act to induce the sun "to start back to its summer home and thus bring suitably warm weather to permit the Hopi to plant their fields" (Titiev 1944, 146). Talayesva again gives a detailed account of his participation (170–86), toward the end of which he receives another new name, "Tanackmainewa, which means the shining feathers of the Road Runner." But, he says, "This name did not stick like the Wowochim name, which seemed to be glued to [him]" (184). Although there is a great deal more of Talayesva's life story to come, this chapter nonetheless closes with strong determination. He says, "I had learned a great lesson and now knew that the ceremonies handed down by our fathers mean life and security, both now and hereafter. I regretted that I had ever joined the YMCA and decided to set myself against Christianity once and for all. I could see that the old people were right when they insisted that Jesus Christ might do for modern Whites in a good climate, but that the Hopi gods had brought success to us in the desert ever since the world began" (186). Talayesva will indeed take part in further ceremonial activities, affirming what he had previously stated, that he "saw the importance of the Powamu [Bean Dance] ceremony for successful farming," and "resolved never to neglect the ceremony or to fail in its proper performance"[24] (205).

After further illness and a cure achieved by a medicine person, Talayesva prepares to marry Irene in a double wedding with his brother Ira; the brothers

are both marrying women of an appropriate clan. Shortly before the marriage ceremony, however, he has a letter from Mettie away at school. She
writes, "when I return home, I shall have you again in spite of your wife and
all the gossip in the village" (228). Nonetheless, the marriage goes forward
and it is not long before Talayesva, despite having stated his determination
to be a good Hopi, poignantly acknowledges that it is not always easy for
him to do. "With marriage," he says, "I began a life of toil and discovered
that education had spoiled me for making a living in the desert. I was not
hardened to heavy work in the heat and dust and I did not know how to
get rain, control winds, or even predict good and bad weather" (232). This
is definitely an instance of "the problem of the returned student," but from
the perspective of the student, not the American government.

　　Talayesva labors on, going on a sacred salt journey with his father and
others (243–55), and, later, on learning that Mettie has returned, he wonders whether he "had made the mistake of [his] life in marrying instead of
returning to school" (258) with her. Sadly, he states that he "regretted [his]
marriage more than ever" (258). But he continues to participate in ceremonial activities, and, when a dry spell affecting the crops occurs, he along with
others decide that the reason for this might be the fact that the Reverend H.
R. Voth had stolen "so many of our ceremonial secrets and had even carried
off sacred images and altars to equip a museum" (261). On learning that Voth
is visiting in his mother's house, Talayesva enters and calls him "a thief and an
idolator who can never go to heaven" (261). Voth would doubtless have been
a more formidable Christian to challenge than Nequatewa's Miss McLean,
but both Hopis strongly confronted the missionaries.[25] Talayesva also continues his adventures with women, including one with a white prostitute,
who charges him two dollars (273).

　　Assessing Talayesva's account of his life after his return from school,
Clyde Kluckhohn wrote that Talayesva "goes back to the Hopi and stews
there for years, getting into more and more trouble. Finally, the anthropologists come along and do what no other white man has done—treat him as
a person worthy of respect, are interested in his thoughts, feed his ego with
prestige. He therefore responds to them" (270). Apart from Kluckhohn's
patronizing manner, it needs to be said that there is much more to it than
that. For one thing, Talayesva's accounts of his efforts to become a better
farmer, a better herder, and a better provider are very moving—and it is good

that Leo Simmons included them in some detail. When Talayesva's uncle, who is old and frail, tells him that it has been decided that he, rather than his older brother Ira, should succeed to the position of Sun Chief upon the uncle's death (296), Talayesva agrees, stating that he "was thirty years old and glad to succeed [his] uncle in office," resolving to do his "best to serve [his] people and insure rains and a good life" (297).

He survives a further encounter with Maasaw (297) and painfully endures the fact that of four children born to him and his wife, Irene, none long survives. His Spirit Guide comforts him (301) and traditional remedies cure him of further illnesses, although nothing seems to remedy the impotence he reports suffering for a time (307). In 1928, he adopts a sick little boy named Norman whom he cures, and who becomes the center of his affections and anxieties. About this time, Talayesva delivers an intense criticism of the whites and, most particularly, of "the missionaries." He says that "When [his] Bible was all gone, I got a Sears Roebuck catalogue and used its pages for toilet paper" (310), the pages of the Bible, it seems clear, having previously been used for that purpose. The Sears catalog, Talayesva says, "was also more interesting reading" (311). Yet in the following paragraph he says—it's not possible to tell what the actual order of Talayesva's statements was, as distinct from the order in which Simmons presented them—that he came to feel "a little better toward the whites," and "took more pains to be polite to them" (311), especially when some "who called themselves 'anthropologists' asked [him] to tell them stories and paid [him] very well" (311). Knowing most whites' attitudes toward sexual matters, he says that he "edited the old Hopi stories" (311), although he certainly did not "edit" his own stories of sexual encounters. .

And, to be sure, "In the summer of 1932 Professor Leslie A. White came to Oraibi with the anthropology students Fred Eggan, Edward Kennard, and Mischa Titiev." Eggan "hired [him] to tell them about Hopi life and to act as interpreter when they talked with others" (318). Talayesva finds that he "liked this work very much and earned a good sum of money," and, although "careful" as to what he told them at first, he decides that after all, "these were fine fellows" (318). The following year, as noted earlier, Titiev rented a room in Talayesva's house, began to work with him, and paid him what seemed "a good sum of money." Then, six years later, in "July, 1938, another white man came into [his] life" (339). This is Leo Simmons, introduced to Talayesva by a letter from Titiev. Simmons also rents a room in Talayesva's house, and, as described earlier, pays him for formal interviews, instructs him in how to keep a diary, and compensates him for each written page. Not only does Talayesva believe that his "Guardian Spirit approved" of their work, but he wonders whether it was his "Guide [who] has brought [them] together" (339).

His potency having returned, he resumes sexual relations with his wife and also with other women. He reaffirms his strong rejection of Christianity, telling a proselytizing Hopi missionary that when he "returned from Sherman" he examined Hopi "religion and found it good enough," much as Albert Yava had felt after attending Chilocco. Now that he is "fifty [he] will never take on Christianity" (387–78). Nonetheless, at this point in his life Don Talalyesva is well satisfied with his white friends, even boasting that quite "a number of students have been picked from the universities and sent out here," and that he is "proud to say that some of them call [him] a teacher" (385). When letters arrive for him at the post office, he is pleased that the postmaster thinks "perhaps, that [he] was a big man" (386).

As he nears the end of his "autobiography of a Hopi Indian," Talayesva remarks that while Hopis "might be better off if the Whites had never come to Oraibi" (392), of course that is not the way things happened. He is fond of his "special friends" (392), but, in general, "There is not much that he wants from the Whites," for all that he would be pleased to have some few of the material comforts they can provide. Near the end of the book he has a "very good dream," (392–94), one in which his Guardian Spirit Guide appears to him and shows him "a pleasant future to look forward to" (381). Talayesva concludes saying that he "would like to keep on writing [his] diary as long as [his] mind holds out," and then to die in his sleep and "be buried in the Hopi way" (394).

As Cora Dunn said of the boarding schools, the schools "change them"—the Native students—"forever." But the exact nature of that change for one or another boarding-school student is by no means simple or predictable. There is no doubt that Don Talayesva was changed forever by his attendance at the Keam's Canyon School on the Hopi reservation and by the Sherman Institute off the reservation, and, as I have said, what it meant for Don Talayesva to be a "real Hopi" was assuredly different from whatever being a "real Hopi" was to those who did not attend the schools or, indeed, to others who did. What is clear is that while his boarding-school education made Don Talayesva a different kind of Hopi, it never remotely made him anything other than a Hopi.

Polingaysi Qoyawayma's
No Turning Back

THE FRONT COVER OF *NO TURNING BACK* SAYS THAT THE BOOK IS "BY Polingaysi Qoyawayma (Elizabeth Q. White), as told to Vada F. Carlson." But this is not an "as told to" Indian autobiography. Rather, Carlson narrates Qoyawayma's life in the manner of a biographer, referring to her in the third person. Nonetheless, because the work Carlson and Qoyawayma did together is very much like the work engaged in by other non-Native editors and the Indian subjects they represented autobiographically, in the first person, I've thought it reasonable to include *No Turning Back* among the texts making up the Hopi autobiographical canon, despite the editor's choice of narrative pronoun.

ৡৢ

Polingaysi Qoyawayma was born in Orayvi on Third Mesa about 1892. Like most Hopi people of her time, she did not know the exact date of her birth, although she eventually adopted April 9 as her birthday, sharing the birth date of a white Christian friend also named Elizabeth. Her father, Qoyawayma, known as Fred or Freddie, worked for and with the Mennonite missionary to the Hopi, H. R. Voth, although he and all the family were Hostiles, opposed to the government schools. I will have a good deal more to say about both Voth and Qoyawayma.

In the book's second chapter, Carlson writes of the time materials were brought to build the Orayvi Day School and, then, in the paragraph immediately following, she tells of Qoyawayma's fearful parents attempting to hide her from government troops and Indian police trolling for prospective students (17). This is very confusing, in that the school first opened in March of 1892, around the time of Qoyawayma's birth, and her parents would not then have needed to hide her. But Carlson's narration is extremely vague in terms of chronology throughout.[1] We are then told that Qoyawayma's sickly younger brother is the first of the children in her family to be taken to the school (18). As Carlson depicts it, in spite of the fact that Qoyawayma "didn't understand what was going on, . . . she was intensely interested in" the school, observing that the children who attended "came back up the mesa trail in the evening, talking and laughing, even singing," and that "her sick brother seemed none the worse for spending a few days there" (21).

Soon Qoyawayma's "sister and her friends were trapped . . . and taken to [the day] school" (23) as well. On her sister's return in the evening, Qoyawayma is fascinated with "the striped cotton dress her sister wore home," so much so that she went to "the home of one of her playmates," a girl who had also been to school, to ask about the "new garment" (23) and to try it on. How old was she at this point in her life story? I can only guess: as we will see, Qoyawayma chose to go to the Sherman Institute in Riverside, California, in 1906, at fourteen years old. In that she probably would not have attended the day school for more than four years (that is not certain, and I have not been able to find any records), she would appear to have become interested in the Orayvi Day School in about 1902 when she would have been ten years old.

After trying on her friend's new garment, Qoyawayma, the following day, descends the trail to the school "of her own free will," knowing that her "mother would be very angry with her" for doing so (24). She allows herself to be taken in to the school by the "white man with the red face and white whiskers" (25), perhaps principal teacher Herman Kampmeier.[2] There, she submits to the initiatory Cleanup: "There was a big tub in the room to which Polingaysi was taken. [An] older girl poured water into it, instructing Polingaysi to undress. She helped her into the tub, scrubbed her from head to toes, then rinsed and dried her body" (25). After her bath, Qoyawayma is given "one of the ticking dresses" she had coveted.[3] If her hair was cut, we are not told of it; if she received a new name when she went to class and was "walked . . . to a desk where two other little girls were sitting" (25), we do not hear of it. When she returns home at the end of the day, her mother is indeed angry with her, and it is worth examining Carlson's representation of the scene between mother and daughter.

Carlson has Qoyawayma's mother asking, "'Who took you to school?'" with Qoyawayma truthfully answering, "'I took myself.'" Her mother reproaches her for being a "self-willed, naughty girl," who has taken a "step away from [her] Hopi people," and brought grief to her family. From this point on, her mother says, she "'must continue to go to school each day... and there is *no turning back*'" (26, my emphasis). It is not possible to know whether Qoyawayma remembered her mother's exact words, spoken in Hopi, nearly sixty years earlier. In any case, Carlson's rendition of them here in English establishes the interpretative metaphor governing the book as a whole. It is a metaphor that oversimplifies a complex matter, and, moreover, one that again and again is undermined as the book proceeds; indeed, it is ultimately abandoned without comment.

First, we may note that some Hopi children who willingly or unwillingly went to the schools did not "continue to go to school each day" (for example, Don Talayesva's sister "Nellie" or "Gladys," and some others I will note below). Although Hostile families might well believe that attendance at school represented "a step away" from being Hopi, that was not necessarily the case. Don Talayesva came from a Hostile family and also chose on his own to go to the Keam's Canyon boarding school. He would, as we have seen, preach for Jesus, dress in "citizen's" clothing, and explicitly state that he wanted to be a white man at more than one point during his school years. Yet he most certainly took steps *back* toward becoming "a real Hopi again" (141). His life story, published more than twenty years before Qoyawayma's, makes clear that there could indeed be a "turning back."[4]

Like Don Talayesva, Edmund Nequatewa, having spent time at Keam's Canyon School and the Phoenix Indian School, nonetheless remained substantially (if differently) Hopi, something true of Albert Yava as well. Unlike Talayesva and Yava, Nequatewa did not reject Christianity—he became a Jehovah's Witness—yet all three of these Hopi men "integrated" (Shillinger) a great many things from the dominant American culture, adopting some "white ways" while remaining firm in their particular "tribal"—Hopi— identity. Qoyawayma's story in many ways differs from those of Nequatewa, Yava, and Talayesva. But the question of how the day school and boarding school affected her vocational choices and her subsequent sense of self is far more complex than anything the apparent definitiveness of a phrase like "no turning back" can convey. Indeed, well before the conclusion of the book, Qoyawayma contemplates several ways in which she might "turn back."

Further, the "no turning back" metaphor that serves as the title for the life history is undercut by the book's structure even before it is offered thematically. This is to say that the chapter I have discussed in which Qoyawayma decides on her own to go to the school, with her mother responding that "there is no turning back" (26), is the second chapter of the book, not the first. And what that first chapter represents is nothing less than a literal *return* for Qoyawayma. The book begins some time before its actual composition, with the "small, brown-skinned woman in the red dress," Qoyawayma obviously, stopping her car at the "ruins of the ancient village of old Oraibi," getting out, and, with a gesture of "indecision and confusion," saying—to herself, perhaps, but to Carlson and the reader as well—"That is my home"[5] (1). That Carlson assigns her the present tense seems significant. She next goes on to represent what Qoyawayma "thought" at that moment (1), in particular the question, "Is that where I belong, now?" (1).

Curiously, the two just happen to encounter old Chief Tawakwaptiwa, leader of the Friendlies in 1906 and in attendance at the Sherman Indian Institute along with Qoyawayma many years earlier. Qoyawayma introduces herself, speaking to him in Hopi. Recognizing her, he says, "Polingaysi! Oh-ee-e! You are the little one who wanted to be a white man" (3). This, Carlson novelistically writes, "brought tightness to the woman's throat and sadness to her mind" (3). She goes on to ventriloquate what Qoyawayma's "heart [was] crying out": "I am still a child. A lost child. I cannot find my way. Where is the pathway of peace? Where can I find the harmony of the true Hopi?" (3). There is much worth comment here.

The trip that opens the book took place sometime in 1959; even without Carlson's testimony, one would know that it had to have taken place before 1960, because that was the year Tawakwaptiwa died.[6] By then, Qoyawayma was approaching the age of seventy. (She was seventy-two when the book was published in 1964, eighty-five when it first appeared in paperback in 1977.) By that point in time, as I'll note further, she had had a successful career as a teacher to Indian children, having been initially criticized but ultimately praised for bringing Native culture into the classroom as an aid to teaching literacy. Upon her retirement in 1954, she was presented with a Distinguished Service Award by the Bureau of Indian Affairs. She had by then built a large house with a piano on land her father had offered to her many years before. While she surely had taken a path different from most Hopi women of her generation, it seems that she was on her way to achieving a sense of harmony and balance that might well compare to the ideal of a "true Hopi" of her generation. Indeed, it is possible that working through these materials with Carlson may have helped her to do exactly that, and in important ways to "turn back." Qoyawayma would live for twenty-six more years after her autobiography was published, dying in 1990, at the age of nearly 100.

Carlson continues this first chapter with a representation of Qoyawayma's early childhood that is both carefully detailed in regard to Hopi culture yet replete with unexamined value judgments. Hopi people, Carlson writes, "believed in *strange* sights and sounds" (7, my emphasis), they baked in a "*primitive* oven of flat rocks" (9, my emphasis), and believed in *katsinam*, "*supposedly* supernatural beings" (11, my emphasis). It was in Qoyawayma's early childhood, Carlson writes, that "a glimmer of *hope* came to her with the thought that she could *better* her condition.... It was, perhaps, the first stirring of *ambition*" (9, my emphasis). These *hopeful ambitions* of *betterment* would seem to have come to Qoyawayma even before she knew about the day school—although, as I have said, it is difficult to determine from Carlson's narration here and throughout the book when any given event occurred.

Looking back, Qoyawayma might indeed have viewed her childhood curiosity about the day school at the foot of the mesa as deriving from an interior movement of "hope" and "ambition." But these thoroughly American or Western terms surely would not accurately describe her motivations as a child. The desire in some fashion to "better her condition" is, I think, another matter. If, this is to say, you have a bow and arrow that you use for hunting or warfare, and you see what a repeating rifle can do for both endeavors, it should come as no surprise that you might want the latter, for all that, as I'll note further, there might indeed be some who would continue to prefer the former. In the same way, one might also think it "better," at least most of the time, to have a pickup truck than a burro; "better" to have electricity and running water than not—although Fred Eggan had noted that "'Traditional' and 'Progressive' factions were arguing over the introduction of electricity and water into the [very conservative] village [of Hotevilla]" in 1970, and, at the time he wrote, "The traditionalists have temporarily won by tearing up the water pipes" (1970, 172). Clearly it was possible to disagree, but it is not hard to understand why many would want to have running water, just as one can understand why young Polingaysi Qoyawayma might find those ticking dresses more appealing than whatever she was wearing as a child. But of course the question arises—as the Hostiles shortly past the turn of the twentieth century and "the traditionalists" in the 1990s were well aware—to what extent can you adopt "white ways" before those ways do indeed threaten your "tribal identity"?

On first encountering invaders from more complex societies and the useful material goods they bring, as Marshall Sahlins has written, "The first commercial impulse of the people is not to become just like us but more like themselves" (388), and the indigenization of modernity on the part of small-scale societies around the globe has been well documented. But, as Sahlins's argument continues, the power of the colonial state interrupts and alters the possibilities of experiencing change as continuity. There is a tipping point at which it becomes harder and harder to assimilate the new into the old without the old becoming—something else, something which no single word suffices accurately to name for all the various colonized peoples of the world. As is well known, the power of the colonial state, its relentless efforts to achieve and extend its dominance, can lead to the internalization on the part of the colonized of the worldview of the colonizer. Still, in a great many cases, peoples experiencing the onslaught of colonial ideology do manage, to borrow a phrase from Craig Womack, to keep "their values and worldviews" (42) intact, although these are inevitably altered in some measure.

I think it is indeed true that any number of Native boarding-school students who adopted "American ways" nonetheless kept their "tribal identities" (32), as Amanda Cobb has written. But past a certain point, the adoption of those ways, to return to Sahlins, no longer enriches "native self-conceptions" (386). One can understand why Chief Tawakwaptiwa saw Qoyawayma's choices as indicative of a desire "to be a white man," although that was not necessarily the case early on, nor was it the case ultimately. Early in her life, as we will see further, Qoyawayma did indeed feel that she had to choose *either* to be a (fairly traditional) Hopi, *or*, as Tawakwaptiwa would put it, a white man (or woman). Over time, however, she would explore ways that might allow her to be *both* Hopi *and* American. The book provides enough detail to raise interesting questions of this kind for the reader, although it does not explore them.

Chapter 3 continues the depiction of Qoyawayma's early education, and it begins by describing punishments Hopi children had to endure at school. When some of the boys become "unruly"—perhaps acts of resistance or simply what children do—a "few of them were booted, others were slapped in the face" (27). "Even one such case was enough to arouse the ire of Hopi parents," who, as Carlson accurately observes, "do not believe in whipping except ritually by the proper persons and at the prescribed time" (27–28). This whipping, Carlson continues, occurred during "initiation in the kiva" (28). Although she mentions ritual whipping at initiation, she does not specify that it is part of the *katsina* initiation that all Hopi boys and girls undergo. By this time Qoyawayma is about ten years old and would probably already have had her *katsina* initiation. As we have seen and will see further, that experience had a strong impact on Hopi children, but nothing is said of it until later in the book (and then very little).

Qoyawayma "remembered vividly the punishment of one of her friends" at school. Because the girl "did not stop talking at once when told to do so, she was placed on top of the big-bellied stove, unheated at the time, of course, and an eraser was shoved into her mouth. She sat there, stiff with fright, head bent in shame and saliva dripping until the teacher's *sadistic appetite had been satiated*" (28, my emphasis). This is a very strong judgment, and while Qoyawayma could not herself have made it at the time—nor, I would guess, would she use this particular language even later—Carlson writes that the incident was sufficiently impressive that she "developed a deep caution, becoming suspicious of the motives of the school personnel and of white people in general, however kindly" (28). This very reasonable conclusion attributed to a bright child does not, however, deter her in the least from wholeheartedly pursuing the schooling offered by white people.[7]

Curiously, it is in this context—that of a punishment—that Carlson describes Qoyawayma's Naming: "One day Polingaysi came home with a cardboard hung around her neck on a string. Lettered on it was her new name: Bessie" (28). Her mother and grandmother—they obviously could not read the sign she wore—respond to "The change of name [as] merely one more evidence... that the white man was unfeeling" (28). I'd guess this is a fortunate rendering in English of whatever Qoyawayma's mother and grandmother had said in Hopi. The "unfeeling" dimension of white naming—here, a largely unconscious failure of feeling, although one that is hurtful—has to do with the fact that, as I've noted several times, it undoes the individuation that Hopi naming confers on the named person, as it obliterates the clan-derived, and so communal, context of each name. Again, there are lots of people named Tom, Dick, or Bessie, but probably only one (or very few) named Polingaysi.[8]

A bit more on the subject of naming: early in chapter 2, Carlson had written that Qoyawayma, shortly after her birth, "had been accepted by her grandparents, named Polingaysi, Butterfly Sitting among the Flowers in the Breeze, and presented to Father Sun on the twentieth day of her life" (13). As Albert Yava had made clear, a baby is named by "aunts on the father's side . . . , and they usually selected a name that revealed the father's clan affiliations"[9] (3). If the grandmother represented as speaking here was involved in the naming, she is Qoyawayma's father's mother, not her mother's mother. (What Carlson means by "accepted by her grandparents" is unclear, and insofar as she implies that those "grandparents" together did the naming she is mistaken.) "Gathering in the house of the newborn (traditionally twenty . . . days after birth), several paternal clanswomen each bestow a name associated with their clan," to cite Whiteley once more. "Typically, a child receives half a dozen different names, only one of which will *huurta*, stick" (1998, 109), a matter addressed by both Albert Yava and Don Talayesva.

Her paternal grandmother says, " 'It was I who named you Polingaysi. It is a beautiful name. It fits you well" (29). This means, as we may learn from H. R. Voth, that her paternal grandmother's clan—and thus her father's clan—is the Povoli or Butterfly Clan, and her name, Polingosi in Voth's orthography, means "Butterfly Follows," as in "one butterfly pursues another" (1905, 104). This would indeed have been her "child-name" (Voth 1905, 67), so that when Carlson has her grandmother continue, "You are a daughter of the Kachinas, as any Hopi will know by your name" (29), her meaning is unclear. A child does indeed receive further names, when, from ages six to ten, she "is initiated into either the *Katsina* or the *Powamuy* ritual society" (Whiteley 1998, 109). And, although this isn't confirmed until a good while later, Qoyawayma had indeed been initiated into the *katsina* society by the time she took herself down to the day school, so that she would already have been given other names than Polingaysi by her sponsoring godfather or godmother. I would guess that one of those names would "stick," so that, in the same way as Don Talayesva relinquished his child name, "Chuka," for "Talayesva" on his Wuwtsim initiation, so too would Qoyawayma have relinquished her child name, Polingaysi.[10] But if, for reasons I can't explain, she retained that "child-name," it would not identify her as "a daughter of the Kachinas."

When Qoyawayma's grandmother asserts that "This silly name the white man has given you means nothing" (29), the young girl responds, "I am Polingaysi... I will always be Polingaysi. But when the *Bahana* calls me Bessie, I will pretend I have forgotten my own name" (29). According to the boarding schools' usual practice, one would expect Qoyawayma to have been called Bessie Polingaysi, her "own name" used as a surname presumed to be derived from her father, despite Hopi matrilineal practice. But her father, Qoyawayma, or Fred Qoyawayma, was surely known to the school personnel who discarded Polingaysi entirely, gave her her father's name as surname, and bestowed Bessie on her as forename. (The other name that appears on the book cover, Elizabeth Q. White, adds Qoyawayma's [ex-]husband's name to her father's name, as if it were a "maiden name." See below.)

Yet a few words more on the subject of names: Carlson had earlier written that the Reverend H. R. Voth called Qoyawayma's father Fred or Freddie "because his name, Qoyawayma was too difficult for English-speaking tongues" (17). This instance of arbitrary and de-individuating naming is not, however, presented as "unfeeling." Meanwhile, what might or might not have been difficult for "English-speaking tongues" is not relevant for Voth, who had been born in a German Mennonite colony that had taken religious refuge in Southern Russia, and whose first language was German. Moreover, Voth had for some time been working on the study of Hopi names that he published in 1905, from which I have quoted, and he had listed among the names given by a member of the Coyote Clan, "Qoyawaima," a male name, literally translating to "Gray Walks," and referring to a "grayish fox... or to the coyote" (1905, 81). Voth had taught himself Hopi to the point that he could understand and speak it fairly well,[11] so that pronouncing the name Qoyawayma would hardly have been "too difficult" for him. Further, in Voth's 1905 text, *Traditions of the Hopi*, the twenty-eighth story, "A Journey to the Skeleton House," to Maski, the Land of the Dead, is credited to "Qoyawaima (Oraibi)" (109), as I had noted earlier. It is also Qoyawayma who is listed as the narrator of the first story in the volume, titled "Origin Myth" by Voth. Of the 110 stories that comprise the volume, no fewer than 26 are ascribed to Qoyawayma, more than to any other named narrator. Polingaysi Qoyawayma's father will be important to her story.

Carlson herself refers to Qoyawayma as Polingaysi throughout the book they produced together. She and Qoyawayma had first met "in Flagstaff in the late 1956's [*sic*]," as Carlson wrote in the letter dated August 13, 1982, that I have cited (Lindner 1983, 127), and I have no doubt that in conversation Carlson addressed Qoyawayma as Polingaysi, Bessie, or Elizabeth. But just as I found it unfortunate that Leo Simmons, Mischa Titiev, and others would refer to Don Talayesva everywhere in their writing as Don—and I found it admirable that Mathew Sakiestewa Gilbert refers to him as Talayesva—so, too, is it unfortunate that Qoyawayma's biographer refers to her in print as Polingaysi. To be sure, that *is* her name (e.g., *not* Qoyawayma). But I strongly suspect that Carlson's practice, along with that of a number of reviewers and some few commentators, does not stem from ethnographic acumen.

To return: at this time in Qoyawayma's early life, says Carlson, "Progress was rolling across the Hopi mesas as relentlessly as the white man's wagon wheels" (29), with the further difficulty that "the missionaries," Voth most certainly, "were doing their best to convince the Hopis of the utter folly and abysmal sinfulness of their ancient beliefs" (29–30). Carlson writes that the Hopis' response is to "endure this thing that is happening," to "give in," and to "let the white man learn his mistakes in his own way" (30). This once more over-simplifies the matter. Hopi people had long feigned resignation and acquiescence when faced with a situation in regard to which they gauged the odds of resistance to be against them. Their apparently passive "endurance" of some "thing that is happening" may not be that at all, however, but, instead, the consequence of a strategic assessment, a specific form of agency, not its abandonment.

The narrative now approaches 1906, and Carlson's presentation of the events leading to the expulsion of Yukiwma's Hostile faction from Orayvi gets much of the complex situation right, for all that it is very confusingly represented. She first describes "friction, smoldering but intense ... developing between Chief Lololma and Yeokeoma, leader of the Spider Clan" (31), the former "taking the pencil," to sign agreements with the whites, and thus apparently having "betrayed the Hopis," while "Yeokeoma wanted no compromise with white ways" (31). There "would be a time," Carlson writes, "when the issue between [Yeokeoma] and Lololma would come to a head" (32). I'll note that while leaders of the Spider Clan had contested Loololma's authority earlier, by the late nineteenth and early twentieth century his chief opponent was indeed Yukiwma—but Yukiwma was head of the Kokop or Fire Clan, not the Spider Clan. In any case, before developing these important matters further, Carlson brings the narrative back to the present very briefly to emphasize the "no turning back" thematic. She has Qoyawayma experience a "Confusion of mind" (34), which leads to another childhood memory, albeit one that fails to dispel that confusion. Carlson writes, Qoyawayma "needed nourishment of spirit now" (35), "now," I think, meaning somewhere about 1959. Further memories of childhood do or do not nourish her spirit or allay her confusion, and the story quickly returns to the events of 1906.

Carlson picks up her account of intolerable differences between the "two strong ideas"—friendship toward the whites and hostility to them—seeking prevalence "in one small village" (32), Orayvi, as if intra-Hopi deliberations and concerns had nothing to do with the matter. For some reason, she interpolates a commentary attributed to Qoyawayma's grand-mother at this point in the narration. Grandmother apparently had spoken of a time when Hopis, dispersed for long, "will come crawling on their knees up the mesa trail." With them, she says, "will be a white brother and a white sister, the only survivors of their race, and we will give them shelter, though it is foretold that they shall have caused the terror and the death by their magic knowledge" (34). This vision would seem more nearly to derive from late '50s and early 1960s fears of nuclear annihilation than from Hopi prophecy about the *pahaana*.

Carlson notes Loololma's death and the succession of Tawakwaptiwa as Bear Clan chief and leader of the Friendlies. Meanwhile, "[a]cross the ever-widening Oraibi Wash in the valley," she writes, "the home of the Voths became a mecca for Yeokeoma and his followers ... under the cover of dark-ness the Spider Clan [*sic*] man and some of his closest followers visited the missionary, seeking to find some gem of wisdom in his teaching that would prove their case" (40). This, like much else, is confusing. Carlson appears to be describing events just prior to the pushing match of Friday, September 7, 1906, between Yukiwma's Hostiles and Tawakwaptiwa's Friendlies to decide who would leave Orayvi. (See appendix A.) But Voth had been replaced by the Reverend J. B. Epp in 1901. He stayed on for a time to help Epp get settled, but he was gone by 1902. Whiteley notes that Voth did make "short visits thereafter" (1988b, 84)—and Don Talayesva had seemed to place him as a visitor in his mother's house at a considerably later date than 1902—but Voth was not present early in September, 1906. Given these facts, it's hard to know what Carlson means by saying that Yukiwma's party met at the "home of the Voths," because—if we are indeed talking about the lead-up to September 7, 1906—the Voths hadn't lived there for years.[12] It might also be noted that insofar as "mecca" has no particular significance in either Christian or Hopi thought, it's rather an odd choice of word to use as a synonym for "the home of the Voths."

Carlson says that Fred Qoyawayma, a Hostile (but as I've noted and will note again, just what Friendly and Hostile means for any particular individual at any given time can never be taken for granted) who not only worked with and traveled with Voth, was not invited to these nocturnal meetings. But, in Carlson's telling, he came on "the tracks of the visitors as he went to the Voth home [?] one morning." As a consequence of his discovery, instead of leaving at the end of his workday, he remains nearby, falling asleep and waking "to hear Yeokeoma talking" (40). Carlson says that he then joins Yukiwma and those with him.

But, again, Voth was not in Orayvi in the late summer and early fall of 1906; if someone had been in residency at "the Voth home," it was not Voth. Moreover, even if Voth had been in Orayvi in the early fall of 1906, it's hard to imagine why the Fire Clan leader along with several prominent Hostile men would go to him "seeking some gem of wisdom in his teaching that would prove their case." Voth could offer only Christian "wisdom" of a sort that was, for the most part, unacceptable to most Hostiles (but not, ultimately, as we will see, to Fred Qoyawayma), nor would Voth's "teaching" serve to "prove" anything to most of the Friendly Bear Clan Hopis.

It's Carlson's curious suggestion that "In their innocence, [the Hostile men] confused the word 'Messiah' with their own word 'Masau-u'" (40). The two words have some phonic resemblance, to be sure, although if the Hopis understood anything whatever about the meaning of Messiah in the Judeo-Christian tradition, they would readily dissociate Messiah from Maasaw. Qoyawayma's father, "a conservative, as was his sturdy wife Sevenka,"[13] apparently realized that "resistance [to the white man] was useless" (40), and Sevenka has a dream that tells her that "Yokeoma and his followers cannot win this struggle. They are already beaten" (40). This becomes an occasion for Carlson to assert that "Fatalism is a part of Hopi nature ... What is to be will be"[14] (41).

As should be clear by now, there is no question that Hopi *culture* does, indeed, base itself on the fact that all things to come have been foretold in prophecies of old. But Hopinavoti, what Whiteley, as I have cited him, calls a kind of "Hopi hermeneutics" (1988b, 255), is always operative in the present. This is to say that while there is no doubt that what has been predicted will, indeed, come to pass, it is nonetheless a matter of a good deal of interpretative thought to determine just what exactly has been predicted, what ancient prophecy means in the current moment, and what actions are to be taken on the basis of that meaning. Let me note in passing that when some Christians, later in Carlson's narrative (82), are said to believe that all is in the hands of God apart from the actions of any given individual, this does not qualify as "fatalism."

Carlson writes that it was the "bickering that had marked the establishment of Oraibi," that had "continued, flaring up, then subsiding until September 1906, when it became evident that a showdown was unavoidable" (42). "Oraibi was founded prior to 1150 AD" (Titiev 1944, 69; also E. Sekaquaptewa, 240), and it is often considered to be the oldest continuously inhabited town in the United States. Others have dated the village's "establishment" a bit later, even a couple of hundred years later, although all the dates I have seen long precede Columbus. There are indeed legends about "bickering" at the time of Oraibi's founding, and "bickering" of one sort or another is described in the earliest collective memories of the Hopi. Thus, Albert Yava had noted that "the theme of dissension and evil . . . starts with the emergence story" (41), which tells of the upward migration of the Hopis to this, the fourth world, and, too, that "Hopis have always been prone to quarrel among themselves" (132). But neither Yava, nor Carlson, nor anyone else can say for sure whether what took place in September of 1906 was or was not a "continuation" of ancient dissension.

What can be said is that leaders of the Bear and Fire Clans had indeed been debating these particular matters at least since the 1880s. Carlson offers a further curious interpretation, writing, "*Ironically*, though their leaders had known this conflict would eventually take place in the *legendary* pattern, the people were surprised" (44–45, my emphasis). The leaders of both factions, as I have several times noted, arranged for the conflict to take place at the time it did consistent with their interpretation of prophecy. And, while some people might have been surprised, a fair number were fairly well apprised. (See appendix A.) In much the same way, there's no irony to the fact that Hopi society entrusts more knowledge to certain persons than to others.

Returning to the events of 1906, Carlson melodramatically writes that Qoyawayma's father "remained on the mesa, an interested spectator during the final hours of Oraibi's greatness" (43), her mother having been sent from the village for her safety. Carlson's account has a "rough and tumble scrimmage" (43) taking place between "both factions" (43). She accurately notes the line "running east and west" (44) drawn in the sand by Yukiwma, who, once pushed over the line, remarks "it is done. . . . It had to be this way" (44). Although the Qoyawaymas have been described as Hostiles, it does not appear that they leave Orayvi with the others of their party, a time when, as Carlson writes, "Oraibi lost its heart" (45).

A couple of pages later, Carlson, in something of an anticlimax, reinterprets the events of 1906, providing some accurate detail, but also confusing matters further. She states that "A sad factor of the episode was that it was foreknown to both Bear and Spider Clan [sic] chieftains" (47). More than foreknown, as we have seen, it was planned by them (although not exactly in the way events ensued). Once more mixing chronologies, Carlson quotes a Bear Clan man who "was asked some years later," "What would you say caused the split in 1906?" (47). He answers, "That was planned from the beginning," adding that the Fire Clan, leaders of the Hostiles, "were said to be tricky, unmerciful, and wicked" (48)—this, to be sure, from a Bear Clan man. But this does at least give some sense of the split as a result of "deliberate acts," to cite the title of Whiteley's important book, on the part of the Bear and Fire Clan leaders, rather than a merely topical dispute about the American schools. Carlson writes that the "Bear Clan lost face by the break in Hopi ranks" (48), although why and to whom is unclear.

Qoyawayma's family, conservatives who somehow had stayed behind, "began to feel uneasy on the mesa," Carlson writes. She says that "Perhaps it was the missionaries who interested them in . . . building a dwelling below the cliffs at Kiakotsmovi—New Oraibi" (48). This is yet again accurate and also slightly misleading in that there was no "New Oraibi" at the time the Qoyawaymas moved; it didn't exist until 1911. "By 1911," as Mischa Titiev had written, "there were so many settlers at Kikotcmovi that it began to take on the appearance of an independent village and came to be known as New Oraibi" (94). The Qoyawaymas would have been in residence for several years before the name of the village changed.

Chapter 4 begins with Carlson writing, "Tawaquaptewa was right. Polingaysi had wanted to be a white man. . . . She had a desire to share the good things of the white way of living" (49). As with her notions of "ambition" and "betterment," Carlson affirms Tawakwaptiwa's view that

Qoyawayma's "desire to share the good things of the white way of living" means that she desires "to be a white man" (51), and that this desire had motivated the young Qoyawayma to "daydream of going" to Sherman with other young Hopis in the fall of 1906. At that time, as Carlson writes, she was small, and although she is fourteen, "she might well be mistaken for a ten-year-old" (49). When she encounters a wagon with children from the Keam's Canyon boarding school, and learns that the children in it are "going to the land of oranges.... Far away. In California," and that they will be traveling "on long houses on wheels, drawn by an iron house that screamed with ear-splitting loudness" (50–51), she hurries home and asks her mother to "teach her to make a plaque" (51). Her mother observes that she had not previously been interested in learning to make these decorative objects, and Qoyawayma explains that she wants the plaque to trade at the local store for an orange. She manages the task, finishing "the plaque, not too skillfully." Taking it to the trader, she receives in exchange for it the orange she desired and she is pleased by its "sweet and tangy" taste (52). The problem, however, is that parental consent is necessary for a child to travel to Riverside and the Sherman boarding school, and her "parents flatly refused to let her go" (53), the situation of other would-be students as well.

But Qoyawayma, again like others, is not to be deterred. She climbs into the wagon that is to take the students to the train for Riverside, and, when confronted by the driver, who asks her "for 'the paper'" (53), which she does not have, she persuades a Hopi girl to go and get her parents. They come, and her kindly father says to his wife, "'I think we should allow her to go.... She will be well taken care of. She will learn more of the writing marks that are in books.'" He concludes, "'I think we should sign the paper.'"[15] (54). And they do. "Thus," writes Carlson, "Polingaysi won her weaponless battle for another sample of white man's education" (54). And, "Again, there was no turning back" (55).

Apart from the fact that Qoyawayma—as Albert Yava had done on the train to Chilocco—spends some of the money her father had given her to purchase a banana, a strange fruit that she does not like, we are told nothing whatever about the long trip to California. Once in Riverside, "the nervous and frightened strangers," Qoyawayma among them, "were taken to dormitories" (58). She is not only the smallest, but, Carlson writes, the "youngest" (57). Told to take a shower, she is frightened by the mechanism, worrying about a "Water Serpent"[16] (58). Urged on by the "matron in charge" (59),

Qoyawayma manages to shower. "That night," says Carlson, "for the first time, Polingaysi slept in a *real* bed" (59, my emphasis), in a dormitory in which not a single girl was a Hopi. She cries herself to sleep, and, Carlson writes, "For weeks, each night was a repetition of the first" (59): "Riverside. Land of oranges. Land of perfume. Time of torture. After more than half a century, Polingaysi could not recall that interval without a surge of emotion" (59–60). What tribes did her dorm mates come from? Did she speak to them in English? In that Chief Tawakwaptiwa along with his wife and daughters were at Riverside, did she see or have any contact with him or with the many other Hopis with whom she had traveled from Orayvi? Nothing is said of these things.

Like Don Talayesva, also at Sherman at this time, Qoyawayma does not mention the school's military regimentation, something that as Viola Martinez would note many years later, girls did not escape. Indeed, as Robert Trennert writes, at most of the schools, "By the mid-nineties most girls were fully incorporated into the soldierly routine.... [A]ll students were organized into companies on the first day of school. Like the boys, the girls wore uniforms and were led by student officers who followed army drill regulations" (1982, 281).

As we will soon see, Qoyawayma spent some of her time in Riverside living in the home of one of her teachers. Did she wear her uniform at the teacher's house? It is surely the case that any time she spent at the school involved marching and drilling.

A "happier memory of that time" (60) is the fact that Qoyawayma was able to sing: "Song was Polingaysi's salvation" (60). Her English was poor despite her day-school education. But, although she "mispronounced many words" (61), her singing was encouraged and "she was singled out to take a leading part in one of the school's programs." Despite a typical Hopi aversion to "being spotlighted" (61), she nonetheless agrees to perform. Just what sort of "program" she performs in is not mentioned, nor is there another word about her singing. From what Carlson tells us, it would appear that Qoyawayma sang only in English. But, as it happened, Hopi students at Sherman had an unusual opportunity to express themselves through traditional Hopi songs and dances.

Although, as Sakiestewa Gilbert writes, "The United States government had instructed [Superintendent Harwood] Hall to destroy American

Indian culture through the boarding schools" (2005, 8), Hall, in charge at Sherman, "allowed the Hopi to share their traditional culture through song and dance to promote Sherman Institute as a progressive, talented, and enlightened institution" (2005, 8)—in this regard, it was well ahead of its time—and also to raise money for the school by showcasing the Hopi performances. Chief Tawakwaptiwa played a prominent role in these. In March, 1907, only four months after the Hopis arrived, Tawakwaptiwa, along with eight others, "performed a traditional Hopi song in the school's auditorium" as "an impressed audience looked on" (Sakiestewa Gilbert 2005, 7). The early ethnomusicologist, Natalie Curtis, spent time with Tawakwaptiwa at Sherman in 1908, having earlier worked with his uncle, Bear Clan chief Loololma, whom she had visited at Orayvi.

As Curtis herself would later report, she had pointed out to the old Chief that the Hopi children who are going to school will be "singing new songs—American songs instead of Hopi." But, as she says she had put the matter, "Hopi songs are beautiful; it is sad they should be forgotten" (475). She could write them down on the page, she explained, so that in the future, Hopi children "could look upon the written page and say: 'Thus sang Lololmai, our chief, in the long ago. Thus sings Lololmai today'" (475). Perhaps as a consequence, Tawakwaptiwa showed considerable "leadership in the area of music" at Sherman (Sakiestewa Gilbert 2005, 6), and Curtis's work with him and her earlier work with Loololma and a number of other Hopi singers led to the inclusion of no fewer than fifty-three pages of words and musical notation in her influential *The Indians Book: Songs and Legends of the American Indians*.[17] At Sherman, Tawakwaptiwa organized a group that became known as the Hopi Singers who performed not only for the school but for the surrounding community (Sakiestewa Gilbert 2005, 9). If Qoyawayma was singing only in English, however, she would not have performed with them.

Carlson does tell the reader that Qoyawayma's mother, Sevenka, "had a strong, lovely voice and Polingaysi had inherited some of her ability" (60). Sevenka belonged to the women's Maraw society. "Initiation into the Mamrawt (an approximate equivalent to the [men's] Wuwtsim society) was an important mark of adult female identity," Whiteley writes[18] (1988b, 325n1). While most young men were initiated into the Wuwtsim, many but not most women, "usually between ages sixteen to twenty" (Whiteley 1988b,

59), were initiated into the Maraw, one of three women's societies. Women who had chosen not to be initiated could nonetheless attain status as adult members of the community "through such means as marriage, reproduction, and, for some, roles in other religious societies" (Whiteley 1988b, 325n1). It's also important to note that the women's Maraw ceremonies, which take place twice a year, in January and September-October, a few weeks before the harvesting of the corn crop in the fall, emphasize what Mary Black calls "the fertility theme" (285), something to which I'll return.

Carlson's account of "the Mazrau" trivializes it by referring to it as "a dancing and singing group" (60), conjuring, for the book's late-1960s readers, the activities, perhaps, of the local high school. She further says that Sevenka not only "composed songs for her own society," but "at one time composed a song which was used for years afterward by the Niman Dancers in the late-July ceremony that closes the Kachina calendar for the year" (60). This, she writes, "was a stepping out of her woman's place to compete with the men" (60). In that different kivas "rotated" in sponsoring the Niman, and that the Marau had its own kiva (Titiev 1944, 111), Sevenka may indeed have had a role in composing some of the songs, although I think it unlikely that the sort of protofeminist "competition" Carlson describes would have occurred. In any case, Sevenka's daughter appears, as I have said, to have sung only in English at Sherman and not in Hopi. Is this to be interpreted as a gesture of rebellion against her mother—who had, of course, disapproved of her desire to go to Riverside? Is it simply a more general further step away from an integral relation to the Hopi culture in which she had grown up? This subject, like many others, is not engaged.

Qoyawayma is befriended by a teacher who invites her "to live at the home of the teacher and her husband and help with the housework" (62). Does this mean that she has no further experience of the Dormitory? Did she not eat with the other students in the school Dining Room or have occasion to observe and evaluate what they were served? Does it mean as well that she escaped the military discipline, the marching, the regimentation, and the religious services at Sherman? Most of Qoyawayma's English, we are told, is learned at the home of the teacher and her husband (62), both unnamed—but didn't she attend any academic classes at the school? Didn't she participate in any of the "domestic science" classes? If she did, there is no mention of what she studied, and not a single teacher is named.

Meanwhile, she surely did spend time at the school; we are told that she scrubs floors, does dishes, makes beds, and helps "in various other departments" (63). She would have been forbidden to speak her own language while engaged in these activities, just as she had been at the Orayvi Day School. But her own language would not in any case have been understood by the girls from many other tribes who were also set to scrubbing floors and doing dishes. If she had spoken to them, it would surely have been in English and one may wonder what that was like. Did she suffer or observe any punishments, as she had at the Orayvi Day School? Did she make any friends among the other girls? There is decidedly no mention of the Hopi boys or of any other Indian boys.

During her first fall at Riverside—this would be 1907, although Carlson consistently avoids any kind of dating—Qoyawayma "was detailed to pick tomatoes at the Institute's Arlington farm" (63). We are told that "There was a classroom at the farm where Polingaysi learned a great deal about vegetables and fruits, as well as routine [*sic*] subjects such as spelling and arithmetic" (63). "The Hopi children" are assigned to peeling potatoes, something they, "including Polingaysi, seldom minded," since they are permitted to "eat as many sweet, raw potatoes as they could hold, while peeling the bucketfuls that went into the huge cauldrons to be cooked."[19] (63). Were there, then, a very great number of students at the Arlington farm, so many that it took "huge cauldrons" to cook potatoes to feed them? Or was food being cooked at the farm to be taken to the Sherman Institute?

Thus engaged, Qoyawayma, Carlson says, "had no desire to return to Oraibi during the summer vacation period" (64). "She was learning at Riverside," Carlson writes—although, again, apart from learning English at the home of the teacher and her husband, there is no word as to what she was learning—"and she was earning a little money." This comes from her work in the school laundry; she also engaged in "the new adventure of sewing"[20] (64). This leads to her first entrepreneurial endeavor, sewing, patching, and making clothes for the other girls, so that "Soon she was making more than the small wage of three dollars per week" (64). Qoyawayma would go on to a successful career as a teacher, but there is not even a suggestion in Carlson's account of the slightest critical thought on her part at this formative period about the nature of the education she is receiving or how she might use it. Nor is there any mention of her response to the Christian religious training on which Sherman insisted, an especially glaring omission in that Qoyawayma, as we will learn, developed a religious vocation so strong that it led her to pursue training as a Christian missionary.

Then, Carlson writes, her four full years at Riverside (most of the Hopi students who had come in 1906, among them Talayesva and Tawakwaptiwa, stayed three years), with not a single trip home, are up; these four years are covered in only seven pages. Indeed, Qoyawayma "almost dreaded the day when her four years at Sherman would come to a close and she would return to her home. She was certain she would not like it" (64). Carlson again resorts to metaphor by way of explanation, writing that "She had outgrown village life. She had burst like a butterfly from the confining chrysalis of her Hopi childhood" (64). There is no awareness on Carlson's part of the aptness, or, indeed, irony of such an observation regarding one whose name, Polingaysi, means "butterfly." Qoyawayma realistically worries that people "would laugh at her behind their blankets," and believes that she "was no longer a true Hopi" (65). Carlson writes, she "asked herself angrily, what it was she wanted. What must she have to make her contented with life? She was reaching out, but for what?" (66). The answer would seem to be a large house with a piano, and missionary Christianity.

Qoyawayma packs her suitcase for the train trip home knowing that "she had learned the white man's way of living and liked it," pleased that "she had a small nest egg in the bank" (67). "A sewing machine would be one of her first purchases" (67). Thus far, it would appear that the aim of the boarding-school educators to "kill the Indian" in Qoyawayma has been successful. David Adams writes that "the primary challenge before Indian educators was to awaken 'wants' in the Indian child. Only then," as he cites Merrill Gates, president of the Lake Mohonk Friends of the Indian, "could the Indian be gotten out 'of the blanket and into trousers,—and trousers with a *pocket that aches to be filled with dollars*'" (in Adams 1995b, 35, my emphasis). Including as well those Indians who did not wear trousers, Commissioner Francis Leupp in 1907 had affirmed that "it is the dollar that makes the world go around, and we have to teach the Indians at the outset of their careers what a dollar means" (in Adams 1995b, 35).

The long train ride back to Arizona is not described, although Carlson does note Qoyawayma's "Excitement... when she saw the San Francisco Peaks looming against the sky" (67). That, recall, is where the *katsinaam* reside. Her father picks her up at Winslow, and drives her home in his wagon. Apparently she had let him know she was coming, although there had been no mention of how and when she had done so. Carlson has Qoyawayma "amazed" at the "desert distances.... So much land, so little growth" (68). And when she arrives home, "The poverty of the scene made her heartsick. This life was not for her. She would never again be happy in the old pattern. She had gone too far along the path of the white man" (69). In Cora Dunn's phrase that provides the title for this book, she had been changed forever. But the "old pattern" is more resilient than it would here appear to be.

Although the family now has an iron cook stove, there is no table, there are no chairs, and "no bedsteads" (69). Her father, again kindly acceding to his daughter's wishes, has someone "make a crude bed ... for this demanding, headstrong girl" (69). Even more troubling to Qoyawayma is the fact that her mother has made "a stack of beautiful plaques" for her wedding. But, as Carlson writes, although she is now eighteen years old, and "had had some schoolgirl crushes"—no one of these ever having been mentioned—"she had never been seriously attracted to any young man" (70). Marriage "had not entered Polingaysi's mind" (69). Just as it was difficult to believe that the teen-aged Edmund Nequatewa didn't know what was going on when his fellow Hopi students visited their girlfriends at night, it is difficult to believe that by the time she was eighteen the idea of marriage "had not entered" the mind of a Hopi woman born in 1892.

Carlson writes that Qoyawayma "was not ready for marriage.... She loved children, but was *not ready* to assume the role of mother" (70, my emphasis). But the timeliness issue, as it were, has already been undermined in that it is made clear that Qoyawayma finds the image of herself on her knees grinding corn "to fine flour for the *piki* wedding bread ... appalling.... Nor would she be willing to marry in traditional Hopi fashion" (70). She tells her mother that she "intend[s] to have a home of [her] own ... some day. A good home" (71). After some further conversation, her mother says, " 'It is sad that the white man's way has caused you to forget the Hopi way' " (71). At this point, however, it seems clear that Qoyawayma hasn't so much "forgotten" the Hopi way, as she has rejected it to embrace "the white man's way." Just as she finds the image of herself on her knees grinding corn "appalling" (70), so too is she "annoyed ... to see her mother on her knees day after day" grinding corn (71). Carlson has her ask her mother why "she didn't use a machine?" (71). Should this desire for women's "betterment" be equated with an intuitive, organic, as it were, movement for women's liberation on Qoyawayma's part? There is much here that needs further explanation.

Hopi girls born toward the end of the nineteenth century would have begun learning to grind corn as early as four or five years of age (Schlegel 1973, 453), and "Sometime during her adolescent years, the girl goes through a corn-grinding ceremony for three days" (Schlegel 1973, 455). It is likely that Qoyawayma had avoided this ceremony by remaining a full four years in California with no return home. Still, the suggestion that her mother grind corn with a machine engages a matter far more important than preferring to sleep on a bed rather than on sheepskins, preferring to eat at a table, sitting on a chair to eat rather than sitting on the floor. Indeed, it provokes from Sevenka a brief but moving discourse on the traditional importance of corn to the Hopi.

Mary Black has written that "The Hopi say... that Maasawu, who greeted the Hopi on their emergence into the Fourth World [the world we live in today], gave them corn and the digging stick for planting it... saying '*Pay nu'panis sooya'yta*,' 'I have only the digging stick; if you want to live my way, that's the way you have to live'" (279). Black goes on to analyze the "Two... most prevalent Hopi metaphors pertaining to corn—'People are corn' and 'Corn plants are females" (279). Further, as we have seen, Sevenka is an initiate of the Maraw society, and, as I've noted, "the women's Maraw ceremonies... take place a few weeks before the harvesting of the corn crop in the fall," emphasizing "the fertility theme symbolically in ritual" (Black 285). She would, to state the obvious, expect her daughter to marry, as almost all Hopi women did, and to have children.

Qoyawayma has pronounced "appalling" (70) the three-day corn-grinding at the groom's house, a task the prospective Hopi bride must undergo. There is no notation of the fact that while the bride is grinding corn, the groom's "male relatives are weaving her wedding robes" (Schlegel 1973, 457), an activity in which, as Titiev wrote, "Every man in the pueblo is invited to participate" (1944, 37). These garments are important beyond the actual marriage itself, because the "wedding robe is used as the woman's shroud, and on this her spirit floats into the Spirit World" (Schlegel 1973, 457; Titiev 1944, 38).[21] No wonder, then, that "For a moment," as Carlson writes, "the old way, with its depth of meaning, beckoned," for all that "the new way won" (72). But Qoyawayma, as we will soon see, is already a devout Christian, so she would no longer believe she would enter the afterlife on her wedding robe. Still, it will take some time before she can sort out these complex matters.

At this point, Qoyawayma's choices have been specified strictly in terms of binary oppositions, *old way/new* way, *Hopi way/white man's* way, and these binaries seem to pose an *either/or* choice of one or the other. Before long, however, these binary *either/or*'s will come to be seen as capable of restatement in *both/and* terms, Qoyawayma integrating *both* old ways *and* new, *both* Hopi ways *and* white man's ways, rather than rigorously choosing between them. Achieving what Michael Coleman called "adaptive, syncretic responses" (121) was indeed something many of the boarding-school students managed to do, some with greater difficulty than others. It also must be said that while for some it was possible also to integrate elements of traditional Native religion with elements of Christian religion, for some who became Christian there was indeed an exclusive choice to be made.

Qoyawayma insists on bringing "new kitchenware" (73) into her parents' house, and cooking in what seems to her mother and to other Hopi women a very wasteful fashion. Carlson writes, "Polingaysi was not then wise enough to see that her lessons in home economics were wrong for her as a Hopi" (73). Apparently she had had—like all the female students at Sherman—"lessons in home economics," although she described no such lessons. Carlson then writes, "Not that it was the fault of her teachers who, being white, had no conception of the true needs of Indian people" (73). This is put blandly enough, but it is an outrageous statement. If, indeed, all of Qoyawayma's teachers were white, "being white," hardly serves as excuse for their having "no conception of the true needs of Indian people," especially given the fact that they were persons who had taken a position teaching "Indian people."

Leo Crane, whom I quoted in the introduction, had certainly grasped the problem by 1917, only seven years later than when Qoyawayma returned home—in spite of the fact that he was white. Perhaps the young Polingaysi Qoyawayma, eighteen years old at the time, was "not then wise enough" to see the folly of some of her education. But, as David Adams notes, the school officials themselves "ignored altogether the charge of superintendent Crane that the nonreservation boarding school ... prepared the Indian student for a life that did not exist on the reservation" (1995b, 43). These people, not surprisingly, were unwilling or unable to engage in "a painful reexamination of the entire rationale by which white Americans had justified the dispossession of the Indian's land and culture" (Adams 1995b, 44). Contrary to Carlson, I would say that her teachers were very much at "fault," not for "being white," but for being ignorant and unthinking.

On the same page from which I have just quoted, Carlson writes that Qoyawayma "was especially bitter about the use of ceremonial foods," which she now sees as "'Food for the Devils'" since that is what "some of her missionary friends called it" (73). Of course we hadn't known that she had made any "missionary friends," or that she had so strongly adopted their beliefs. Had she met them at Sherman? She had described no participation in religious services there. Nonetheless, when Qoyawayma now refuses to "eat food sacrificed to the Devil" prepared by her mother for Niman, "the Homecoming Dance" (74), her situation at home worsens. Her mother, Sevenka, "had not, at that time, developed any desire to become a convert to Christianity," Carlson writes, adding that her "father had more insight, thanks to his long association with the Reverend Voth" (75). Diane Notarriani has written that Fred "Qoyawayma . . . did not convert until 1925, . . . but his wife and children . . . were baptized much earlier" (601). Thus it would seem that Polingaysi Qoyawayma's mother converted to Christianity before her "more insightful" father did, although neither of their conversions is mentioned anywhere in the book.[22]

At this point, Qoyawayma's consistently kind father—the story of his interesting life does not appear ever to have been written—arranges for his daughter to live with the Mennonite missionary Jacob Frey and his wife, Aganetha, "at Moenkopi, about forty miles away" (75). She will "live in their home, help with cooking and housework, and in return continue to study . . . this study to include religion, as well as other subjects" (75). With the prospect of this change, chapter 5 concludes, "Again, life seemed to be opening out before the Hopi girl, Polingaysi. She looked forward eagerly to living with the Freys" (77).

Before she leaves for Moenkopi, her father walks with his daughter to a nearby piece of land. He is represented as saying, "You talk much about building a house of your own. . . . I want you to know, before you leave us again, that there is room on my land for all my children. I will continue to plant my crops here until you are ready to build, but you may have this plot of land, if you like the location" (77).

Carlson notes that "The site he indicated was about two blocks from his rock house as a white man would measure the distance" (77). In fact, she has also presented this bit of talk between kindly father and wayward daughter also "as a white man would." This is to say that strictly speaking the land he offers is not Qoyawayma's land to give; the field is not his nor is "his rock house" *his* house. Hopi women are considered to own the houses in which their husbands reside and also to own the land on which their husbands plant crops.[23] I think what Polingaysi Qoyawayma would have understood from her father's words is that her parents had discussed this matter, and that her mother had agreed that her husband might offer their daughter *her* land. I am not, on this occasion, criticizing Carlson—who in many other regards I find a very unsatisfying writer—for her presentation. Western readers would find it "natural" for a kindly father to speak this way, and a discourse on Hopi matriliny would probably be out of place here. Still, these are matters of which any reader attempting a fuller understanding of the book should be aware.

Qoyawayma's father has recently planted a young cottonwood tree on the land he offers his daughter, and she is moved to say that "This is where [she] will build [her] house. Here beside the tree [he] planted" (78). It's at this time that she is also paid a visit by her mother's brother, a maternal uncle, someone who, as we have already noted—and as Carlson accurately states (90)—serves as the family authority figure. Going on at some length, he upbraids her for "straying from the Hopi way of life" (90). Qoyawayma, in tears, responds, also at some length, that she "won't go back to the life of a pagan" (91). Despite this assertion, the school girl is still Hopi enough to marvel at how she "could... have dared to talk in those defiant terms to an uncle" (91). Qoyawayma "could see the chasm between her two worlds widening," Carlson writes, employing once more a phrase from the subtitle she had given to the book for explanation. This will be a matter that will occupy us further. Carlson goes on to say, in rather free-associative fashion, that the uncle's "words had stung like the lashes of the Whipper Kachina on the day of [Qoyawayma's] initiation into the Kachina *cult*" (91, my emphasis).

What has seemed to me a free-association on Carlson's part rather than a considered narrative decision now leads to a flashback describing Qoyawayma's actual *katsina* initiation, many years before. We are told that the "whipping she received *was not painful*" (93, my emphasis), careless writing here undercutting the comparison of her uncle's words to the "lashes of the Whipper Kachina," both of which had, just a page or so earlier, apparently "stung." Vowing to "forget" the "pagan rite" (93) Qoyawayma has been recalling, she arrives at the Freys' home, and, still troubled by the encounter with her uncle, immediately lets down her hair to wash it, recognizing the gesture poignantly as "automatic ... how Hopi" (93). Now we learn that in "ancient days, her mother had told her, it had been considered a sin to cut the hair, except as ritual decreed," but that the whites had insisted on it, cutting the hair of the men by force if necessary, "disgracing them in the eyes of their people" (94). Although Qoyawayma's hair would now seem to be long, hadn't it been cut short at school?

At this point Carlson introduces an interesting, if oddly placed discursus on Hopi thought about hair, in which, among other things, she mentions its resemblance to corn silk. She assigns these reflections to Qoyawayma and states that they "calm" (95) the young woman. The Freys had earlier changed Qoyawayma's name from "Bessie to Elizabeth Ruth" (80), and the chapter in which she comes to live with them ends with an invitation for her to accompany the Reverend Frey to Newton, Kansas, where she "might learn the type cases, so that she could assist him," when they returned, "to print translations of Bible verses and stories in the Hopi language" (95) on his small printing press. She is pleased to go.

H. R. Voth has for some time been living in Newton, and Qoyawayma is taken to visit him. Voth reminds her that her father had earlier traveled with him to Kansas, where Voth had shown him the Bethel Bible Academy, now Bethel College. Voth reports Qoyawayma as having said at that time that he "hoped some one of his children would be able to go to school here" (98) and train to be a Christian missionary. This appeals to his daughter, who, on her return home, announces to her father that she "will be the one of [his] children to attend that school" (102). This, he acknowledges, "would be a good thing" (102), although he will not himself convert to Christianity for almost ten more years. Before returning home, Qoyawayma becomes friendly with a German religious family, the Schmidts, and it is Elizabeth Schmidt's birthday, April 9, that Elizabeth Ruth Qoyawayma takes as her own (104). "She returned to Kansas the next summer" (102), and in the fall "enrolled at the Bethel Academy" (103), although "She dreaded the active work in the religious field that she would be expected to do among her own people" (107).

When she "returned to Hopiland in the early summer of 1914" (108)— from this point on some few dates are provided—she discovers, as she had feared, that her "work on the reservation did not bring her satisfaction.

(See figure 7.) Her Hopi friends listened politely but were not converted from their pattern of life" (109). Qoyawayma is pleased "when the Reverend Frey asked her and another Hopi girl to go with him to a Mennonite general conference in Pennsylvania" (109). The girls get to see Philadelphia, Mount Vernon, and Washington, DC, stopping in Indiana on their way back to Arizona (110). Whatever may have taken place in the years immediately after her trip with Frey, the story jumps ahead to "the fall of 1918."[24]

It's at this time that Qoyawayma is "asked to go to Kayenta"—the "Kayenta Indian boarding school, about seventy-five miles north of Tuba City, near the Utah state line," a "school attended mostly by Navajo children" (110)—as the matron's assistant. She has been invited, we are told, on the basis of having earlier met and liked the matron, who liked her as well. When that meeting occurred and what took place between the two are once more missing from the narrative. "[G]lad to have a respite from missionary work" (111), Qoyawayma accepts the position. Before she can embark on her responsibilities, however, the great influenza epidemic of 1918 breaks out at the school, and Qoyawayma is forced to turn back. She "soon succumbed to the disease and took her turn in the hospital. When she was well enough, she returned to Moenkopi and the Frey home" (113). It is not long before Jacob Frey tells her that the war is over (114). "The War," Carlson writes, "had never seemed real to her" (114); indeed, as I have noted, it had not ever been mentioned.

Another opportunity to teach arises "because of the epidemic" (114), when Qoyawayma is "asked to serve as a substitute in the Tuba City boarding school." Her pupils are Navajos, people of whom her

7 Polingaysi Qoyawayma, about 1914.

early experiences had made her wary (114). Although her success is mixed, she finds herself engaged by the work, to the point of discussing with the Freys the possibility that she was not "really qualified to be a missionary" (116). They urge her to persevere, and "offered to enroll her in the Los Angeles Bible Institute" (116). She goes to Los Angeles and does housework "to help pay for her schooling" (116–17). On one occasion, "she went on the train to Riverside to spend a Saturday with friends at Sherman Institute" (119). Of course we had not known that she had made friends at Sherman, or—this is at least eight years after she left the school—that she had kept in touch with any friends she had made. Soon Qoyawayma leaves Los Angeles to return to Arizona "with mixed feelings of reluctance and eagerness" (120), still not sure what success she might have as a missionary to her people. She is pleased, however, to be coming home with "a thousand dollars in the bank" (120). It is now a "little more than a decade since she had returned from Riverside" (121), that is, about 1920.

From the account provided by Carlson, most important to Qoyawayma on her return home is the possibility of building the house she had dreamed of on the land offered by her father. With the aid of the Reverend Frey she obtains materials that allow for construction to begin. We have now advanced to 1924, when, on "a summer day" (123), she is offered "the position of housekeeper" (123) at "the government day school at Hotevila" (123). Her diligence and hard work there lead to her being offered a teaching position, even though "she had taken no examinations for government employment" (124). Her students here are Hopi, but she is not permitted to speak Hopi to them. Nonetheless, rather than trying to get them to read stories like "Little Red Riding Hood," "she substituted familiar Hopi legends, songs, and stories" (125), providing English-language versions of them. Although there are objections to her methods, she persists and goes on to experience "her first real taste of success" (126). It's at this point that the "no turning back" interpretative metaphor is specifically called into question, perhaps even rejected, although—unfortunately but predictably—there is no acknowledgement of this on Carlson's part.

Working with the Hopi children, we are told, Qoyawayma "saw plainly that she must try to help them blend the best of the Hopi tradition with the best of white culture, retaining the essence of good, whatever its source" (127). She is said to realize that the "struggle was not 'to be a white man' but to keep from rejecting everything good she had gleaned at such cost of time

and energy from the white man's world" (128). This is an important realization, one from which it follows that "bridging the gap," "turning back," or
not "turning back" are not at issue after all; rather, what is at issue is finding
a way to integrate the two cultural systems. It is not traditionalism versus
assimilation, but some integration of the two in Shillinger's sense; syncretic
adaptations, in Coleman's; or affiliation, as Wendy Kozol writes, a term that
"acknowledges the dialogic nature of identity formations" (68).

This becomes clear as Qoyawayma—she is about thirty years old—
recognizes that despite her adamant rejection of the traditionalism of her
upbringing on her return from school, she "was . . . uneasily aware that it
would not be difficult to shuck off the thin veneer of the white man's ways
and return to the familiar mores of her Hopi people" (128). In spite of her
ongoing commitment to Christianity, "she hung Kachina dolls of carved
cottonwood root on her wall"; although she had insisted on baking all
sorts of cakes and pies, "she still liked the Hopi food of her childhood . . . as
though she could escape her heritage" (128). This is a substantial recognition. Qoyawayma prepares for "an examination for Indian Service teachers
which she would soon be asked to take" (129), and she passes. Now "she was
a bona fide employee of the government" (131), a teacher of Indian students.

She continues to work on her house and takes advantage of the opportunity to purchase a piano "at an absurdly low price" (133), for all that many
of her Hopi neighbors treat her endeavors with derision. Carlson offers
a flashback to Hopi stories Qoyawayma had heard as a child, attributing to
her the observation that "Much superstition was mixed in the culture pattern
of the true Hopi, yet there was good in it also" (141). This rather patronizing
Christian estimate may nonetheless accurately represent Qoyawayma's view
of the matter, at least at that time. Emphasizing what has just been fore-
shadowed as the direction Qoyawayma will take, the penultimate paragraph
of chapter 12 articulates as a question something that had earlier seemed to
have been decided in the negative: "Could she, perhaps, help to blend the
best of Hopi culture with the best of the white culture, retaining the essence
of good from both?" (142).

Qoyawayma's self-esteem as well as her reputation are heightened by
a favorable visit "in late March of 1927" (144) from Henry Roe Cloud, the
"Yale Indian" (Pfister), a Winnebago, and a member of Lewis Meriam's
team studying Indian boarding schools for the secretary of the interior. Roe
Cloud and others are presently "doing a field survey of schools on the Hopi

reservation" (143). He observes Qoyawayma's work, and later sends her a praising letter from which Carlson quotes extensively (144). Nonetheless, she is twice transferred, both times to schools with predominantly Navajo students. It's at this point that she accepts a proposal of marriage from Lloyd White, who "was part Cherokee but looked like a white man" (146), and about whom we learn almost nothing. They are married in 1931, and settle in Orayvi, where her large house has been completed. Although no details of the couple's relationship are given, before long, we are told, Qoyawayma's "marriage was not going well" (148), and soon "she and Lloyd parted" (149). Qoyawayma now takes a position at the day school at Polacca, at the foot of First Mesa, the school Albert Yava had first attended. She benefits from the changes taking place in government thinking about the Indian schools, and, Carlson states, "It was Indian Commissioner John Collier who eventually gave her the greatest support" (151), although not, of course, personally or directly.

After "two successful terms at Polacca," Qoyawayma is "transferred to Oraibi" (152). Although the principal is welcoming, much of the staff is not. This is because a popular teacher "had been transferred to make room for her" (152). It is now that Qoyawayma undergoes a period of what Carlson, accurately, I think, calls "depression." She writes of Qoyawayma that "Nothing cheered her. Feeling that she was a failure, she began to dread each new day" (153). It's at this point that "Finally, in desperation, she reverted to the Indian way." But this once more oversimplifies a complex negotiation on Qoyawayma's part. Leaving her house in a troubled mood one day, Qoyawayma puts her hand "on the rough bark of the cottonwood," which Carlson describes as an "old tree that struggled, year in and year out against the cutting grains of sand and tearing winds" (153).

If this is "the" cottonwood, it would be the one that her father had planted years before on the land he offered his daughter to build her house. But then—I don't mean to be splitting hairs—the tree would not be "old" for a cottonwood. Southwestern cottonwoods, depending on the variety, live as few as 50 years, although many have been known to live 150 years, and there was a cottonwood reputed to have been 400 years old. My point is that if, as seems certain, this is indeed the tree Fred Qoyawayma planted somewhere between 1910 and 1914, and it is now about 1930, it's not a very old cottonwood at all and therefore not a good choice of image for what Carlson wishes to convey, the image of an aged and gnarled tree that had long braved and survived the elements. Meanwhile, we may note that the cottonwood Fred Qoyawayma planted was surely still alive in the early 1980s, in that the volume Jo Linder published of letters of tribute to Qoyawayma in 1983 is titled, *When I Met Polingaysi Underneath the Cottonwood Tree*, surely *that* cottonwood tree. Carlson now, melodramatically, provides some detail about Qoyawayma's painful introspection.

She has Qoyawayma walking home thinking about what she calls "the Hopi tenet of nonresistance" and what is "in essence the teaching of the missionaries. Turn the other cheek" (155). Although neither of these principles for Hopis or Christians is absolute, their concurrence is substantial; apparently no choice between them is necessary, and Qoyawayma continues to work out her integration of Hopi and Christian principles in a way that might make the two cultural/religious systems compatible. She says that because of her instruction in Christian doctrine, she does not "await the coming of Our Brother as [her] unconverted people do" (155), referring to the expectation of the *pahaana*'s return to the benefit of the Hopis. For her, "and for many others," Carlson has her say, "He has come" (155). "He" is capitalized midsentence, and Qoyawayma is represented as further stating, "I have given Him my heart and soul" (155), so there can be no question that she is referring to Christ.

The book goes on to detail Qoyawayma's development of her methods of using Hopi culture to teach English literacy, and of the broad recognition and many accolades that came her way. Qoyawayma, sure of herself now, recalls her first days experimenting with curricular materials as a teacher. Carlson writes that Qoyawayma "had been so positive her approach to teaching had been correct... because the way she had been taught was so very wrong" (158). This is stated casually, in passing, but it is a strong negative assessment of the schooling Qoyawayma had so avidly pursued. Indeed, there is an extraordinary paragraph late in the book that elaborates and provides the details on which such a generalization might be based. Carlson has Qoyawayma "reflect" on the tremendous "change in educational methods through the years, thinking back to her first school days" (174):"the saucer of syrup and the hardtack, the ticking dress, the stupid, brutal whippings and humiliations. She and her companions had been treated like little dumb animals because they did not speak the language of the school authorities" (174). Here are referenced the initiatory loci of the Dining Room and, perhaps, the Dormitory; here are the topoi of poor and unpalatable food, and

Corporal Punishment. That the ticking dress, the dress so avidly desired by the young Polingaysi Qoyawayma, is included in this litany of suffering comes as a surprise. But then, if one had not read the histories of the boarding schools, if one had not read the autobiographical accounts of Edmund Nequatewa, Don Talayesva, and any number of other boarding-school students, all of this would come as a surprise. So far as these things had been experienced or even witnessed by Qoyawayma herself, none of them had to this point been mentioned.

On the penultimate page of the book, Carlson puts quotation marks around words she attributes to Qoyawayma that would seem to sum up the understanding she has achieved. She has her say, "I tell the young people this: 'Your foundation is in your parents and your home, as well as in your Hopi culture pattern. Evaluate the best there is in your own culture and hang on to it, for it will always be foremost in your life; but do not fail to take also the best from other cultures to blend with what you already have'" (179). Again, this sort of syncretic adaptation, integration, or affiliation is something many boarding-school students managed to achieve. But such an achievement on Qoyawayma's part is one that completely undermines the metaphor in the title to Qoyawayma's life story, *No Turning Back*, as it also abandons the metaphor of "bridging the gap" offered in the subtitle. It is a conclusion consistent with what I have called the *both/and* logic of traditional, small-scale indigenous cultures rather than the *either/or* logic of the post-Aristotelian West.[25]

I had earlier cited Peter Whiteley's assessment that the life stories of Don Talayesva and Polingaysi Qoyawayma were the best-known texts of what he called the Hopi autobiographical canon. I think he is right. But apart from a number of reviews, *No Turning Back*, unlike *Sun Chief*, has received almost no critical attention. David Brumble's *Annotated Bibliography* accords it little space because, as Brumble accurately notes (and as I have noted), it is, strictly speaking, a biography not an autobiography. Early studies, my own *For Those Who Come After* (1985) and Hertha Wong's *Sending My Heart Back Across the Years* (1992), do not mention it at all, while Gretchen Bataille and Kathleen Sands's *American Indian Women: Telling Their Lives* (1984) references it only briefly in passing. Jo Linder's 1983 *Polingaysi* has proven to be unavailable either through interlibrary loan or for purchase. (Amazon lists it but says no copies are available.)

While there is no direct correlation between the quality of any published text and the amount of critical attention it receives over the years, the book's neglect may indeed come from the fact, to cite Beatrice Medicine in her review of it, that Qoyawayma was badly served by her biographer-editor (123 passim), a judgment I obviously share. LaVonne Ruoff found *No Turning Back* "marred by a highly fictionalized method, complete with flashbacks," along with "an often melodramatic style" (24), a particularly egregious example of which she quotes. Yet, as Leo Simmons wrote, in a brief but insightful review, it's almost surely the case that the book "relates and interprets largely what the writers wish the reader to know about the real life of the heroine—not much of what the reader would want to know" (1,567). I think this is accurate, and I can only wonder to what degree "the writers" were conscious of how very many things "the reader would want to know" they were omitting. I'll conclude by citing the anthropologist Edward Spicer, who captures very closely my feeling about the book. Spicer wrote that to him, the book was "fascinating and disturbing. It fascinates because again and again it comes to a point where one expects illumination concerning the continuous struggle of a strong-minded woman to find herself in a difficult world, and then moves away with the bases of the struggle hardly suggested. I put the book down with a sense of sadness" (185). I, too, put the book down with "a sense of sadness"—but a strictly *literary* sadness, one that is mitigated by the knowledge that, in human terms, Polingaysi Qoyawayma's long life eventually brought her a great many years of affirmation and, no doubt, joy.[26]

5

Helen Sekaquaptewa's
Me and Mine

LIKE DON TALAYESVA'S *Sun Chief*, HELEN SEKAQUAPTEWA'S *Me and Mine* HAS gone through a great many printings; my old 1993 paperback was the tenth since the book first appeared in 1969, and by 2009 it had gone through another four printings, fourteen in forty years. In 2015, the University of Arizona Press issued a Kindle edition and another paperback printing with a new cover (the book has had several different covers). The first edition contained an epilogue by Louise Udall, who worked with Sekaquaptewa in the production of the book. Unfortunately, only Udall's name appears on its spine. The book dealt with Sekaquaptewa's children, listing some of their impressive achievements, and also noted the debilitating arthritis suffered by her son, Abbott. According to P. Jane Hafen, "the editorial and authorial representations in the book were mostly as Helen [*sic*] wanted, except for Louise Udall's epilogue published in early editions of the book"[1] (156). The epilogue was removed from later printings, the publisher substituting for it "a short remembrance of his parents by son Emory and a 'Retrospect,' Helen's eulogy delivered at Louise's funeral in 1974" (Hafen, 156). I haven't been able to find every one of the printings so I can't say exactly when the epilogue was removed. It still concluded the 1981 sixth printing, but it was gone by the time of my old tenth printing (1993), which still had only Udall's name on the book's spine.

Sekaquaptewa converted to Mormonism in 1953 at age fifty-five. In the autobiography, she provides an exact date for that event, noting that she was "baptized ... on May 3, 1953" (242). It was around this time that she met Udall, five years her senior and a formidable Arizona Mormon woman.[2] Udall (1893–1974) was the granddaughter of Jacob Hamblin, who had been

113

sent by Brigham Young as a missionary to the Hopis in 1858 (James, 86); she was the mother of Arizona Congressmen Morris and Stewart Udall. As Udall said in a brief preface to *Me and Mine* called "How the story came to be written," the two had met when Sekaquaptewa "was living in Phoenix, keeping a home for her children who were attending high school and college" (n.p.). As members of the Relief Society, "the women's organization of the Church of Jesus Christ of Latter-Day Saints" (Udall, n.p.), they visited the Maricopa reservation southwest of Phoenix once each week, and, on the way, they chatted.

Similar to what Vada Carlson had said about her relationship with Polingaysi Qoyawayma, Udall notes that "The many things [Sekaquaptewa] told [her] about her life, prompted [her] to say, 'You should write the story of your life for your children and grandchildren.'" Udall reports Sekaquaptewa responding to her in much the same way as Qoyawayma had to Carlson—she had "thought of doing it, but didn't think [she] was capable" (n.p.). The two worked together for ten years (Bataille and Sands, 100),[3] with Sekaquaptewa eventually writing two of the chapters herself, one on bartering with Navajos, one on her marriage (Bataille and Sands, 100). She did this, Sekaquaptewa said in a 1978 interview, because Udall "couldn't understand some things that the Hopis believed or did"[4] (Sekaquaptewa 1978, n.p.). It "was more about the customs and the things that we did ... and so I sat down and wrote those chapters in my own words, and then she edited it down" (1978, 1).

Although she realized she might indeed have written the book on her own, in the end, as she agreed with the 1978 interviewers, "the book came off pretty much like [she] felt then" (1), something her daughter, as I have said, confirmed in 2000, ten years after her mother's death. Bataille and Sands note that Sekaquaptewa's "only regret" was that Udall included less detail than she had apparently offered "concerning her mother's admonitions to guard herself sexually from men" (101), a matter to which I will return. Udall also deleted an event Sekaquaptewa had recounted about "a threatening situation in her youth," also involving sex (Bataille and Sands, 101). The book has as epigraph a page-long set of quotations from Proverbs. I would guess that that was Udall's idea, but if so, it seems certain that Sekaquaptewa approved of it. So, too, must she have approved of the title—I have found no information as to how or by whom it was chosen—*Me and Mine*, a somewhat unusual title for the life story of a Hopi person who, as Fred Eggan had noted, is "taught communal virtues," and not "to think primarily of oneself and one's family" (411).

∞∞

Born in Orayvi in 1898, in her first chapter, "Childhood," Sekaquaptewa states that when she was "five or six years of age" (8) her parents, Hostiles, hid her to keep her from the government officials and Navajo police seeking forcibly to take their children to the day school at the bottom of the mesa, a story by now familiar to us from her Hopi contemporaries. Although she describes in some detail the efforts to hide her, Sekaquaptewa was "finally caught and went to the Oraibi day school . . . when [she] was about six years old" (9). She also mentions that Emory Sekaquaptewa[5]—he would become her much-loved husband, although she seems not to have known him until they were both at the Phoenix Indian School—had also been hidden on the mesa as a boy, in his case by "an older man" (10). When she was finally "caught," her mother, by this time largely resigned to the likelihood of her being caught, put her arm around her because, Sekaquaptewa says, "Tradition required that it appear that [she] was forced to school" (12). This is not "tradition" so much as Hostile practice at the time.

Sekaquaptewa recounts several of the boarding-school primal scenes. First, she describes the Cleanup she and the other captured children experienced and its locus, the kitchen: "Each was given a bath by one of the Indian women who worked at the school. Baths were given in the kitchen in a round, galvanized tub. Then we were clothed in cotton underwear, cotton dresses, and long black stockings and heavy shoes, furnished by the government. Each week we had a bath and a complete change of clothing" (12).The children were "permitted to wear the clothes home each day" (12), something that Polingaysi Qoyawayma had said earlier of the Orayvi Day School girls. Sekaquaptewa's mother, however, removed "the clothes of the detested white man as soon as [she] got home" (12). A bit later she refers to the underwear the girls were given as "cotton union suits," noting once more that her mother would "make [her] take it off because of her deep scorn for the white man and his trappings" (50).

Then comes the topos of the Naming: "Names were given to each child by the school."The one given to her "was Helen. Each child had a name card pinned on, for as many days as it took for the teacher to learn and remember the name she had given us" (12). The Naming is not represented as something unpleasant or, as with Qoyawayma, in the context of punishment. This is about 1904, and Sekaquaptewa describes the "feud" (13) that had already developed between the Friendlies and the Hostiles, remarking specifically that at the school "The children of the 'Friendlies' made fun of . . . [her] and other of the children of the] Hostiles" (13). Nonetheless, as she states simply, "I liked school. It was pleasant and warm inside"; she also "liked to wear the clothes they gave us at school" (14), as had Polingaysi Qoyawayma. She indicates an interest in the nearby Mennonite church, although her "parents would not let us go even to their Sunday school" (14). Nonetheless, she "came to the Sunday School by a back path," and, although she "did not understand much that they said . . . it was nice to be there" (15).

Apart from school and an occasional surreptitious visit to the Mennonites' Sunday School, Sekaquaptewa describes the typical activities of Hopi girls of her time, in particular, fetching water (an entire chapter, 17–22). The chapters are not numbered, but her third chapter is called "Kachinvaki," and in it she explains that this is "the first ceremony in which Hopi children participate" (23), and that "it is also called 'The Whipping.'" Her first mention of it states that it "occurs in the spring of each year in connection with the Bean Dance" (23), Powamuy. She interprets this for Udall and her non-Hopi readers as being "in the nature of a baptism—that is, to drive out the 'bad'" (23). How accurate this is in regard to *katsina* initiation and, too, in regard to baptism, I will leave an open question.[6] She notes what we have remarked earlier, that for some boys it might be said, "Whip him hard. He is naughty. Don't be lenient with him" (28). Perhaps this is driving "out the bad." She does not refrain from stating what we have also observed earlier, that there might be "big welts on the back of the boys and sometimes they are bleeding" (28). She also briefly references the "Disenchantment"—she will return to it soon—by remarking that children "too young to be initiated . . . don't discover that the kachina is only a man with a costume and a mask" (24), someone impersonating a supernatural. That discovery will come with their own initiation.

Here, as in a great many places, Sekaquaptewa offers richly detailed descriptions. She recounts how her godmother for the initiation was chosen, how corn is used in the ceremony, her descent into the kiva, the costumes of the *katsinam*, and the fierceness of their appearance (25–27). She says, "It was quite an ordeal." Indeed, "when [she] went back home [she] wished [she] didn't know that a kachina was a man with a costume and a mask, when all the time [she] had thought they were real magic" (29). This was, as I have noted, the response of many young Hopi initiates.

Her next chapter is called "Emory's Early Years" and it gives some of the life history of her husband, Emory Sekaquaptewa. She describes his being taken to school at the age of six, his very brief stay at the Orayvi Day School, and his immediate transfer to the Keam's Canyon School in 1901. Sekaquaptewa quotes her husband's own brief account of his arrival at Keam's Canyon, something of an autobiography within an autobiography. He describes a familiar locus, as he and the other children are "herded into the dining room." There, "the evening meal [having] been over for hours," they were given "hard tack and syrup in a saucer" (32), meager rations that other boarding-school students had also described, Polingaysi Qoyawayma very belatedly. Then comes the Dormitory: "The next thing I knew," Emory Sekaquaptewa reports, "I was in a big room full of boys and put into a bed." He mentions no Cleanup. "In the morning," he continues, "we were issued regular government clothing—blue shirt, mustard-colored pants, and heavy shoes" (32). He seems to have remained at the Keam's Canyon School for a full seven years before being transferred to the Sherman Institute when he was "thirteen" (33). This would be 1908, just two years after Chief Tawakwaptiwa and a large contingent of Hopi boys and girls had arrived at Sherman, Don Talayesva and Polingaysi Qoyawayma among them.

At Sherman, Emory Sekaquaptewa worked on the "outing" program picking oranges (33–34) and strawberries (34) and driving a team on a hay bailer (34). "After three years in Riverside," he "was sent home to the Reservation" (34). Then, at the end of the summer, he "went to the Phoenix Indian School" (34), where he and Helen Sekaquaptewa would become acquainted. Emory Sekaquaptewa's story is dropped for a return to historical and ethnographic detail that is offered in a lengthy chapter called "Food, Clothing, and Shelter." Among other matters Sekaquaptewa considers is the fact that land division and labor among the Hopis were very unequal; she also states the simple fact that food was often scarce. She notes here the prophecy "that there would come a time when the Chief would so stray from the traditions of the past that the best corn land would be destroyed" (45). She says that this has indeed come to pass "as a result of the schism in the village and the events of 1906" (45), events that she will discuss two chapters later. If this arrangement of the materials strikes Western readers as somewhat unusual, Bataille and Sands state that it was Sekaquaptewa herself "who set up the sequence of the narrative" (100). Perhaps her assertion that Udall "edited" everything refers primarily to style, not structure.

It is in the chapter called "The Line" that Sekaquaptewa recalls "the happenings of September 6 and 7, 1906," when she "was only seven years old" (63). She gives some of the history leading up to the conflict on September 7, noting in particular the arrival of the Shongopovi Hostiles to Orayvi (66), and also referencing once more her awareness of the "prophecy that there would come a time when the village would be divided and one of the groups would be driven off the mesa forever" (67). Udall, in what she calls an "Author's Note," writes that she "supplemented and augmented and verified" the account given by Sekaquaptewa and her husband with materials from the National Archives, including letters and documents by whites present at the time—J. B. Epp, the Mennonite missionary who replaced H. R. Voth at Oraibi in 1901, and his guest Gertrude Gates, along with Elizabeth Stanley, school principal at Orayvi, and Miltona Keith, a field nurse (84). She later—pages 85–89—includes excerpts from reports by Agency Superintendent Lemmon.

Sekaquaptewa's presentation of the events leading to the departure of the Hostiles from Orayvi differs somewhat from other accounts. She first describes a struggle in which Tawakwaptiwa insists that the Second Mesa Shongopovis who had come to support the Orayvi Hostiles leave the village. When Yukiwma "said they should not leave," Tawakwaptiwa responds that in that case, Yukiwma will also have to leave (74). A struggle then ensues, pitting the Shungopovi and Orayvi Hostiles against the Friendlies. The Friendlies prevailing, "the Hostiles were taken bodily, one by one to the northern outskirts of the village, and put down on the far side of a line which had been scratched in the sandstone, parallel to the village, some time before. After evicting the Hostile men, the Friendlies went into each home and forcibly ejected each family, driving them out to join their menfolk on the other side of The Line" (75).

As I've tried to make clear in appendix A, those events occurred early on September 7, at which time there was not yet a "line ... scratched in the sandstone," or in the sand. Sekaquaptewa, however, would seem to have these events taking place on September 6, in that she says her father spent that night "in the Hostile council" (76). There had indeed been meetings long into the night of September 6 before any Hostiles were put over the line. It appears to be the next morning when Sekaquaptewa's mother hears "the rumor that [they] might be expelled from the village" (76). In response to "the rumor," Sekaquaptewa's mother hides her and her siblings in "an underground little room in [their] house, [their] secret hiding place in case of war or trouble" (76), and, while the children are in hiding, her mother "watched and kept telling [them] what was happening" (76). What is actually happening is not, however, described. (I believe what is happening is what was described as already having happened, the events of early September 7.) It is just as mother calls for the children to come out that "Tewaquaptewa's men" arrive and pull them out (76). It is at this time that her family is "driven out of the village with the others" (77), assembling to the northwest of Orayvi.

But the pushing match is yet to take place. Whatever line in a sandstone rock Sekaquaptewa said had been drawn earlier, she now has Yukiwma draw what would seem to be another "line on the sandrock," not in the sand, while speaking approximately the words memorialized in the later inscription. She reports Yukiwma saying, "'Well, it will have to be this way now. If you pass me over this line, then I will walk'" (80), meaning, Sekaquaptewa says, that "he and his people would leave" (80). When he is indeed pushed over the line, he "started walking the trail to the Hotevilla spring" (80), and she and her family "gathered [their] bundles and followed him" (80). The chapter ends with Sekaquaptewa noting that Robert Selena, "a student at the Indian School at Keams Canyon [who] was home in the summer of 1906," was the one to scratch "an inscription" in one of the "many big flat sandstones cropping out of the ground on the outskirts of old Oraibi" (83), to mark "The Line." The inscription, as noted earlier, is dated September 8, 1906, and reads

WELL IT HAVE TO BE DONE THIS WAY NOW THAT WHEN YOU
PASS ME OVER THIS LINE IT WILL BE DONE SEPT. 8, 1906 (83)

As a consequence of the events of the 7th, she notes that Emory Sekaquaptewa's father was among those sent to the Carlisle School in Pennsylvania, while her father, along with "Some of the older men . . . were given a punitive sentence of a year in prison at Fort Huachuca in southern Arizona" (87).

The next chapter, "To School in Keams Canyon," has Superintendent Lemmon arriving in the village in October of 1906 to see to it that the children of the Hostiles attend school (91). Eighty-two children, Sekaquaptewa among them, are taken "to the schoolhouse in New Oraibi" (92), where they spend the night.[7] The next morning they are taken by wagon to Keam's Canyon. "It was after dark," Sekaquaptewa says, when they "reached Keams Canyon boarding school and were unloaded and taken into the big dormitory." It was "lighted with electricity," and she "had never seen so much light at night"[8] (92). In that it was past dinner time, the children are given "hardtack and syrup to eat" (93), a familiar, meager repast, and one that her husband-to-be had also described. In that there "were not enough beds," in the dormitory, "they put mattresses on the floor"; even so, "Three little girls slept in a double bed." Evenings they "would gather in a corner and cry softly so the matron would not hear and scold or spank us" (93), corporal punishment being a near-constant of boarding-school life.

Once more the girls' clothes are taken, and they are "issued the regular school clothes" (93), which she describes in some detail. The military nature of the Keam's Canyon School is conveyed when Sekaquaptewa notes that "Boys and girls marched to the dining room from their separate dormitories" (94). There are a number of Navajo children in attendance "even though it was a school for Hopis," and she describes them as having "their plates heaping full, while little Hopi girls just got a teaspoonful of everything" (94). As a result, she "was always hungry ... and thought [she] would just starve." Worse, she notes, "You can't go to sleep when you are hungry" (94). "For breakfast," Sekaquaptewa says, "we had oatmeal mush, without milk or sugar, and plain bread" (94–95). In that the "Navajos didn't like the mush, ... they took the bread and [the Hopis] had the mush" (95), hungry enough, it would seem, to consume it whether they liked it or not.

She describes other of the meals served to the children, recalling that "Day after day, the food had a sameness," and that the children "longed for some food cooked by [their] mothers" (95). Remarking on "the few occasions ... the girls did beat the boys to the dining room," a time when they "fared better," she mentions, for the first time, the children saying "the blessing on the food" (95). I suspect that the "blessing" preceded each meal, although Sekaquaptewa offers nothing further about the saying of grace, nor does she—despite her early interest in the Mennonite Church and Sunday School—say anything about religious services or instruction at Keam's Canyon.

Sekaquaptewa tells us that "early one morning," the girls "wondered what was making the approaching clinking sound. Running to the high, woven wire fence around the playground, [they] saw a long line of men walking down the road. They were some of the seventy or so fathers from Hotevilla [i.e., Hostiles] who had been arrested for resisting the government and had been sentenced to ninety days of hard labor.... They were fastened together in twos with ball and chain" (96). The men "walked four miles out to the job every morning" (96), surely a difficult walk "with ball and chain," and the children, "each morning... ran out to see if [their] fathers went by" (97). Sekaquaptewa poignantly remembers, "We would cry if we saw them and cry if we didn't" (97). She sees her father only once more; this is because, as she again states, he had been "sent to prison at Fort Huachuca" (97).

"Being a little girl and away at Keams Canyon," she speaks of what she wouldn't learn until later, the "very sad plight" of her mother, "along with the other exiles back at Hotevilla" (98). In retrospect, she realizes how difficult it was for them to survive the winter while she "had three meals each day and a comfortable bed and a warm building to shelter [her]"[9] (98). At the end of her first year at Keam's Canyon, she is not allowed to return home because the "parents from Hotevilla... would not promise to bring [the children] back to school in September" (98–99). For that reason she "was left to spend the summer at the school along with other boys and girls of Hostile parentage" (99). With fewer children "and no Navajos," the girls' nutrition improves. It's at this time that Sekaquaptewa remarks on the sweetness of the raw potatoes some of the big girls who had kitchen duty "would slip... to us little girls" (99). I have earlier noted Polingaysi Qoyawayma's fondness for raw potatoes.

In September of 1907, the students who had gone home return to school at Keam's Canyon, and, soon, all "were back in [their] regular routine again" (99). But, then, one October morning, Sekaquaptewa along with some others watches "a few government wagons as they wended their way... into the canyon," bearing "the prisoners being returned from Fort Huachuca. They had come by train to Holbrook, and then by team and wagon on out to Keams Canyon." She recognizes her father, "dressed in an old military uniform," and looking "fine and young and straight..., and [she] was proud of him" (99). Sekaquaptewa gets to talk to him that "night and again in the morning," and, although he says that the soldiers had treated the Hopis well, his "attitude had not changed, and it was many years before he could even begin to tolerate any part of the white man's culture" (100). The men must walk "forty miles on home to Hotevilla," a walk, she says, that "probably seemed a short forty miles to them" (100).

As others had, so, too, does Helen Sekaquaptewa recall parents and relatives visiting the children at Keam's Canyon School bringing "piki, parched corn, dried peaches, and the like" (100). The children, she says, "learned by sad experience to have [the] housemother lock up" this food, "otherwise it would be pilfered" (100). Sekaquaptewa will soon describe other abusive behavior by some students. She experiences her "first Christmas at Keams Canyon," and, again like Nequatewa, she remarks that she "had never known about Christmas." Although the girls receive apples, oranges, and candy for gifts, she says that "they didn't tell us any Christmas story" (102), the religious nature of the occasion being left unclear to her. She remarks that "The second year, Christmas was just the same as the year before." While she now "understood more of the English words," she appears still not to know what it is all about—although she "got a very nice doll . . . from a group of children from the Baptist Church" (103).

It would seem that her hair was not cut at the Keam's Canyon school but left long. Nonetheless, how one's hair was treated at the boarding schools is consistently a topos of the boarding-school autobiographers, and so, too, is it in Sekaquaptewa account. She says that she "had lots of hair and had never tried to comb it [herself]," so that "certain bigger girls were detailed to come and braid the hair of the little girls" (103). Unfortunately, her "long hair got matted and snarled, and they were rough, and it pulled" (103). One of the girls says that unless Sekaquaptewa gives her some of her food, she would pull her hair (103). Others also threaten her and take the little that she has. There seems to be a fair amount of bullying on a regular basis, although not of a sexual nature. Sekaquaptewa also notes that although she "was really serious at school" (104), "some of the teachers were unkind" (104), and once when she "gave the wrong answer, the teacher boxed [her] real hard on the ear" (105), injuring her seriously enough so that to this day she "can't hear very well out of that ear" (105). She does not name this teacher or indicate his or her gender; to this point, she has also not named any of her fellow students.

The condition of the children's hair, in particular, the issue of lice, is dealt with at the school every "Saturday afternoon [when] it was hair washing time." Sekaquaptewa describes the children lining up—"seems like that was the first English we learned, 'Get in line, get in line,' all the time we had to get in line" (105)—and getting "the delousing treatment": first the application "of kerosene, provided by the government... to hair and scalp," and after, a fine-tooth comb run through the hair (105). "If it came out clean you could shampoo and go out and play, but if the comb showed 'nits' the word was, 'Go to the buggy bench'" (105). There, more "kerosene was applied, fine-tooth combs were passed out, and the girls combed each other's hair or just picked nits from the strands of hair" (105). Eventually "the matron would inspect again," and those not "given a clean pass" would have to wash their hair once more with "a bar of yellow laundry soap," after being warned that "next week you will still be on the buggy bench" (106).

"Most of our teachers were women," Sekaquaptewa says, although Mr. M., one of the few male teachers, as I'd noted earlier, fondles one of the girls, "sometimes taking her on his lap." Although "Some of the girls seemed to like it," she "was scared that [she] would be the next one called to his desk" (106). When she is, he puts his arm around her, and "put his strong whiskers on [her] face." She screams until he lets her go, then runs out of the room to the dormitory (107).

"One, two, three, and four years passed by, and each spring [the] girls from Hotevilla saw the children from the other villages go home... while [they] were kept at school." Then, "one fine day in June, 1910," the Hostile girls' fathers come to ask "permission to take their children home for two weeks to be there at the Home Dance" (107–8), the Niman when the *katsinam*, in July, return to their place in the San Francisco peaks. She describes the superintendent—this would be Horton H. Miller, who had been in charge since 1906 (James, 107), when Sekaquaptewa first arrived at the school—as "a pleasant man [who] gave his consent, with the understanding that [the] parents would bring [them] back when school started on September first" (108). But their fathers do not bring them back and thus Sekaquaptewa "spent a year at home, and enjoyed the old life, learning from [her] mother the things a Hopi girl should know" (108). Clearly her four years at Keam's Canyon boarding school have not yet "changed" her.

Sekaquaptewa begins the chapter titled "Home for One Year," stating that "Grinding the corn is the most important homemaking skill" (109).

She goes on to provide a wealth of detail, explaining that "All daughters in the family grind," and that "Girls take pride in filling storage bowls and rounding them over the top" (111). Younger and with less boarding-school experience than Polingaysi Qoyawayma had when she returned home and pronounced the near-endless round of corn-grinding "appalling" (70), Sekaquaptewa recalls grinding corn in her year at home with fondness, even providing several pages (112–16) of instruction on how to make *piki*. Her subsequent conversion to Mormonism obviously has not changed her relation to corn-grinding and *piki*-making in that she recalls with pride the fact that her "eldest son Wayne [as] a little boy in Hotevilla ... would gather his friends and bring them home and want [her] to give each one of them some fresh piki" (115).

It is also while Sekaquaptewa is at home that her "mother told [her] about the sex side of life ... although even when [she] was younger she had not neglected that subject" (117). Perhaps Sekaquaptewa has revised her recollections of traditional Hopi practice in these matters; perhaps she is editing them for Louise Udall's Mormon sensibilities, or it may be that Sekaquaptewa's mother thinks about this particular "subject" in a manner very different than most Hopi women of her generation. In any case, Sekaquaptewa here, for the first time, offers an account of Hopi belief and practice that is questionable.

Sekaquaptewa says that "When a girl starts menstruating, then her mother teaches her the Hopi moral code, which is that she is to keep herself a virgin until she is married—that before marriage it is wrong, but at the time of her marriage it is right and proper" (117). This runs counter to an enormous amount of evidence. I will begin by citing Mischa Titiev, and in doing so, I need to make clear that I am not blandly replicating the (neo) colonial error of trusting the anthropologist rather than the "native." On these matters we have already had a fair amount of commentary from Hopi people, which I have cited and will cite further.

Titiev had written that while Hopis had "developed a tacit understanding" of "the white man's professed standard of morality," and thus were usually—Don Talayesva was an exception, as he notes—very circumspect in discussing sexual practices with whites, it was nonetheless the case that "pre-marital affairs are taken for granted and readily condoned" (1944, 30). On Third Mesa "a ceremony ... was formerly performed annually for unmarried girls ranging in age from about 16 to 20" (1944, 203), but Titiev specifies that "It was in no way connected with the start of the menstrual cycle, nor do the people of Oraibi... recall that any ritual was ever attendant upon menstruation" (1944, 203). Thus, one may wonder what Helen Sekaquaptewa means when she says that her mother did, in fact, use the occasion of her first menstruation to teach her "the Hopi moral code." Titiev further states that his investigations made clear that "sex actions as such, are not regarded as reprehensible, and youthful love affairs are lightly treated as perfectly natural occurrences" (1944, 205) by the Hopi people he had consulted. The young men's practice of *dumaiya*, when, as we have already noted, they "go to call on the girl of their choice, sometimes by pre-arrangement, and sometimes on the mere chance of getting a favorable reception" (1944, 31), Titiev writes, is "now widespread in all the Hopi villages. It goes on with the connivance of the elders although it has never received open sanction" (1944, 31). "To summarize the situation up to the eve of marriage," writes Titiev, "we find the sex life of the Hopi beginning early in adolescence for both sexes, with young [men] soon learning the trick of visiting girls by night, with the choice of lovers supervised in varying degrees by parents and other relatives, and with pre-marital pregnancy carrying no stigma and almost invariably resulting in marriage" (1944, 33).

Finally, and contrary to what Sekaquaptewa says her mother emphasized, "Virginity, while recognized, is not requisite for marriage" (Titiev, 33). Although Sekaquaptewa recalls her mother saying, "After marriage be true to your husband as long as you live" (117), Titiev's interviews with a great many Hopi consultants, did not find such advice widely followed. He writes, "loose marriage ties and frequent adultery are long-standing Hopi traits. That this has not been more clearly brought out in the writings of former students of the Hopi is due in part to Victorian conventions" (1944, 41).

But we have, of course, already heard from a Hopi older than Helen Sekaquaptewa on these matters, Edmund Nequatewa. Describing his time at the Keam's Canyon School, Nequatewa said that "the boys were so well acquainted with the girls. Naturally they had their sweethearts, and it was customary with the Hopi"—I had quoted him to this effect earlier—"that the boys would call on their girls at night" (92). Don Talayesva, sexually active since the age of thirteen, on his return home from the Sherman Institute had stated his desire "to become a real Hopi again," thus "to sing the good old Kachina songs, and to feel free to make love without fear of sin or a rawhide" (141). Theirs are, to be sure, the accounts of Hopi males.

But Nequatewa made it entirely clear that the boys' nocturnal escapes from their dormitories to visit their "sweethearts" "must have always been planned ahead" (92) with the girls, who "hung down their sheets to pull up the boys" (92). Talayesva's many sexual encounters with Hopi girls (and several women from other tribes) were not only consensual but on more than one occasion initiated by the young woman herself.

Sekaquaptewa continues her account, describing gestures of Hopi modesty, and offering the recollection that in her "time, if a young man wished to court a young lady, he was allowed to call at her house where he would stand outside, looking in through a small window. First the girl learned who was calling. If she liked him she would carry on a conversation. If she didn't like him, she would ignore him. The parents could lock the door and go to bed, but if things got too quiet, if the girl stopped grinding [corn] for too long, the mother would come to investigate" (119). Apart from the fact that most Hopi homes at the time did not have locks on the doors—nor did all of them have doors—and the fact that such visits took place at night when the parents were (ostensibly) asleep, there is little here that conforms to most of the information available on Hopi sexual practices in the first decades of the twentieth century.

Sekaquaptewa returns to school at Keam's Canyon in September of 1911. She describes a new superintendent in charge, a "hard-boiled" (122) and unpleasant man. This would be, as she will state later (133), Leo Crane. Whether this is a new regime initiated by Crane or not, now, she writes, "Each older girl was assigned to a work detail.... Some worked in the morning and went to school in the afternoon, and vice versa" (122). Her "first assignment was bathroom detail," something she hated, for all that she is assigned it again and again (122). Sekaquaptewa writes that years later, when she "met the woman who used to be in charge of detail duty and asked her why [she] always had to have that assignment" (122–23), the woman answered that it was because "No one else would keep it clean like you did, my dear" (123).

In the spring of 1912, the "year after [Sekaquaptewa] had been at home," she receives a visit from her mother, who brings along her new baby, and also some "boiled corn and jerky which she had cooked." This "tasted so good"(123). The following year, when she is fifteen, she is put in charge of the school laundry over the summer (124), once more not going home. For her work, she "was paid fifteen dollars a month" (124), her first experience of a cash economy. Sekaquaptewa repeats that she "enjoyed school and was eager to learn"; "she was a good reader and got good grades" (125). But, as frequently happens in schools everywhere, her "ability did not help [her] socially, it only made the others jealous" (125). Moreover, she "was a wallflower," who, at dances, "sat back in the corner with another girl and watched" (125). Bullying is again referenced when Sekaquaptewa describes an occasion when the other girls hit a girl named Ella, although she herself "wouldn't do it" (127). When Ella tells the matron, the matron promises that "the next morning all would be severely punished—except Little Helen" (127). (Sekaquaptewa had told us that "There was another Helen in school known as Big Helen" [127].)

She then goes back in time to introduce an anecdote from when she "was about twelve years old" (128), which would be about 1910. Out of place as it seems to be, it is nonetheless charming, as Sekaquaptewa describes exchanging letters with a fellow schoolgirl in which she pretends to be Mrs. Holmes of Philadelphia while her friend pretends to be Mrs. Judson of New York (128). Their letters are intercepted but the teacher is approving of and amused by the girls' efforts, and "gave [Sekaquaptewa] a good grade in English composition because of that letter" (129).

It's just after this story that Sekaquaptewa returns to the present to inform the reader that "Sunday was a busy day at boarding school. We had to go to Sunday School where we were separated into age groups for Bible Instruction"(129). She notes that "Different churches came and held services," and that the students "were required to go to evening services too" (129). "The different sects," she says, "were always urging and bribing us with little presents to join their church." This is off-putting to the young woman who had been interested in the Mennonite Sunday School on the Reservation (she and her husband would be married by a Mennonite minister), and who would later become a Mormon. As for the "different sects" and their "bribes," she says that "It didn't appeal to me and I didn't join any of them" (129).

Sekaquaptewa begins her next chapter, "Phoenix Indian School," stating that "Time passed by, and I grew older, and it was better for me at school." Quite undramatically, she recognizes the important fact that she "was weaned away from home" (132). Thus, "At the end of the school year in 1915"—there is no mention of the war—she "had finished the sixth grade, which was as far as one could go at Keams Canyon" (132). She "wanted to go somewhere else and continue [her] schooling," but, as was the case with Albert Yava and Polingaysi Qoyawayma, the case, too, as we will see with Fred Kabotie, she "could not go without the consent of [her] parents which they would not give" (132–33). Along with "a few others of like mind"—students wanting to continue their education—"[they] begged the Superintendent, Mr. Leo Crane, to let us go to Phoenix Indian School" (133). "He finally agreed to let [them] go on [their] own responsibility" (133).

Consistent with her sense that she had been "weaned away from home" (132), she spends the summer "humoring" her parents, dressing "in Hopi traditional clothes… anything to please them" (133). Now it would indeed seem that Sekaquaptewa has in strong measure been "changed." She says that she "had lived at school so long that it seemed like [her] home." She "stayed with [her] parents in Hotevilla only ten days and went back to the dormitory at Keams Canyon" (133). In "the fall of 1915," she and several boys and girls travel by team and wagon to Holbrook (133), from where, as Edmund Nequatewa had done, she goes "by train—about seventy of us, all in one car" (133), to Phoenix.

There, the train is met by Emory Sekaquaptewa, whom she does not immediately recognize. The group from Keam's Canyon is taken out to the Phoenix Indian School where they are "met by the school band, a military type of welcome"; then they are "formed into lines and marched to their assigned dormitories to the music of the band" (134). Affirming what Edmund Nequatewa had only mentioned briefly, Sekaquaptewa repeats that Phoenix "was a military school" (134). The students "marched to the dining room three times a day to band music," "arose to a bell, and had a given time for making our beds, cleaning our rooms, and being ready for breakfast"[10] (134). Clock time rules mercilessly: "Everything was done on schedule, and there was no time for idleness" (134).

She describes the clothing "furnished by the government," and observes that the students here, too, "went to school half a day and worked half a day" (135). The girls work in the "home economics department," the laundry, and also do "home-cleaning" tasks, while the boys are assigned to "janitor work," to "learn shop skills," and to take care of the cows in the school dairy (135), where the girls "learned to care for the milk" (135). "Sunday morning all pupils had to be in their uniforms and stand for inspection at 7:30"; the "boys gave a military salute as the officers passed and the girls held out their hands to be inspected." "Following inspection," she says, the students "marched to the auditorium for church services" (135).

Discipline as well, Sekaquaptewa notes, "was military style. Corporal punishment was given as a matter of course; whipping with a harness strap was administered in an upstairs room to the most unruly," although girls "were not often whipped" (136–37). It is no surprise that she follows description of these punishments with the topos, Running Away. Sekaquaptewa notes, as Nequatewa had, that although both the boys and the girls who slept in separate dorms "were locked in at night, they managed to get out somehow. Often a boy and a girl would have it planned and go at the same time. They would usually start to go home" (137). It's likely that the boy and the girl were sometimes, as Nequatewa referred to them, "sweethearts" (92).

"Older boys with records of dependability would be sent to find and bring them back," and Sekaquaptewa's husband-to-be, Emory, is one who is "often sent" (137). Sekaquaptewa describes the punishments of those runaways who were caught and returned to the school. "Punishment for the girls might be cleaning the yards, even cutting grass with scissors, while wearing a card that said, 'I ran away'"; "Boys were put in the school jail"—we had not been told thus far that the Phoenix School had a jail. (But it must have been closed at some point since it was "reopened" by Superintendent Brown in 1915. See endnote 13.) "Repeaters," Sekaquaptewa notes, "had their heads shaved," and the boys "had to wear a dress to school." She then observes that "Some of them forgot how to wear pants" (137), a sentence whose meaning I can't unpack.

Well aware of what the punishment for running away might be, one family, Sekaquaptewa says, nonetheless "had children on the road most of the time" (137). "Sam, the eldest, left his dress on the doorstep of the house of the disciplinarian and went home" (137). "Another time he took his younger brother out of the hospital, discarding the hospital garb and going 'as is'" (137–38). She notes that this "was later than my time" (138), so that she must have kept in touch with people who knew what was going on at the school in the years after she left. Although her husband Emory had been one of those who'd gone to bring runaways home, Sekaquaptewa displays a certain pride in Sam the runaway, who later in life received "recognition for outsmarting the 'Japs' in the jungles of the South Pacific" during World War II. She adds, with more ambiguity I'd guess than irony, the observation that Sam's "training did not go for naught" (138). But she seems already—and soon will be further—adept at integrating her Hopi heritage and the values of mainstream American society.

Also at the Phoenix Indian School at this time was Anna Moore Shaw, an Akimel O'odham (Pima) woman, the same age as Helen Sekaquaptewa, whose autobiography, *A Pima Past*, I have already mentioned. In their autobiographies, Shaw does not mention Sekaquaptewa, nor does Sekaquaptewa mention Shaw. Nonetheless, it "was at the Phoenix school that Anna Moore and Helen became acquainted and shared a room in the dormitory"; indeed, "they shared living quarters for three years during boarding-school... respected one another but were never intimate friends." I have this information from *Native American Women: Telling Their Lives* by Gretchen Bataille and Kathleen Sands (85 and105). They have it on the basis of interviews Sands conducted, as I'd noted, with Sekaquaptewa and her daughter, Alison, and also with Shaw, her daughter, her daughter's husband, and her editor at the University of Arizona Press, Karen Thure. Their account of the two women and their autobiographies, "Two Women in Transition," is the only full treatment of either of them I have found. The authors offer only two brief quotations from Sekaquaptewa herself (100), paraphrasing or abstracting from the interviews Sand conducted. Bataille and Sands write that Sekaquaptewa "was made a lieutenant, Anna a captain" (105) in the military organization of the Phoenix School, and that it was "the privileges given the Hopi girls" that "caused resentment and prevented a close friend-ship—in fact, Anna would not speak to Helen—between the two"[11] (105). "In time, they met again when Helen set up a temporary household [in Phoenix, about the same time she met Louise Udall] so her children could attend urban high school" (88).

As Bataille and Sands point out, Shaw was essentially a generation ahead of Sekaquaptewa so far as Americanization was concerned. "The adjustments required of Helen," they write, "are actually more similar to those required of Anna's mother than of those made by Anna herself" (94). Her father, Red Arrow, had taken the name Josiah Moore, and both parents were Christians at the time of her birth. They had already named her Anna (she had formerly been called Chehia) when they sent her off, at eight years old, to the Mission boarding school in Tucson, her mother first having "dressed her in [her] best clothes, then braided her long hair and tied it with pink ribbons!" (124). When she gets to the school in Phoenix and is assigned "to an upstairs dorm," she notes with pleasurable anticipation that she "had never climbed a stairway before" (126). When she sees the beds, she thinks, "'Oh, this is going to be fun!'" (126). On first encountering the dining room, and seeing that the girls "repeated Grace in unison" (126), she is entirely familiar with the practice because her father, "Josiah Moore, is an ordained elder of the Gila Crossing Mission" (124). Rather than being put off by any mush served her, she finds that the "cornflakes [she] ate for breakfast were delicious"[12] (126).

Then, "On September 1, 1908," Shaw and her older brother "enrolled at the government boarding school in Phoenix" (132), a "semi-military institution" (133), as she calls it. "They had a boys' and a girls' battalion, called the First and Second battalions respectively. The companies were named alphabetically from A to F, and [she] was placed in the E Company" (133). Shaw describes the military routines in detail and with appreciation, such as when "the famous Indian School Band ... would commence to march to rousing Sousa compositions" (133). Nonetheless, she notes that the "matron was strict and frequently used her strap" (134) on the girls, in particular, as I had quoted her earlier, when they "were still on their hands and knees" (136) scrubbing floors. She mentions the presence of a non-Indian girl at the school, and notes that there were "many Mexican-American boys and girls" and that although "for the most part," the students were "Arizona Indians...," there were also representatives of tribes from Oklahoma, the Dakotas, and California. Together," she writes, "we were one big happy family" (135). She does not make clear that the majority of the Indians from Arizona were Hopis and that, as Bataille and Sands learned, and as I have noted, Shaw was not very "happy" regarding what she perceived as Hopi privileges. Shaw would meet her husband-to-be, Ross Shaw, at the Phoenix School, just as Sekaquaptewa would meet Emory Sekaquaptewa there.

Some of Sekaquaptewa's recollections of the Phoenix School recall Don Talayesva's at the Sherman Institute in Riverside. That is, she describes "going to town on a Saturday afternoon by streetcar," going "to a show," or shopping "at the dime stores" (138). These are things Edmund Nequatewa had not mentioned, if, indeed, they were available at the time he had attended the school. When summer comes, Sekaquaptewa and the Hostile children once more do not return home. She had earlier been chosen to work in the home of school superintendent John Brown[13] and his family, and, during her "third and last summer" (139) at Phoenix, she works for a Mrs. Scott, who, when Sekaquaptewa announces her decision finally to go home, prom-ises her a sewing machine if she will stay on another year. This is an offer Sekaquaptewa refuses (139). While she is still working in the Brown home, she remarks an occasion when the doorbell rang, and "there stood Emory with a package in his arms" (140) for her. She steps out on the porch, thanks him, and they talk. In a parenthesis, Sekaquaptewa offers what is hardly par-enthetical at all: "(P.S. Emory has been the light in my life ever since.)" (140).

"After three years" at the Phoenix School, Sekaquaptewa writes, she "had completed the eighth grade and should have graduated, but that year there were no graduates," because "They"—this would, I think, mean the government's Indian Bureau—"moved graduation up to the tenth grade" (142). Although she had completed the three-year maximum time a student "could stay without the consent of [their] parents," "Superintendent Brown said that [she] could go home or stay on" (142), as she preferred. Her deci-sion is to go home for a visit, planning, after, to "go away to high school and learn good English" (142), another confirmation of the fact that even Native students who'd completed eighth grade were often far from fluent in English. Looking further into the future, Sekaquaptewa hopes after high school to establish a laundry at Keam's Canyon (142). In "September, 1918"—there had been no mention of the war to this point, nor is there any mention of its end—she and a friend go by train to Holbrook, "and on to Keams Canyon by mail truck," where they "were delayed for two weeks," after which they finally return home to Hotevilla.

Somewhat less intensely than Polingaysi Qoyawayma, Helen Sekaquaptewa nonetheless experiences difficulties on her return. She does not wish to wear Hopi clothing (144–45) and encounters great hostility on the part of her sister, Verlie, who "had gone to school only one year, . . . married young . . . remained a true Traditional all her life, strongly opposing schooling for her own children" (145). Verlie is, of course, one of the many boarding-school students whose experiences were never recorded. When the 1918 flu pandemic comes to Hopi-land, Sekaquaptewa's brother becomes ill but for a time improves, although her mother dies of the disease. (Her brother will later have a "relapse" [150] and die soon after his mother.) Sekaquaptewa offers moving passages in which her father, during her moth-er's illness, speaks to her in traditional terms, saying, "If you have the will to get well, it will be so, and you will recover" (147), an example of what we have seen earlier as a complicating aspect of Hopi belief in fate, destiny, and the fulfillment of what has been predicted long ago. Sekaquaptewa also provides much detail on Hopi burial practices.

Although she "should have inherited [her] mother's house" (151), Sekaquaptewa's sister Verlie takes it for herself and her family, placing her "in an awkward position" (151). Emory Sekaquaptewa, having returned from Phoenix to see about his own sick relatives, observes Helen's difficult situation, and, although "Boys do not visit their girl friends when they are in mourning" (152), he leaves her a note saying that when both are through with their period of mourning he will come see her. He does and proposes marriage (152). "He had a job at the government school at Hotevilla," and, Sekaquaptewa says, "it looked good to me" (152). The two marry in traditional Hopi fashion, with Sekaquaptewa providing, once more, abundant ethnographic detail (153–61). "About halfway through the rites," however, their "consciences" trouble the young couple who feel "the Hopi way was not quite right" (161). Therefore, Emory Sekaquaptewa applies for a marriage license, and the two are "married in the evening on February 14, 1919, in the living room of the home of Mr. Anderson, principal of the school in Hotevilla, by Reverend Dirkson of the Mennonite Mission" (163). She notes that "in the morning… a wedding breakfast" was served, and then the young married couple "went back to finish the tribal wedding rites at Bacabi" (163), rites which she again describes in detail (163–66). The extent to which Sekaquaptewa and her husband seem untroubled by—or at least comfortably able to manage—the very different marital customs observed by Mennonite Christians and traditional Hopi people seems to me extraordinary, and I will return to this by way of conclusion.

Because her sister continues to behave in a hostile manner, "after about a month," Sekaquaptewa gathers her belongings and decamps to "the house where Emory lived near the school" where he taught shop. Soon she gets "a job teaching beginners at the school," and, she says, "we were real happy" (166). She next describes moving with her husband to the Nez Percés reservation in Idaho, to "work in the school and tuberculosis sanitarium" (167). There, the young couple also does some small-scale farming, successfully producing enough potatoes and gathering enough eggs from their chickens so that Sekaquaptewa "traded them for groceries at the store" (171). The two return to Hotevilla in 1920, where they are again industrious, and where their first child is born (173); Sekaquaptewa provides a rich description of traditional childbirth and the aftercare of the newborn (178–84). Unfortunately, the child dies "of dysentery when she was about a year old" (184), and Sekaquaptewa now offers details about the burial of children who have died in infancy (184–85). Soon, a second child, a son, is born (185). Reflecting on this period of their life, Sekaquaptewa says of herself and her husband, Emory, that "Our lives were a combination of what we thought was good of both cultures, the Hopi way and what we had learned at school" (186). She will repeat this in her final chapter. She uses her penultimate chapter, called "My Church," to convey what the "good of both cultures" means in terms of her Mormon beliefs.

"My Church" begins with a brief account of the origins of the Hopi people "in the underworld" (224), and their ascension to this world, the "upper world" (225). In that they find that world in darkness, the people themselves go about creating the sun (226), after which they "headed east for Oraibi" (226). It's at this point that Sekaquaptewa tells a version of the story of *pahaana*. He is, she says, the older of "the two sons of the Chief," and is told "to go to the East where the sun rises.... This is the origin of the white man. The younger brother was to live in Oraibi. He was to send for his older brother in time of trouble.... The time will come when the white chief brother will come and bring peace and right living" (227).

In the meantime, the Hopi live, Sekaquaptewa says, by what she calls "'Pbutsquani' which is like the Ten Commandments" (229). This, she says, is taught to the young by the "uncles (mother's brothers)" (228). She affirms that "Whenever an uncle comes to visit, little Hopi boys [girls, too] are as good as they can be, because the uncle is the official disciplinarian of his nephews [and nieces, e.g., Polingaysi Qoyawayma] the year round" (233). The Hopi dictionary defines *pötskwani* as "law, rule, regulation; the way one should live one's life, plan of life laid out for one, knowledge and rules for the proper understanding and maintaining of the Hopi way."[14] I will speculate that when Sekaquaptewa explained *pötskwani* to Udall, the latter may have responded, "Oh, then it's just like the Ten Commandments," because the Ten Commandments also specify "the way one should live one's life." Of course while every Judeo-Christian child who learns the Ten Commandments learns exactly the same words—they are written words—every Hopi child's knowledge of *pötskwani* will vary as one or another uncle's words—spoken words—may differ on one or another occasion.

Sekaquaptewa also mentions "One Hopi ceremony," which, she says, "re-enacts the confusion of tongues at the Tower of Babel" (233–34). Without naming it, she says the ceremony involves "making a babble of sound, yelling loudly. Certainly a dramatic reproduction of the Tower of Babel" (234). I learn from Peter Whiteley that the ceremony she has in mind is the Wuwtsim, with "bells . . . used by the Kwaakwant (One Horn society—one of the four Wuwtsim orders)." Some of the "multiple languages used during the babble, may be real" in that "some Wuwtsim songs are in Keresan or have Keresan words" (Whiteley, personal communication, 12/17/15). Whiteley agrees that "the idea is to communicate chaos, so the Tower of Babel analogy . . . is appropriate," although he suspects—I agree—that the notion that this is "a dramatic reproduction of the Tower of Babel," is "more likely to be Udall" (12/17/15) than Sekaquaptewa.

Although she states that "the ritual part of the Hopi religion had no appeal to [her]—it was crude," nonetheless, "the things [her] parents taught [her] about the way to live were good" (234). It's at this point that Sekaquaptewa quotes some of what her father (not her uncles) had taught her during "the long winter evenings." She calls them "the teachings of the kiva" (234). I'd guess she means by this that her father had had many discussions about these things with other Hopi men in the kiva and spoke of them at home in winter. She quotes her father as having said that a time will come—he sounds a bit like Edmund Nequatewa's paternal grandfather here—"*when the written record will be brought to the Hopi by the white man. There will be many religions taught*" (235, italics in original) indicating his awareness of the different Christian denominations. Therefore, "*You will need to be wise to recognize and choose the right church.*" But "*There will come a time when all the people of the earth will belong to the one true church*" (235). Sekaquaptewa notes that she and her husband heard her father "say this long before [they] ever heard of the *Book of Mormon*" (235–36), but when they "heard of and read the *Book of Mormon* it sounded like a familiar story. Reading the *Bible* and the *Book of Mormon*," she asserts, "helped us to understand the Hopi traditions and the Hopi traditions help us to understand these books of scripture" (236). She later reaffirms her belief in the compatibility of the teachings of the Mormons and the Hopis, saying, that what the Mormons "taught sounded good to [her], like the teachings we were used to, like the Hopi way" (241).[15]

For Sekaquaptewa and her husband, it would seem, in religious matters as in the matters of everyday living, there could be "a combination . . . of the good of both cultures." For daily life, they could combine "the Hopi way and what [they] had learned at school" (186); for religious life, they could reconcile the teachings of her father and uncles with the Bible and the *Book of Mormon*. Near the end of her story, she once more states that she and her husband "chose the good from both ways of living" (247). Thus the Sekaquaptewas, boarding-school students both, managed successfully to integrate a strong Hopi identity with a mainstream-American identity, to call it that. For them, it is not a matter of "bridging two worlds" or "living in two worlds." They are not part Hopi and part American Mormon but a "combination" of the two. Theirs is not a "hybrid" identity, but, rather an Indian identity of a different kind. While there can be no doubt that their schooling "changed them forever," as Sekaquaptewa presents her life story, it was a change that amplified and in no way undermined their strong Hopi identity.

6

Fred Kabotie's
Hopi Indian Artist

BORN IN SHUNGOPAVI ON SECOND MESA IN "LATE FEBRUARY, 1900, AS far as anyone can remember"[1] (1), Fred Kabotie (d. 1986) was an internationally known painter and silversmith. He travelled widely, visiting India, Egypt, Europe, and various parts of the United States. He was a recipient of a Guggenheim Foundation award, and counted Arizona senator Barry Goldwater as a friend. He made one of his first silver pieces expressly for Eleanor Roosevelt (78), and Mrs. Harold Ickes, wife of the secretary of the interior, commissioned a painting of a *katsina* from him. He shook hands with President Dwight Eisenhower (102), served on the boards of many institutions, and played an important role in the work of the Hopi Cultural Center, which he helped to found. A substantial list of Kabotie's honors, awards, commissions, and one-man shows follows the conclusion of his autobiography.

Active as he was in the broader world of art, Kabotie was also intimately involved in Hopi projects nearer to home. He participated, for example, in the search for a land grant supposed to have been given to the Hopis by the Spanish that would establish Hopi rights to lands encroached on by Navajos, and he helped revive the Hopi Shalako ceremony that was performed in July of 1937 for the first time in seventy-five years.[2] He continued, almost into his eighties, to tend his cornfield. Of the six Hopi boarding-school autobiographers under consideration, Fred Kabotie was by far the best known to the wider world.

His editor, Bill Belknap, was a travel writer, photographer, and river-runner. He'd met Kabotie while still in his teens, so the two men had known each other for many years by the time they collaborated on what the

137

title page of the book calls "an autobiography with Bill Belknap." It was published in 1977 by the Museum of Northern Arizona in a handsome, oversize
volume that includes many full-color reproductions of Kabotie's paintings
and drawings. Sadly, *Fred Kabotie: Hopi Indian Artist* has not appeared in
a paperback edition, the only one of the Hopi boarding-school autobiographies I am considering not to have done so. The narrative proceeds in
chronological order, and reads fluently; nowhere, this is to say, is Belknap's
presence felt, nor are there passages that seem likely to derive from Belknap
rather than Kabotie. In a brief prefatory note to the book, Belknap writes
that Kabotie narrated with a "rich Hopi accent" (xv). That means, I believe,
as was the case with Edmund Nequatewa, Don Talayesva, and others, that
his English was not strictly standard.[3] In the book as we have it, however,
I don't find that "accent" discernible at all, although the narrative is indeed
marked by an oral, conversational ease of manner. There are, as I will note,
problems with chronology in some places, because Kabotie had either forgotten when some things occurred, or because, as he said, he regarded exact
dates as meaningless (although he does provide several exact dates). I suspect that Belknap was either not aware of these inaccuracies or chose not
to correct them.

Kabotie begins with a memory from "early spring when [he] was six."
It was in that spring that soldiers from the Keam's Canyon Agency attacked
his father and other men "from the *Wuwuchim* kiva" (1). Kabotie's "family
were Hostiles," who not only "did not want their children in school," but
did not approve of the government "surveying the land and cutting it up,"
as it was doing at that time, "giving an acre or so to each man." According
"to Hopi tradition," Kabotie says, "each clan already had its own land"
(1), for all that the Friendlies nonetheless did wish to accept the government's arrangements (2). The dispute between Shungopavi Friendlies and
Hostiles leads, Kabotie says, to the latter "being exiled from [their] village"
and going to Third Mesa, where "the Oraibi people were offering [them]
a place to stay" (2). I have noted Peter Whiteley's observation that "about fifty-two people" from the Hostile faction at Shongopavi moved to Oraibi "on
1 March 1906," and that "Many Hopis cite this influx from Second Mesa
as the precipitating cause of the Oraibi split" (1988b, 105).

But, Kabotie says, "If things had been bad between the factions in
Shungopavi, they were worse in Oraibi" (4). He was present during "the
historic struggle" between the Friendlies and the Hostiles on September 7,

1906, although, when "the trouble started that morning," the morning of the Split, he says, "our fathers put us kids down in a dark room, like a cellar, in the main part of Old Oraibi." Curious, the children "peeked out through a small hole," but, he acknowledges, they "saw nothing" (4). Later in the day, Kabotie joins his "mothers and grandmothers" who have been put out of their homes "north of the village a little way." He remembers "seeing a lot of men pushing back and forth; they struggled and pushed on each other until they got tired, then sat down to smoke while others took their places" (4). "I don't believe," he says, "I actually saw Tewaquaptewa's people push Youkeoma across the line" (4). As for just when all this took place, he notes that he's "since read that the date was September 8, 1906" (4), the date of the inscription on the sandstone rock. (See appendix A.) After the pushing match, his family, along with the other Hostile families, "walked six miles to where the village of Hotevilla is now, and camped for the night" (4).

The Hostile leaders continue to keep their children out of school and their resistance leads to some of their men being arrested, as Helen Sekaqauptewa had also noted. Along with a number of others, Kabotie's "fathers and uncles were… taken to an army camp" nearby (6), a place the Hopis called Bahana Wash. Shortly after the removal of the Hostile men, "the agent at Keams Canyon ordered that all the Second Mesa families who had settled at Hotevilla be moved back to Shungopavi" (6). This entails a fourteen-mile march made especially difficult by the absence of the "fathers and uncles" whom the government had detained. On their way, the party makes a stop at Bahana Wash, where a brief visit with the prisoners is allowed. Kabotie's Uncle Andrew and five other Hopi men "would be sent to Indian school at Carlisle, Pennsylvania," while Yukiwma "and the older men would be sentenced to prison as troublemakers" (6).

Once back in Shungopavi, Kabotie's mother and grandmother persist in their attempts to keep him out of school. Soon, however, several of his fellow-resisters are "caught," and, although his grandmother continues to hide him "carefully," it is not long before "Honani, leader of the Friendlies," comes and insists that he go to school. Honani "led [him] away" down the mesa, before giving him over to an older boy who "he ordered to take [Kabotie] to school at Toreva" (10), three miles away. Once there, the six-year-old encounters several of the initiatory topoi of the boarding schools in very short order. Kabotie says that "The first person [he] saw [at school] was [his] friend Homer, but [he] hardly recognized him with no hair. The next thing [he] knew, [his] head was being clipped, and [he] looked like Homer" (10). He notes that "All of us Hostile kids had no hair," that "it felt queer," and that the boys "were ashamed to go home" (10). In that Kabotie speaks of the hair-cutting as "the kind of humiliation [the Hostiles] were subjected to," it is possible that the Friendly scholars were spared, although I suspect this school policy applied to all the students.

Kabotie next encounters Clock Time and Discipline. In particular, he says, he "hated the school bell" marking the beginning of the school day each morning. The Second Mesa students "had to run from Shungopavi to Toreva and back every day, and if [they] were late and heard the bell [they'd] say to [themselves], 'Ahhh, that means punishment'" (10). Nonetheless, some of them were always late, and when that happened, "after school you'd pay for it." He says that "They would line everybody up in the carpenter shop, and a very mean teacher named Mr. Moran would put a thin board in the vise and make a handle on it. Then he'd start down the line, hitting our backsides" (10). There was a further punishment to be endured, however, for after Mr. Moran had finished, "they'd make us haul water for the school." Not only Mr. Moran, but "Jessie, a blonde Hopi albino from Shipaulovi,... a Christian who worked at the school... was as mean as Mr. Moran, and would make [the boys] carry water from the spring to fill big caldrons. After the caldrons were filled [they] could go home, although some evenings she'd make [them] chop wood, too" (10).

Kabotie reasonably says that he "never could understand how they expected [the students] to tell time. There were no clocks in Hopi homes and most of [them] had never seen a watch. Sun time was all [they] had" (10). Nonetheless, the students from Shungopavi try to be punctual; "to avoid being late [they'd] leave before breakfast," taking along "parched corn in one pocket and dried peaches in the other," attempting to eat as they ran to school (10). Toreva Day School's concern for clock time seems also to have involved the imposition on each student of a specific date of birth. "When you first started attending school," Kabotie remarks, "they looked at you, guessed how old you were, set your birthday, and gave you an age" (10). This, too, can make for confusion. Kabotie says, for example, "According to our families, Elmer"—a brother? a cousin?—"was much older" than he was, although "at school [they] said [he] was older" (10). It is in this context that Kabotie describes his acquisition of a Christian name; he will describe a further name change later. After setting the child a birth date, he says, "they'd assign you a 'Christian' name. [His] turned out to be Fred" (10). His time at Toreva Day School is short. "I think I attended school at Toreva only one year," he says, "Then the Shungopavi Day School was built below the mesa, much closer, and we went there" (11).

"The first teacher" he remembers at the new school is Mr. Chipper. Mr. Chipper is chipper indeed: he plays a sort of game of tag with the students in which he shows himself to be "fast and strong" (11). He also organizes a dinner intended to encourage the children from Mishongnovi and Shipaulovi to become more friendly with their Second Mesa neighbors from Shungopavi. The results are disappointing. Nonetheless, "while he was there"—would his fraternizing with the students have led to dismissal?—"we ate well," Kabotie observes. "We even had things like meat and stew." It is not clear why these things were available only during Mr. Chipper's time at the school. All in all, Kabotie thinks of Mr. Chipper as "a fine person" and "a wonderful guy" (11).

In regard to religious training at the school, Kabotie says only that "Missionaries . . . came to teach [the students] hymns." One of them is Miss Beaman, who "always wore a white shirt and black tie, and she would bring her Hopi interpreter"; the two would "lead the singing" (11). He notes disapprovingly that "these Christians never have any new music." Unlike the Hopi "who make up new music each time" for their *katsina* dances, hymn-singing "gets monotonous" (11). It's in this context that Kabotie speaks of singing "Hopi words to 'Jesus loves me, this I know' that sounded like English, but had funny meanings. Miss Beaman never caught on" (11). So far as cultural and religious matters are concerned, Kabotie states early in the book what he would affirm later. He says, "I've found that the more outside education I receive, the more I appreciate the true Hopi way. When missionaries would come into the village and try to convert us, I used to wonder why would anyone want to be a Christian if it meant becoming like those people" (12).

The "wonderful" Mr. Chipper is replaced by a Mr. Buchanan who was, Kabotie says, "the meanest teacher that we ever had." It is because of Mr. Buchanan that he "began running away from school" (11). He provides a vivid illustration of Mr. Buchanan's "meanness," which is a good deal more than that. When some of the boys ignore the school bell to continue playing marbles, Mr. Buchanan grabs one of them and knocks him down. Wishing to avoid similar treatment, Kabotie "ran up toward the mesa where he couldn't catch [him]" (11). "Mr. Buchanan treated [the children] so badly that [they] began looking for ways to get back at him," engaging in acts of resistance. One of these involves the Dining Room, of which Mr. Buchanan was in charge. The students are served "oatmeal, hard crackers, and water. The cooks put salt in the oatmeal, but no sugar, no milk." The oatmeal has the appeal of the Mush to most Indian students; as Kabotie states simply, "We didn't like it." They demonstrate their dislike by playing with the oatmeal, although "one time," as he says, the boys went further and "got playing around, lifting up the tables and banging on them." As Kabotie recalls, "We knew we'd be punished, but we didn't like the food!" (12).

It is Mr. Buchanan who will do the punishing. Although he is not in the dining room at the time, but "in his house eating," he is alerted to the state of affairs by "One of the Hopi girls, the teacher's pet." Buchanan enters the dining room "mad. He got [the boys] all in the classroom and [they] sat down." This is clearly serious business in that, as Kabotie recalls, Mr. Buchanan "had his razor strop—it was leather, with a metal hook on the end—and [he] was going to beat them" (12). A boy named Claude— Kabotie reports that Claude is "now *kikmongwi*, chief of Shungopavi"—"is first" (12). But Claude actively resists. "Mr. Buchanan put him out in the center of the room and swung hard. But Claude was watching carefully, so when the blows came he could jump or duck, and Mr. Buchanan ended up hitting himself!" (12). "Fortunately," as Kabotie explains, "Mr. Buchanan must have realized how foolish he'd been and stopped." There is no doubt, as he says, that "Claude could have been hurt badly" (12). And, I think, there is also no doubt that Mr. Buchanan had been worse than "foolish."

Mr. Buchanan's willingness to wield "a razor strop . . . with a metal hook on the end" is sufficient cause for Kabotie to run away. "After that," he says, he "quit school and hid out. Even when [his] sister said she was being punished for [his] absence, [he] couldn't make [himself] go back" (12). He had already noted that he "couldn't see that we were learning anything. We had books—I remember that they were blue—but we couldn't read" (11). Much as Albert Yava had done when put back to the fourth grade, Kabotie says that "in class all [he] did was make funny sketches" (11). As a runaway, he is aware that the "Indian police were after [him]," although, since "they were lazy and never got up early," he could, for a time, elude them. "Finally," however, "a Hopi policeman . . . caught [him]." He takes Kabotie "to the edge of the mesa," and says, " 'Now, you go to school!' " (12). "Halfway down the trail," Kabotie says, he "looked back and he was gone," so he "circled around and went home.... They never caught [him] again" (12).

It is during his time running "wild, some place different everyday" (12), that Kabotie reports the return of his "uncles and fathers... from Carlisle" (14). He notes that his Uncle Andrew, "Except for the inhuman way he was taken from his family, and not having any word for five years,... liked Carlisle" (14). There, he and Louis Tewanima had run on the Carlisle track team with Jim Thorpe. (Tewanima would become a member of the 1908 and 1912 American Olympic track teams.) Uncle Andrew goes into the livestock business and Kabotie works with him and finds it satisfying. He notes that he "enjoyed the free life for maybe two years—no school, outdoors all the time, good horses to ride" (16). But, as Kabotie's next chapter, called "Santa Fe," begins, he "had a feeling that [his] cowboy life was too good to last" (17).

He is aware that his sister "was still being punished at school for his absence" (17)—quite a long term of punishment—and "in the summer of 1915 a man named Archuleta came to interview Hopi boys and girls who might be interested in attending Santa Fe Indian School" (17). Mr. Archuleta explains that "under government policy," if he were to attend "boarding school for three years, [he] could forget about further schooling" (17). It's not clear whether this accurately represents government policy. That is to say that while most of the Hopi students who went to the Sherman Institute in California after the Orayvi Split stayed for three years before returning home, John Gram, in a fine study of the Albuquerque Indian School and the Santa Fe Indian School, writes that "At off-reservation boarding schools, students were to stay for a minimum of *five* years" (29, my emphasis). At any rate, Mr. Archuleta's offer appeals to Kabotie, who also finds interesting the things the man tells him about the school. After Andrew "and two of [Kabotie's] clan uncles... advised [him] to go," he signs up and so does a friend[4] (17). There is no mention of the war in Europe.

The students bound for Santa Fe are driven to Winslow in wagons.[5] But because there "must have been trouble about [the] railroad tickets, [they] spent four days in Winslow eating well and enjoying the town—the smells from the restaurants, the clothes in store windows, the Santa Fe station and Fred Harvey hotel."[6] (17). This is, to be sure, an education in itself. Kabotie says that, "We never tired of watching people get off the trains, women in long dresses and fancy hats, men in fine suits." He also acknowledges that "it all made us somewhat uneasy because our lives were so different" (17). Finally, the Hopi students get "on the train . . . an overnight express to Lamy, New Mexico. The next morning a horse-drawn herdic took [them] out to Santa Fe Indian School."[7] "It was a cold, foggy day," and the School "seemed like a depressing place to spend the next three years" (17). He will, in fact, spend double that time at the Santa Fe Indian School.

The Santa Fe Indian Industrial School opened in 1890 with nine Pueblo students. By the end of the year, their number had grown to ninety-three, and by "1900, there were three hundred students, sixty per cent Pueblo and the rest from the southwestern tribes of Apache, Navajo, Pima, Papago, and others" (Hyer, 5). The "others" eventually included some Hopis but not many in any year. The school closed in 1962, but re-opened in 1981 under the direction of the All Indian Pueblo Council (Hyer, 83). When he arrived, Kabotie reports, the school "was run like a military academy," as all the Indian boarding schools were. "We were divided into companies, the big boys in A and B, the small ones in C and D" (17). He "was assigned to Company C, down toward the tail end" (17–18). This is because, although he is fifteen years old, he is short and slight of build. "We lived on the second floor in a dormitory filled with double-deck bunks," he says. "They issued us coats, but nobody could find one small enough for me, so I got to keep my old one. We had to give up our moccasins for shoes and stockings" (18). He describes no initiatory Clean-Up or Haircutting, nor does he indicate that the dormitory serves as a locus for sexual activities of any sort. He does describe the dormitory's "disciplinarian, Mr. Saenz, [who] was short and stocky and had a loud voice. He always wore a military cap with a shiny band around it" (18). It is Mr. Saenz who, "when the bugle sounded reveille . . . would yell, 'Roll out! Roll out! Everybody roll out!'" The students would "all jump up and run to the washroom." Then, when another bugle call sounded, "everybody would rush into a big room and line up for roll call"[8] (18).

Although he has already had the name Fred bestowed upon him at the Toreva Day School, a further change of name is in store, although it is not an actual renaming. Kabotie says that when he first arrived at the Santa Fe school "he wasn't called Kabotie." He had given "his name as Nakavoma, [his] real Hopi name; it means 'day after day,'" and his company's sergeant from San Juan Pueblo "could pronounce it perfectly. He'd call out, 'Fred Nakavoma!' It sounded good the way he said it, and I'd answer, 'Present!'"

(18). But "Months later when . . . school records arrived from [the Agency at] Keams Canyon, [he] was called into the office and told, 'Your name is not Nakavoma, it's Kabotie'" (18). At that "point [his] English wasn't good enough," he says, to explain Hopi naming practices, and how he'd been given the teasing nickname, Kavotay, a shortened form of Nakavoma, which meant "tomorrow" (18). What had happened, he realizes, is that he had provided that nickname to a teacher "at Toreva Day School [who] hadn't listened carefully, and had written 'Kabotie' on a paper that would follow [him] forever."[9] (18). He offers no further comment here on this particular change of name.

Returning to daily routine at the Santa Fe School, Kabotie says that after morning "roll out, before breakfast we'd be out marching—left-right-left, and the captain would call out orders. 'Company, halt! Right, face! About, face!' If you didn't understand and obey quickly he'd come around and kick you, so we learned fast. We'd march into the dining room by companies, boys on one side, girls on the other, and sit at long tables" (18). He does not mention grace being said at this breakfast or at any other meal (but see below), and he says nothing further about the girls at the school (who also marched regularly). He does, however, remark, as many boarding-school students did, that "Sometimes there wasn't enough to eat."[10] Hungry students might "try to put bread in [their] pockets to eat later. But they had a rule that you couldn't take food outside." He recalls an occasion when a boy named Morris "got caught. Mr. Saenz put a chair out in the middle between the boys' and girls' sections, and made poor Morris stand on it, holding the bread in his mouth all during the meal. He was on exhibition: 'There's Morris who stole a piece of bread!'" (18).Rather a substantial shaming for a minor infraction.[11] As far as other disciplinary measures taken by the school, Kabotie does not speak of corporal punishment or mention the fact that there was a jailhouse at the Santa Fe Indian School (SFIS) that served as "an alternative to corporal punishment in the minds of the superintendents" (Gram, 91). Gram also notes that "Surprisingly, former students at . . . SFIS recalled never being punished for speaking their native tongue" (112), which was not the case at most of the boarding schools.

It is probably not meant as a commentary on Mr. Saenz's lack of charity that Kabotie next engages the subject of religion at the school. He recalls that he "was asked through an interpreter"—his time at day school, as we saw when he received his new name, had not taught him to understand or speak English very well— "'What denomination are you? What church do you belong to?'" His Uncle Andrew "had warned [him] that at Indian School you had to attend church whether you wanted to or not," and on the basis of his own experience had "advised [him] to go Methodist as he had at Carlisle." Thanks to his uncle's advice, Kabotie is ready, when questioned, to answer, Methodist (18). He notes that "all of the students from the New Mexico pueblos were Catholic," and, while they would "go off to Mass on Sunday," he "was the only Methodist, but [he] couldn't go"—to the Methodist church, it would seem—"because there was no one else to go with [him]" (18, 27),[12] no other declared Methodists among the students. In that there are some "Mescalero Apaches and some Utes" who attend the Presbyterian Church, the superintendent—this would be Frederick Snyder, in charge from 1915–1918—suggests that Kabotie go with them, and he does. No further religious instruction is mentioned.

Kabotie states that "School was hard at first because we knew so little English," a situation shared by not a few others. "As classes began," he says, "the teachers had trouble deciding what grades we should be in, but they kept testing us, seeing where we stood and how we studied. They started me out in second grade, I believe, but within a few weeks I was in third" (27). Curiously, "After [the students] had learned a few words [they] were told to write letters home to [their] families" (27). Although Kabotie had relatives who had been to Carlisle and could read, one may wonder whether and how widely that was the case with others. As for his own letter home, he remembers "writing, 'How is my enemies?' . . . just something [he'd] heard; [he] had no idea what it meant" (27). It is probable that his uncles would not know what it meant either, and perhaps they would question the wisdom of attending the Indian school at Santa Fe to learn English.

Nonetheless, Kabotie says that "Once we settled into the routine, classes and military life weren't so bad" (27). Apart from that general assessment, he tells us nothing further about academic or industrial training at school, changing the subject with the phrase, "but summers were the times I liked most" (27). A considerable number of Santa Fe's Pueblo students—their homes were not far away—would go home for the summer. Those whose homes were more distant, like Kabotie's, or who chose to remain at school for other reasons, did what Indian students from Chilocco, Riverside, and other boarding schools had done: they went to Colorado "to work in the sugar beet fields" (27). The Santa Fe students go to Lamar rather than

Rockyford, Colorado, where Albert Yava had gone from Chilocco, and Don Talayesva from Sherman.

Kabotie wishes to join the work party but is told that he is "too young, too small" (27). Remaining at school for the summer turns out to be pleasant enough, however, in that he "worked on the school farm in Santa Fe." The farm is "self-supporting" and raises "corn, potatoes, carrots, parsnips, and peas," all but the first of which crops would probably be new to Fred Kabotie.[13] The school also has chickens, cows, and pigs; Kabotie, unlike Don Talayesva, has nothing in particular to say about pigs. One of his jobs, however, is to feed them, something he does with the help of his "friend Joe, the horse," who is "so educated that you could harness him up and he'd trot over to the kitchen and wait to haul slops" (27). Like other boarding-school students, Kabotie is paid for his work: "That summer [he] earned six dollars" (27). This would probably be the summer of 1916 and six dollars for some two months labor does not seem like much, even for the time.

He notes that when "school started in the fall we had classes in the mornings and learned various trades in the afternoons," the general practice in the Indian boarding schools, as we have several times seen. The school "switched [the students] around so [they] could try different things." Kabotie is "in farming" first, although he already knows something about growing vegetables and feeding pigs at least. He also works in the tailor shop, learns to make horseshoes, and "for a while... was boilerman, stoking the fires so the buildings had steam heat" (27). It is about this time that he meets a series of white friends who take an interest in his artistic abilities, opening many doors. The first of these is Elizabeth DeHuff, the wife of the new Santa Fe superintendent, John DeHuff. Kabotie observes that "When the De Huffs came they changed everything, the whole attitude of the school toward the pupils." It's his sense that "they were understanding people with a deep interest in our Indian cultures" (27), and they will play an important role in his life.

John David DeHuff became superintendent of the Santa Fe Indian School in 1918 and served until 1926. DeHuff, much less known than Pratt, was like him a complex and interesting man. If Pratt, in the remark I'd quoted ascribed to Dr. Martin Luther King, was very fond of individual Indians while thoroughly hostile to Native culture(s), DeHuff was a great admirer of (Pueblo) Indian culture(s)—John Gram calls DeHuff "probably the superintendent most sympathetic to Pueblo cultures" (88)—while often unsympathetic to individual Indian students. Gram, for instance, notes his beating three runaways from the SFIS with "buggy whips" (98), and his strong disdain for other of his students (99).

Elizabeth Willis DeHuff, the superintendent's young, Barnard-educated wife, shared her husband's positive view of Native cultures and seems to have also been more sympathetic to at least some of the individual students she encountered. Ms. DeHuff comes into Kabotie's fifth-grade classroom where the teacher has hung maps of the United States that the students had been asked to color with water colors. She singles out the one Kabotie had done because, he notes, "she liked the way [he'd] used his colors" (28). When he is introduced to Ms. DeHuff, "she asked if [he] would like come to their [the DeHuff's] house in the afternoon and paint" (28). Kabotie states simply, "That was how my painting began, in the school year of 1916–17. Mrs. De Huff got me some drawing paper and water colors and I started painting things I remembered from home, mostly kachinas" (28). But this is mistaken. As I've noted, the DeHuffs did not arrive at the Santa Fe school until 1918 so Elizabeth DeHuff could not have encouraged Kabotie to paint in 1916–17. Kabotie was in his mid-seventies when he began work on his autobiography with Bill Belknap and, as noted earlier, it is possible that his recollections of just when certain events had transpired some fifty years earlier were slightly off. And, again, it is also quite possible that, as he had said, the exact dating of events just did not seem important. For these or other reasons, the dates he gives for this important period in his life are occasionally inaccurate, as I'll note again below.

To accept Ms. DeHuff's invitation, Kabotie must obtain the permission of "Mr. Jensen, a new instructor from Denmark," who is in charge of the carpentry shop to which he had been assigned. When "Mrs. De Huff asked him if [Kabotie] could paint at her house instead of taking shop,... he allowed [him] to go"[14] (28). Kabotie is joined by another student, "Velino Shije from Zia Pueblo, who also wanted to paint." Eventually, other aspiring young Indian painters would come to work at the DeHuff's home.[15] Kabotie, as he'd said, began "by painting things [he] remembered from home, mostly kachinas" (28). Shije also "began painting ceremonial things that he remembered from home, but when the Zias found out what he was doing, he was ostracized from the pueblo" (28). Kabotie seems not to have encountered any resistance of this sort.

For a time, Kabotie finds life at the Santa Fe School good. If the rations in the dining room continue to be meager, at least he and the other young Indian artists get "tea and delicious homemade cookies" served by Ms. DeHuff at her home. (Apparently he is a Hopi who likes tea!) Mr. Jensen, the shop teacher, becomes "the first collector" of Kabotie's work, purchasing "single kachina figures ... for about seventy-five cents, per dozen," "a lot of money" to him at that time, Kabotie says. He knows that Mr. Jensen is "buying all [he] could paint," and sending the paintings to Denmark (28), almost surely to sell them at a considerably higher price, but he offers no comment on this. Jensen also orders "a large painting; ... a Snake Dance picture" like one he had done for Ms. DeHuff. He begins work on the painting, but the Santa Fe heat causes the colors to run and there is "no picture for Mr. Jensen." Kabotie observes only that the accident meant he'd "lost money" (29), clearly something of which he is now aware. Some ten years later, Kabotie would affirm that his "carpentry teacher was interested in [his] paintings, and he was [his] first customer.... He was a good guy, and [they] were friends" (in Seymour, 243).

"Meanwhile," he says, he "was getting promoted in military life" at the school. He "became an officer, and instead of sleeping in the dorm ... had [his] own room where [he] could paint" (28). Such a privilege had not been reported by any other Hopi autobiographer, regardless of the rank he or she might have attained. "Suddenly," he says, he "had more friends than ever, all eager to help" (28). One "eager" new friend washes and irons his clothes; another, "a friend from Zia Pueblo," during weekly inspection "cleaned [his] room and waxed the floor" (28). He does not indicate the possible reasons for his sudden popularity—can it only be his newly elevated rank?—nor does he say whether or in what way he returned these favors.

Things get even better when "Mrs. Welch, an enthusiastic new teacher from Pennsylvania," (29) arrives at the school. She "started an art club which met in the evenings" in "an empty classroom" where "everybody would paint" (29). Mrs. Welsh and the DeHuffs make school "much more enjoyable." Indeed, they sponsor "an art club dance." The proceeds from the sale of a "bundle of [student] drawings" to "a Jewish man who had a store on the plaza" allow them to hire "an orchestra from town." Kabotie tells us that "the girls invited their boyfriends and [the boys] invited [their] girlfriends" (29). He has not, to this point—he is about eighteen—said anything about relations of any kind between the girls and boys, certainly nothing about romantic or sexual relations, nor will he say anything further on these matters. With the students' "best paintings … exhibited around the auditorium," and a "big punch bowl up on the stage" from which "you could help yourself," Kabotie says, "we had a great party" (29).

There are yet further opportunities for the young Indian students to express themselves in that "Mrs. De Huff and Mrs. Welch wrote and produced several plays. Usually there'd be one performance for the school and three nights for the public. One of Mrs. De Huff's was about a Pueblo grandfather who told animated legends to the young people."

Although he is a young person himself, Kabotie's role is that of "Taytay, the grandfather"[16] (29). He notes that it was about this time that he "met Julian Martinez and Maria, the potter from San Ildefonso. They came to the play, and whenever [they'd] see each other after that they'd call [him] Taytay"[17] (29). Unfortunately, there is a snake in this garden. Kabotie reports that "An elderly librarian at the Indian School, … her name was Mary Dissette," "didn't like what the DeHuffs and Welshes were doing." Her dislike was such that she "reported to the Commissioner of Indian Affairs in Washington that our superintendent and staff were reviving Indian culture instead of eliminating it, as the schools had been ordered to do … to encourage [Indian students] to become Christian and live like white men" (29). Kabotie surely did not know then—and, if he learned later, he did not choose to include what he'd learned in his autobiography—that the clash between the DeHuffs and Mary Dissette was a classic confrontation in the history of changing white relations to Native people in the Southwest in 1920s America.

Mary Dissette was indeed "an elderly librarian" at the Santa Fe Indian School when Kabotie encountered her, but she had had a long career in the Southwest prior to coming to Santa Fe. Margaret Jacobs writes that "In 1888, the Presbyterian Board of Home Missions sent [Dissette] to convert and civilize the Indians at Zuni Pueblo" (1999, 29). Tisa Wenger adds that "nine years later [she] became principal of what had become the government-operated day school in the pueblo" (44), after which she held several positions in schools run by the Bureau of Indian Affairs. She and a co-worker, Clara True, Jacobs writes, were "moral reformers," committed to female purity as a basis for the moral authority of women (Jacobs 1996, 180). On the one hand, they advocated for better treatment and proper advancement for women employed by the Bureau. On the other, Dissette in particular "argued that the sexual immorality she had seen in the Zuni dances led directly to female subordination"[18] (Wenger 175). Dissette and True would become "two of the most vociferous opponents of Pueblo Indian dances in the 1920s" (Jacobs 1996, 181). Opposition to the dances on the part of people like Dissette and True was intense enough to persuade the commissioner of Indian affairs, Charles Burke, in 1921, to issue Circular 1665 urging all in the Indian Service "to stop dances that they judged to be 'degrading'" (Wenger, 7; see also Jacobs 1996, 181, and Gram, 21–23). This was followed two years later by a "Supplement to Circular 1665," advising agents to "consider measures such as forbidding some ceremonies outright" (Wenger, 7). Jacobs finds that for all their fervor, Dissette, True, and many other like-minded reformers "displayed an enormous contempt for the cultures of the Indians with whom they lived," predicated on an "enormous ignorance" of those cultures (Jacobs 1999, 32).

Elizabeth DeHuff, to the contrary, was among those Jacobs calls the "new feminists," women less interested in female purity and moral authority than in self-fulfillment and the expression of sexual desire (Jacobs 1996, 180). She might also be placed among those Tisa Wenger refers to as "cultural modernists," persons who sought to "unseat the Christian reformers as the dominant voices in this arena" (4). John Gram simply calls these men and women "romantics," white Americans who, in the first third of the twentieth century, looked to the indigenous cultures of the Southwest for an antidote to the industrialization, modernization, and alienated individuality they saw everywhere in American society.[19] Charles Lummis, for example, long a champion of the Indians, was still active in the 1920s, and entirely as "romantic" as his younger contemporaries.[20] So, too—and importantly—was John Collier. Collier, John Gram writes, would find in the Southwest "a renewed passion that would lead him all the way to the office of Commissioner of Indian Affairs" (84) under Franklin Roosevelt.

Also among these romantics were the writer, Mary Austin, and the socialite, Mabel Dodge Luhan. It is Luhan who "is generally credited with bringing [John] Collier to New Mexico and introducing him to the Taos Pueblo" (S. Smith, 247n2), where she and her Pueblo husband, Tony Luhan, would also host D. H. Lawrence and his wife, Frieda von Richtofen Weekly Lawrence, and other artists. John and Elizabeth DeHuff, like these better-known people, had, Gram writes, fallen "in love with a romantic notion of the Southwest... what [they] really treasured about the cultures [they] encountered was not their inherent worth but the ammunition they provided for criticizing the dominant American culture" (24). Because they "believed that it was American society not the Pueblos that needed saving, they sometimes came into conflict with the boarding schools" (Gram, 85). Indeed, John DeHuff was in the impossible position of heading a boarding school whose mission went directly counter to his personal beliefs.

The Lawrences were looking to Pueblo cultures to revitalize art and save it from a formalist sterility as threatening to it, in their view, as Puritan morality was to the broader society. Elizabeth DeHuff would go on to participate in what Margaret Jacobs calls "the Indian Arts and Crafts Movement" (1999, 149ff.), in which she strongly opposed any "modern" elements or "realism" in art produced by Native Americans. In these regards, it must be acknowledged that where the reformers had contempt for and ignorance of Indian cultures, the romantics had admiration for but also a fair measure of ignorance of those cultures.[21]

Doubtless because Mary Dissette was someone well known to the Bureau of Indian Affairs at a time when the Bureau was still committed to ethnocide and (an increasingly confused) notion of Indian assimilation, it was not long after her complaint that, Kabotie says, "a man came from the commissioner's office to investigate Miss Dissette's charges" (29). After "days of talk, it was announced that Mr. DeHuff would be transferred to Sherman Institute at Riverside, California, as principal—a demotion"[22] (29). Although the DeHuffs by this time have many friends in Santa Fe who intervene on their behalf, it is "to no avail" (29), the Bureau finding in Dissette's favor. Kabotie says nothing about the fate of the Welshes, allies of the DeHuffs, nor does he say anything about life at the school after they are gone. This may be because he was no longer a student at the SFIS at the time the DeHuffs were forced to leave in 1926. (Although, as we will see, he continued to live at the school for a time.) Indeed, he had begun attending Santa Fe Public High School in 1921! As I've said, the autobiography presents the chronology of this period in Kabotie's life in a very confusing manner.

I'd already noted that Elizabeth DeHuff could not have begun procuring "drawing paper and water colors" for Kabotie to begin painting "in the school year of 1916–17" (28) because she and her husband did not come to the school until 1918. The afternoons painting, the evening socials, and the dramatic performances that were disturbing to Mary Dissette appear, in Kabotie's account, to have occurred shortly after the arrival of the DeHuffs. But if, as Margaret Jacobs has written, it was only "in the 1920s" that Mary Dissette was "working as a librarian at the SFIS" (1999, 29–30), she could not have objected to practices the DeHuffs had introduced around 1918, when she was not yet employed by the SFIS. We know that John DeHuff had (deliberately?) courted trouble with his superiors by allowing Indian dances at the 1924 graduation ceremonies at the school, an action in direct opposition to Commissioner Burke's 1921 "Circular" and its "Supplement" in 1923, and this was something that angered Burke, as DeHuff noted in his diaries (Gram, 23). If Mary Dissette was at the Santa Fe School at this time, as I believe she was, such a move on DeHuff's part might have served as a last straw, impelling her to appeal to the Bureau.

I offer this conjecture because Kabotie's narration strongly suggests that the DeHuffs left the school very soon after the "man from the commissioner's office came to Santa Fe to investigate" (Kabotie 29) at the behest of Mary Dissette. Again, at the time they were forced to leave in 1926, Fred Kabotie was no longer a student at the SFIS, having enrolled at public high school no fewer than five years earlier. Kabotie includes a photo of himself with the caption, "On the Santa Fe High School football team, 1921" (37), his first year at the high school, also noting that he "graduated from Santa Fe Public High School in 1925" (40). Further confusing matters is the fact that Kabotie presents his decision to attend Santa Fe Public High School in the first place as based on advice given him by John DeHuff on DeHuff's *return* to Santa Fe from Riverside, California. But DeHuff could not return until some time after he left in 1926—by which time Kabotie had already graduated high school.

Kabotie says that when his time at the Santa Fe School was almost up, he had begun to wonder "what to do after finishing." In large part because of the recent death of his sister, Hattie, he is reluctant to go home, and, too, he is interested in furthering his education. But Carlisle, attractive to him because of his Uncle Andrew's stories about it, has closed; this leaves, he says, "the other big Indian schools—Riverside, Phoenix, Albuquerque, Chilocco—to choose from" (33). It's in this context that Kabotie announces the DeHuffs' return to Santa Fe. John DeHuff, he says, "quit the Indian Service," and came back to Santa Fe, where he soon took a position as secretary of the Santa Fe

Chamber of Commerce (33). About this time, Kabotie says, the two have "a good long talk" in which DeHuff advises him "to stay away from Indian schools" (33), about which he surely knows a good deal, and to attend Santa Fe Public High School instead. There he can "keep on with [his] art and music," and his "English would improve much faster," too. Kabotie takes this as "good advice," because Mr. DeHuff surely knows "what a handicap 'Indian School English' could be" (33). Kabotie gives as an example the fact that even after "completing the eighth grade" Indian students "were still saying, 'You get wanted from Mr. Saenz,' and, 'Oh, I was not know it this time, but I get know it'" (33). "That fall... ," he says, he "enrolled in Santa Fe Public High School" (33), his time at Indian boarding schools at an end. But, again, things cannot have transpired this way. If Fred Kabotie was on the Santa Fe Public High School football team in 1921 and graduated from the school in 1925, he obviously could not have entered it after a conversation he had with John DeHuff in 1926.

After a space break in the text—it would have been inserted by Belknap—the story continues, but from an earlier point in time, "After the United States entered World War I" (29), in April of 1917. Then, Kabotie says, the "workers from school were more needed than ever in the Colorado beet fields" (29). For that reason, the school superintendent—we are back, now, to Frederick Snyder in that position—despite remarking that Kabotie had not grown any bigger, decides that nonetheless he'd "better go." The student work crew is taken to "Lamy where [they] got on the train for Lamar, Colorado" (29). What most impresses Kabotie there are the mosquitoes: "You couldn't walk through an alfalfa field," he says, "without getting eaten alive" (29). The work is "hot, dusty, and sweaty"; the Indian students "were paid twelve dollars per acre," and Kabotie says "it took several days to earn twelve dollars" (30).

When the company cook "had to return to Denver," Kabotie is asked to replace her, "so she began teaching [him] how to cook." He also gets to take over her room and "all the Hopis moved in with [him]." It's not clear whether "all" these Hopis are from the Santa Fe School or from other schools as well. Fortunately, "Being camp cook gave [him] more time to do other things" (30)—not painting, as it happens, but fishing and hunting. Because "of the war [the Indian students] didn't go back to school that fall but stayed longer in the beet fields." Their work earns them a two-week vacation to Colorado Springs. On the way there, the students stop at Rocky Ford; Kabotie does not say whether he encountered other boarding-school beet-field workers there. Once in Colorado Springs, Kabotie "kept looking for springs," but he "saw only city." The students are put on "streetcars for a sightseeing tour," treated to a big picnic meal, and, when they are taken to "an ice cream parlor downtown," Kabotie says they'd "never tasted anything that good" (31). They also rent and somewhat recklessly ride bicycles before returning to the beet fields (31).

Kabotie tops beets, then gets "work driving a wagon." The crew foreman "knew more cuss words than anybody [Kabotie] had ever met," an introduction to cussing much like that Don Talayesva had experienced. He is next assigned "to the hay mill" (31), where his job is "sewing up gunnysacks." In regard to this work, he says that his "training in the school tailor shop paid off" (32). He notes the closing of Carlisle toward the end of World War I and the fortunate coincidence that "Carlisle's band instruments came to Santa Fe Indian School, and had just arrived when [he] returned from Colorado." Kabotie had heard an Indian marching band play in Rocky Ford and at that point, he says, he "made up [his] mind to learn band music, learn an instrument" (32). The instrument that most appeals to him is called, he discovers, a French horn, but, unfortunately, there is only one, and "somebody had taken it." He gets a clarinet, although it was "not at all what [he] wanted." Soon, however, he realizes that the clarinet is "more versatile than the French horn," and also "how good it sounded in the band"; he is "happy to have it" (32).

Having spoken of his early efforts as a painter, Kabotie now shows himself to be a more-than-competent musician, playing in "a little orchestra in the Presbyterian church," and then joining "the Santa Fe City band" (32). At school, some of the students "organized an Indian orchestra" in which Kabotie "played clarinet and saxophone." They "name it *Weniman* Orchestra which means 'dancing' orchestra in Hopi" (32), he says. The adoption of a Hopi name for the orchestra suggests that there might have been a number of Hopi students in it, although Hopis were very much in the minority at the SFIS at any given time. Kabotie says that he "was a great admirer of John Philip Sousa," and had the opportunity, with a friend, to travel to Albuquerque to hear him in concert. Kabotie is surprised to find that "Sousa was a small man," as he is himself, although "he had a big band with a wonderful sound" (32–33). Noting that ever since he "first got started in music [he'd] used school instruments," Kabotie says that he now "looked forward to owning [his] own" (33).

It is in this context that the DeHuffs are mentioned again. Kabotie informs us that "During Indian school Mrs. De Huff had started [him] on a book illustration project" that "carried out the idea she'd written as a play"[23] (33). This would indeed be 1918 when the Carlisle band instruments came to the SFIS, the war was over, John DeHuff has assumed the position of school superintendent, and Elizabeth DeHuff is producing Indian-themed plays. *Taytay's Tales* "came out in 1922, with a second volume, *Taytay's Memories*, following in 1924" (33), Kabotie says. These bring him "$200, more money than [he'd] ever had," and he spends most of it not on painting supplies, but on a saxophone "ordered from Conn in Elkhart, Indiana. If John Philip Sousa used Conn instruments," Kabotie proudly announces, he "would, too" (33).

In any event, having enrolled in public high school by this time, the difficulty for Kabotie is that he is "the only Indian among hundreds of white faces" (34). He is fortunate that "he still lived out at the Indian School, two miles away," bicycling "back and forth." With the help of the DeHuffs who, he states, "became almost like parents" (35)—they are still at the SFIS during Kabotie's high school years—he begins to make a number of further contacts with influential whites, in particular, Dr. Edgar Hewett, director of the Museum of New Mexico. He works on a dig with Dr. Hewett, and when that is done, he is asked whether he'd like to go home. He remarks that he'd "been away seven years and there'd been little communication. [He'd] tried writing letters but nobody would answer" (38). Kabotie went to the SFIS in 1915, so if he's been away for seven years, it must be in 1922, early in his high school career, that he completed work on the dig with Edgar Hewett.

Although "there'd been little communication," Kabotie does indeed want to go home. Once he is back, however, he feels the degree to which he has been "changed forever" by his time at boarding school. As Polingaysi Qoyawayma had so intensely experienced, as Don Talayesva had at least partly experienced, as other boarding-school students had also found, home is less comfortable than it had once been. "All those years [he'd] looked forward to coming home," Kabotie says, "but once [he] was there, everything seemed foreign. [He] hardly knew anybody, just a few here and there." He makes no mention of his parents, or of Hattie, the sister who had died. He sees his Uncle Andrew and some clan relatives in Hotevilla, but, "soon

[he] got lonesome for Santa Fe. There [he] was, in [his] own village at last, but [he] felt uneasy. After one month [he] was glad when it was time for school," not the Indian School by this time but Santa Fe Public High School. A friend takes him to Winslow, where he "caught the train back to Santa Fe" (39).

Still "in high school," he works "vacations and spare time at the museum," (39) the Museum of New Mexico, and soon joins a group of musicians to play at the opening of a "new hotel up at Espanola" (39). His experience there mostly teaches him that "doctors, lawyers, judges, even the governor, paid no attention to Prohibition" (40), which had gone into effect in 1920. He also does some drinking himself, even, as he says, "drinking quite a lot" (42). Dr. Harry Mera, a friend involved in establishing "the Indian Arts Fund," tells him that his "paintings are not as good as they used to be," a judgment that moves Kabotie to recognize that indeed he "was drinking too much" (42). Dr. Mera suggests he go back home, and Kabotie once more decides to take the advice of a well-meaning white friend (42).

He only gets as far as the Grand Canyon, however, accepting a job offer from the Bright Angel Lodge there to give tourists "telescope tours" of the Canyon. This pays well, and he earns even more money by joining "a dance orchestra." But he "was still drinking too much," and, acknowledging that he "hadn't followed Dr. Mera's advice," he decides he had indeed "better go home" (43). Making a brief stop in Phoenix to do a friend a favor, he meets Alice—the book gives no other name for her—the young woman who would later become his wife.[24] Then, from "Phoenix [he] finally came home to Shungopavi" (43). The return, once more, is not easy. Kabotie says, "That winter was a difficult time," and when "the money [he'd] saved from Grand Canyon ran out, [he] was broke" (43). He works "herding sheep, as [he'd] used to; but the sheep didn't bring [him] any money." After that, he says, he "started hauling wood, harder work than [he'd] done in years, out in the cold." Making things more difficult is the fact that he "wasn't getting enough food" (43). But he does have "a lot of time to think, to sort out what was important" (43–44).

Hard as life is, Kabotie nonetheless "began to appreciate [his] Hopi heritage as never before" (44). He spends "winter nights around a stove, hearing the old folks tell about the earliest times they remembered, or listening to the men rehearse a song." "Taking part in these things," he says, "made his bahana life in Santa Fe seem less important" (44). Neither boarding school

nor public high school has weak-
ened his Hopi identity, although
he does return to Santa Fe once
more. There he participates in
a number of cultural projects
sponsored by white friends, and
"worked more on [his] art and
cut down on the music." Looking
back, he finds those days to have
been his "most productive time"
(44). Making and selling paintings, he "made enough money to
buy [his] first car, a brand-new
Chevy coupe" (47).

The following chapter, enti-
tled "Initiation and Marriage,"
tells of both these events in
Kabotie's life. (See figure 8.)
He hears from Alice—she is in
Shungopavi, and, apparently, the

8 Photograph of Fred Kabotie. GRCA
22600. Circa 1933.

two had been in touch after the initial meeting Kabotie had mentioned—that
his uncle wants him to come home for the "*Wuwuchima* initiation," which
"was to be held during the coming year" (48). Kabotie says that Wuwtsim
"takes place every four years, and requires a year to complete" (48), something not conveyed by other male Hopi autobiographers.

To this point, Kabotie has not said a word about his initiation into the
katsina society or about any other ceremonies in which he might have participated by the age of fifteen, when he went off to Santa Fe, nor will he say
anything further on this subject in the autobiography. Tryntje Seymour wrote
that Kabotie at eighty-five was still "a diligent and studious participant in the
ceremonial activities of Shungopavi," "a good Hopi [who] was initiated into
all levels of Hopi life and ceremony, with the accompanying responsibilities."
Indeed, she quotes him as saying, "I have done that all the way through . . .
so I am a full-fledged Hopi" (246). The paintings reproduced in his autobiography would certainly attest to that, and I cannot say why he chose not to
mention any ceremonial activity on his part other than Wuwtsim initiation.
"This time when [he] went back to Shungopavi," Kabotie states, his "Santa

Fe days were over. [He'd] been away fourteen years instead of the three [he'd] originally planned" (48). Since he'd left for Santa Fe in 1915, when he was about fifteen years old, he must now be close to thirty. This makes him older than most Wuwtsim initiates, although it is entirely appropriate that he undergo initiation prior to marriage.[25]

Fred Kabotie and Alice Talayaonema were married "pretty close" to "June 30, 1931" (48), after his Wuwsim initiation. He tells the reader nothing about that, nor does he provide the new name he would have received. He also says nothing about the actual wedding, which would most likely have been a traditional Hopi wedding, Kabotie never having accepted Christianity. (Alice's religious beliefs are not mentioned, although the couple's general agreement on these matters is strongly implied.) But neither Wuwtsim initiation, as had been the case with Don Talayesva in *Sun Chief*, nor marriage, as had been the case with Edmund Nequatewa in *Born a Chief*—quite serves as a climactic moment for *Fred Kabotie: Hopi Indian Artist*. Kabotie continues to paint, and he also benefits from the fact that some of President Roosevelt's "federal job programs reached out into the Hopi Reservation" (50). He will teach, travel, and participate in many institutional endeavors that engage him with mainstream American society. These things, like everything else in the book, are narrated with an even tone, and scenes of conflict are absent or avoided, in a typical Hopi manner. Nonetheless, as Kabotie approaches the end of his story, issues of identity come to the fore in a powerful if mostly implicit fashion.

The autobiography, this is to say, reports no deeply reflective moments like those found in Don Talayesva's *Sun Chief* or in Polingaysi Qoyawayma's *No Turning Back*, moments in which the narrator articulates serious concerns about being or again becoming "a real Hopi." This simply does not seem to have been a problem for Fred Kabotie—as it was not, to be sure, for Helen Sekaquaptewa or Albert Yava. Nor has his rich experience of both Hopi culture and mainstream American culture presented Kabotie with something like the difficulties of "living in two worlds" or of "bridging the gap." The book includes no (Western) climactic narrative moment of choice or an epiphanic moment of sudden insight. Rather, since his early teens—again, like Yava or Sekaquaptewa—Kabotie has navigated with an even keel the historical conditions encountered by Hopi people in the decades just after the turn of the twentieth century. Like all Hopis of his time, Fred Kabotie was well aware of the threat these conditions presented to traditional ways of life—he'd first encountered this threat before he was six years old—but he was also increasingly aware that these conditions presented a number of opportunities. As he tells his story, he would seem to have integrated aspects of modernity and long-established traditional lifeways successfully and with little pain and strife.

But, in the third to last chapter of the book, the reader learns of at least one stressful time in Kabotie's life, and this involves his Uncle Andrew. It was in "the spring of 1961," Kabotie tells us, that Andrew "passed away in a tragic accident." He'd been "herding sheep far out below the mesa at a place where," Kabotie says, he himself "still [has] a cornfield" (106). Andrew had cleared and, on a windy day, "was burning masses of tumbleweeds that accumulate in the arroyos." A "sheet of flame must have caught him," and "he fell down the steep bank into the fire" (106). "As far back as I remember," Kabotie says, "I'd looked up to Andrew and sought his advice. When he returned from Carlisle he was more of a hero to me than Lindbergh or the astronauts ever were" (106). But "as [Andrew] grew older," Kabotie says, the two "drifted apart until he was working against everything I was trying to do." This is a very strong statement, although to this point Kabotie had made no mention of any adversarial relation having developed between himself and his once-beloved uncle. "No one," Kabotie affirms, "could be more for preserving our religion and culture, the Hopi way, than I. But I'm also for using modern inventions and technology when it's to our advantage. Andrew wasn't" (106).

The two had most recently disagreed on obtaining a dependable water supply for Second Mesa, and the title of the chapter presenting these things is "After Centuries, Water." Water here is used both literally and figuratively. "There's no point in living primitively," Kabotie argues, "Our young people need water and electricity and sanitation, and the best education we can give them. Then if they grow up healthy and participate in our ceremonial calendar, that's the best we can do" (107). He adds, "You can't stop progress. It's like a flood coming down a wash. How can you hold it back? My uncle was trying to hold back the flood" (107). The matter is dropped with no further comment, and Kabotie moves on to discuss his part in inaugurating the Hopi Cultural Center.

The book's penultimate chapter is titled, "Hopi Cultural Center," and in it, Kabotie moves forward in time, proudly describing an evening in 1975 when he and his wife have come to the Center—it had been operational since the late 1960s—for dinner. "Friendly Hopi girls in traditional costume greet guests and wait on tables," he says, "The food is good. The menu even offers *piki* bread and *nokquivi*, hominy stew" (113). Wayne Sekaquaptewa, Helen and Emory Sekaquaptewa's son, "is in charge of the restaurant," and another Hopi, "Ferrell Secakuku[,] manages the motel," all thirty-three rooms of which are full on this particular night (113). Thinking back, Kabotie recalls another night, years earlier, when "Henry Allen Moe and his wife came out to visit us." He is glad "that Henry at least saw the site of the cultural center before he passed away" (114), for Moe had helped Kabotie obtain funds from the Tiffany Foundation to decorate the then-projected Center.[26] But the Moes get to see more than the Center's site. "There were kachina dances going on down in the kivas that night," Kabotie tells us, and while it isn't clear whether the Moes got to observe those, they are invited to the "Kwakwan kiva," which the One Horn Society members have just rebuilt (114). Kabotie mentions "the Bean Dance in February" (114), and the Niman or "Home Dance in July" (123), when the *katsinam* return to their homes in the San Francisco Peaks, but he again says nothing about any part he might have played in these ceremonies.[27]

But he does go on to discuss the *katsinam*, a great many of which he had represented in his paintings. He explains that "A kachina is a supernatural being, but is not a god, as so many bahanas believe" (123). He had not, as I have noted, mentioned his own *katsina* initiation, or told us much about the *katsinam* earlier. He explains that until their initiation, "until they're about ten years old . . . Hopi children are taught that the [kachina] dancers are actually the supernatural kachinas" (123). The general reader would have to guess that he is talking about what we have several times noted, that at their initiation the children learn the *katsinam* are not supernaturals and that each *katsina*, as Kabotie says, is "impersonated by a properly initiated Hopi, wearing the appropriate costume and mask" (123), someone the children know and recognize once the mask is removed. Several pages more are devoted to the special roles of Hopi clowns, and further details are given about various *katsina* dances.

This belated, albeit very general, excursus into Hopi ceremonial culture is followed by a similarly belated, although more specific, turn toward Hopi history. Kabotie's final chapter, "The Hopi Way," begins with the surprising fact, as he tells us, that by "1976 it had been twenty years since [he'd] done any painting!" In that year, however, he is asked "to paint something for a bicentennial show" (129) at the Museum of New Mexico. Kabotie accepts the commission because the idea he had "for the picture was one [he'd] been thinking about and wanting to paint for a long time" (129). His idea has to do with an event near the successful conclusion of the Pueblo Rebellion of 1680 against the Spanish, a rebellion in which Hopis participated. It is a quite extraordinary painting, a watercolor reproduced on page 122 of the autobiography. It "shows the destruction of San Bartolome Church at old Shungopavi and the death of its priests, according to the way [his] uncle [Andrew?] and grandfathers told it" (130). Although, as I've said, the painting is reproduced for any reader to see, Kabotie offers a detailed description of it nonetheless, something he had not done for any of the other paintings reproduced in the book. "My picture," he says, "shows the Mishongnovis, armed with bows and arrows, piling firewood under the priest." The priest has been hanged from a church-beam supported by two large rocks. "A woman brings more wood," Kabotie continues, "as one of the men makes fire with a hand-rotated fire drill, just as we still do in ceremonies. In the background the church is being demolished, rocks and beams thrown down from the roof. An old man with his arm upraised urges those above to knock down the cross. Another runs out the front door with a *santo* [a wooden representation of a saint] to throw on the fire." The description concludes with a new paragraph consisting of a single sentence: "That was my bicentennial painting" (130). One may wonder what the Museum people thought of this "bicentennial painting," one which shows the Hopis regaining their independence by ridding themselves of the first European colonizers to oppress them. Could the painting somehow imply that Hopi independence might once more be achieved by ridding themselves of the American invader-settlers? The American Bicentennial, after all, was only four years short of the Tri-Centennial of the Pueblo Rebellion. So far as one can know Fred Kabotie from his autobiography, these possibilities do not seem likely to me—although we have indeed been told that this is a picture the artist had had in mind for some time. That the hand-rotated drill used to start the conflagration beneath the priest is, as Kabotie says, the same kind of tool still used to start a fire in Hopi ceremonies today makes of it a symbol of Hopi continuity, and, indeed, autonomy: the fire-drill is something Hopis had long before the arrival of both the Spanish and the Americans.

As Kabotie approaches the close of his story, he engages in some retrospection. He notes that he and his wife, Alice, "often talk about how different our life is now than when [they] were first married" (130), more than forty years earlier. "Food now comes mostly from the outside.... Electricity is available but expensive," and they "have television, as do several other families." But they have "no bathroom; there isn't one in Shungopavi" (130), Kabotie says, something that may come as a surprise. Although there is a "new artesian well in the middle of Shungopavi," getting the benefit of it, he tells us, required overcoming the opposition "of our so-called traditionalists." Like his Uncle Andrew in regard to modern conveniences, the "*kikmongwi*, or village chief, and his followers were dead set against it" (130), he says. Having "felt all along" that a reliable source of water "had to come," Kabotie "took a petition around from house to house," and, although "there were twenty-nine who didn't" sign, nonetheless, because "Most people signed up" (130–131), the village now has "good water" (131). Just as Kabotie's painting had represented the past, so, too, do these actions on his part look toward the future as he outlines other projects he hopes to advance. He is working "on plans for a much larger museum" at the Hopi Cultural Center, and for the construction of "the four-year Hopi High School" (131) he had long envisioned as part of the Center.

Thinking of the future, he once more reflects on the past, recalling his grandfather, "the hardest-working man [he'd] ever known," and a man who had lived through the famine of the 1860s (136). "To remind themselves that hard times like those can come," Kabotie says, offering another linkage of past and present, "Hopi women traditionally use their left hand when they start to serve a meal, dipping four times with the left before using the right. They call it *nakiatani*, which means 'lasting.' It's like a prayer that the supply of whatever they're serving will last" (137).

These recollections conclude with Kabotie's assertion that his "grandfather was a real Hopi." "The older I get," he says, "the more I appreciate everything he taught me" (137). He adds, "Alice and I hope most of all that the things we're teaching our grandchildren, the Hopi way"—"The Hopi Way" is the title of this last chapter of the autobiography—"will mean as much to them." There is, then, no doubt about the identity of this boarding-school student who is at one and the same time a man celebrated internationally as an artist, and, at home, a television owner, and circulator of petitions for an

9 Fred Kabotie and Eleanor Roosevelt at the exhibition "Indian Art of the United States." January 25, 1941. Photograph ©1999 The Museum of Modern Art, New York

indoor supply of water (although not for a bathroom). However differently from his grandfather, Fred Kabotie is "a real Hopi" as well.

The last paragraphs of the book illustrate Kabotie's extraordinary ability to integrate American and Hopi lifeways. "In my office over at the craft guild," he says, "I have a big appointment calendar. Somehow each year it gets busier" (137). There are "Tiffany Foundation meetings in New York, . . . teaching in California, judging exhibits at . . . Gallup, . . . Tribal Council meetings" (138). (See figure 9.) "A year or so ago," Kabotie says, he received an invitation to serve on the board of the Hopi Center for Human Services, an invitation he declined. The reason he gives for this sets up the quite-formal conclusion to his book. He won't be able to serve, he tells the board members, because "You fellows call meetings in the summer at seven-thirty, and I'm still out in my cornfield. I have no more time for meetings; I'd rather stay out in my field and work" (138). The book concludes: "Each morning when I get up early and go outside at Shungopavi, the business and confusion seem far away. I split off some juniper chips for kindling and look out on the world from the top of Second Mesa. Then I see my real calendar— the Sun's forehead coming over the horizon—day after day" (138). This is lyrical, lovely, a set piece, and a statement. But is it too easy a statement? A statement too simple or sentimental? Any answer to these questions will depend to a large extent on the temperament and taste of the individual reader. But any answer also needs to take into account a complicating factor: Fred Kabotie's name, as he had told us earlier, is "Nakavoma"; although it is not the name given him after his Wuwtsim initiation, it is still his "real Hopi name" and it "means 'day after day'" (18). Because he'd given a shortened form of that name, "Kavotay, which means 'tomorrow,'" to a teacher at the Toreva Day School who "hadn't listened carefully, and had written 'Kabotie' on a paper," Kabotie was indeed the name "that would follow [him] forever" (18). That may be the name by which the whites know him, but in the last sentence of the book, the sun speaks the name by which it knows him, his "real Hopi name," Nakavoma, "day after day."

PART II

NAVAJO BOARDING-SCHOOL AUTOBIOGRAPHIES

IN A REVIEW OF TIANNA BIGHORSE'S *Bighorse the Warrior*, H. DAVID BRUMBLE wrote that "The Navajos are the most numerous of the American Indian peoples—and they are by far the most frequent autobiographers" (1993, 144), a judgment that may well hold today. Brumble names three books he considers to be "the best known" Navajo autobiographies, but makes clear that his 1981 *Annotated Bibliography* had listed many more.[1] And indeed there are enough full-length texts to speak of a Navajo autobiographical canon, in much the same way as Whiteley (and I) spoke of a Hopi autobiographical canon. Here I will examine only those Navajo autobiographical texts that represent their subjects' boarding-school experiences, relegating to an appendix a brief survey of the others.

Unlike the Hopi boarding-school autobiographies I have just examined, the Navajo boarding-school autobiographers' experiences don't overlap, but with one significant exception, occur later than a period of acute crisis in the People's history. I am referring to the Long Walk of the Navajo, the People's forced removal by government troops in 1864 from lands in what is now Arizona to Bosque Redondo—"Round Forest" in Spanish, *Hweeldi* in Navajo—in eastern New Mexico, a distance of over 300 miles. There, some 8,000 or 9,000 people were held in an area of about forty square miles under harrowing conditions that some writers have likened to those of a "concentration camp" (see below). The Treaty of Bosque Redondo, signed in 1868, permitted the surviving Navajos to return home. It has been widely noted that this historical trauma, like the Cherokees' Trail of Tears, continues to play a part in contemporary Navajo identity. The 1868 treaty committed the government to construct schools for the Navajos and the Navajos to send their children to them once those schools were built, a development that would begin to occur in several years' time.[2] A twentieth-century trauma for the Navajos was the government's stock reduction program of the 1930s, and I discuss that below.

7

Frank Mitchell's
Navajo Blessingway Singer

FRANK MITCHELL DICTATED A VERSION OF THE NAVAJO BLESSINGWAY CER-
emony some time in the early 1930s to Father Berard Haile. The Blessingway
expresses for Navajos the culture's "main values of harmony, order, good
health, long life, and beauty" (Shepardson 1995, 161). It is "concerned with
peace, harmony, and good things, and should exclude all evil" (Wyman, 4).
Generally speaking, "Navajo ceremonials are personal and occasional rather
than group-oriented and calendrical"—Hopi ceremonials, as we have seen,
are "group-oriented and calendrical"—"and their purpose is to restore an
individual to a harmonious relationship with the physical, social and psycho-
logical worlds. At the base of all the ceremonials is one that is preventative
in purpose, prophylactic rather than curative; this ceremony is known as
Hozhooji or Blessingway" (McAllester and Frisbie, in Mitchell, 1).

Father Haile did not live to publish Mitchell's version of the Blessingway,
and Leland Wyman took on the task of editing his notes and papers, aided
eventually by David McAllester, an anthropologist and ethnomusicologist. In 1963, Charlotte Frisbie, a graduate student at Wesleyan University
where McAllester taught, joined the project,[1] and in June of that year, she
"asked Frank if he would be willing to record his life history"[2] (McAllester
and Frisbie, in Mitchell, 3). After giving the matter some thought, Mitchell
commenced speaking into a tape recorder in Navajo and continued until "a
total of twelve hours of narration had been recorded" (Frisbie and McAllester,
in Mitchell, 3). This was only the beginning of their work together. Frisbie,
joined by McAllester, continued to consult with Mitchell until his death in
1967, and remained in regular contact with his friends and family for some
eleven years more before publishing his autobiography in 1978.

Navajo Blessingway Singer was met with acclaim at least as great as that that had greeted *Sun Chief* forty years earlier.[3] The editors' work was lavishly praised, and Mitchell himself recognized as a "philosopher and theologian" by Martha Knack (412); a "thoughtful and articulate Navajo leader," and a man to be regarded as among those "whom anthropologist Gary Witherspoon has called 'Navajo intellectuals'" (273), in the words of Barre Toelken. Frank Mitchell does not talk a great deal about his time at boarding school, but I will look closely at what he does say.

Born in 1881, Mitchell was "enrolled to go to school" when he was "maybe fourteen, fifteen, or even seventeen" (57), he didn't know, and like many Native people of his generation, probably didn't think his exact age at the time made much difference.[4] The school he went to was the government boarding school at Fort Defiance, Arizona, at which he arrived for the second half of the school year of 1894. Completing the spring semester, Mitchell returned home for summer break and did not return to school for almost ten years. In his time, he says, the children Navajo parents were willing to send to the schools were the "black sheep" of their families. Indeed, it is his recollection that some of the first to go "were actually half-witted." He says of himself, "I was the ugliest in the family so they put me in school and kept the others back" (57). Although his clan "uncle Charlie Mitchell, and other relatives tried to persuade [his mother] to put one or more of her children in school," she nonetheless, "really objected to [his] going to school; she did not want to release any of her children for school" (57). The treaty between the Navajos and the government in 1868 had provided for the construction of schools for the People, who committed themselves to sending their children, as I have noted, and Mitchell says that it was "The leaders who were appointed after they returned from Fort Sumner [in 1868] ... who went out and did the recruiting" for the schools. Chee Dodge,[5] who would have a long career on the Navajo Tribal Council, and at that time had recently been appointed head of the Navajo police, was of the opinion, Mitchell says, that " 'If we had any sense at all ... we would have enrolled the best Navajo children in school'" (56).

Mitchell and some other prospective students are first taken to Round Rock, where "the recruiters prepared [them] for the trip" to Fort Defiance (58). Shortly before leaving, he is told by uncle Charlie Mitchell "that [his] name would be Frank Mitchell" (58), thus making it unnecessary for him to undergo the usual renaming done at the schools. As part of the preparation, "the recruiters ... brought clothes along" for the children; their "old ones were pulled off, and [they] were given some new clothing to put on" (58), although he speaks of no cleanup preceding the change of apparel. This is Mitchell's first encounter with "white man's clothing" and he describes it in some detail, observing that the "material was all the same, like corduroy ... a yellow-brown color, and the coats, pants and vest were all made out of that brown material." The boys also "had a cap, something like golf players wear, out of that brown material" (58). This does not sound like military attire. The shoes provided, he says, had "a wide toe, and ... no shape to them." The prospective students are also given "some underwear, in one long piece, like a Union suit." This causes problems with excretory functions because, as Mitchell explains, "We didn't know how to unbutton those, so that's why we dirtied ourselves" (58). Two more paragraphs describe the clothes and, again, the problems caused by those buttons. Some of the people at the Round Rock trading post kindly offer instructions in how to handle the pesky buttons, but, nonetheless, "it took a lot of explaining and a lot of work to get used to how to do those things" (59).

"While we were being prepared for the trip [to Fort Defiance]," Mitchell continues, "this was the first time that we had our hair cut. We all had long hair." He notes that "those boys with their long hair had lice. Some of them even had open sores on the back of the neck from them" (59). But with their hair cut short he says, "When they returned home for visits, the older people used to ridicule them, just because they were cleaned up" (59). It takes his party four nights on the road to get to Fort Defiance from Round Rock (59), a distance of about seventy miles, and, although they "got ... [there] after dark," Mitchell finds the place lighted. This was "the first time [he] had seen artificial lights" (61). The lights are sufficiently bright for him to observe several of the buildings, including what he refers to as "the old hospital ... the general hospital," although "they were just then digging the foundation for the [new] stone hospital." He will come to know the old hospital well because, like many Indian boarding-school students, he "had trouble with his [eyes], and ... had to go there and get treatment at that general hospital," probably for trachoma.

Once at Fort Defiance, his group "saw that there were ... a lot of children already in school. So they just dumped us among the children who were already there" (62). Mitchell is about thirteen years old, and, unlike what other Native children had felt on their first days at school, he says that he "was not afraid of anything; [he] did not know what fear was at that time." He then observes that when he "entered school there was plenty to eat there, more food than [he] used to get at home" (62). Other students at other schools often were hungry, but not Frank Mitchell at Fort Defiance. Rather than mush, the meals include "meat, beef.... So [he] was happy about that. [He] was willing to go to school if they were going to feed [him] like that." Even more, "The clothing that [he] got there too gave [him] joy. He was proud to look at the clothes and the shoes"—they are more appealing to him than what he had first been given for his journey—"and to walk around in them" (62). This new apparel does constitute a uniform of some sort since Fort Defiance, as Mitchell will observe, is, like the other boarding schools, run on a military model.

He experiences the familiar topos of the Cleanup: "When we entered school," he says, "they [again?] cut our hair short and they kept us clean all the time." He mentions the school's use of a "louse medicine," and the fact that they "checked our heads every now and then and would give us treatments." He says that "they kept us clean by bathing us every so often," and "once a week, usually on Saturdays, we used to change our clothes so there was no chance for lice to be on them" (62). Looking back, Mitchell states that he "learned a lot from that experience." Indeed, he has "taught [his] family all about it, so you will not find any bugs around here" (62), he told his editors, McAllester and Frisbie, probably in the 1960s. When he "started school," Mitchell says, he "used to go all day," not the usual boarding-school practice. He does say that "later on ... [he] went for only half a day.... The other half of the day [they] would do chores around the school, whatever there was to be done around there," this schedule being typical of the boarding schools.

He is introduced to Clock Time: "They rang a big bell to tell us the time of day. We learned what the bell meant" (63). Before elaborating on life by the bell, he describes the classroom. "We had desks and chairs," he says, "and writing materials were provided for us. We had a blackboard and a big, wide book which had pictures of various animals in it, like cat and mouse and things like that with the names under them. They told us what those were and what their names were, and how you spelled them. Then they taught us the ABCs" (63). Along with the ABCs they taught "1, 2, 3 and all that. As soon as you get up to 10 you know you were qualified as educated." "That was the beginning of our schooling." Unlike what students at other schools reported, Mitchell says "We never had tests or grades," and so "we never knew who was on top of anyone else" (63). If he recalls the names of any of his teachers or fellow students, he does not provide them, using, as above, a generic "we" and "they," a practice he will consistently maintain. He now returns to the subject of Clock Time.

"At school," he says, "we just went by the bell.... At a certain hour we would go to bed. Every time that bell rang, it meant that we had to get in line, or go to bed, or get up and get ready for breakfast, or dinner or supper" (63). He elaborates on bedtime procedure in the dormitory, and also gives the morning routine: "morning exercises, drill around"—the standard military model—"and exercise for about one hour" (63) before breakfast. In the dining room, "One of the problems [the Navajo students] faced there was that [they] did not know how to eat at a table. [They] had to be told how to use the knife, fork, and spoons" (63). The students, he says, "were so used to eating with [their] fingers that [they] wanted to do it that way at the school, and [they] had to be taught" (63). Mitchell's account is again general; he describes no particular incident, nor does he name any teacher or fellow student. He will explain this, at least in regard to the teachers, a bit later.

Like Fred Kabotie, Frank Mitchell is "detailed to feed the hogs all winter, to haul the slop to the pig pen." He does that not with a particularly "educated" horse, as Kabotie had, but with "a team of horses," that he used to drag the slop "over to the pig pen and feed the pigs that way." "For doing that," he notes, he "used to get twenty-five cents a week" (64). He "also had a job in the horse barn," feeding, watering, brushing the horses, and cleaning out the stalls. He describes other tasks that occupied the boys, and observes that the "girls had jobs, too ... sewing, mending, cooking, washing and ironing, helping in the kitchen and baking bread for the school" (65). Boys worked in the bakery as well, and "that was the highest paid job in the school. They were getting about thirty dollars a month, a lot more than any of the others did" (65). If he remembers accurately, we may note the substantial difference between twenty-five cents a week and thirty dollars a month! "On Saturdays," he notes once more, the students "used to take [their] showers and put on clean clothes," and "On Sundays, the next day, [they] all went to church." As was frequently the case with boarding-school religious services, "The preacher or whoever was there of course did not have any interpreter in those days, and of course [the students] did not know much English, and ... did not understand what they were talking about half of the time. They talked about God, and most of us did not understand it.

So I guess they were just talking to themselves" (65). Mitchell notes that at "that time they did not have any Protestant missionaries. Everybody that went to school there was eventually baptized a Catholic" (65). He would also become a Catholic.

Although he had specified church on Sundays, he doubles back and gives an alternate account of religious services at the Fort Defiance School, an account I will soon consider. This mode of proceeding is typical of oral narration, and Mitchell, as I have noted, told his story orally in Navajo, speaking into a "tape recorder's microphone without interruptions, directions... or translations" until "a total of twelve hours of narration had been recorded and Frank announced that he had finished telling his story" (McAllester and Frisbie, in Mitchell, 3). This material was transcribed, translated, and studied by the editors, and, then "in the spring of 1964," McAllester spent a week interviewing Mitchell. Later, in August of that year, Frisbie "began directed interviewing with Frank on his life history." This work "resulted in a total of 1,155 pages of typescript" (McAllester and Frisbie, in Mitchell, 4). The editors, as I have noted, continued to work with Mitchell in the years following, and, after his death in 1967, with the Mitchell family, which had been involved throughout.

"Part of our job as editors," McAllester and Frisbie write, "has been to render the widely different styles of the various interpreters," who had translated a great many materials relevant to the life-history project "into a translation that seemed consistent with Frank's Navajo in flavor, style and implication" (8). Although it was the editors who put "the narrative in chronological order," thereby altering Mitchell's "own scheme—an undated progression of events from his youth to the present" (8), they nonetheless "tried to maintain the unity of narrative style" (8). Mitchell's account of religious services at the Fort Defiance School, to point only to this single instance—there are many others—would seem very much to follow what I take to be his oral "narrative style," and it is a tribute to the great care and sensitivity of his editors that it has been preserved.[6]

"They had church in the classroom," Mitchell continues, "because they did not have a church building there at school." Nor was "church" only on Sunday. He explains, "I think the priests came out twice a week, on a Sunday in the morning, and then on Wednesday in the evening, too; in the winter it was Thursday. When they came we were all sent to listen" (67). Once more he makes clear that he did "not know what they talked about; we never could understand it" (66). He then relates the sort of anecdote common enough at the boarding schools, of a well-meaning priest who attempts to address the students in Navajo as "my dear children," but unfortunately mispronounces the words so that what he is actually saying is "abalone shell" (66).

At Fort Defiance, Mitchell observes, "None of the officials, teachers or other employees of the school knew any Navajo. . . ; not even enough to translate the talks there"—of the priests, it would seem—"to the children." Nor does the school, in his account, seem to have any Navajos or other Native people among its employees. This is different from what some Hopi boarding-school students said was the case at schools they attended, as it is different from what several other Navajo students found elsewhere. "We did not talk much English," he says, "most of the time we talked Navajo, our own language, to one another." He does not say that this was forbidden, or—similar to what Edmund Nequatewa had reported—that there was any punishment for the practice. "They did not understand us and we did not understand them" (66), he states simply. This lack of understanding extends to an inability on the part of the students to "memorize the names of the teachers" (66), so that the children "give them names in [their own] language," names that fix a physical or behavioral trait—for example, there was "Miss Chipmunk" and also "the Woman Who Makes You Scream" (66). Mitchell notes that "there were no men teachers there, just women" (66).

At Fort Defiance, too, there are runaways—"A lot of boys ran away from school," Mitchell says—but those who do run away do not, in his brief account, head for home. Rather, "A lot of them just took off and worked somewhere on the railroad" (67). We have noted that he was thirteen years old at this time, and I'll guess that any runaway intending to work on the railroad could not have been much younger. Of course, "Whenever a child was missing from school, they went out and hunted for him; they did not just let him go" (67). This was the case when Mitchell himself, along with another young man, ran off. He does not say what prompted them to do so, although he notes the fact that although they ran away "not during the school year, but after school let out . . . just the same they had a search party out for [them]." He says that "When they located children missing from the school, they brought them back but they did not whip them." Instead, "they just punished them by having them do some chores, or stand in the corner for a certain length of time" (67). He offers an apparently contradictory account of these matters only two sentences later when he says, "When I was there, if a boy ran away and was caught before he was very far away, when he was brought back, why of course he used to get a whipping" (67). It does not seem likely that returned runaways got a whipping or not depending upon how far away they had got before being caught, so it is hard to know what to make of Mitchell's account, nor is it possible to know whether he and his runaway friend—they certainly were caught and brought back—did or did not get a whipping. Girls as well as boys must have run off, in that he notes "It was mostly the girls who had to stand in the corner for the whole day or something like that" (67). Whether they were also on occasion paddled or whipped is not stated.

Mitchell recalls that whippings were also administered to students caught stealing. Thus, when he and "some other boys" were caught stealing apples, "They locked [them] up in the disciplinarian's office. When he came in he got a great, big, long strap." The strapping is not described; Mitchell says only that "After the spanking, he locked us up all day. That's the way we used to be punished" (67). When it "happened to be big boys who deserted the school"—boys, I will guess, older than he—"then when they were caught, they would get punished in a different way. They would make them carry a big log, a piece of fence post, over their shoulder walking back and forth" (67). This recollection prompts Mitchell again to contradict an earlier statement, his admission to having stolen apples. Now, he says, "I was never naughty like that or punished that way" (67)—although he had said he'd been punished by a "spanking" with a "long strap." He says, "I was always obedient because I was a little scared of them and so I always did what I was told" (67). A reader might wonder just when, in his short stay at school, the young man "who did not know what fear was at that time" (62), the time of his arrival at school, had come to be "a little scared of them" (67).

He returns home in the summer of 1894, and his appearance proves upsetting. "When I arrived home," he says, "my folks were crying.... 'My goodness, look what they did to you; they surely must have been abusing you. Look at your hair. They even cut your hair!'" (67). This is a response he had earlier reported other families having upon seeing their returned students. In any case, Mitchell says, "I just spent one winter there in school, and when it was time to go back, I did not go" (68). He does "not remember exactly how long [he] stayed home"; "maybe it was three years before going back to school again" (68). In Letter Book 30 of records kept by the Fort Defiance Agency, McAllester and Frisbie found that 1903 "would have been around the time when Frank returned to school with his brother Tom" (75), at least nine years from the end of his initial school experience.

During his lengthy time at home, Mitchell says, he "wore ... out" the clothing he had been given at school; "even [his] shoes were worn out," no surprise over so long a period. And, when he "realized what condition [he] was in again, [he] got to thinking about going back to school" (68). When his "family finally gave in. . . , they decided they would send [his] younger brother, Tom Mitchell, along with [him] to school" (68). In that he "and [his] brother stayed there about another three years," he says, "altogether the schooling [he] had was about four years." Or, he recalculates, in that "one was not a full year at that time in the beginning," it was more like three-and-a-half years.

But, as the editors write in their Chronology of Events, records show that "the second time Frank went to school he stayed only a year" (76), leaving in 1904 to work "on the railroad"[7] (358), so that the length of his time in school was "altogether" no more than a year and a half. What I am pointing to is the editors' admirable decision to preserve what they had earlier referred to as Mitchell's "Navajo sense of time" (73), a sense of time we have encountered again and again among people raised in a primary-oral culture. On the one hand, as I have noted for others, Mitchell, narrating at the age of eighty-three, may not have accurately recalled just how long he had been at school some sixty years earlier. But, again, on the other hand, it may not have mattered much to him whether his total schooling had been one-and-a-half or three-and-a-half years.

Whatever the length of his stay at the Fort Defiance School, Mitchell states that "The reason we decided to leave school and go out and work was that we had seen men go off to work like that and come back with good clothing. They also had money which they would then use to buy things like jewelry and dry goods for their families. Of course, we wanted to have some of those things" (77). The "we" here does not, as I had first thought, refer to Mitchell and his younger brother, Tom, but, rather, to an unnamed "friend." *Navajo Blessingway Singer* continues for a great many pages, but this concludes Frank Mitchell's account of his education at boarding school. His further life-learning will come from traditional Navajo singers.

8

Irene Stewart's
A Voice in Her Tribe

IRENE STEWART (1907–1998) AND MARY SHEPARDSON (1906–1997) MET AT Chinle, Arizona, in 1955 when Stewart was running for the Navajo Tribal Council, and Shepardson—almost fifty years old, and, as she writes in her Foreword, "a graduate student in anthropology from Stanford University" (5)—was doing research on Navajo government.[1] The two women kept in touch and became friends, and, in 1965, Shepardson writes, she "conceived the idea of asking Irene Stewart to write her life story" (7). Stewart did this "in a series of letters" to Shepardson that Shepardson herself did not edit, but, rather, turned over to Doris Ostrander Dawdy.[2] *A Voice in Her Tribe* is the result of Dawdy's editing. Stewart's life story is followed by an appendix by Shepardson titled "From My Notebooks," which contains a good deal of further information about Stewart along with many quotations from her that are not included in the autobiography.[3]

Irene Stewart was born in Canyon de Chelly in 1907, "a typical Navajo birth," she says, "in a hogan, far away from a hospital" (11). Her grandmother named her "*Gli Nezbah* (Goes to War With)," because her "Father wanted so much that [she] would be a boy" (11). Although this is not made clear in the narrative, Stewart had told Shepardson early in their acquaintance that her father "was Jake Watchman from Fort Defiance. . . . His father had been the first night watchman at the Fort after the Navajos returned from Fort Sumner [1868], and that's how he got his name" (80). As for her name, she was "christened by a white missionary and named Irene Elinor," although she kept her Navajo name "until [she] went to the off-reservation school,"[4] (11), Haskell Institute in Lawrence, Kansas. She will tell us more on the subject of names and naming.

179

Stewart's mother—her "English name was Eleanor Bancroft," we learn from Shepardson's notebooks (80)—died in childbirth in 1910, when the girl was about three. "After Mother's death," Stewart says, "Grandmother… took me. I was only four years old" (12). This would have been her mother's mother, for Stewart had told Shepardson that "she had seen her grandmother on her father's side only once" (80). But Stewart had also told Shepardson that it "was the missionary, Mr. Black, who took [her] in when he found [she] had lost [her] mother" (81), so it is possible that she was with Mr. Black for about a year before going to live with her grandmother.

It is at Chinle some years later that Stewart sees "a tall Navajo girl dressed in school clothes. She had long braided hair hanging down her back. Grandmother said she was a school girl working for the people at the trading post" (13). This recollection serves as lead-in to a chapter called "School and White People." Stewart recalls that she "felt secure" with "the love of [her] grandmother," living "far away from school and white people" (15). Nonetheless, "one fall day around noon, a mounted Navajo policeman came," and he "took [her] on horseback all the way to the school at Fort Defiance" (15), the school Frank Mitchell had attended some twenty years earlier. She learns that the policeman had come at her father's bidding. Because, as she explains, "Grandmother wouldn't give [her] up to be put in school," her father "had told the agency superintendent, Peter Paquette, to send a policeman to pick [her] up" (15). "This sudden change in [her] life," Stewart writes, "was a shocking experience." Suddenly, she "was homeless. No one cared for [her] as [her] old home folks had," and she "feared everything, especially the people and the strange facilities" (15) at the school. While her characterization of her early life as "a primitive, wild, Navajo life" (15) would seem to reflect her many years as a "civilized" Christian, it also reflects her father's negative opinion of how her grandmother was raising her. For Stewart had told Shepardson that her "father used to say that if the policeman hadn't taken [her] to school, [she] would have been just like [her] grandmother. [She] would have gambled just like her and been a wild Navajo" (80). Father's disapproval of grandmother will come up again.

"Upon being brought into the girls' home" at the school, the dormitory, Stewart finds it to be the locus of the Clean-Up. She "was taken to a huge bathtub full of water," and, although she "screamed and fought… the big girl in charge was too strong. She got [her] in and scrubbed her. Then she put [her] into underwear and a dress with lots of buttons down the back" (15).

No one cuts her hair; rather, the big girl "combed [her] hair until it hurt. And the shoes she put on [her] feet were so strange and heavy. [She] was used to moccasins" (16). "At night," she says, the girls "were put to bed in beds that seemed so high. Some of us fell out during our sleep," something we know to have happened to other young Indian students on their first nights in the dormitories. "There was always someone crying," Stewart says, "mostly because of homesickness. One time [she] cried all night long." This was not, however, because of homesickness, she writes, but, rather, "because [she] had an earache; it was so painful" (16).

This is not the only illness she will suffer. During her "first winter in school," Stewart says, she "became very ill with double-pneumonia which nearly took away [her] life." She was put in the hospital, where "a kind missionary nurse took care of [her," and "forced jello into her mouth, the first jello [she] had ever seen [*sic*]" (16). As she remembers the kindness of the nurse, so, too, does she remember "Miss Shirley [her] teacher. She was kind..." as well, "and her teaching was such that we loved to learn. She taught us with colored balls," Stewart writes, although it's not clear whether the colored balls were keyed to lessons in literacy or numeracy. From them Stewart writes, she "learned there were all kinds of colors" (16), or, rather, she learned the names for these particular colors in English. Although Frank Mitchell had said he never knew what grade he had been in during his time at the Fort Defiance School, Stewart says that Miss Shirley—she seems to have no problem remembering the teacher's name—"divided her pupils into what she called her Baby Class, Sunbeam Class, and Big Class" (16). These names suggest that all of Miss Shirley's pupils were girls, at least in the first two classes.

"At the end of the school year," Stewart says, "Grandmother came after [her] older sister who had completed five years of schooling" (16). We had not been told that Stewart had an older sister at school; perhaps this is the "oldest half-sister... named Doris" (80) she had mentioned to Shepardson. Although she does not speak of her in the autobiography, Stewart had told Shepardson that her "cousin Rose Watchman was in school with [her]," too, and when "they started to call her [Stewart] 'Watchman' over there" (81), it was Rose who "explained about it being [her] last name" (81). Although Stewart knew that her father was called Jake Watchman, she did not know that Watchman would be her name as well, since Navajos, like Hopis, did not take their fathers' names as their own.

But grandmother has not come to take Stewart home along with her older sister. Rather, she "said that [her] father would take [her]" (16). Stewart observes that her father's having arranged for her to be taken to school had only "increased" grandmother's "dislike for Father" (15), a dislike that is mutual. Because father "had not arrived," Stewart "became frightened and hysterical," hanging on to her "sister, begging not to be left behind." Grandmother is sympathetic, and employs an interpreter to obtain "permission to take [Stewart] with her" (16). The three women, with some difficulty, make their way to a clan relative's home where they spend the night. Father arrives there the next morning.

But he does not take Stewart home. "As soon as we had breakfast and the horse was saddled," she writes, "we went back to Fort Defiance" (16), where "we were to be with my father's brother, Lewis Watchman" (16). What it means for her and her father "to be with . . . Lewis Watchman" is not explained, nor does it ever become entirely clear. Stewart reports her father saying, "You have no one but me. Your mother has been dead these three years," and "Someday you will take advantage of your education" (17). After reproducing Father's words, Dawdy begins the next paragraph with Stewart saying, "I remember entering elementary school in a large building where the studies were very hard for me" (17). But what happened to the summer of that particular year? It seems to have passed in the blank space between paragraphs.

Stewart's father, this is to say, had found her with her grandmother no more than a day after "the end of the school year" (16), and they returned to Fort Defiance the very next morning. In that the school would not have taught elementary students during the summer, Stewart could only have resumed her education in the fall. In mentioning the return to Fort Defiance, Stewart had indeed said that she and her father "were to be with [her] father's brother, Lewis Watchman" (16), and it is almost surely the case that the two of them spent the summer with him. Stewart will confirm this—see below—but only later and in passing. In this regard—I'll note others—Doris Dawdy, like Charlotte Frisbie and David McAllester, did not try to "anglicize" (Toelken) the chronology of an oral storyteller's narration—although unlike Frisbie and McAllester—she did not comment on the matter so far as I have been to discover. She did not, in this particular instance, this is to say, insert phrases that would have clarified such things as how much time actually passed between the end of one school year and the beginning of another.

Another instance of Stewart's oral style left intact by Dawdy's editing—and Stewart's oral style manifested itself in writing, in letters that she wrote Shepardson—concerns Stewart's presentation of her school experience once the new school year begins. What she says now is very different from what she had said just a bit earlier—and her evaluation will change yet again, with none of these changes noted or acknowledged. Thus, whereas Miss Shirley had been "kind," and learning previously had been fun, the new teachers, to the contrary, "were mean and strict. [The students] were always being punished for not knowing [their] lessons. Once [Stewart] was slapped in the face for gazing out of the window, and once for chewing gum in class. [They] were never allowed to talk to one another in school, or to speak [their] language" (17). Stewart gives a description of almost three years of "elementary school" in similarly condensed fashion. The students, Stewart writes, "were always being put in line to march to school, to meals, to work, to the hospital," all but the latter—I do not know why the students would be marching "to the hospital" all together—the typical military routine of the Indian boarding schools. "Four hours of each day were for school work," she notes, "four hours for industrial education," domestic science for the girls. "Saturday afternoons," she continues, "were for play; Sundays, we went to church." Here, she turns back to say that "Getting our industrial education was very hard. We were detailed to work in the laundry and do all the washing for the school, the hospital, and the sanatorium" (17), a part of the school she had not mentioned. "Sewing was hard, too," she writes: "We learned to sew all clothing, except underwear and stockings, and we learned to mend and darn and patch. We canned food, cooked, washed dishes, waited on tables, scrubbed floors, and washed windows. We cleaned classrooms and dormitories" (17). One does not doubt her when she says that "By the time [she] graduated from the sixth grade [she] was a well-trained worker" (17), quite thoroughly "proletarianized."

The rigors of this aspect of her "education" took a significant toll on her. "I have never forgotten," she writes, "how the steam in the laundry made me sick; how standing and ironing for hours made my legs ache far into the night. By evening I was too tired to play and just fell asleep wherever I sat down."[5] (17). This sounds like the experience of a nineteenth-century child laborer. Indeed, Stewart says, "I think this is why the boys and girls ran away from school; why some became ill; why it was so hard to learn. We were too tired to study" (17). The subject of runaways will come up again when Stewart is at home and her father raises the issue.

Stewart herself does not seem ever to have run away, and her prospects improve when, "During the third year of elementary school, a missionary named Mr. Black took us into his home for almost three years" (17). This is the same Mr. Black who had taken her in for a time after her mother's death, something she does not here mention. She uses the plural first person all through her brief account of living with Mr. Black, although it is not clear who—her sister? a friend? a cousin? someone else?—might have been there with her.[6] "At his home," she says, she "had the privilege of learning out of Old Mother Goose books and singing songs" (17). If she and whoever was with her provided domestic help for Mr. Black, as I am sure they did, it is not mentioned. She writes, "We had become very attached to Mr. Black," and so it was "a sad parting" when he married and "we returned to the school dormitory" (17).

"During the closing years of school days at Fort Defiance," Stewart recalls, she "began taking part in school programs—something [she] was too shy to do before" (17). From what she had said earlier, readers might think it was not shyness but extreme fatigue that caused her to take no part in school programs. Stewart is told by her "fifth grade teacher" that she has "been chosen to sing a song with a boy on Easter Sunday" (17). She is "surprised" at the thought of singing with a boy because "Before, [she] had sung only with a group" (17). Apparently she has participated in at least that school program. Although she has a high-pitched voice "which sometimes cracked" (17), the performance goes well and "From then on [she] was interested in singing," something she "continued to do throughout the years" (18). The teachers who enable her singing do not seem to be "mean" at all, and Stewart's account of school at this point more nearly parallels the one she had given at the outset.

"When I look back at my elementary school days," Stewart writes, "I remember that there were happy times when we played on merry-go-rounds and swings" and engaged in all sorts of children's games. In the winters, she says, "We made snowmen, threw snowballs, and skated," and during "evenings we told Navajo stories"[7] (18). Indeed, winter is the proper time for telling Navajo stories. After a while, she "was no longer always lonesome and homesick. And when [she] went home on summer vacation, [she] missed the fun [she] had at school" (18). These recollections of singing, playing, telling stories, and having fun are, obviously, very different from Stewart's recollections of being so ill and exhausted from her labors that she could not study.

The differences in her accounts of life at school are neither acknowledged nor reconciled in the text, but, as I have noted with other narrators, this is not to say that Irene Stewart contradicts herself. Several of the boarding-school autobiographies have prominent instances of what has been called "writing in the oral tradition," as noted earlier, that is to say, passages in which translators or editors have not rearranged or altered orally delivered narration, sometimes leaving it—as I'd quoted Barre Toelken in reference to the style of *Navajo Blessingway Singer*—"comfortably diffuse and usefully repetitious" (273). Thus, Stewart tells of the times and the ways in which her experience of the school at Fort Defiance was positive and she tells of the times and the ways in which her experience was negative. She doesn't distance herself from them in order to weigh whether, all in all, they were more positive or more negative, nor is she is inclined to employ an abstraction like "ambivalent" to convey that her experience was *both* positive *and* negative.

Although Stewart may have "missed the fun [she] had at school" (18), life at home is broadly instructive in how to live the Navajo way. She "learned to herd sheep, prepare wool, and weave; to clean the hogan floor and wash dishes." She also says that she learned "to clean [herself], wash [her] hair, and keep it combed and braided" (18). These are things she had also learned to do at school—although she makes clear that Navajos do these things differently; for example, "they wash their hair often with yucca soap suds to clean and soften their hair"—as Hopi people also do. Because Stewart "is allergic to this wild plant," she is instructed in alternate means of washing her hair. She also learned "to make [her] own dresses. . . ,[8] wash clothes, to cook, milk goats, haul buckets of water. . . ; and when there was a garden [she] hoed and watered the plants" (18).

It is her father who teaches her "how to grow up to be a good girl," and among his precepts is "Above all, don't ever try to run away from school. You know the punishments for this," he says, warning as well—as Don Talayesva's father had warned—that "there are wild animals in the forests and canyons like bears and wolves. They eat people" (18). Stewart promises him that she would not do this, not so much fearing the wild animals as "the punishments meted out to runaways." These she describes here: "They were spanked, and either locked up in a room or made to walk back and forth in front of the girls' and boys' dormitories. If a boy, he was dressed in girls' clothing; if a girl, in boys' clothing" (18), the latter punishment being used at some of the other boarding schools as well. Although she had not indicated this earlier, she makes clear that she "had known about those girls and boys who had tried running away. Few succeeded. The others were caught and brought back. One boy ran off in midwinter and froze his feet. A girl, caught not far from the school, received a whipping from the head matron" (18).

In the next chapter, Stewart articulates something that a great many boarding-school students also found, that her "attempt to live the traditional Navajo way of life was chopped up with school life" (19). Thus, for example, she says that "the customary puberty ceremony was not made for [her] because [she] was in school at that age" (19). This is an important ceremony for Navajo girls, called Kinaalda.[9] Although she did not herself experience it, Stewart does describe the ceremony as she had seen it performed for another girl. Early in the story as she is, she nonetheless offers some poignant reflections on her life thus far. "As a child," she writes, she "was shifted back and forth from [her] Navajo life to the white man's schools," something that perhaps "accounts for some of [her] varied characteristics." For example, she writes that "It was in [her] early years that [she] began to give way to feelings of inferiority and insecurity. It seemed as though hardly anyone cared for [her] after [she] was taken away from Grandmother" (20).

Stewart writes that she "had an unusual number of fears on into adolescence" (20). This might well be because she entered adolescence without the support of a mother or her grandmother, and it also might be because she entered adolescence without having the puberty ceremony performed for her. She says that she was "afraid of darkness, people"—Navajo people? whites?—"lightning and thunder, and to this day [she is] afraid of lightning. Three times [she] was nearly struck by lightning, once so close that [she] fainted." It was "shortly after this experience that [she] became sick, and was in bed for two months of [her] school vacation" (20). "During [her] illness," she says, she "had strange experiences," being visited by "owls, and coyotes" by night, and "mice and blue jays" by day. Her father keeps a fire going through the night, she says—this is during summer vacation—and her "stepmother took care of [her] by day" (20). Her illness persisting, her father, with "tears in his eyes," undertakes to effect a traditional cure. After, she sleeps deeply and then "felt a sudden urge to get up." But she is so weak that she needs "some sticks for support" in order to walk. (21). "Two weeks later [she] returned to school." There, a friend of hers says that she'd heard Stewart had died "from some awful sickness." The friend is pleased to find her "very much alive, but ... awfully pale and skinny." Stewart notes that she had not gone "to the hospital when [she] was sick, because [she] was afraid of the doctors," and had also "been told that many people died there" (21).

Having ended chapter 4 with Stewart's return to school, Dawdy does not pick the narrative up from that point in time. Rather, in chapter 5 she has Stewart offer recollections of her "father's brother," Lewis Watchman, and his five children, noting that she "was raised with these children, especially the first four" (23). The oldest of these is Dadi, "five years older" than Stewart, and the two, she writes, were "very close to each other" (23), Dadi perhaps serving as a mother to her as well as an older sister. Stewart will tell us much more about Dadi. Here, however, it is worth remarking that these few sentences confirm the fact that when Stewart's father had taken her from her grandmother and brought her back to Fort Defiance only a day after school had let out, she had indeed spent that summer with her uncle and his family before returning "to elementary school" (17).

Stewart tells of Dadi's marriage to a man considerably older than she, "a Navajo marriage" first, "and later a Christian marriage" (24), offering the opinion that Dadi "should have gone to school" instead of marrying when she did. In regard to Navajo marriage customs past and present, Stewart refers to things that "Greyeyes told [her]" (24), concluding the chapter with Greyeyes's explanation of the "mythical origin" of the mother-in-law taboo. (Mothers-in-law and sons-in-law are to avoid each other.) She does not, here, impart the information that Greyeyes is her husband, a man also considerably older than she, and one who like Dadi and (probably) her older husband has also not been to school. Again with no transition, Dawdy goes from concluding chapter 5 on Navajo marriage ceremonialism and the origins of the mother-in-law taboo, to chapter 6, which she titles, "Four Years at Haskell Institute" (27).

The chapter begins with Stewart providing an exact date for when she "received [her] first hard-earned diploma" (27), June 2, 1922. "It was," she writes, "the happiest event. [She] was graduating from the sixth grade at Fort Defiance after long, hard years, although the last two had been happy ones as well" (27). She recalls that the school "superintendent, Peter Paquette, told [the students], 'This is only your Commencement Day. Finishing the sixth grade is just the beginning of other school years ahead'" (27). Paquette, who, Stewart writes, "had a genuine interest in [the] children," apparently "persuaded all the graduates to continue by enrolling for off-reservation schools" (27).

Stewart's preference is the Phoenix Indian School, but she discovers it is full and "only Haskell was open." She and several others register for Haskell, and although it is far away in Lawrence, Kansas, they are buoyed by Paquette's assertion that "'It is one of the best Indian schools, with more training and high-school subjects'" (27). She "told [her] father that [she] was determined to continue [her] education, and that this time no policeman was going to pick [her] up." She had then, she notes, "that youthful fancy to become educated in some off-reservation school among other tribes." Her father, she sees, "was proud of [her] sixth-grade education, because he told relatives and visitors that [she] had finished school at Fort Defiance" (27).

That summer, Stewart writes, "was spent preparing to leave for Haskell. [She] made two dresses, and Father bought [her her] first suitcase and a pair of white high-topped shoes. The trading post at the Fort wasn't selling new style shoes yet in 1922, nor was it selling dresses" (28). (But clearly her father had found a way to obtain both.) "There were twelve of us girls and boys," she recalls, "who had enrolled in that far-away Eastern school," and she notes that her father "was perplexed" over the fact that she is "going so far away from him, parting for four long years, maybe never to see each other again" (28). Full of youthful fancy, the fifteen-year-old tells him, "I am going toward the sunrise." He thoughtfully reminds her to tell the doctor about her illness the summer before (28).

Stewart provides a full account of the long journey to Haskell. On the day "when [the Navajo students] were to go away from [their] people" (28), they pile, with their luggage, first into "an old army truck"—she had indeed been at school when the United States was at war, although she did not mention it—with their "folks and school friends [standing] around to see [them] off." She notes movingly that just "before she climbed in, Father hugged [her] and blessed [her] with his corn pollen" (28), causing her to cry as she took her seat.

Let me make explicit here what the reader has probably gathered: that father, much in favor of educating his daughter—I suspect that he himself had not had any schooling—and worldly enough to know what kind of stylish shoes she would like, is also thoroughly traditional. Indeed, Stewart's narrative all through has fine pieces of description of this period, roughly 1913 to 1926, when Navajo people were very much a mix of unschooled traditionalists of different ages—Uncle Lewis's daughter Dadi, among the younger ones, and both Stewart's father and her own husband, Greyeyes, among the older, and schoolboys and girls like Stewart herself. During the summer of preparation for Haskell, for instance, Stewart related that her father's proud talk of her graduation had prompted a visit by an old man who "thought this might be a fine chance to obtain a young girl for a wife" (27). He offered "nine goats, a silver belt, and one pair of beads" (27) for her, an offer her father turned down. Stewart notes that "we all laughed about what happened," although it becomes less funny when her "stepmother started to worry because the old man was known to be a witch" (28).

The old army truck takes the students on a dirt road to Gallup, New Mexico, where the students board "two cars at the end of a long locomotive. It took three and one-half days to get to Haskell because the train traveled so slowly" (28). As other students onboard the trains had done, Stewart also notes the food situation. She writes that the "cook at Fort Defiance had packed three large boxes of sandwiches and some apples" for the students. They "were not allowed off the train . . . during train stops," probably "because one of the students was missing when [they] boarded the train at Gallup. Evidently," she writes, "he sneaked away while the man in charge was buying . . . tickets" (28). It would seem, therefore, that not all of those bound for Haskell were voluntarily "going toward the sunrise" (28). "At noon on the fourth day," Stewart writes, they "arrived at a dingy, isolated platform at a little town near Haskell Institute," where "another big army truck" awaited the tired Navajo students. Like Fred Kabotie on his arrival at the Santa Fe Indian School several years earlier, Stewart is "disheartened" by "the old grey stone buildings of Haskell." They were "far from [her] happy imaginings about [her] new school" (28).

Haskell had opened in 1884 as the United States Indian Industrial Training School, with twenty-two students. Its name was changed to Haskell Institute in 1887, in honor of U.S. Representative Dudley Haskell, who had been instrumental in bringing the school to Lawrence. Among the "old grey stone buildings" Irene Stewart would have seen in the fall of 1922 were the adjoining Osceola and Keokuk Halls from 1884; Hiawatha Hall, opened as a Methodist Chapel in 1898; Winona Hall (1897); and Tecumseh Hall, opened as a gymnasium in 1915.

Stewart writes that the students are told to hurry to the dining room "and get ready for the noon meal... other students were already in line"; she doesn't remember what was served (28). She is "car-sick and lonesome, and barely touched [her] food" (28–29). She next encounters the "girls' dormitory" which "impressed [her] no more than the campus" (29). She and another girl are "led to a large room" on the third floor, "where eight or nine other girls of different tribes roomed." She and her companion both begin to cry, and one of the others "tried to console" them. A floor matron intervenes and takes them to her room, where she offers comfort by informing them that "there were some Navajos there, two from Fort Defiance and six from Tuba City." Unfortunately, as Stewart writes, "It didn't help much; the lonesomeness stayed with [her] for almost two years" (29).

In her second year at Haskell, "Mr. Paquette," the superintendent from Fort Defiance, "came to check on [his former students]." One Navajo girl cries, tells him "how much she missed her folks," and "asked to go back with him." Paquette, however, is not immediately going back, but continuing east, to Washington; he attempts to cheer the girls by noting that they "all looked fine and up in style." This prompts Stewart to note that "some girls had their hair bobbed and used make-up" (29). She will discuss the matter of hairstyle further, although Dawdy interposes two paragraphs on the subject of dress and loneliness first. Stewart notes that while at Fort Defiance, they had "dressed in uniforms, at Haskell [they] wore the clothes [they] brought from home," although "There was plenty of clothing issued by the government for those who couldn't afford to buy their own" (29). At this point, it seems, Haskell is run on a military model less strict than at most of the boarding schools. But if some days the students wear the clothes they had brought from home, "Sundays everyone dressed in uniforms," and marched in "a military dress parade in the afternoon which was attended by people from the nearby towns"[10] (29).

Elaborating on the subject of lonesomeness raised in the earlier paragraph, Stewart writes of her "own lonesome days" on which she "wrote to [her] uncles about how lonesome [she] was, and asked them to let [her] come home" (29). They respond—they are apparently literate—that she "will get over it soon," urging that she "stay there and do [her] best to finish the four years" (29). She notes that her Uncle Lewis—this is the first time she calls her father's brother "uncle"—advises her, perhaps teasingly, to "Learn to bake good cakes," so that when she comes home the family "can have cakes for [their] meals" (29).

Stewart returns to the subject of hairstyle, writing that "that first fall at Haskell in 1922, bobbed hair had come into style. Nearly all the girls had their hair curled and nearly all used makeup" (29), the 'twenties having arrived in Kansas. The matron tells the girls "not to overdo painting their faces, and to keep skirts below the knee" (29). Most fashionable among the students, she says, were the Oklahoma Osage, who had oil money. "We Navajo girls," Stewart writes, "did not go out for style for some time because we did not have money." Nonetheless, after "two years at Haskell," she, too, had her "hair bobbed" (29). This requires that she first have her hair cut, something that had not been done by the school staff earlier, and a task that is undertaken by a Pima friend named Effie. Stewart describes this experience and its unfortunate result: she thinks it makes her look like "the Navajo boys and men who had haircuts like [hers]" (30). Effie tells her not to be concerned, because with the use of an electric hair curler she will soon look like "Clara Bow . . . the 'It Girl' in the 1920s"[11] (30). Effie performs her magic, and Stewart is pleased—although it "was then time to work in the kitchen—of all places to go with a nice hairdo" (30). Indeed, the steam of the kitchen undoes all her new curls. Further, she recalls, that haircut "also cost her a friend . . . who was almost a mother to [her]." This is Mrs. Swingly, the head cook, who had "advised . . . against the haircut and the use of makeup." She calls Stewart a "bad girl," and does not speak to her "for almost two weeks" (30).

Her last years at Haskell are accounted for in three short paragraphs. "At the end of her second year," Stewart writes, she "had begun to like Haskell" (30). During her third year, she makes some new friends and mingles with "the high-school students," for she was "already in the ninth grade." She joins "the Glee Club and the girls' basketball team [and] took a home economics course to fulfill [her] vocational training requirements." She notes that she "acquired many friends among other students and among the employees, and . . . admired the matrons despite their strict attitudes toward" (30) the students. This is a view expressed by a number of other boarding-school students as well. Then, "Before [she] knew it, the four years were up." She is "anxious to go home, and at the same time reluctant to leave Haskell"

(30). The school principal, she writes, urged her "to re-enroll" but she "was undecided" (30). The chapter ends with Stewart attending the "bright June Commencement Day for twelfth-grade graduates," which she finds "inspiring" (31). "These happy and wonderful memories," she says, she "took with [her] back home that summer" (31).

The return is difficult. "When Father met [her] at Fort Defiance," she writes, she "hardly knew him. He had taken on years and was old and thin" (33). It would also seem that he hardly knew his daughter. Stewart remembers: "He looked at me for some time. I think he wondered about my bobbed hair and all the new style, perhaps even my actions" (33). "How these sudden changes make a Navajo student feel"—or, as we have seen a Hopi or other returned Indian boarding-school student—"is only to be understood by one who has experienced them" (33). Looking back, Stewart has a broad and insightful view of the matter. "Back in the 1920s and '30s," she writes, "the returning students' problems were very much unsolved" (33). They were also not very well understood. Of her own situation, Stewart says that "Unless a Navajo family were well off and could give their children a good home," along with "some stock and land to start them off—they would in time drift away to nearby towns, or even farther away," as, she notes, she herself had done (33). I'll quote her on this subject at some length. "Once having left hogan life," she writes, "and having gotten used to living where there are hygienic facilities, it is very hard to live again in the old hogan way of life. A Navajo boy or girl wants a suitable home, a chance to live the life he has been taught, and an opportunity to find suitable work to support himself and later his family. The school regime was hard to break away from; it had left me with problems unsolved" (33).

Indeed, she does not actually return home with her father but remains at Fort Defiance, where she works as a housekeeper for about ten weeks, after which time she "visited [her] father and his family"—this would be her stepmother and any children the couple had had—"for two weeks." She notes what Polingaysi Qoyawayma and others had noted, writing, "When I had left the Navajo country years before, I felt heartbreak; now I was disappointed in it. . . . Hogan life—once a great pleasure to me, *and in later years so satisfying*"—the phrase I have emphasized is a matter to which we will return—"was not for me" (33, my emphasis). At this time, she says, "I looked forward to the white man's ways and decided to go back to school, this time to Albuquerque Indian School" (33).

Having again been ill—she has had to have her tonsils removed—and concerned that every cold she caught might turn into something more serious, Stewart decides to take up "practical nursing at the Indian hospital in Albuquerque as the vocational part of [her] training." As at Haskell, she writes, "part of [the] training was vocational, part was academic" (34). One thing that is different, however, is that whereas at Haskell "the students were expected to speak English, at Albuquerque it seemed that more spoke their native tongue than they did English." Stewart says that "In order to be better equipped to learn, [she] spoke English with those few who tried to keep from speaking their native language." Because most of the students at the Albuquerque school were from the New Mexico pueblos, Stewart would have to have spoken English to them to communicate at all. She makes clear that "The one thing [she] never stopped regretting was not having gone back to Haskell to finish high school" (34). "In 1928," she writes, she "switched back to home economics from practical nursing, and in 1929, [she] received her diploma" (34). She describes no bright June Commencement Day for her own graduation from Albuquerque as she had for the Haskell high school graduates. As for her next step, she notes that during her "last years of high school, a Christian woman encouraged her to take Christian training in California" (34). This she will do.

Stewart only now reveals what the reader had not known before, that her "Christian training began as a small girl when [she] was sent by Uncle Lewis to learn the Presbyterian teachings" (35). It's not possible to know the order in which Stewart described incidents in her life in her letters to Mary Shepardson—I have found no record of them—although the decision to treat her Christian training as a flashback from this point in the book is almost surely Doris Dawdy's. Stewart's Christian training continued "during [her] childhood at Fort Defiance school," she writes, although she had said nothing of that or of any other religious instruction.

Stewart takes a Bible study course for nine months in Oakland, California, hoping to become "a missionary's helper" (35). Then she goes home to "work among [her] people at the Presbyterian Mission Hospital of Redrock near *Lukachukai*, Arizona" (36, italics in original). Before long, however, the Mission closes. After a time, she says, she "left for Oakland," and apparently "was soon back where [she] wanted to be." She writes that she "worked a year for a woman who ran a pawn shop," and then, "got married to an Oneida boy" (36). These are the years of the Great Depression, and her husband, whom she does not name, "was always out of a job" (37). Although the marriage produced "four small children," it does not last. The couple separate and "then years later, with much legal red-tape" (37), Stewart got her divorce.

She once more returns home and gets work "as a field-nurse's helper," but this too does not last, leading her to go to "Chinle to see [her] Father and to look for work" (38). The next two chapters, 10 and 11 of Stewart's story, are called "The Navajo Way," and "My Father." Both serve as preparation for chapter 12, "Greyeyes." In "The Navajo Way" Stewart describes her childhood in relation to the broader topic of "the role of the Navajo woman" (41). In "My Father," Stewart describes something of the life and death of her father, who fell from a tree in 1944 and died several months later at the age of eighty-seven (46). He was, in Stewart's depiction, a typical Navajo man of his time: "a small-time medicine man," a sheep and goat herder, a gambler, a railroad and construction worker, and a blacksmith (45–46). Stewart's thoughts about the role of traditional Navajo women in her time and of her father, a fairly traditional Navajo man of his time, lead her to "Greyeyes."

Greyeyes became Irene Stewart's husband in "the year of 1942," when, she writes, they were "joined by common-law marriage. Greyeyes was 20 years older than [she was]; he had been married three times before and had daughters and sons"[12] (47). They later "had a church marriage... as common-law marriage became illegal on the reservation about 1945" (47). "Greyeyes is a narrator of Navajo ways in stories and chants," Stewart writes, and "Married life with Greyeyes has been good" (48). "Greyeyes' family," she observes, "are hard-working, traditional Navajos. They believe in the Navajo religion, which they often use for sickness, bad dreams, prosperity, and well being. They own sheep and goats[13] and the women are good weavers of rugs." Greyeyes was raised like the typical Navajo "of his time. He never attended school. He was taught stock raising and how to be a medicine man" (48). It may well be that a union with Stewart, whom he had known since she was a child, served Greyeyes as a meaningful connection to the future just as Stewart's union with him served as a meaningful connection to the traditional past. In any case, this successful marriage explains the phrase Stewart had used earlier when describing her return to Navajo country from the Haskell Institute when she wrote that "Hogan life—once a great pleasure to me, *and in later years so satisfying*" (33, my emphasis), was not, at that point in her life, satisfying any longer. But for Irene Stewart there decidedly was—as there had indeed been for Polingaysi Qoyawayma—the possibility of "turning back" without rejecting what she had learned at school. This allowed her to run for a position on the Navajo tribal council, while her marriage to Greyeyes kept her in touch with the traditionalism of her youth. Irene Stewart's integration of the Navajo way and the boarding-school way, of tradition and modernity, was very much a success.

9

Kay Bennett's
Kaibah

IN A REVIEW OF KAY BENNETT'S *Kaibah: Recollection of a Navajo Girlhood* (1964), Flora Bailey wrote that "The reviewer is puzzled concerning the intended audience for the book," noting that it read very much like what she called a "junior novel" (1,567). Maureen Reed, whose substantial work on Bennett I will cite, dismissively refers to it as a "children's didactic novel" (2005a, 207), and Edward Spicer, in a brief review, apparently agrees; he describes the book as "a series of pleasant sketches . . . told in simple, declarative sentences, as though for middle teen-agers" (185). The book often does read like fiction for young adults, like a "junior novel" with an "intended audience" of "middle teen-agers"—although it is nowhere "didactic," not consistently "a series of pleasant sketches," and not fiction. It is, to be sure, often less than fully satisfying to more experienced readers, but it is a very interesting book nonetheless, one worth careful attention.

Kay Bennett (1920–1997), like many of the boarding-school autobiographers considered in this study, is very little known today.[1] Susan Brill de Ramirez's chapter on "Postcolonial Navajo Ethnography: Writing the People's Own Stories from Within Tribal Culture," speaks glowingly (if briefly) about Franc Johnson Newcomb's biography of Hosteen Klah published in 1964 (see appendix B), but does not mention Bennett's *Kaibah*, published the same year. In part this is because Bennett is not easily seen as a postcolonial champion of traditionalist authenticity, a matter I will consider further. Bennett first came to public notice as a singer, performing at the Gallup Intertribal Ceremonials, and Spicer, in his 1966 review of *Kaibah*, recalled her as "Princess Whitefeather, singer of Navajo songs and promoter of Navajo crafts" (185). In 1953 she was crowned Queen of the Flagstaff

"Southwest All-Indian Powwow," and she became a finalist, in 1954, in the "Miss Indian of [*sic*] America" Beauty Contest (Waltrip, 12; Reed 2005a, 194). (See figure 10.) Spicer's reference to her as Princess Whitefeather, "a performance name she used at that time [1954]" (Reed 2205a, 322n61), along with the negative associations many readers may have to titles like "powwow queen" or "beauty-contest winner" need to be interrogated if one is to avoid simplistic assumptions about Kaibah Bennett.

She also ran unsuccessfully "as the Republican candidate for the Mckinley County, New Mexico, assessor's office" in 1968, (Reed 2005b, 127), the year in which "she received New Mexico's 'Mother of the Year' award, a first for an American Indian Woman" (Waltrip, 10; Reed 2005a, 119). Years later, in 1986, she became the first woman to run for president of the Navajo Nation; after her defeat, she ran again in 1990. All of her many endeavors may be seen as attempts to resolve the dilemma, in Maureen

10 Kay Bennett, in black, third from right, at the American Indian Miss America contest in 1954. On the back of the photograph she is identified as "Miss Kay Price, Navaho, Sheep Springs, NM." Second from right is the eventual winner of the contest, Mary Louise Defender, identified as Yanktonais Sioux. Courtesy of the Stanford University "American Indian 'Miss America' Archive." #MO810, Box 1, Folder 8.

Reed's words, of a woman "caught between tribal models of femininity"—
more accurately the traditional social role and status of Navajo women—"and
the 'modern' models [she] had learned at school" (2005a, 172), an issue faced
by every boarding-school student. With her third husband, Russell Bennett,
she published *A Navajo Saga* (1969), a novel very specifically for juvenile
audiences, although it is based on incidents in Bennett's grandmother's life
before and after the Navajos' detention at Bosque Redondo from 1864 until
their return to their homes in 1868.[2] But *Kaibah: Recollection of a Navajo
Girlhood* is not, as I have said, fiction. Bennett presents it as autobiography
(in the third person), stating that it is the "true story of an average Navajo
girl as lived by the author during the period from 1928–1935" (n.p.). Among
that Navajo girl's experiences are three years at the Toadlena, New Mexico,
elementary school, and it is well worth listening to this Navajo boarding-school student's voice.

The story begins with Kaibah's mother, Mother Chischillie, a widow
living with her children in the area of Cross Hills, New Mexico, on the
Navajo reservation. There, Bennett writes somewhat simplistically, "the
people were happy. They lived an uncomplicated existence, free from the
worries which beset most people who live and work in urban communities" (11). A complication arises, however, in chapter IV, "The Visit From
the Superintendent," when a "tall white man" from "the boarding school at
Toadlena, about twenty-five miles to the north" (21) drives up. He has come
to take Kaibah to school "as she is of school age" (21), about eight years old.
The little girl is horrified at the thought of leaving home, and her mother
tells the superintendent that he would do better to take her son, Keedah,
who is fourteen. The superintendent agrees to return in two days to do so
(23). The young man, reluctant though he is, will obey his mother's wishes.[3]
We hear almost nothing of his schooling.

School is not mentioned again until the seventeenth chapter of the
book, when Keedah, home from school, is told by his mother that she is
thinking of sending her granddaughter Glenbah to school. Glenbah, about
seven, and so a year younger than Kaibah, lives with the family. The boy
responds that "There are some girls smaller than Glenbah in school and
the Navajo matron takes good care of them." He thinks "she'll be all right"
(145). Glenbah is indeed sent to school, for, six chapters later, we meet her
"toward the end of May [when] the children came home from school." To
Kaibah, Glenbah, on her return, "seemed more grown up. Instead of being

a silent little girl, she was full of talk about what had happened at the school. She spoke a few English words, and Kaibah felt very much left out when the other children talked in this new language"[4] (185). Seeing this, "Kaibah made up her mind that she would return to school with them when they left in the fall. She was now ten years old" (185). Chapter XXVII is called "Kaibah Goes to School" (209).

When the other children return to school, Kaibah's mother does not let her go with them. Instead, "about two weeks after the children had gone," she discusses the matter with Keedah, who also must not yet have left for school. He offers the opinion that "Kaibah should go to school." "It is not right," he says, "that all of the other children learn to read and write while she is kept at the hogan" (209). Although mother will find it "very lonely without [her]," she agrees that her daughter "must go and learn the ways of the white man like the other children" (209). Mother and daughter set out for school early the next morning. Mother will bring "some corn bread for the children," knowing that they "don't get any at school and are probably hungry for it" (210).

Mother seems familiar with the school at Toadlena. On arriving, she knocks on the door of the superintendent's home, and, finding he is not in, goes "to the school house," where "they entered and saw him sitting behind a large desk" (211). After mother has "explained that she had brought her daughter to school"—it is unlikely that mother knows any English or that the superintendent understands Navajo, but no interpreter is mentioned—the superintendent "shook hands with Kaibah," who may or may not have seen the practice of shaking hands before. Then he "said he was glad she had come to school ... [and] motioned for them to follow him ... to the girls' dormitory" (211). It is there that "the girls' advisor," a Mrs. Taylor, calls for "a Navajo woman interpreter," a Mrs. Begay, "and told her to take them to the dining room" (211). Bennett provides a description of the dining room, a familiar locus of boarding-school narratives: "There were about forty tables in the room, with glasses, plates and silverware set on them for the next meal. Kaibah had never seen so many dishes. The wood floor was very clean and polished. Mrs. Begay gave them each a plate, with a slice of cold meat loaf left over from lunch, some bread, a glass of water, and an apple" (212).

Kay Bennett, who not only attended the Toadlena School but was also a dormitory attendant there from 1946 to 1947 (Reed 2005a, 192), probably remembers this accurately, although her description differs from that of other Indian boarding-school students.

Because "Kaibah was too excited to eat," she attempts to take "the apple ... outside," only to be told by Mrs. Begay that eating outside the dining room is not permitted. They now move to "the girls' building"—the dormitory—where Kaibah will be given "new clothes" (212). Her mother admonishes the girl to "do everything [she] is told to do," and, in Mrs. Taylor's office, she explains to the woman that "Kaibah was afraid of white people," asking "that they be kind to her." Mrs. Taylor assures mother that "There are two Navajo ladies to help the girls." Mother, who clearly knows about these things, next states that she does not want her "daughter's hair to be cut" (212). Mrs. Taylor, noting that Kaibah "has come voluntarily to be with us," agrees to "accord her that privilege," adding, however, that "her hair must be kept washed and combed all the time" (212).

They then proceed to the topos of naming. Of all the English names suggested, "none seemed to satisfy Mrs. Taylor," who finally said to mother, "'What is your daughter's Navajo name?'" (212). Learning that it is Kaibah, Mrs. Taylor responds that she likes that name, so "'We will call her Kaibah here at school'" (213). "Kaibah was a little disappointed. She had hoped to be given an English name like the other children. But she said nothing, and kept her eyes on the floor" (213). Mrs. Begay will now get Kaibah her new clothes.

They descend to "a basement room" with "many boxes on a shelf," from one of which Mrs. Begay took "a pair of black shoes and told Kaibah to put them on. Kaibah took off her moccasins and put them on. Then she was given a pair of brown stockings, an underslip, bloomers, and a striped print dress" (213). Although she has already put on her shoes, before donning the other clothes, it is still necessary to undergo the Clean-Up: "From the storeroom she was taken to the washroom. A long sink stretched across one side, with faucets about two feet apart. A door led to the shower room. Mrs. Begay placed the new clothes, a cake of soap, and a towel on a wooden bench in the shower room" (213).

She tells Kaibah to take off her clothes and to wash; after, she will once more put on the new clothes. Her old ones will be given to her mother to take home (213). Not having ever "undressed completely in her life," the girl is "embarrassed." Mrs. Begay, assuring her that there "is no one around to watch" her, urges her to "take a good bath," and adjusts the water temperature.

Kaibah washes, Mrs. Begay hands her a towel, "and turned Kaibah around to see if there were any sores on her body," perhaps, as Frank Mitchell had noted, sores from lice. Satisfied with what she sees, Mrs. Taylor "told her to dress quickly" (214). Bennett nicely conveys Kaibah's sense of her transformation: "When she was dressed, she felt like she had nothing on. The clothes were very light compared to those she was accustomed to wear." Then, "Mrs. Begay combed and braided her hair, and took her upstairs to a large room with many beds. She led her to one and said, 'This is your bed. This is where you will sleep every night while you are at school. You must always keep it clean and neat. Now let us go back to your mother, and show her how nice you look'" (214). Her mother does indeed think Kaibah looks "nice and clean." By this time classes are over, and Glenbah along with two boys from the extended family come running to see them. They "were happy to have Kaibah with them" (214). Mother leaves the happy scene, mounting her horse and riding away. Once she is "out of sight," Glenbah offers Kaibah a tour of the school. They visit "the playground," which has "swings and seesaws," and they see some "of the girls ... playing ball, others walking in groups ....[or] sitting on benches" (215). There are "about one hundred and fifty girls," and some of them "welcomed Kaibah in Navajo." Glenbah explains that they "are supposed to speak English while [they] are at school," and that tomorrow Kaibah "will start learning some English words" (215).

Kaibah encounters Clock Time when the "five o'clock siren blew while they were walking around the playground, and it made Kaibah jump." Glenbah assures her that she will "get used to that noise," explaining that this particular siren "means that everyone who works here is finished for the day" (215). Reinforcing the regimen of Clock Time, Mrs. Begay "came out of the dormitory and blew a small whistle. It was a signal for all the girls to go to the washroom to clean up before supper" (215). Bennett writes that the "girls lined up, and were each given a towel as they filed into the washroom" (215). The school would seem to have learned the dangers of students' sharing towels.

"Kaibah watched the other girls as they washed," remarking that "Most of them," unlike herself, "had short hair, which was easily combed." As Irene Stewart had noted of some of her classmates in the early 1920s, Kaibah sees, now in the late '20s, that "the larger girls fixed their hair, powdered their faces, and brightened their lips with lipstick" (215). Mrs. Begay keeps Kaibah with her "while the other girls lined up to go in to the dining room." Then she "blew her whistle, and spoke to the girls in Navajo"—this is apparently allowed—telling them, "'This is a new girl.... Her name is Kaibah.... You will help her learn how to live here" (215). To help her most particularly, Mrs. Begay has chosen "one of the older girls, named Nancy," to whom she explains that it is her "job to help Kaibah," who will sit at her table and sleep in the bed next to her (216). "Kaibah, feeling not so lost now that she had a friend, followed Nancy to the dining room" (216). Despite its different physical arrangement than that of most of the boarding-school dining rooms, Toadlena's operates in similar fashion.

Bennett describes how "A line of boys entered one side, and moved to the chairs assigned to them on the boys' side of the room. The girls did the same, until all the children were in, and each standing back of their own chair. The smaller children entered first, and stood, three at the side of each table, then the older children entered and one stood at each end. When everyone was in place, the boys' advisor, a white man named Mr. Johnson, blew a whistle, and everyone sat down" (216).

Grace was not said. When "all was quiet," Mr. Johnson "again blew his whistle, and Nancy and the other table leaders started dishing up the food" (216). There is no competition to be served; each child is given a plate, and a "larger girl, sitting at the other end of the table, poured ... cocoa, and passed the cups around" (216). We are not told what Kaibah thinks of cocoa or of the meal she has just been served. When Johnson sees that they have finished, he blows his whistle again, and the children stand and file out of the building (216).

The rest of the evening is spent pleasantly, with some girls returning to the playground, some going "to the sewing room to mend their stockings, and others ... to the living room to read the library books or listen to the radio" (216). Kaibah had not encountered a radio before, and her mentor, Nancy, who "liked the radio, ... tried to teach Kaibah how to operate it" (217). Bennett confirms what one can easily believe, that Kaibah's "first evening at school passed very quickly" (217). Mrs. Taylor, once more blowing her whistle, signals that it is time for bed. "She handed Kaibah a nightgown," and "Nancy showed Kaibah how to fold her clothes, and hang them over the iron bedstead." Sleeping on a bed does not seem to cause her any difficulty; like the other girls, Kaibah "put on the soft flannel gown and pulled the sheet and blanket over her head" (217). At this point, she feels "suddenly very lonesome.... Tears came to her eyes and she was crying as she dropped off into an uneasy sleep" (217).

Although it was "uneasy," her sleep must have been deep, for when Kaibah hears another whistle, she finds Nancy shaking her, saying "softly, 'it's time to get up'" (217). She rises from her bed, dresses in the new clothes that are "still strange," and watches as Nancy makes her own bed, folds her nightgown, and "then rolled gown, blanket and sheet to the foot of the bed to form a neat bundle." Nancy teaches Kaibah how to perform these tasks, warning her that Mrs. Taylor will make her do it over or "assign some extra work" if it is not done to her satisfaction. No corporal punishment is mentioned. The girls go next to the washroom where Nancy again helps, combing and braiding Kaibah's hair (218). There is as yet no marching or drilling, nor are there any chores to perform; rather, "the girls went out-side, and sat on the porch until the whistle blew for breakfast" (218). Then, after breakfast, "the girls swept and dusted and cleaned up their dormitory until it was time to go to their classrooms." The "girls lined up by grades" and they do indeed march to their classrooms, with Nancy taking Kaibah "to the first grade teacher," before going to her own "fourth grade class in another building" (218).

The teacher shows Kaibah where to sit and "then continued writing the ABCs on the blackboard. She would point to the A, and pronounce this letter, then the children would try to imitate her" (218). Kaibah does the same, remarking that "the teacher had very black hair, cut short, and [she] thought she might have her hair cut some day like the teacher." For an hour the children attempt to draw a rabbit like the one in a picture "tacked to the walls" (218). Then, an "old man with a white beard came into the classroom." He is the doctor and the teacher points Kaibah out to him as "our new girl." When the man asks her to open her mouth, the other girls tell her in Navajo what it is that he wants. After looking at her throat, "he looked at her eyes, and told the teacher to send her to his office" (219). Before going to the doctor's office, Kaibah learns from the other girls that the doctor "had stuck needles in their arms, and put medicine in their eyes." Several days later, Kaibah herself is "taken to the hospital to be inoculated for typhoid, and small pox, and to have one of her eyes operated on" (219). The medicine the girls had received was probably for trachoma, as Kaibah's surgery almost surely was.

Kaibah's experience at school continues to be presented in positive fashion. She "worked hard to catch up to the other children," and the "teacher kept her after class to help her" (219), Bennett writes. Kaibah "learned the names of most of the things she came in contact with in the dormitory and dining room, but it was difficult to pronounce the names correctly, and more difficult to learn how to form sentences" (219). Bennett notes what we have often found, that "Many of the children who had been in school three or four years had the same problem with the strange language." This is because, as Bennett writes, "English was not spoken in any Navajo hogan, and during their summer vacations, the children forgot much of what they had learned at school" (219), something we have also remarked earlier.

Mrs. Taylor is indeed strict; she "expected everything in the dormitory to be kept neat and clean." When Kaibah, on her first "turn to sweep the floor," leaves "dust in the corners," "Mrs. Taylor inspected ... and pointed [it] out" (219). The little girl has to tend to it, but there are no raised voices or punishments. "On Saturdays, after the dormitory and dining room were thoroughly cleaned and polished, the girls who wished to go to the nearby trading post were marched down the road to the nearby store" (219–20). We are told that "Most of the girls had ten to twenty-five cents, which they had been given by their parents," and they buy fashion items or candy. Although the girls were "marched" to the store, they are certainly not in military attire. "On cold days they wore long red sweaters and tam-o-shanter hats, and were quite a colorful sight swinging along in double file" (220). Sundays, the students "marched to the church to hear the preacher tell them that they would all go to hell and be burned up if they were bad" (220). That, at any rate, is what Nancy tells Kaibah he has said. She doesn't understand why that should be, and thinks that in any case "the Navajo gods were better" (220).

When cold weather comes, Bennett writes that a "heavy snowfall blanketed much of the reservation west of the Turquoise Mountains ... and army helicopters were sent to drop food to the people who lived in isolated locations." This fascinated the children, who, Bennett writes, "saw the helicopters several times over the mountains" (220). But this could not have happened when Bennett says it did. *Kaibah* represents Bennett's recollection of "the period from 1928 to 1935," and the first (military) use of helicopters did not occur until 1942. Reed suggests that Bennett "probably mixed up this winter with a later one during which she saw helicopters conducting relief efforts" (2005a, 320n23). Kaibah's first year at school ends with the reader having been told nothing more about it—academics, domestic instruction, sports, and the like—than what transpired during her first week there. "Spring came," Bennett writes, "the snow melted, and the grass was plentiful. Soon Kaibah's first year at school was over, and the children were on their way home in the yellow buses" (221). Whether the grass is or is not plentiful each spring is a matter of great importance, and something sure to be noted by Kaibah, who, like most Navajos of the time, grew up a sheep herder.

Soon, Kaibah is with her mother and brother, "dressed in their Navajo clothes and grouped around the fire, drinking coffee and eating fried bread" (221). Mother notes that Kaibah has gained a good deal of weight; clearly she has not known hunger at school as so many other boarding-school students had. In the afternoon, Kaibah and Keedah sit "on a small hill watching the sheep spread out as they grazed below." Keedah asks his sister, " 'How do you like school?' " to which she answers, " 'I like it very much' " (221). This summer, also, "passed quickly" (222), and, except for a visit from the Toadlena preacher—he points out that he wears "a short coat instead of a long coat like some other preachers" (224), thus identifying himself as a Protestant rather than a Catholic cleric—it is uneventful. Soon Kaibah is back at school.

She has been promoted to the second grade; there are "about forty children in her room," and her teacher is Miss Cornell (226). "Each child was given a reading book and an arithmetic book,... and told to write his or her name on the label pasted inside the cover" (220). Bennett notes some "usual infractions of rules," but once more does not describe punishments for them. "The first few weeks, in order to force the children to resume speaking English as quickly as possible, extra duty was given those caught speaking Navajo" (226–27), but, again, no soap in mouths or consequences of that nature. Meals are "prepared by a white man, with the help of three Navajo women," but other kitchen chores—with the exception of dish washing, which is done "in the automatic dish washing machine" (227)—are "done by the older boys and girls" (227). Kitchen duty, Bennett writes, is in great demand here, too, because students assigned to the kitchen "would get extra food, and extra apples or cookies." "The detail most disliked was cleaning the washroom, toilets and the showers," Bennett writes, and, while "Everyone took their turn at this duty. . . , it was also assigned as extra duty to those who broke a school rule" (227).

Although discipline has been presented as mild, duties not particularly onerous, and learning taken seriously, nonetheless, "Shortly after the children had returned to Toadlena, four boys and four girls ran away from the school" (227). The boys' absence is not immediately noticed since boys are ordinarily permitted to leave the school grounds. This is not the case with the girls, who "were missed when the children lined up to wash for supper" (227). Bennett writes that the "superintendent felt that an example had to be made of these children," the runaway girls, and the next paragraph describes just how they are punished. But first it seems worth noting the many things missing from Bennett's very brief mention of the runaways. We haven't been told, for example, whether these are younger or older boys and girls, or what may have caused them to run away. And nothing is said of the fate of the boys who ran off. Were they caught and brought back, as is likely? If so, what was their punishment? The girls, obviously, were found and brought back to the school. But we are not told anything about how that was accomplished.

In any case, "All of the girls were assembled at the playground," the run-aways among them. Then, "a chair was brought and the guilty girls, one by one, were told to sit on the chair while an attendant cut off all their hair and shaved their heads" (227). "The girls"—those who are not guilty—"watched in shocked silence, thinking what if this should happen to them" (227), "a great disgrace." As for the girls to whom this does happen, all we are told is that they "hastily put a shawl over their heads" (227). In a few days "their parents arrived and removed them from school" (228), having by some means learned of their daughters' "disgrace." Losing these students surely cannot have been the superintendent's intent.

With no further reflection on the serious events just described, Bennett writes that "Kaibah became more and more sure of herself as the year passed. She could speak a little English and her quick smile made friends of the teachers and the other girls. She was stronger and heavier than the other girls of her age and more active in their baseball and volley ball games" (228). The coming of spring turns the children's thoughts toward home, "and then one day school was over, and it was time to leave" (228).

Chapter XXIX detailing this summer at home is called "The Drought," and it begins with Keedah's "worried" observation that "There will not be much for the sheep to eat this winter," because "all the families have more sheep than they had a few years ago" (229). Also current is a rumor that "Washington wants to take all of our sheep and horses"; and, too, mother has "heard that Washington wants our land" (231). This is partly confirmed, partly complicated when a "white official" comes with a message from Washington to the effect that Indian Commissioner John Collier—his name is well known to the Navajos, although who he is exactly and what he actually intends is far less well known—"wants you to sell some of your sheep and horses" (234). This is the first announcement of what would come to be known as "the stock reduction" program, a development arguably as traumatic and life-altering to Navajo people of the twentieth century as the Long Walk and exile at Bosque Redondo had been to the Navajos in the nineteenth century. Bennett writes that "No one wanted to sell their animals. Most families had increased their herds. The grass had been plentiful until this year. . . . They did not realize that the land was becoming over-grazed" (235). A great deal has been written about—I cite the title of Broderick Johnson and Ruth Roessel's book—the *Navajo Livestock Reduction: A National Disgrace* (1971).[5]

Teresa McCarty begins her brief but excellent discussion of the stock reduction program quoting "Agnes Begay, a young girl during that time," who said, "when they took the sheep, we used to cry" (57). As McCarty explains, the land was indeed overgrazed and "the rangeland vegetation became depleted and the topsoil it held in place was washed and blown away" (56). A drought exacerbated and hastened this depletion. "The tribe's solution was to increase Navajo rangeland," McCarty continues, but "White politicians in the newly created states of Arizona and New Mexico resisted returning 'public' (more accurately, publicly seized) lands to Navajos" (56). In 1935, the last year Kay Bennett's *Kaibah* "recollects," "The Federal government declared the Navajo reservation '100 percent overgrazed,' and, under Commissioner Collier, instituted a program of voluntary, and subsequently forced, herd reduction" (McCarty 57). (See figure 11.)

Bennett ends the chapter called "The Drought" with the People being asked to mark ballots with an X or an O to indicate their position in regard to the proposed stock reduction. The distinction between the two, as the book presents it, is unclear and essentially meaningless, just one aspect of the "confusion" Irene Stewart had said the program had caused (46). (Voting X means voluntarily reducing the herds; O is to be marked "if they wanted the sheep to die" (241), a vote, it would seem, to have the herds forcibly reduced.) Kaibah returns to school for a third year in chapter XXX, titled "The Reduction of the Sheep," a chapter that begins with the sentence, "At school the reduction of the sheep was not discussed" (243). Nor will Bennett discuss it in this chapter, although as we will see, the stock reduction program is ongoing and will have important repercussions for the Navajo people, in particular for Navajo women, and for Kaibah herself.

In this third year of school, in "home economics class Kaibah learned to operate a sewing machine, and made a bright yellow dress to wear to her first dance" (243), an occasion that is not described. "Kaibah was a good student, and Mrs. Taylor"—she is still in charge of the girls—"rewarded her efforts by assigning her work of cleaning up and washing dishes at the employees' club" (243). This is indeed a reward—one that Nancy, her former mentor, shares—in that they "can eat better food ... take leftover cake, and they would receive three dollars a month" (244). Although this is not very good pay, in these years of the Great Depression Kaibah and Nancy are envied by the other girls. "This was especially true of Lena," Bennett writes, "the largest girl in school," a young woman who "was quarrelsome," and "constantly threatened the smaller children" (244).

Kaibah and Nancy come into conflict with Lena on a trip to Gallup where those children who could raise the money for a ticket are to attend

11 Bureau of Indian Affairs Commissioner, John Collier, and two unidentified Native men, about 1935. Courtesy of the National Archives and Records Administration, NARA #519179

a circus. The group arrives early and Lena orders Nancy and Kaibah "to steal a lipstick for [her]" from one of the stores they will visit. If they don't do this, she threatens, she will "beat [them] up when [they] get back to school" (245). To avoid that fate, Nancy and Kaibah enter a store and consider the theft, only to find that "the sales girl watched them so closely that neither of them had a chance to steal a lipstick" (245). After the circus performance, which the students find impressive—"This had been the greatest experience of their lives" (246), Bennett hyperbolically writes—they return to school. On the following day, when classes are over, "Lena and two of her friends" stop Nancy and Kaibah and Lena announces her intention to do what she had promised since she had received no stolen lipstick. She pushes Kaibah, who first tried "to avoid the big girl, and continue on her way to work" at the employees' club. But Lena grabs her hair, slaps her, "and soon the girls were on the ground" (247). Mrs. Begay arrives, breaks up the fight, and as punishment tells both of them, "you will... stand in the hall, facing the wall, until bedtime" (247), still several hours away. This is the last we hear of Kaibah's schooling at Toadlena.

The book's final chapter is called "Kaibah Leaves the Reservation." At the end of the school year, Kaibah returns home where "the drought [had] continued through the winter and spring of 1935" (249). Recognizing this, Kaibah is "a sad and sober girl as she got off the bus and walked slowly toward the hogan. The other children, too, did not alight with shouts of joy and race around the prairie," for they "had seen the bones of sheep and horses along the highway" (250). Caring for their remaining sheep is the primary task of the family this summer, and although "Some sheep died,... most of them regained their strength" (252).

It is during this same summer that "a missionary and his wife asked Mother Chischillie if they might pitch their tent near the spring" (252). She is welcoming, and, in that "they did not preach or try to interfere with her way of life," mother and the missionary couple "became good friends" (252). That is all we learn of this couple; their names are not given, nor do we learn their business in Navajo country. Nonetheless, when "it came time for them to return to Los Angeles"—apparently where they are from—they "asked Mother Chischillie if they could take Kaibah with them" (252), to act as housekeeper "and go to a nearby school" (253). This request prompts mother to ask Kaibah whether she would prefer "to return to school at Toadlena.... Or to go with these good people" (253). "Kaibah," Bennett writes, "said, 'I will go with them to California.' And so Kaibah bade her mother and her home farewell" (253). And there the book ends. But why, as Maureen Reed puts the question, "did a girl who had planned to take over her fami-ly's sheep herds decide to take a job as a maid instead?" (2005a, 189). Why did she choose not "to return to school at Toadlena" (253), where she had seemed to be having a very positive experience? A good part of the answer to both questions may be found by considering the change in the status of and opportunities for traditional Navajo women wrought by the years of the livestock reduction.

The "livestock reduction era must appear as a tragedy" to Navajos, Maureen Reed has written, because "Regardless of the good intentions held by Collier and Navajos who acted as agents of stock reduction measures, the inconsistency, inefficiency, and waste produced by these policies devastated something more important, even, than the Navajo herds: Navajo confidence in a way of life and in the potential to work with 'Uncle Sam' to achieve it" (2005a, 188).

The first of these—"Navajo confidence in a way of life"—weighed particularly on Navajo women. What Bennett had learned as a young girl, "that being a Navajo woman meant being a powerful person with many important responsibilities" (Reed 2005a, 180), suddenly seemed threatened, and this threat seems to have affected the life choices and sense of identity of a boarding-school student like Kay Bennett.

Laila Shukry Hamamsy's "The Role of Women in a Changing Navaho Society" (1957) studied the Navajo community of Fruitland, New Mexico, in the northwestern corner of the state, not far from where Kay Bennett was born, from approximately 1933 and the development of a federal irrigation project there to the time of her work in 1951–52. "Raising livestock and subsistence farming are the major economic activities" among the Navajos, Hamamsy wrote, with men "generally responsible for the horses and cattle, women for the sheep and goats" (102). But, about 1933, as the federal government began to enforce the stock reduction program, "the women," Hamamsy found, "in losing their sheep... lost their economic independence" (109). Moreover, locally, "There are few job opportunities for them, and their duties in the home make it impossible for most of them to seek work outside" (109).

Some thirty years later, Mary Shepardson set out "to compare Navajo women's status in three different periods: in traditional society before stock reduction (1868–1933); during and after stock reduction (1933 to early 1950s); and at the present day (1980s)" (1982, 149). *Kaibah* chronicles its author's experiences during the last five years of the "traditional" period and the first two years of the stock-reduction period, and Bennett also was actively engaged in a number of activities in Shepardson's third period (and after). In agreement with Hamamsy, whom she cites, Shepardson wrote that "Stock reduction dealt a devastating blow to Navajo economy," and that "The blow fell heaviest on Navajo women who were offered few alternatives" (1982, 151).

Kaibah's choice to go to California may have come from a nascent realization of how times were changing drastically. Whether she had chosen to continue with her education at Toadlena or not, there once would have been the chance to attain the traditional high status of Navajo women like her mother by keeping a substantial flock of sheep. But by 1935, at the end of only her third year of schooling on the reservation, it began to be clear to young Kaibah that this status would be "lost," as Shepardson wrote, "with stock reduction" (149). Not yet bound by "duties in the home" (Hamamsy 109), she sought to gain status by the means available to (some) Navajo women in the second period through "education and wage work" (Shepardson 1982, 149). But, as Hamamsy had noted, "When the women do find work, they are usually poorly paid in comparison with the men. There are a few openings in government institutions such as schools and hospitals, but the major sources of employment are in such areas as seasonal agricultural work, and domestic service" (104).

Kay Bennett went to Los Angeles precisely to engage in "domestic service," although with some intention as well of furthering her education. It is not known what life was like for her at the home of the missionaries she accompanied west, or whether she continued in school there. By the late 1930s, however, she was back in New Mexico, married to Ned Kelleywood, a Navajo. He worked "as a property clerk for the Indian Service; she worked as a ward attendant at the hospital in Fort Defiance" (Reed 2005a, 191), near the border between Arizona and New Mexico. Then the couple went back to California, where two daughters were born. At some point in the 1940s, Bennett left Kelleywood and, now with her children, returned once more to the Southwest. As I'd noted, she spent 1946–47 "as a dormitory attendant at the Toadlena Boarding School," where she had earlier been a student, and then worked "as a teacher and interpreter at the Phoenix Indian School" (Reed 2005a, 192). She would not have had her daughters with her while she held either of these positions. It was only a bit later that Kay Bennett would first perform as a singer (1951), going on to become a powwow queen (1952), and a beauty-contest winner (1954), before, some thirty years later, venturing into tribal politics.[6] All of these endeavors may be seen as complex negotiations between "Indian and national citizenships" (Kozol, 68), attempts to negotiate the "competing expectations of authenticity and modernity" (Kozol, 70) in such as a way as to bolster her status as a Navajo woman.[7]

Jennifer Nez Denetdale offers a warning about valorizing "Navajo women as princesses and beauty queens who represent ideal Navajo womanhood" when it is done predominantly by Navajo men as a tactic to deploy "Navajo nationalist ideology to re-inscribe gender roles based on Western concepts" (2006, 9). But Wendy Kozol notes that several of "the powwow princesses" studied in the 1990s "incorporated their ideas of tradition with contemporary popular culture to carve out identities meaningful to their modern lives," and that their doing so is "Far from betraying tradition" (75). Both observations are important, and there is a rich critical literature complicating these matters that I cannot engage here. I would ask only that neither Kay Bennett—nor any beauty-contest entrant or boarding-school student with a positive view of that education—be dismissed simply as someone who has internalized colonial values.[8]

Bennett married her third husband, Russell Bennett, an engineer, in 1956, and spent time with him in Afghanistan, where she learned the art of doll-making, a craft she soon adapted to Navajo subjects. It was only much later, in 1986, that she ran for tribal chairman of the Navajo Nation, the first woman ever to do so. She lost badly to Peter MacDonald[9] (Reed 2005a, 218). In 1990, she once more attempted to run. Initially "disqualified as a candidate because of a tribal law that required all candidates running for tribal chairman to have served in an elective position before or have been an employee of the tribe," a ruling by the Navajo Supreme Court "allowed her to run as a write-in candidate because the ballots had already been printed" (Denetdale 2006, 25n37). Again she did not win. As I have noted, neither had Irene Stewart won election to the tribal council when she ran in 1955 and 1959. Stewart's life story included her mention of a traditional bias against Navajo women serving in tribal government, a bias that persisted into Kay Bennett's time as well, and it is worth a moment's attention here.[10]

Stewart referred to a "legend about a woman leader ... Asdzaa Naat'aani (Woman Chief)," as a source for the Navajo view that men are to be the leaders, and that there "will be confusion within the tribe whenever a Navajo woman takes office" (61). Ruth Roessel refers to this as the story of "the Separation of the Sexes," which chronicles "an attempt ... never ... repeated, for women to occupy the top leadership positions in Navajo society" (1981, 132). Asserting that "accounts of women in Navajo history reveal a very important leadership position for them" (1981, 132), she nonetheless finds that "when knowledgeable Navajo women today [1981] discuss politics, the traditional ones usually refrain from wishing or believing that someday a woman will be a Chairman of the Navajo Tribal Council" (1981, 133). These women, "some of whom are highly educated," she writes, believe that while "it is proper and someday possible that Navajo women may occupy the position of Vice-Chairman," nonetheless, "the traditions of the Navajos make the seeking of the office of Chairman unwise and out of keeping with Navajo culture" (1981, 133). Roessel acknowledges that "there are young articulate Navajo women… who publicly declare their intent to run for Tribal Chairman," but she finds that although these women may be "well-educated… [they] do not have their roots in Navajo culture" (1981, 133). This was five years before Kaibah Bennett, who most certainly did have her "roots in Navajo culture," ran for the office of tribal chair.

More recently, Jennifer Nez Denetdale points to this same story (2006, 16), and Lloyd Lee adds to it a number of Navajo creation legends, all of which contain what he also terms "separation of the sexes" stories (280). Denetdale and Lee agree with Stewart and Roessel that these stories are invoked to support the claim that "tradition" dictates that men be—to use Stewart's word—"rulers" (61), and predominate in tribal government. But Denetdale points out the paradox involved in "declaring that women should not vie for the top leadership in the Navajo Nation government because of traditional restraints," when such a declaration ignores the fact "that the hierarchical structure of the modern government itself is not traditional" (2006, 17). Lee affirms that it is not Navajo traditional logic, but, rather, "Western logic [that] dictates women should not be leaders" (283). Indeed, he makes the case that "it was not… prior to the 20th and 21st centuries… that men are supposed to be the leaders" (284). Thus, to call on "separation of the sexes" legends to justify denying women top leadership positions in tribal government is, Lee writes, borrowing a term from Clyde Kluckhohn and Dorothea Leighton, "retrospective falsification," a process whereby past practice is falsified "strategically to conform the history of the people with existent forms of governance" (Lee, 284). The "falsification" here involves the assertion that because Navajo women had not "traditionally" taken leadership roles in public affairs, they should not do so now. Indeed, as Lee and other scholars (e.g., Gladys Reichard, Peter Iverson, Jennifer Denetdale) have shown, whatever selective invocations of tradition may claim, this was, historically, not the case. Kay Bennett thus was both modern and traditional at once in choosing to run for the office of Navajo tribal chair.

Bennett's various self-fashionings richly complicate any simple dichotomy between conservative and progressive, traditional and modern, authentic or inauthentic. I'll close this discussion by citing a quotation Maureen Reed found in an interview Bennett gave to "the Women's Section of the *Scottsdale Daily Progress*" soon after the 1964 publication of *Kaibah*. (Reed 2005a, 118). Bennett is quoted as saying, "I may drive a Cadillac and wear contemporary clothes instead of traditional velvet tunics and gathered skirts when I return to my old mother's hogan at Sheepsprings, N.M., but that does not make her words of wisdom nor the practices of the medicine man any less valid for me. What is invalid is living in a mud hut and tending sheep. That is not my way of life and I cannot accept it" (in Reed 2005a, 118–19).

I will leave it to the reader to parse this statement of the complexities—in Wendy Kozol's phrase—of "historically specific notions of identity and experience" (66) on the part of this Native boarding-school student.

10

Stories of Traditional Navajo Life and Culture

IN ASSOCIATION WITH NAVAJO COMMUNITY COLLEGE AND THE NAVAJO Community College Press, Broderick Johnson published *Stories of Traditional Navajo Life and Culture* in 1977. The book is a collection of life histories from twenty-two "traditional" Navajo people born between about 1882 and 1920, all of whom narrated in Navajo. Fourteen of the twenty-two elders attended boarding schools. The following discussion, arranged chronologically according to the birth date of the narrator, for the most part allows some of these people to speak for themselves. I'll quote substantially from the narratives that are either the most detailed or that provide details and perspectives we have not encountered in other boarding-school accounts. Something that may be said in advance of all of these Navajo boarding-school students is that—like Irene Stewart, Kay Bennett, and certainly Frank Mitchell before them—each of them left school fully, if differently, Navajo.

∾∾

The oldest narrator in Johnson's collection is Ch'ahadiniini Binali, born about 1882. He speaks of schools being built some two years after the Navajos' return from Fort Sumner in 1868 (227), and of strong resistance to them.[1] But by the time a school "appeared in Chinle," his home, Binali says he "was grown up ... and had a wife" (228), so there was no schooling for him. The oldest of the group who did attend school was Howard Bogoutin, born in 1890. His father wanted him to have an education, he says, and so he "placed [him] in a mission school at Aneth, Utah, when [he] was nine years old." He thought that nine "was a late age for starting to school," and he stayed "only one year" (280). But some years later, when he was "a big

217

boy," his "father told [him he] should go back to school," so he "entered the Shiprock boarding school and stayed for six years" (281). Whatever his exact age may have been at that time, the "school officials said [he] was far over-age," leading them to "put [him] in a vocational training group." Although he did not learn to read and write, his training did enable him to be "hired in the trade that he had learned," and although he "did not graduate from high school," he nonetheless was able to qualify as a "supervisor" (281) and to earn a good living.

∽∾

Mrs. Bob Martin—no other name is given for her—was born in 1892. She says she "was enrolled at the Fort Lewis School" in Durango, Colorado, when she "was 10 years old," not knowing "a word of English" (121). At Fort Lewis, she says, "There were members of other tribes attending, such as Utes and Plains Indians, as well as some Chicanos." She remembers that "When I first got there it was frightening, and I almost died of loneliness. It took me a year to become accustomed. The teachers taught us what we had to learn, and we worked hard to be good students. We did what we were told to do. I enjoyed my school days. At times it was difficult, but I managed to get along well" (121). So well did she manage to get along that during her "first summer at Fort Lewis [she] did not want to go home for vaca-tion," apparently lonely no more. There were no summer classes, and like other students who did not go home for vacation, she obtained employ-ment, "worked hard . . . and . . . did what [she] was told" (121). She doesn't indicate the nature of her work—housekeeping of some sort I'd guess—nor does she say how much she was paid. But she does state clearly that she "was learning things which [she] never had known before," and that she "enjoyed going to school and being in Durango" (121). Although she has offered only a bare outline of her educational experience to this point, she will later provide further details.

First, however, her narration turns to a description of traditional Navajo life as she has known it. She tells of gathering wild plants, of cooking, and of her puberty ceremony, the Kinaalda. Mrs. Bob Martin describes this important occasion in a Navajo girl's life at some length (126–28). On the final day of the ceremony, she says, the girl is to "race to the east and to the west, boys yelling right after her" (127). She, however "was not a fast runner," and "ran just a short distance" (127). That she is a slow runner will come up again. She next mentions the Navajos' exile at Fort Sumner, noting that her "father was born there," and that he "was two years old when his people returned to their homeland" (129) in 1868. Then she declares, "My story, from here, will pertain to my education." With no acknowledgment of the fact that she had said this earlier, Mrs. Bob Martin repeats, "I was 10 years old when I entered school" (129), and offers details she had not given before. Despite her schooling, this is to say, Mrs. Bob Martin's narrative manner is very much that of an oral storyteller, and neither her translator nor the editor seems to have rearranged the material.

At this point, the reader is given fascinating recollections of the horse-back trip she, her father, and her mother made through Ute country to get to Fort Lewis; about visits to relatives along the way; and about how her father and some Ute men killed and butchered deer for meat. When the family arrives at their destination, they go to "the superintendent's office at the Fort Lewis School in Durango, Colorado" (130). Then, after some discussion carried on through an interpreter, Mrs. Bob Martin heads to the girls' dormitory with her mother. There, she encounters the Clean-Up: she is told to take a bath, and to discard her "traditional clothes" (130). Her new clothes, she says, consisted of "a brand new pair of shoes, a dress, under clothes and stockings. I washed my hair and combed it neatly. I felt so good all dressed up in my new clothes and was very refreshed. I turned myself around admiring my clothes. It made me happy. It was in 1902" (130). "That night," she says, she "was given another dress. [She] learned this was called a nightgown to be slept in; and [she] slept in a nice clean bed with white sheets." She acknowledges the strangeness of it all, and "thought of [her] sheepskins that [she] had slept on at home" (130). She seems to have had no problem sleeping in the bed.

Nonetheless, the "next morning [she] suddenly became homesick. [She] felt so lonely that [she] began to weep" (130), as had been the case with many other Indian boarding-school girls, and not a few boys. Then, she says, "It was time to eat." Before eating, she is "told to go to the washroom, which was in the basement of the girls' dormitory." There, the girls "washed [their] faces and hands. Then they were told to line up, and [they] marched to the dining hall" (130). Although the Fort Lewis girls were lined up and told to march, it does not appear from Mrs. Bob Martin's account that the school was run according to the usual boarding-school military model—although (as was the case with Kay Bennett at Toadlena) there is a good deal of marching. The dining hall, she finds, "was very large, with many tables," with, probably, the boys' tables on one side of the room and the girls' on the other. The students "were told to be very quiet; someone"—we are not told whether this is one of the older students or a staff member—"was to say grace before [they] ate. After grace was said"—she could not yet have understood its meaning—"[they] sat down and were served… breakfast" (130). At this point, Mrs. Bob Martin, like many another boarding-school student, found that the food served "was strange and did not taste good to [her]; so [she] did not eat" (130). When the others have finished, "a bell rang," and they "marched out of the dining hall back to the dorm… to clean up for classes" (130–31). She is still lonely and once more begins to cry, nonetheless lining up with the others "to march to the school building" (131) where classes are held.

Once in her classroom, she says, she "was given a stick called a pencil, a large piece of paper and also a book of A B Cs" (131). Told by the teacher to copy the letters, she "scratched lines all over the paper, trying to learn" (131). Saying nothing more about her lessons, mentioning no church attendance, nor any punishments, she notes her first Christmas at Fort Lewis. The students all receive "a large present," and hers consists of "a new dress, shoes, stocking and underclothes" that made her "very happy, and… proud of them." Mrs. Bob Martin recalls that at home, her "mother had made [her] clothes from flour sacks," not unusual on the reservations at the time, and that as a girl she "hardly wore any shoes or any kind of store-bought clothes." Her present situation she finds more fortunate. "Here at school," she says, "we had plenty to eat, and warm clothes" (131).

Although she begins to comprehend a few English words, and to write a little during her second year at school, she still "did not understand [her] teacher at all," finding "learning… very slow," although the older students helped her (131). Mrs. Bob Martin says nothing more about her second year at school, and soon "it was vacation time again, and the parents began to come for their children to take them home" (131). She, however, "refused to go home. [She] actually wanted to stay" (131). She is not the only student to remain at Fort Lewis during summer vacation. "A man came to the school to recruit boys and girls for summer employment," she says and these students—probably only the girls—"were placed in private homes to work as housekeepers" (131). This does not appear to be part of any formal "placing out" program, although as Mrs. Bob Martin describes her experience, it would seem to have served the purposes of boarding-schools' outings: "I learned a lot that summer," she says, "how to cook, wash and iron clothes and keep the house clean" (131). Perhaps a bit more English as well.

"In the fall," she says, she "went back to school," where the girls now "wore black shoes and black stockings," and "were measured for [their] new dresses," made by "the girls in the sewing class" (131). Aware on this occasion that she is indeed repeating herself, she states that the students "had good clothes to wear and good food to eat" (131). She follows this positive judgment with a description of what she calls an "important incident... in [her] life that [she thinks she] should mention" (132). This "incident" occurred during her third year at school, the year whose beginning she has just described. She notes that "some girls were planning to run away from school," and when they "invited [her] to join them," she agreed. She seems to have been impelled by what is now called peer pressure rather than the desire to resist, for she has expressed no dissatisfaction with conditions at the school, and reflects that she "was foolish to do such a stupid thing." In any case, as events transpire, she "got tired" before the group has gone very far, and the other girls urge her to turn back, because she "was too slow." There are "wolves in the woods ," they tell her, and they "would have to run fast to escape them"; slow as she was, she'd "never make it" (132). The prospect of being caught by wolves persuades her to do as they wish. Climbing a tree, she sees that after all school is not that far behind.

It is while she is up in the tree that she observes "three big boys" from school in pursuit of the runaways. They discover her, pull her down "roughly," and order her to return to the school. This she does. There, in the dorm, she is scolded by the matron and sent "upstairs to bed without any supper." Although she is "very hungry," she says that she "knew [she] deserved the punishment" (132). The following day she is questioned by the school superintendent and his wife about who planned the runaway and where the other girls might now be. She is warned that should she run away again, she would be punished "harder"—she has thus far suffered no worse than a missed dinner—indeed, that she "would be hanged on a tree!" (132). I have seen no mention, apart from Mrs. Bob Martin's here, of returned runaways being hanged, and I hope the threat was an exaggeration. But it has the intended effect; she says, she "believed them" and "did not run away again." As for the other girls, they "never came back" and she does "not know what happened to them" (132). This "important incident" in her life is mentioned no more. The next paragraph begins, "Fort Lewis was a wonderful school, and I learned a lot there" (132). She also continued to work "during summers for families in town, and . . . earned money and learned good things" (132–33).

As her narration approaches its close, Mrs. Bob Martin, having now spoken of her government schooling a good deal, once more mentions that during "the early stages of [her] life [she] was taught the traditional Navajo ways"[2] (133). Then, returning to the subject of schooling, she offers the judgment that "the schools then were far better than they are now." Although "Today's facilities are much better," nonetheless, there is, in her estimate, currently an absence of the "disciplinary rules," which, in her time, "were good for us." Although she has said very little about discipline, she adds, "We knew we had to learn—or else!" (134). She recalls this, it would seem, fondly, and she concludes, saying that she is "always happy to tell about [her] life . . . for the good of [the] young people" (134).

තඥ

Tillman Hadley was born in 1896, although he notes that "When [he] was born, months and years did not mean much to the Navajos" (285). He doesn't know how he got the name Tillman, although Hadley, he says, he got from his grandfather, Laughing Medicine Man, "*Hataalii*" in Navajo. "Anglos had difficulty pronouncing [it] . . . so, they called [him] Hadley" (285). He "was just a little boy when [he] was first enrolled" at the newly built school at Blue Canyon (also known as the Western Navajo Training School), which opened with fourteen students in 1900 on the site of a trading post that had been abandoned in 1889. Hadley says that "If there was a subject to learn or a reason to go to school, [he] never did know them" (285). But he went anyway, and, "After several weeks of school," he says, he "became lonesome and wanted to go home," a familiar response on the part of boarding-school students. Since Blue Canyon, where the school was located, also was "the region that [he] came from," home was not far off. That meant he could wander off every now and again and spend a day going around and eating cantaloupe melons that people in the area had planted (286). Someone "always would take [him] back," someone from school or perhaps just one of the local people, but the "person who did it would have to take along a couple of cantaloupes for [him]. That was the only way [he] would return to school" (286).

His relationship to the school appears to have been casual indeed. He mentions a stocky man named "Mr. Meetham" who was called "Red Mustache" in Navajo. Meetham, he says, "was the superintendent" (286). This was Milton Needham, who had opened the school. "As for the teachers, there were two women," he recalls, along with "some Navajo helpers, and . . . dormitory aides who were Anglos" (286). Girls and boys had separate dorms and the west wing of the girls' dorm contained the kitchen. There were runaways, he notes, "both boys and girls." He follows this recollection with the statement that "We had a jail that was located in the hollow of a rock. It had a pile of dirt around it and wood on top" (286), an edifice somewhat hard to envision. "Pupils were locked in it," he says, surely returned runaways among them. The jailed students "had to stay long enough to cause crying, for crying always could be heard" (286). Unlike Frank Mitchell and Mrs. Bob Martin, Tillman Hadley found that the school "food situation was very poor," although "now and then," he says, "we would have a feast," with food being brought in wagons from Flagstaff. At the time of his attendance, water had to be brought in "from a rocky place . . . in pails" (287), for washing and cooking. He also recalls that firewood was brought to the school to heat water, for it was "steam [that] provided heat in the school dorms" (289).

He speaks of a time when "a bad illness struck the people," and someone, perhaps a doctor (287), gave inoculations. Curiously, Hadley says he has "a scar on his arm where [he] received the medication." This sounds as though it was a smallpox vaccination that he had received, although he says the illness was "Some sort of flu spread among us" (287). If this was indeed an outbreak of flu, it was one that preceded the 1917–18 pandemic. At this point in his narrative, Hadley offers several recollections of life in his youth, although it is difficult to determine which of the incidents he describes occurred at the Blue Canyon School and which among Navajo people living in the general area of the school.

He reflects that, "For education, we really could have learned, but [he] did not notice doing so," because the students "just played games" (289). Hadley says that "Paperwork we did not do because the Navajos did not realize the value of education for many years" (290). As we have seen and will see further, this was certainly not the case with all Navajos, nor is his sense of the shoddy quality of the education provided widely shared. "As for reading materials," Hadley continues, "I don't know what we read," again stating that "we played much of the time." This time he adds that "We could have learned something worthwhile, but, instead, we would steal for boys who were mischievous" (290), older boys who "picked on" the younger boys, pressuring them to petty thefts. "About school again," he says, "I attended in Tuba City for a while," where he "would go to school, and . . . would be able to be at home, too." And "At times, [he] would be absent from school" (290).

His reference to going to school at Tuba City will be confusing to readers unaware that the Tuba City School Hadley now attends is, essentially, the Blue Canyon School he had gone to before. In 1902, the federal government had bought Tuba City, Arizona, on the Hopi Reservation near the village of Moenkopi, from the Mormons, who had established it some thirty years earlier, and in 1902–3, Walter Runke, superintendent of the Western Navajo Indian Agency, moved both the agency and the Blue Canyon School to Tuba City. Although Hadley's Blue Canyon home was about twenty-five miles east of Tuba City, that distance does not seem to have been great enough to prevent him from, as he put it, going to school and being at home, too (290).

Another contributor to Johnson's book is Lee Kansaswood. He does not give his date of birth but he also attended the Tuba City School in the years after World War I (275), a good many years later than Tillman Hadley, and I'll take a moment to note his recollections of it here. Kansaswood speaks of many Navajo people who "moved from Blue Canyon to Tuba City before or after a school was built there" (273), recalling that the "schools had hard times getting the Navajo children to attend. Many parents did not want their children to be away, and the policemen had to go out to the homes and fields to gather young children and take them to school" (274). This does not seem to have been the case with Tillman Hadley, although as we have seen, he was a very reluctant scholar, nonetheless. Kansaswood himself was taken to school at Tuba City not by "the policemen" but by his parents. He remembers "the big bedroom in the dorm" where there "were two beds to a bunk." Because, like most Navajos, he "used to sleep on the ground floor at home," he "fell off the bed a few times for several nights" until he "got used to it" (278). Unlike Hadley, Kansaswood does remember several things about his early education other than playing games and petty theft. He remembers "learning the numbers system; then the ABC's—writing animal names and names of articles of clothing; also arithmetic, spelling and reading." In the fourth grade, he says, he had a Sioux music teacher named "Black Hoop" who had "all the instruments" for the students (278).

The girls, he recalled, "learned to play basketball, while the boys had classes in baseball, football, track, wrestling and boxing" (278). One rationale for the boxing, he says, was that "there might be another war in the near future." It also served "if one boy got in a fight with another fellow." In that event, the "administrators would put boxing gloves on [them], and [they] could fight all [they] wanted." They also "did much running and wrestling every day" (278). He worked in the carpentry shop, although "there weren't enough tools," and learned "to raise crops, and to handle horses and cows.... In geography class [he] learned about the lands and their locations"; in "civics class [he] learned a little about laws" (278). Kansaswood says that he "left Tuba City and attended Fort Wingate High School in New Mexico for a few years." Then, for reasons he does not provide, he leaves Fort Wingate to spend a year at the Sherman Institute in Riverside, California. Kansaswood returned to Fort Wingate for the eleventh grade, and graduated the next year (279). His single year at Riverside, however, was only a little later than Tillman Hadley's attendance there, and I will return to Hadley and his account of how he came to go to California.

Hadley says that at some point during his time in Tuba City, a "young man came around to visit. He had been attending school in California" (290). This young man is Hadley's clan uncle, who, sizing up the situation, tells him that he "is getting out of hand ... getting mischievous. It's not good. Somehow, you should get more education" (290). Reminding his nephew that he has just come from school in California, he advises Hadley to go there as well (290). It's not clear just how long Hadley had been both going to school and also being absent from school in Tuba City, but it must have been several years in that the returned uncle's advice came "around the year 1914." In any case, Hadley decides to heed his advice. "The superintendent's name at my school was Sullivan," he says. (290). This is William T. Sullivan, who resigned the superintendency of the Tuba City school in that same year, 1914, after an investigation by the commissioner of Indian affairs into charges brought against him.

Hadley says that it was the superintendent who "took us down there" (290) from Tuba City, Arizona, to Riverside, California, a distance of more than 500 miles, and thus quite a gesture on Sullivan's part. Hadley "attended

Sherman Indian Institute at Riverside for four years," from the advanced age (but see Max Hanley's account just below) of eighteen to twenty-two. (Sherman, like Carlisle, did not go beyond high school.) Those four years are summed up very succinctly. Hadley says, "At that time, young people did not go to school in the same manner that they do today," for back then, they "were taken care of real carefully, in the fashion of a military school." Although he says nothing more about it, he seems clearly to approve of the "manner" of education at Sherman, stating that "A boy or girl really could learn under that method, and [he] picked up much useful knowledge" (290). This estimate differs considerably from what he had said about Blue Canyon and Tuba City.

So much "useful knowledge" did he pick up that upon his return home he finds that "Our way of living, our land and our everyday doing just did not look right to me" (290), an observation made by many returned students, as we have seen. "There was much common sense in having schools for education," he says, and, although he "hoped for success and improvement among our people ... things would not move because [he] was just by [himself]." He is disappointed to find that "No Navajos around Tuba City could speak English when [he] returned" (291). This is a surprise in that many Navajos had by then attended the Tuba City School. Can they have had as wasteful an experience as Hadley had described? He would hold many jobs after his return home. One of them was that of police officer, something he regards as a great "honor" (295). Tillman Hadley was instrumental as well in organizing various "returned-student organizations" (295).

∞

Born in 1898, Max Hanley was encouraged to attend school by one of his youngest uncles, although his grandmother was opposed to the idea. Time passed, the matter was much discussed, and finally, it was decided that he should indeed go. When he heard the decision, he "became real excited" (31). Hanley does not name the school he attends, although from other things he says, it would seem to be the school at Shiprock. Once there, his "hair was cut short," and his "earrings cut off and given back to him." Then, his "head was shaved, which made it look like melted lard." Told to "take a bath in a white bath tub," he discovers "something that looked like black lard that made a ring in the tub," leading him to conclude that he "must have been real dirty" (31). He is given new clothes that he finds "smelled with a nice aroma. They were blue; and [he] received some underclothes, too, along with shoes that were black, and the soles were hard and felt like boards" (31). This hardly displeases him; to the contrary, he recalls thinking, "Boy, the things I wanted have been given to me." He notes that he "was 18 years old—and happy about starting to school" (31), even at his advanced age for a beginner.

Pretty soon, he says, he "got used to the place," although he "did not understand the white man's language then—not one word" (31). He is put to work milking cows for several months and then "placed in the blacksmith shop." He is growing tall, and because eighteen, his actual age, is too old by two years for the school, his mother sees to it that they "wrote '16 years old' for [him]" (32). As it happens, there is no teacher available for the new arrivals, who "just worked until past Christmas, when a teacher came" (33). Meanwhile, Hanley says, "Whenever the English language was used, [he] would pay close attention." The first words he learns are "yes" and "no," soon followed by "all right" and "okay" (33). He is intrigued when one of the Anglos says, "The sun is shining," asking "one of the boys who understood English" what it meant. The boy explains it to him and also writes it on paper. Hanley "practiced and practiced writing it," and "The sun is shining" becomes "the first thing [he] learned to write" (33). Called on, he goes to the front of the classroom and writes the phrase in chalk. His teacher is proud of him, he says, something he has "always remembered" (33).

He goes home for the summer and returns in the fall: "Now it had turned 1917," he says, "and I had learned a lot" (33). He works again in the blacksmith shop, mastering the craft "really well" (34), and goes back to "the dairy department again." He notes that after "our country got into World War I, hunger was felt by everyone" (34), and he, along with some other student farm workers, keeps back some of the eggs they gather and cook them up out in a grove with bacon and corn. "That was how we continued our schooling," Hanley says, "being constantly hungry." He notes that "hunger and hardship were the reasons why many pupils ran away at that time"[3] (34). When the flu pandemic hit the school in 1918, "a real bad flu," "[w]e had to stay in bed for two weeks until most of us got well again," but "[t]hree persons died" (35). Then school starts up again: "Day after day it was classes and hard work until 4 o'clock"[4] (35).

In 1919, the twenty-one-year-old Hanley is "put into the blacksmith shop again," although there are more and more automobiles in use all around him. As summer approached, he says he "played on a baseball team" (35). The war is over, but an appeal was nonetheless made to the students to "volunteer for the military service." Although Hanley does not explicitly say so, he would seem to have signed up in that he observes that when the time came to depart for "Fort Bliss, Texas," for training, he was ill and in the hospital, and could not leave with the other volunteers. He recalls that "It was July 4 that [he] entered the hospital because [he] noticed that the flags were raised." There, his condition worsens, and, like the seriously ill Don Talayesva, he "started to have dreams" (35). Unlike Talayesva, however, he provides few details. He recalls walking westward with many people with "brand new Navajo blankets... in a green pasture with rolling hills" (36). This is a dream he has again (36), although—once more unlike Talayesva—the dream has no consequences that he mentions. After about a month in the hospital he recovers and moves back to the boys' dormitory (36). It's at this time that a white man comes from California, bringing "some forms which could be filled out if we wanted to go to school there." "Right away," Hanley says, he "signed his name for Sherman Institute, Riverside, California" (36). His age is not an obstacle.

There is an overland trip to Gallup, New Mexico, where Hanley's group is joined by more students bound for Sherman. Because "there were lots of people" (37), he realizes that the "big Gallup Indian Ceremonial" (36), where Kay Bennett would perform some twenty years later, must have been underway. Waiting for the westbound train in Gallup, he sees his first airplane. His group is now made up of students from "three schools put together," more than 300 young men and women. Although he had not described the distribution of new clothing, he notes that their "clothes were dark blue; so we all"—girls as well as boys?—"were dressed something like soldiers" (37). Discovering even some of the older girls crying, he wonders why. "For myself," he says, "I was excited" (37). He describes some sights along the way, then, "just before noontime, [they] arrived at Riverside" (37).

The trip from train station to school is made in cars, while the luggage is transported by some "big trucks." He reckons that the group arrives "at noontime because the students were in line for lunch, looking like military people" (37), girls on one side, boys on the other. Hanley finds the dining room "big in size," and the "Clanging of tableware was loud." There are students from Shiprock already in attendance, and they recognize some of the new arrivals, "for [their] names were called several times" (37). "Those students of the past year," he says, "were the first Navajos to be at Sherman, and we were in the second group. We shook hands with a lot of them" (38).

Only three days later, he says, "the Riverside Fair would begin, and the students were really polishing their shoes and getting ready for it" (38). The entire school goes into Riverside for the Fair, "all riding in the street cars" (38) powered by electricity. Hanley notices "many Anglos, mixed with Spanish, Blacks, and Chinese and members of various tribes of Indians," adding that "We Navajos numbered quite a few" (38).

He is assigned to the laundry, and doesn't mind the work; on Saturdays, he does odd jobs "among the Anglos in town," for which he is very modestly paid. Perhaps because of his age—although Hanley does not say this—he seems to have had no academic instruction at Sherman. Abruptly, we are told that "Another year went by" (38). He returns for one more year, and now he is sent out to work at the Sherman farm, called, he says, "The Indian Farm" (38). He does say that he "was among those who went there to study," but he mentions no classes of any kind. It is not until 1923 that Hanley "returned home," although he does not stay long. His plan to return yet again to Riverside—he is a man of twenty-five now—is undone by "a phone call" that informs him that the school is currently overcrowded, with no room for him (40). Someone from the school at Shiprock advises him to go "to school in West Virginia," where this (unnamed) person has himself studied with "Anglos and Blacks and even some Indians"[5] (40). Then another phone call is received, this time "from a school in Ganado, on the Reservation in Arizona." Told that the school is seeking four students, Hanley decides to attend, noting that it is "just a little way" from his home. Along with two girls and another boy, he travels to Ganado in the snow.

Hanley "spent the winter there—the year of 1923–1924," and the highlight of his stay is that he "learned how to read in Navajo," no small achievement. Also, he says, he "learned how to sing" (40). This almost surely refers to American glee club or choral singing. Then, in August he again "left for Riverside by train. That was in 1924!" This time, when he "started classes"—as I'd noted, he had described no classwork during his last stay at Sherman—he is told that he is "too old for going to school now; you are a grown man." Hanley "kept pleading to let [him] attend" nonetheless, and "they finally agreed" (41). His intention is "to learn a good career," and he pursues several vocations, receiving "certificates... which identified what [he] could do best" (41). That summer he participates in fighting a large California fire, and, rapidly "Another year went by attending Sherman!" (44). When his use of cracked plastic safety glasses while welding causes his eyesight to deteriorate, he "did not go to school for quite a while," and "just worked outdoors" (45). He does not return home until just before Christmas of 1929 (45).

Back home he obtains work as a baker but hurts his back "lifting 100-pound flour sacks and 100-pound bags of sugar" (47). That amount of lifting might hurt anyone's back, of course, but Max Hanley says that in his case the problem began at Sherman. He now tells us what he had not before, that he was on the Sherman football team for two years, and was seriously injured once when he was tackled. He had to quit football then, but later, the heavy lifting he did exacerbated the serious rupture he had sustained. This requires an operation and he is taken to Albuquerque to have it performed (48). Upon his return to Shiprock, he receives a visit from a white man who asks him why he did not finish school, and recommends to him—he is more than thirty-one years old!—that he go back to school in the fall (48). The unidentified man has Hanley's records sent from Sherman, and now he enrolls at the Albuquerque Indian School. He enters the eleventh grade "because at Sherman [he] had just begun the 12th" (48) and, after two years at Albuquerque, he finally completes his high-school education.[6]

During his time at the Albuquerque school, Hanley says that he played in the school band—he doesn't tell us his instrument—and was a member of the "drama group" (48). He travels with the band and the drama group, and notes that the band played at the annual Gallup Inter-Tribal Ceremonial (49), which he had first encountered many years earlier. He "also was a member of the Albuquerque National Guard for two and a half years" (49) and that, too, involved considerable travel.

He speaks of a "white man in Window Rock, and also a lady, who wrote letters to [him]" (49). In one of the lady's letters, he says, she reminded him that he had written, in an essay for an English class at Sherman (how she knew this is open to speculation), that after finishing school he wanted to go "back to [his] own Reservation among [his] own people and be able to help them." She is bringing this to his attention because, as she says, "we need your help now here on the Reservation" (49). I'm not sure what to make of this in that this lady, like the man, seems to be white. "This gentleman and lady," Hanley says, were writing to him because they know that at Albuquerque, he "really got interested in the armed services, wanting to go overseas" (49). This is the early 1930s. Whoever they are, these two appear to be against the idea. They advise him—again, their relation to him is unclear—instead to get married and to have his wife "work at a school by being a housekeeper" (49). He finally does marry a young woman after she graduates from high school in 1935.

By that time, he was already employed by the Bureau of Indian Affairs, for which he did many different kinds of work. One learns this only when Hanley says that "in 1962, [he] was told to retire from the Bureau of Indian Affairs service" (52) having worked there, he notes with great exactitude, "for 32 years, four months, and seven days after [his] schooling" (53). During his retirement he is visited by a "Dr. Gotman" from the University of Michigan, who asks him, as other researchers had asked other Native people, to help with what seems to be a project on Navajo (and Mexican) longevity (53). He works on this for a time, and this leads to his interest in another project. This one, sponsored by the new Office of Navajo Economic Opportunity (53), sought to interview and record the "knowledge, legends and history" of elders "of the western Navajo region" (54), Hanley's own home grounds. He "gathered songs, too." He does this for a couple of years until the "funding ran out, and [they] had to quit the project" (54). He is hopeful that "there will be money available again so that the project can be finished" (54). Making knowledge "about [Navajo] culture,... history,... mythology, and... traditions," available for the "young people who are going to high school and college" (54) is something that at this late time in his life, Max Hanley finds very important.

ката

Myrtle Begay was born in Canyon de Chelly in 1912. Her father was "a medicine man," who "loved her very much"; (56) he died when she was only six. Shortly before his death, her father "placed [her] in boarding school in 1918... because he wanted [her] to get an education" (56). Before speaking of that education, she elaborates on her traditional upbringing, after which she repeats, "I was placed in boarding school when I was five years old. This was a new start in my life. After my father passed away, life changed in our family" (59). But she is not yet ready to detail that changed life so far as it concerned her boarding-school experience. Instead, she recalls stories narrated by her father of "events that had happened many years ago" (59) and also stories told by her mother, all of which serve as narrative lessons in the proper conduct of traditional Navajo life. "All traditional education," she explains, "came to us through actions and lecture" (60), "lecturing" to young people having been mentioned by a number of these Navajo elders as an important instructional modality.

Begay goes on to speak of her marriage and children, and, when her children were old enough, her work for many years as a housekeeper, followed by a position for "the government at the Bureau of Indian Affairs boarding school in Chinle" (62). Perhaps it is her mention of the Chinle boarding school that brings her to say at this point, "I have told you briefly about my education" (62) and then to offer a fuller account of it. She recalls that it was her father who "encouraged [her] to learn English," saying that "'Whatever you learn in school will benefit you in your job.'" It seems clear that by the time of World War I, Begay's father fully understood that wage labor would, in the future, be part of Navajo life. She remembers travelling with her father to school in "a two-horse buggy or buckboard"—almost surely to the boarding school at Chinle—and his telling her "to go to the Roman Catholic Church while in school because the missionaries there instructed the children to be good Christians" (62). That a medicine man and storyteller wants his daughter to be a good Christian once more presents no contradiction. Begay announces that she "stayed in school there for five years," and then goes on to describe some of her experiences during that time.

"At first," she says, "everything was strange," as it was to many Indian children. That initial strangeness probably involved the Clean-Up, a Naming, the Dining Room, and a first encounter in the dormitory with a bed, but she speaks of none of these things. She doesn't "remember what [she] learned that first year," although she does recall "playing with clay" and making "all kinds of silly figurines" (62). The first-year students, she says, "also had crayons with which [they] drew odd pictures in many colors" (62–63). It was only "the following year" that they "began to learn to read and write. First, . . . [the] A B C's," then "short sentences like, 'I see a cat,' 'I see a dog,' and so on." There was "only one matron who looked after all the girls in one dormitory," and "Strict discipline was practiced then. When a girl was naughty she got a spanking with a ruler or a strap" (63). She next recounts an incident that illustrates just how severe such discipline could be.

Begay and some other students are out for a Sunday walk into Canyon de Chelly when one of the girls suggests that a few of them stay behind and hide in an apple orchard. Once the other girls turn back to school, those in hiding emerge and pick some of the apples, which are still small and green. Filling "small terry-cloth bags that [they] had made themselves" with sour apples, they hurry back to school to find that it is past suppertime "and the dorm doors had been locked" (63). They "banged on the doors until the girls' matron heard . . . [and] unlocked the door without a word. . . . When it was time," she says, "we all went to our beds." "Then, everything suddenly became quiet when the matron came in and called [the offending girls'] names. She told us to pull our blankets down and lie on our stomachs. She had a wide strap in her hand. She began whipping us one by one, and we screamed with agony" (63).

Nonetheless, it is Begay's judgment that since they "had broken one of the school's rules . . . [they] all deserved the punishment." Moreover, in this instance the students' "mothers and fathers," when they learned what had occurred, "did not say anything to the matron for strapping us. They all knew we were wrong. It was a good lesson"[7] (63). So good a lesson was it that Begay can attest to the fact that she "never back-talked to [her] teachers or the girls' matron, and . . . learned not to be led into temptation by others" (63), that last turn of speech suggesting that Begay had probably followed her father's advice to seek out Christian teaching.

"In our classroom," Begay recalls, "we learned to keep our desks clean and to be polite to others." Consistent with what she has already said on this matter, she states that although "Discipline was strict," she is "grateful to all of [her] teachers who worked hard to educate [her]" (63). "Our parents wanted us to get an education," she says, "and we learned the hard way" (63). She remembers that when "one of the students got naughty or stubborn in the classroom he or she sat as the 'dunce' in a corner for hours" (63–64) and when "one of us got caught chewing gum the teacher made the student put the gum on the tip of his nose and stand facing the class all day until school was dismissed." She has probably heard similar stories from other Native students, for she states, "All of the government boarding schools were run the same way" (64). Most of them, as we have seen many times, were also run on the military model, but if this was the case at Chinle, Myrtle Begay does not mention it.

In 1923, when she was in the fifth grade, she "was transferred to the Fort Apache Boarding School" (64). She does not say why this change was made. To get to the Fort Apache school, she travels by truck to Gallup, New Mexico, and then experiences her "first train ride" to Holbrook, Arizona, a distance, she precisely notes, of "96 miles by rail" (64). From there, it is truck transport once more to the Fort Apache School. She and the other young people with her arrive in the dark and are "taken to their dormitories and straight to bed, without a meal" (64). In the morning, she looks at the place and finds it "seemed . . . like a desert." Although she has already spent five years at boarding school, now, having "never been that far from home," "Everything was strange," and she "felt very lonely" (64). "That evening," she says, "all the girls [she] came with gathered together. . . [and] sat talking about [their] homes and wept all evening" (64), a familiar scene. Fortunately, Begay says, "After classes began our loneliness disappeared." She "was so involved in [her] lessons that [she] did not have time to be lonely," although often, "in the evenings . . . [she] thought about [her] family and home" (64).

The Fort Apache school at first did not furnish the students clothing, so, Begay says, the girls had to wash their "clothes every evening to have clean ones to wear the following day" (65). Eventually, "the school sewed [them] some new clothing" (65). It's not clear whether these were uniforms and, again, Begay describes no military activities. Nor, for that matter, does she describe a routine based on clock time—bells, whistles, bugles, triangles—which surely was in operation. She joins the school band, another of the many Indian students who took up one instrument or another, and notes that the band traveled with the school's sports teams (65), as was often the case. Having come to Fort Apache in 1923, she does not go home for vacation until 1927, describing almost none of her activities during the summers, nor does she say a single word about what it was like to be home after four years away.

The following summer, she once more chooses to remain at the school, and takes work with a local family as housekeeper. She is the only boarding-school autobiographer I have found to say that "We called this type of work 'outing,'" the term apparently still in use ten years after the closing of Carlisle. Begay's wage on the eve of the Great Depression "was five dollars weekly," a sum that "was a lot of money to [her]" (65). She also worked in the school laundry and, like Max Hanley, did not find that duty as oppressive as some other Navajo students had. She states that she learned to be a good housekeeper at school in the dorm, the laundry, the dining room, the bakery, and the sewing department (66).

She "dropped out of Fort Apache before [she] had finished high school," and says she doesn't "know why [she] never went back" (65). Her last formal relationship to the Indian boarding schools consisted of working for the family of "the school superintendent at Fort Defiance for three years"

(66). It is her opinion "that traditional and Anglo education are similar in many ways. Both teach a student to be independent, to have self respect, to know the facts of life, and so on" (66).

∽

I'll close this consideration of the Navajo elders represented in Johnson's book, with the boarding-school experiences of Paul Blatchford and Hoke Denetsosie. Blatchford was born in 1916 to a Navajo mother (he notes that she had been sent to the Sherman Institute when she was ten years old) and an Anglo father from Superior, Wisconsin. Blatchford was a great grandson of Chief Manuelito, who, he says, "helped mightily in getting the Navajos freed from captivity at Fort Sumner... and returned to their homeland" (173). When he was five, a white man named Mr. Bascher appeared in a Model T Ford. His parents tell him and two cousins who had been visiting "to just take a ride in the car and see if [they] liked it." The three children get in and Blatchford says that he acted as "the interpreter" (174), no doubt having learned some English from his father. After they have gone a ways, his cousins begin to cry, realizing that they "were being hauled away to school somewhere." They are, in fact, being taken "to the Christian School at Rehoboth, New Mexico" (174).

On arriving at the school, they go directly to the dorm to spend their first night. In the morning, they have a wash and, after making their beds as best they can, they hear a bell ring. "The school was a military setup," Blatchford says, and the matron places the boys "in Company C" (175). They are dressed in "Holland military uniforms adjusted to [their] size."[8] They "marched to the dining room ... [their] classrooms ... [and] to church Sunday mornings." An addition to the dormitory has "a small, cellar-type window" through which Blatchford can see two boys. "They were runaway boys, chained to a big iron ball. They told [him] that a punishment for runaways was to be put in jail" (175).

Although they are now aware of the consequences, Blatchford and his cousins run away nonetheless, sleeping "in the open," and hearing "mountain lions" all night (175). They attempt to catch a ride with a passing Model T, only to find that its driver is a state policeman who takes them back to the school. "Corporal punishment was identical at every school," Blatchford says, "whether it was a government or a church mission school." The boys are shown "different lengths and widths of straps." Returned runaways "were told to pull their pants down, lean over a bench and receive 25 straps. Next time they ran away they received more" (175). The boys are not, however, put in the school jail. Blatchford describes other punishments, one of them unique, so far as I am aware, to the Rehoboth school. "Also," Blatchford says, "if one was late for line-ups in going to dinner or to class, one was placed in what they called the belt line. There were two lines facing each other, four feet apart, and the [guilty] person started from one end, running from right to left—and all those who could swing with their right arms, swung their belts at the person. Then he turned back and the other line gave him a strapping" (175).Further, "if anyone wet the bed, he or she had to carry the mattress around in the square between the girls' dormitory and the boys' dormitory—and had to continue to carry that mattress around all day long" (175).

Blatchford details the "general curriculum in the schools... history, arithmetic, English and penmanship." These "were taught the first half of each day while the other half was used to clean up dormitories and perform other jobs if the person was one of the younger students." For the older students, the "school offered vocational training,... and it was taught the last half of the school day" (175). Blatchford makes clear that "The memories of how children were treated—and punished for every little thing they did—made [him] want [his] children to live at home"; "they could attend school nearby," he says, "but not a boarding school or a mission school away from home" (177). At the time of his narration, he was "the counselor for the Public School Board in Tuba City" (177) and he has many interesting things to say about schooling for Indian people. He tells us that after "high school [he] went to the Phoenix Indian School" for vocational training he had not had before (179), only later noting that he had earlier gone to the Albuquerque Indian School, entering the sixth grade and remaining to graduate from high school. He concludes, "That was how education was carried on among the Navajos when I was young; and, in spite of many hardships, harsh discipline and problems that I have discussed, students generally did learn much—and I am glad that I was able to get what was considered a full education at the time" (181).

Hoke Denetsosie was born in the spring of 1920. His "childhood happiness with [his] parents and relatives... living the traditional way in natural surroundings," would be "shattered" when he was "forced to go to school" (78). He recalls the growth of Navajo communities when he was a boy, in particular at Leupp and Tuba City, where boarding schools had been established. "To get full capacity," he says, school authorities "hired young Navajos who had been students and deputized them as school agents and policemen" and sent them out to force parents to send their children to the schools. "In some cases," he says, "they even kidnapped boys and girls" (79). He is warned by his father that before long policemen from the school in Leupp "will be coming to ask for children." He doesn't understand what this means until, in the fall of 1926, "mounted policemen" come and ask his parents how many children they will be sending to school (80). His "grand-mother put up a protest against [his] going to school" (80)—one of many grandmothers who protested—but it is to no avail.

The family attends "an all-night 'Beauty Way' sing," where, in the morning, the police come and assemble some "14 boys and girls, all taller" than Denetsosie, to place them in "two old black Model 'T' Fords." All of the prospective students have long hair, "tied into bundles behind [their] necks." "Just before [they] climbed into the cars," he says, "some of the girls' parents got shears, and cut off the hair bundles and kept them" (81). They travel at "about 15 miles per hour, which [they] thought at the time was quite fast," while some of the fathers ride horses alongside, disappearing on occasion to take short cuts not possible for the automobiles. Having traveled fifty-five miles "on rugged, dusty, unimproved horse and wagon trails," the students arrive at the Leupp Boarding School in the late afternoon. Denetsosie remembers that "Leupp gave [him] the impression of being a big place. And it was just that"; he "never had seen anything like it" (82).

The boys and girls are separated, and he recalls the boys' dorm—the one for the younger boys like him—as "a strange big building." He finds

> an Anglo lady matron... in charge. They cut our long hair off completely, right down to our scalps because some of us might have had lice. After we took showers, we were given new clothes and shoes... the small boys wore blue denim coveralls with red trim around the waist and sleeve cuffs. These were brand new, and we thought they were great, but they were the last new clothes we got. Later we wore clothes that had been laundered a lot... so much that they became threadbare and full of patches. (82)

When it comes time for him to be named, someone suggests Hoke, "after Hoke Smith, a U.S. senator from Georgia." Denetsosie is retained as a surname; it had come from his grandfather "whose name was *Dine Tŝ'osi*" (73) or Slim/Slender Navajo.

Denetsosie is the only one of the Navajo elders in Johnson's book to have attended the Leupp school, and, in his stark and richly detailed memories, it is a grim place.[9] "Conditions at the school were terrible," he recalls. "It was isolated ... Food and other supplies were not too plentiful. We were underfed; so we were constantly hungry. Clothing was not good, and, in winter months, there were epidemics of sickness. Sometimes students died, and the school would close for the rest of the term" (83). Like the other boarding schools, Leupp "was run in a military fashion and rules were very strict" (83). He then gives the schedule for a "typical day." Wake-up is at 6 a.m. to "the sound of bugles." The students washed and dressed and then "lined up in military formation and drilled in the yard." They next formed into companies and "marched to the dining room." There, he says, "we all stood at attention with long tables before us. We recited grace aloud, and, after being seated, we proceeded with our meal. If, during the meal, we got too noisy, an attendant, who was the disciplinarian, usually blew a basketball whistle, and all became quiet. After the meal was finished we went into formation again" (84). And then something unique to Leupp occurs: "One of the boys, who had been selected, rose and took a position where he could be heard, holding a thick sheet of metal about 10 inches square with a rope handle, together with a metal rod. He would "bang" away at this metal, while we kept in step and marched single file out of the dining room, and then back to the dormitories until we were properly dismissed" (84).

Adding to the general unpleasantness at Leupp is the fact, as Denetsosie recalls, that some "teachers and other workers weren't very friendly. When students made mistakes they often were slapped or whipped by the disciplinarian who usually carried a piece of rope in his hip pocket" (85). At last, his family comes to pick him up at the end of the school term in May. Denetsosie wryly notes, "That year was my introduction to so-called 'civilization'" (85). Then, "After two hard years at Leupp [his] folks decided that [he] should go to the Tuba City Boarding School because it was nearer... home. That was in the fall of 1928" (89).

As for the Tuba City School—Tillman Hadley and Lee Kansaswood had been there earlier, as I have noted—[10] Denetsosie "found it not much different from Leupp. Everything was rigid and strict. All students, big and small, had to obey the rules" (90). His description here, too, is full of finely observed (and recollected) details. He remembers that older students were selected not to help the younger ones, as had been the case for Kay Bennett at the Toadlena school, but rather "to assist in seeing that the regulations were enforced" (90). This was particularly hard on the younger children, he notes, "and soon there were runaways" (90), so many that agency police-men are kept "busy hunting them down and returning them to school." The school day ends each weekday at 4 p.m., and the students are allowed to play for an hour. "Then, a bugle called for cleanup, formation, and supper time" (90). As he had done for the school at Leupp, he provides the schedule for a typical day at Tuba City; it is, he says, much the same as at Leupp (90).

He remembers that each "Saturday morning the dorms got a special scrubbing and cleaning for the following week," while in the afternoons "boys were required to get haircuts and shine their shoes for Sunday inspec-tion and church services" (90, 92). He describes considerable preparation for church attendance with both boys and girls cleaning up, dressing for inspection, and assembling "outdoors for a hymn-singing session." Here, too, his description is richly detailed. He describes the boys' "woolen olive-gray-green uniforms styled after World War I, with caps and thick-soled shoes" (92), and the "puttees" worn by the company officers "on their legs from below the knees down to the ankles." Some of the boys "puttees" are too large for them so they "stuff them with white rags to hold them up." "It was comical," Denetsosie recalls, "the way a particular officer would stand out front shouting commands—with swollen-looking legs—while school officials would pass inspection nonchalantly, checking for neatness" (2).

Nor has he forgotten how the girls were dressed. They wore "middies, consisting of white cotton blouses with full-length sleeves and very wide sailor-type collars." Their "skirts were a blue-black scottish type, fully pleated and knee length, worn with black stockings and shoes" (93).

He doubles back to describe the outdoor hymn-singing session on the lawn, where, "after the hymn books were passed around, the group would sing, led by a slim elderly woman who at one time must have been a concert singer." He remembers that "She must have liked to sing because she usually wore a smile after each song" (93). We know well by now that the children may not have understood what they and this woman were singing. "After the singing session the students were marched directly to church—Presbyterian, the only church in the community at the time" (93), he tells us. The church service featured a preacher who went on "for the next two hours ... on righteousness and the evils of sin." Of course, as he observes, "Some of us who did not understand the full meaning of the sermons would get bored and fall asleep." Staying awake is particularly hard because the sanctuary is overheated and the boys are in "tight woolen uniforms" (93).

At least "Sunday dinners were special—about the only decent meals we had," he recalls. There is roast beef or pork and for "dessert ... apple pie, frosted cake, gingerbread or an apple" (93). Unfortunately, "Most of the time," Denetsosie says, "our desserts were not eaten by us." Instead, they are sneaked out of the dining room "in our coat pockets to be given to our captains," who would kick or otherwise punish any boy who held back (94). He also emphasizes the fact that "The school officials ... all practiced various forms of corporal punishment, combined with extra duty for the students" (94) who violated any rule. These "misbehaviors" (94) along with running away, "called for a whipping down in a basement provided for that purpose" (94).

It is in his second year at Tuba City that Denetsosie is diagnosed with trachoma, a disease, he knows, that "was prevalent everywhere on the Reservation" (94). In that "there were no known drugs that would cure it at the time" (94), the "doctors usually scraped the diseased eyelids, which was very painful." In severe cases like his, Denetsosie, observes, "an operation was needed"—something Kay Bennett had also experienced—"with further treatment until the condition was cleared" (94). Nonetheless, his vision "was impaired" (94). Denetsosie completes sixth grade at Tuba City, the school offering nothing beyond that, and in 1932, he transfers to the Phoenix Indian School.

Phoenix is a much larger school than any he has known so far, with "More than 35 tribes of Indians from throughout the United States ... represented ... each tribe speaking a different language." Large as it is, the "school was run in a rather strict and old-fashioned conventional way" (96), for all that there are a great many academic and vocational programs available, along with farm training. There are also, as there had been earlier in Fred Kabotie's time, drama groups, a band, and a national guard company, along with something not available before, movies "called 'talkies' because just about that time talking pictures were new and were reaching their popularity" (96). "For religious services on Sundays," he recalls, there now was "a choice of going to one of the three churches: Protestant, Catholic or Mormon," the last-mentioned not available earlier at the Phoenix school. Denetsosie recalls that he was initially "dazzled" by the sights and sounds of Phoenix, a big city "very different" (96) from what he had known on the Navajo reservation. (See figure 12.)

Otherwise, as he notes, "Dormitory life was nothing new to [him]," and he soon "became adjusted to things—except for the weather" (97). As the Hopi student Edmund Nequatewa had also found, Phoenix "was extremely hot, almost unbearable, from about May to October" (97). Denetsosie does well in his studies, and joins an "art class, in which there were few students." The single art teacher available "wasn't really equipped with the necessary supplies" (97), and no patron like Elizabeth DeHuff shows up to improve matters. Moreover, as he recalls, "No attempt was made to teach us the basics of art . . . so [his] approach was mostly by trial and error." Hoke Denetsosie graduated from "the high school in May of 1938" (97) and, his interest in art ongoing, he "took postgraduate work in it," and "visited local Anglo artists"

12 Undated photograph of the Navajo artist and illustrator Hoke Denetsosie. Photograph by Edward Ellinger. Published in Desert Magazine, 1952.

(97), learning from them, and going on to travel promoting Native art. He continued this work, in 1973 joining "the staff... at Navajo Community College at Tsaile, Arizona, as one of the artists, primarily illustrating... curriculum materials," along with "many books and other publications of the Navajo Community College Press" (99) including this one.

Near the end of his account, he offers several broad reflections on his own schooling. It's his sense that although he learned much, education for Indian children then "was so limited that by the time we left school we were only half prepared to make a living in the dominant world around us." Making things more difficult was the fact that "there was much discrimination and lack of equality, forcing many of us back to our native land" (102) where jobs were few. He concludes by quoting "One of our traditional Navajo leaders." He had said, "Navajo schools should strive to prepare their students for life in the modern world, while, at the same time, keeping the best of Navajo tradition and culture." It's Denetsosie's view that this "is wise and fitting" (102). Hoke Denetsosie died in 2016.

11

George P. Lee's
Silent Courage

GEORGE P. LEE WAS BORN IN THE AREA OF SHIPROCK, ARIZONA, IN 1943. HIS parents were "full-blooded Navajos" (3), he writes, his father receiving the name Pete Lee during his brief service in the army during World War I (3). Neither of his parents had any formal education and both lived a traditional life, his mother herding sheep, chopping firewood, and tending to "all the household cleaning and chores" (3), his father active as a hand trembler—a diagnostician—a medicine man, and a wage laborer when he could get work. His father also dealt with alcoholism most of his life, something Lee several times discusses with great sympathy. ("My father and I were close" [41], he wrote early in his book.) Like many Navajo people, Lee's parents suffered considerably from the livestock reduction program of the 1930s. He writes that "both [his] father and mother have painfully recounted their story to [him]. Their stories of the reduction are bitter and bewildering" (6). Lee's childhood was marked by poverty. "During the first nine years of my life," he writes, "we moved back and forth between our winter hogan and the summer hogan. About the only variation in our life-style was when we left to do migrant work" (11). And, too, as he writes, "There were numerous times . . . when racial prejudice was added to poverty" (21). Summing up his childhood, he observes that "As a boy [he] spoke only Navajo, except for a few English words. . . . [He] ate as a Navajo, thought as a Navajo, and behaved as a Navajo" (40). Reflecting on this time some forty years later, he asserts, "My Navajo roots were strong and would provide stability in the years to come" (40).

Lee attended the Shiprock Boarding School in Arizona for two years in the early 'fifties, next attending a school with Anglo students in Aztec,

New Mexico (96). He eventually went on to graduate from Orem Junior and Senior High School in Utah, and then to receive his bachelor's degree from Brigham Young University. He completed a master's degree at Utah State University before returning to BYU to take a doctorate in education. Of those Native students whose accounts of their boarding-school experience we are considering, Lee, who died in 2010, had by far the most formal education. Nonetheless, as I have quoted him, throughout his life, his "Navajo roots were strong" (40).

George Lee sought to integrate the strong Navajo roots developed early in his life with his later education as a mainstream American (although his strong Mormonism put him at a slight tangent to the mainstream), becoming, like Irene Stewart and Kay Bennett, among others, a different kind of Navajo than his parents had been. With the exception of Kay Bennett (her husband, Russell, may have participated in her book's composition), Lee is the only one of the boarding-school students we have considered to write his book entirely on his own, and both his extensive education and his Navajo roots may on occasion be seen in the manner of its composition.

This is the case in chapter 8 of *Silent Courage*, called "Government Boarding School." The chapter opens in the middle of the night. Lee writes that "The snoring of the boy in the bunk next to [his] was not what kept [him] awake" (85). Awake in his bunk, he "did not even know what time it was" (85). Lee begins the chapter with a statement of two negatives, something self-conscious writers might do but oral narrators do not. (I'll explain further.) He next recalls that "it seemed . . . [he] had been in this place forever," offering an abstraction, "forever," as a measure of time, once more something one does not find in oral narration. What is keeping Lee awake is his "homesickness" and "loneliness" (85). He explains that "No matter how much [he] tried to get home off [his] mind, [his] homesickness only intensified" (85). He then generalizes, "Rules. Rules. So many rules," and compares the strict routine of boarding-school life to "the almost absolute freedom [his] parents allowed at home" (85). "[A]lmost absolute" is an error, just as "very unique" would be, both absoluteness and uniqueness by definition taking no qualification. But the phrase conveys Lee's thought about degrees of regimentation and freedom he has known, in a manner typical of a literary writer.

Consider the very different manner in which someone like Frank Mitchell, for example, might have narrated these nocturnal events. The oral narrator might say, "I was so lonely and homesick that I remained awake late at night," offering positive statements, the condition of wakefulness not being presented as the absence of sleep. He might continue, "It was about midnight or later and the boy next to me was snoring. I had been in this place maybe three months, maybe more," the latter rough estimates of actual, periods of time. Then, finally: "Every day here we had to do the same thing at the same time. When I was home, we did things differently. I felt free."

Lee the writer continues, recalling that the dormitory walls were "bare, smooth, and cold" (86), and once more wishing that sleep would come. Although he "felt like crying aloud" (86), he does not, sure that his crying would be met, like "almost everything [he] had done so far . . . [with] either censure or ridicule" (86). Or worse: as the "stink of the inadequate facilities wafted across the room," he thinks of "the big bully a few bunks down, the one who had beat [him] up earlier that evening" (86). Bare, smooth, and cold more or less parallel rules, rules, rules; having odors "waft" is a literary choice. (In English, of course; an oral narrator might also employ a particularly vivid term in his or her own language to convey the movement of the "stink.")

He explains that the students "had all been made to take showers that night" (86). Lee is in his first year at Shiprock, and he doesn't say whether the showers the students were made to take the night before were like any initial Clean-Up he may have experienced. Nor is it clear whether what he will describe as taking place just after the showers on that particular night had also happened other times during this first year at school. In this instance, Lee's presentational manner is indeed more nearly that of the oral storyteller. (Although the word "literally" in the next sentence is writerly.) Lee writes, "All of us had literally been forced in, two per shower. Some of the older teenage boys made fun of us younger ones. I was just nine years old" (87).

Other than noting the extremely unsanitary condition of the showers, Lee describes no more than teasing having occurred. The showers, in any case, are not the important event of that night. After the shower, he dresses in "those green-colored overalls again," the apparel of all the boys "whose parents couldn't afford to buy [them] new clothes" (86). Apparently referring to his present wakefulness—it is the frame for these recollections—he feels his "eyes beginning to puff and swell," and then his bruised left "eye started to throb" (86). This returns his thoughts to the previous night when the "older boys had lined us up after bed check," with "the younger ones . . . commanded to stand at attention" (87). The "meanest one" demands money, "hitting and shoving to prove he meant business" (87). When approached, Lee truthfully states that he has none because his mother had had no money to give him. For this, he receives a punch in the eye: "Things went black... [he] hadn't seen the menacing fist coming" (87). His older brother Joe is there as well, but Lee forces himself not to "glance at Joe, or [he] might cause something to happen to him" (87). "None of us," he writes, "dared tell on them to the dormitory attendant. Some had registered complaints before, but nothing was done" (87). The bullies use the money they have extorted "to buy luxury items at Saturday visits to the trading post. The food was bad at the dorm mess hall," Lee explains, "so they bought bread, bologna, candy, cookies, and pop" (87). Max Hanley and Thomas Clani's earlier accounts of the Shiprock school (see above) had also noted the poor quality of the food.

A bit later, Lee, reviewing this "first year at boarding school" as "not the most promising experience" (88), mentions his involvement in fights "not of [his] own choosing" (88–89), two more descriptions by negative instantiation, and "rough initiations from the older boys" who "wanted the younger students to know quickly who was in charge" (89). It's at this point that he turns back to describe the day he and his brother Joe first arrived at the Shiprock school and underwent an initiation "into the bare"—like the walls of the dormitory—"reality of boarding school" (89). "As they had done to other incoming children"—so he must have heard or assumed—"the older boys," he writes, "lured Joe and me into a dark, isolated room. They led us on with kind words feigned [*sic*] in false friendship. Being naïve and trusting, Joe and I went. Once in the dark room, they beat us badly, telling us that we had better understand who the real bosses were. And, they promised, if we told any teacher or supervisor about getting beat up, our next brutal session with them would be worse than the first" (89). The unidiomatic verb, "feigned," seems to have been chosen for alliterative purposes with "false" and "friendship." At any rate, it seems sure that Lee has been beaten up more than once since that first day. Earlier, he had noted that because he was an excellent marbles player, if he had no money to give the bullies, he could usually buy them off with marbles he had won (88). He says nothing more about these brutal older boys here, turning to an account of the reg-imen at Shiprock, the rules, rules, rules. Meanwhile, on the basis of Lee's description of enticement into a "dark and isolated room" and the fetid yet bare dormitory, of his depiction of an earlier occasion when the bullies "grin sadistically" (87) as they ate what had been purchased with stolen money, and of the absence or utter irresponsibility of adult supervision, I will guess that a measure of sexual abuse of the younger boys by the older ones also occurred, constituting on one occasion or another a different order of initiation. Nothing of the sort is mentioned and of course no such abuse may have taken place. It is also possible, however, that Lee is reticent in this regard at least in part because of his strong commitment to Mormonism.

For Lee was an Elder and held high office in the Church of Latter-day Saints at the time he wrote his book, and I will close this section with the important change in his relation to the LDS Church that occurred just two years after the book's publication in 1987. Meanwhile, let us note that he was already a Mormon when he arrived at the Shiprock School at the age of nine, having taken the religion of George Bloomfield, the man who ran the trading post at Mancos Creek, Colorado.[1] It is only toward the end of his "Government Boarding School" chapter that Lee writes of these things, offering them out of chronological order, perhaps in a more nearly oral than literate manner.

Lee writes that perhaps a year earlier, "The Bureau of Indian Affairs superintendent of the [Shiprock] boarding school had been to the trading post. He had asked George Bloomfield... if he would help the government by persuading local Navajos... to sign their children up for school" (93–94). Bloomfield must not only have agreed, but also been successful in persuading Lee's parents to do so. For, Lee writes, "The same day that Mr. Bloomfield, the Mormon trader, signed Joe and me up for boarding school, we were also signed up for religion, that is religion other than the Navajo religion" (93). How the parents were persuaded to sign their sons up is not explained, nor is the occasion when Bloomfield brought the papers for school attendance specified. But the papers, Lee tells us, have boxes for religious choice—"other than... Navajo religion"—and when Bloomfield asks Lee's mother which box to check, she answers that she thinks whatever Bloomfield's religion is "will be the best" (94). He replies that there is no box for his religion, "but [he] will write it on here." "In this manner," Lee says, "I unofficially began to be a member of The Church of Jesus Christ of Latter-day Saints"[2] (94).

Lee's next paragraph begins, "When Mr. Bloomfield came to our hogan that day, mother said something about going to school. In filling out the papers, it was necessary to show English names" (94–95). This once more replicates an oral narrator's manner of repetition with variation, as Lee returns to an event that he has already described, although only in part. This is to say that the choice of English names for the school papers would have been made before or, more likely, on the same day as checking the box for religion. He continues, "Joe got his English name then"—its origin is not explained—and "George Bloomfield asked Mother if it would be all right to name [Lee] after himself. She nodded her approval, and [he] became George Lee" (95). I will guess that it is only after this naming that the matter of choosing a religion is broached; but, again, that decision has already occurred in Lee's narration. The only naming done at the school, which Lee and his brother, Joe, attend just a week later (95), is the addition of the middle letter "P." Because "there were already four George Lees" enrolled at the school, and because Lee's "birthday was in March, [he] received the middle name *Patrick*, after St. Patrick's Day" (95). He then writes, "For my two first English names, I'm indebted to George R. Bloomfield, the kindly Mormon trader. To the United States government, I owe my first taste of formal schooling and my middle name" (95).This is a somewhat convoluted way—writerly but not gracefully so—of saying that although Lee would not have had a middle name if the boarding school had not needed a way to distinguish him from the four other George Lees, the name Patrick as well as the name George did not come from the school but from George Bloomfield.

We may return to Lee's further description of his first year at school; thus far it has not been pleasant. After noting that the Shiprock school "did not have much playground equipment," leading the boys—he mentions no girls at the school, although there were girls in attendance—to amuse themselves by playing tag or playing marbles (88), he suddenly steps back to offer an assessment of the "government boarding school historically" (88). He states accurately that their aim had been "to remove [Native people] from the supposedly uncivilized Indian world and teach [them] to appreciate the white man's way," and he continues, "According to boarding-school policy, the Indian was to be assimilated into mainstream America. Ignored was the thought of Navajo language and culture" (88). This is 1952, and, as we have seen with Polingaysi Qoyawayma, Fred Kabotie, and others, at least from the time of the Meriam Report (1928) and John Collier's tenure as Indian commissioner (1933–45), many of the government schools did allow the pedagogic use of Native culture, and by the 1940s, several were also using bilingual and Native language materials.[3] Nonetheless, from Lee's description of Shiprock thus far, it had not at all benefitted from the reforms to the old assimilation model.

Just as students did at Carlisle, Lee writes, so too at Shiprock, "we marched everywhere in military fashion," despite the fact that Commissioner John Collier had put an end to the military model at the boarding schools in the 1930s. "Wherever we went," Lee recalls, "we were told not to get caught speaking Navajo" (89). For this, one would have his "mouth ... washed out with frothy, lye soup [*sic*]" (89), and Lee's "was washed out several times that first year." "Not only was [his] mouth washed out with soap, but many times [he] was forced to stand and stare at a blank wall for hours on end" for unnamed infractions. If the students "used English improperly, such as incorrect grammar, [they] had to wear a sign around [their] necks that said 'Dummy.' If [they] broke any dorm rules, [they] were punished" (89). In a strong critique, Lee says that having been caught "speaking [his] own beautiful language, [he] was called stupid. Soap eating and being called stupid were the daily menu around the government boarding schools in those days" (89). Certainly that menu was still in service at Shiprock.

Shiprock is also something of a throwback in that, as Lee writes, "All of the teachers were Anglos." He says that official policy "in all the reservation government schools" was "regimentation and punishment, including corporal punishment such as spanking with hard, brutal, wooden paddles" (89). But shortly after the publication of the Meriam Report, Indian Commissioner Burke, as I have noted (see introduction), "issued Circular #2526 ... forbidding corporal punishment altogether at Indian schools" (Trennert 1989, 605). By the early '50s, it was allowed to some extent and obviously was in force at the Shiprock school. (Thomas Clani had described it earlier at Shiprock, although Max Hanley, also a student there, had not.)

"Instruction was stiffly formal," Lee writes, "Even the rows of runner chairs were nailed to the floor" (90). As had been the case in many of the boarding schools in the past, Lee says that the teachers at Shiprock were poorly trained, and more interested in "the dollar and not the Navajo." He is well aware, however, that these teachers are in fact very poorly paid (90). "There was no library," he observes, and outside the classroom or work assignments—these, too, seem to have replicated the nineteenth-century model—"there was no supervision"; "[o]ften fights and brawls broke out easily because of the sparse supervision." The days full of rules, rules were "highly organized," Lee writes, "leaving enrollees little time to be on their own" (90), although there was sufficient time, it would seem, to engage in fighting. The routine is "bed making, kitchen detail, and cleaning" before classes, the students having risen "before the sun every day, only not to a kind father's voice, but instead to the clanging" of what he calls "some regulated bell" (90). Clock time is unrelenting: "Our whole day," Lee writes, "was regulated by bells, clear until bedtime" (90).

"The kitchen and dining room were poorly equipped. Meals were eaten in silence along [*sic*] unadorned mess tables" (90), Lee recalls. Although students' parents had had to check off a Christian religion for them, he mentions no grace being said at meals. (Lee will describe religious observances at the school later.) "The fare was usually government surplus food and lumpy powdered milk" (90), considerably worse than what students of some other schools had described. Yet "Sometimes after the meals, we were searched to make sure that uneaten, unpalatable food was not taken out." Would students actually try to take out food that was "unpalatable?" "The boarding-school matron oversaw us to make sure we cleaned our plates" (90), Lee writes, but why this is so is also unclear. While the regular fare may have been "unpalatable," occasionally the students were served a good dessert (90). Unfortunately, they do not get to enjoy the desserts, the bullies insisting that these be smuggled out for their consumption. Lee nonetheless observes that "even though [the food] was poor, it was generally far better than the food at home," better in quantity, I would guess, not quality. "Many of us, when first brought into the school, were very thin because food was scarce at home," he says, and "Most of us went home in spring looking much healthier" (90). When parents visited, "they usually brought some home-cooked food to give us a change from the food we ate at school" (91), something other visiting parents had done.

"In spite of the negative experiences during that first year," Lee writes, "there were also a lot of positive experiences." Other than that he "learned a lot of English" (91), however, Lee does not name a single one of those "positive experiences," noting only that the students "counted the days until school would be out" (91). It would seem that he and his brother went directly home when school was out, but there is no mention of what they did during the summer; the "second year of boarding school" begins in the sentence immediately following the one that announced school was "out" (91). This second year "repeated many of [their] first year's experiences" (91), and Lee and his brother decide to run away. Lee speaks of "friends who had run away but were caught by the Navajo police and brought back" (92), but he does not describe the punishments they surely endured after being returned to the school. He also has heard "stories of others who ran away during the winter months but never made it. They froze to death in their efforts to reach home" (92). Nonetheless, he, his "brother, and a few of [their] friends... had a plan to run away while everybody was asleep one night" (92).

"At the appointed time," the boys "quietly got out of bed and dressed. [They] then crept down the stairs and out of the dormitory into the cold night" (92). It is perhaps late fall or early winter. "Once outside, [they] slid quickly through the fence and into the fields" (92). As "the others hurry ahead," Lee has "a feeling that what we were doing was not right." The sentence continues, "so my brother Joe and I turned back" (92). Joe is the older, but, it would seem, he here follows the lead of the younger George—who suddenly does not "feel" that running away "was ... right!" But there is a great deal more about this decision that the literary reader would like to know. Who were these friends, and were they the ones who instigated the attempt to run away? Was there something that moved them to go just when they did (although the school is bad enough to tempt anyone to run off at any time)? And how curious that George Lee, very much aware of himself as a Mormon, had not "felt" that running away "was not right" until immediately after he began the attempt. Nonetheless, the episode concludes simply, "Not long after we had silently crept back inside and gone back to bed, we noticed that the others did not come back" (92). However, a "few days later, some of them were brought back to the boarding school by the police. A lesson was learned," Lee writes in the passive voice, "it was useless to run away" (92). His own decision ultimately not to do so, of course, had been brought about not by the recognition of the "uselessness" of the act but by the recognition that it "was not right." In any case, we are again not told of the punishment surely meted out to the students who were brought back. (Thomas Clani had earlier told of these things at Shiprock.)

Lee next describes a terrible accident that kept him in the school hospital for six months (93), during which time "Mother visited [him] there," and "wanted to have them release [him], to take [him] home for a healing ceremony, a sing" (93). He tells her that he would prefer to remain in the hospital, in which he recovers and from which he is finally released (93). He turns next to a review of his boarding-school experience thus far, observing that he does not "intend to be too critical of the conditions in the early boarding schools. Perhaps these conditions were not found in every boarding school. They probably did the best they could under difficult circumstances" (93). Of course his critique has not focused on the "early boarding schools"— we could date those to the period from around 1879 to 1928 or 1933—but on the Shiprock school of the early 1950s, a time which may seem "early" enough, looking back as Lee is from the mid-1980s. Although he is generous in his acknowledgment that the schools often worked "under difficult circumstances," he seems to have forgotten his earlier insight that the "government boarding school historically has had one thing in mind for the Indian child—to remove him from the supposedly uncivilized Indian world and teach him to appreciate the white man's way" (88).

As for doing the best one can under difficult circumstances, Lee notes a "dedicated" teacher with whom he studied, someone "who, though lacking in professional preparation, instinctively knew how to develop desirable behavior in us without overcontrolling, punishing, or regimenting," and who "inspired the students with a desire to learn" (93). This man or woman would appear to be the exception; Lee makes quite clear, for example, that he "had another teacher who told us in class that none of us would ever amount to anything, that Indians were all destined to fail in life" (93). Nonetheless, he begins his next paragraph stating that "Looking back, [he] is now very grateful for [his] experiences in boarding school." Like many other boarding-school students, he finds that "In a way, the old-time disciplinary program was effective," and that even the "policy of not speaking [his] own native language was beneficial in that [he] was forced to learn English" (93). One can easily imagine, however, that he might have learned English without having his mouth washed out with soap for speaking his own "beautiful language."

With no transition, Lee here returns to the day that "Mr. Bloomfield, the Mormon trader, signed" him and his brother up for the school and the Mormon religion, and gave him his name. After this brief flashback, Lee describes the practice of religion at the Shiprock school. He writes that "various churches were allowed to instruct the children, usually once during the week and again on Sunday morning." He recalls that "out of the three to four hundred students enrolled, [he] and [his] brother were the only ones signed up to attend The Church of Jesus Christ of Latter-day Saints" (95). Although his brother "chose . . . to attend church with his friends," Lee "decided to stick with the Mormons." This meant that "he endured much ridicule from [his] friends about the strangeness of the LDS church." Each Sunday, after the others had gone off, he waited until "someone from the local LDS branch picked [him] up for Sunday school" (95). Although he "thought about changing . . . religion to be with [his] friends and escape ridicule" (95–96), he nonetheless "decided to stick with the Mormons" (96). He writes that among them, he had "kind, loving, and understanding" religious teachers who "nourished within [his] soul the first seed of understanding of this new religion that would someday bring blessings and direction to [his] life" (96). After his two years at Shiprock, Lee would enter the fifth grade, an advance of two grades, at a school in Aztec, New Mexico; his "brother Joe decided to stay home and not go to school again" (96).

Lee concludes his chapter on boarding school with his baptism into the LDS church "in the summer of 1954." He writes, "All in all, the boarding-school experiences thrust me into new and different encounters. Though I had been degraded as a human being, I had found new life in a religion that was to play a major role in my future" (97). However much the boarding school may have tried to do the best it could, thrusting him into new and different encounters, his overall estimate of his experience—stated quite matter-of-factly—is that he "had been degraded as a human being" (97). His new religion did indeed "play a major role in [his] future" (97), but it did not derive from his boarding-school education.

Lee went on to become an Elder in the LDS Church, when he was called, in 1975, to become a member of the First Quorum of the Seventy, the first Native American to hold a position as "general authority." But in 1989, after several public clashes with Church policy, he was excommunicated. Lee claimed that his problems arose from doctrinal disagreements, and the Church's withdrawal of support for Native American outreach programs. The LDS Church does not comment on internal matters, but in 1993, the Salt Lake *Tribune* reported that Lee's excommunication also involved the Church's having learned that in 1989 he had molested a twelve-year old girl, something Lee had strongly denied at the time. In 1994, however, he pleaded guilty to the charge in court. His autobiography, published in 1987, concludes before these events occurred.

George P. Lee, as I have noted, had a great deal of formal education. In view of that, it is hard to say just what part those two early years at the Shiprock boarding school played in his life. As we have seen, he was, on the one hand, grateful for what he learned at boarding school, but, on the other, felt it had degraded him as a human being. His Navajo roots, as he had written, were indeed strong, and he worked diligently on behalf of his Navajo people, although he did so, to be sure, as a devoutly committed Mormon for as long as he was able.

APPENDIX A: THE ORAYVI SPLIT

THE FOLLOWING ACCOUNT OF THE SPLIT DERIVES FROM A NUMBER OF
sources. First, I cite briefly from documents produced by whites present at the time in either an official or unofficial capacity. For Hopi accounts, I turn to Edmund Nequatewa (2008/1936) and Emory Sekaquaptewa, Jr. (1972), both of whom offer detailed depictions of these events. What Don Talayesva had to say on these matters, both in *Sun Chief* and later in his life, Albert Yava's comments, and the few words devoted to the subject by Fred Kabotie are referenced as well. Still useful is Mischa Titiev's *Old Oraibi* (1944). Titiev knew Nequatewa's account, and he also, as I said above, knew Talayesva well. Finally, the accounts later provided by Peter Whiteley, 1988a and 1988b, and, definitively, 2008, are cited. These are all consistent with those of earlier writers.

On September 9, 1906, only two days after the Split, Keam's Canyon School and Agency Superintendent Theodore Lemmon wrote a long letter to the commissioner of Indian affairs in which he stated that "Tawaquaptewa and his men . . . informed me that it was a Hopi prophesy that all this would come about and that whichever party was vanquished must leave the village and the Hopi country forever. That they must go far to the north to the land of 'Ka-weis-ti-ma,' told of in their religious songs" (in Whiteley 2008, part 2, 996). A bit later, on September 18, 1906, a man named A. M. Woodgate, identified only as a "witness," offered a "Statement" in which he began by noting that he "was in Oraibi at about 9 a.m. on the morning of Sept. 7," and concluded by saying, "From all I can learn from the Hopi the dispute has to do with their own religion and nothing to do with the US School as most people think" (in Whiteley 2008, part 2, 1,014).

Emory Sekaquaptewa, Jr., writes that Loololma, Tawakwaptiwa's uncle and his predecessor as leader of the Bear Clan, "saw himself as the last traditionally ordained chief at Oraibi, fulfilling the prophecy that all *wii wimi* (. . . cultural practices, but more narrowly . . . only religious practices) would be 'put to rest' at Oraibi" (247). Indeed, Albert Yava's sense of the matter was that "Tawaquaptewa proclaimed the end of Oraibi's ceremonial life" (116). Fully to grasp the meaning of the Split, as E. Sekaquaptewa writes, requires an understanding "that the division itself was the substance of the prophecy... [which] held that such a division was necessary to the survival of the Hopis as a people... [and] that the sanctity of the religious authorities had become subject to more and more abuse as Oraibi grew in size and social complexity" (247). Kookop or Fire Clan chief "Yukeoma and his followers," Sekaquaptewa confirms, "were to seek and resettle Kawestima ["a ruin in a canyon near Navajo mountain," (Nequatewa 2008/1936, 64) and an ancestral home of the Hopi people] after their ejectment [*sic*] from Oraibi" (248).

Loololma, who had been hostile to the Americans before a trip to Washington in 1890, appeared to reverse his position after it, entering into agreements with government officials. These were, in Sekaquaptewa's view, essentially "an instrument to dramatize the conflict" (E. Sekaquaptewa, 248) between himself and the leaders of the Hostile faction, as much or more nearly strategic moves as expressions of deep conviction. As Whiteley makes clear, citing Nequatewa and Sekaquaptewa, "the Hopi analysis" of these events highlights "the conspiracy of political leadership; the established practice of leaders manipulating the people to unwittingly fulfill clandestine plans; and the element of self-sacrifice on the leaders' part—in effect, planning their own demise or the demise of their positions of authority" (1988b, 260) to fulfill their understanding of prophecy, and to serve the best interests of the Hopi people. As a Hopi consultant from Bacavi—a village formed by a group of Hostiles who had left Hotevilla—told Whiteley, "All the chiefs agreed and it was decided on in good faith and with no ill feelings toward each other. Yukioma agreed to lead one group out of Oraibi, and in this way he would fulfill his clan's prophecy of return to their ruins at Kawestima" (1988b, 257). Indeed, Whiteley continues, as several "of the whites present reported later... many of the Hostiles did not resist expulsion from the village as they believed this was the fulfillment of prophecy... apparently knowing that despite all the public commotion, the deeper meaning of the events concerned the age-old prophecy about splitting the village" (1988a, 56).

On the night of September 6, 1906, both parties, Friendly and Hostile, met long into the night (Nequatewa 2008/1936, 65; Whiteley 1988a, 52). But as Whiteley's Hopi consultant stated, "Yukioma had a change of heart: he refused to go on his own and carry out his promise. Some of us who knew little of the plan between Loololma [he had died in 1904], Tawaquaptewa, and Yukioma saw the bitterness as real" (1988b, 257). This particular "change of heart" gave rise to two physical struggles on Friday, September 7. Early in the morning of the 7th, Tawakwaptiwa "made his request four times [a Hopi pattern number] of the hostile party. Each time he asked them if they would be willing... to leave of their own free will.... But each time Yukioma said he would have to be forced to move out" (Nequatewa 2008/1936, 65). Finally, one of Tawakwaptiwa's men grabbed Yukiwma and threw him from the house, while the other "men in the house [of the Friendly party] just kept throwing men out... until they had emptied the house" (Nequatewa, 65) of all the Hostiles. The men and the Hostile women who were then driven from their homes, "assembled a little to the northwest of the village," where they "were periodically charged upon by groups of Friendlies trying to force them to move on" (Whiteley 1988b, 109).

Titiev wrote that "by late afternoon on September 7, 1906, the two sides found themselves facing each other on the level ground just outside the northeast corner of the pueblo. Yokioma shouted to his followers, and both sides paused to hear what he had to say" (1944 86). Then, Titev continues, with "his big toe trailing in the sand, the Hostile leader drew a line running east and west. To the north of it... he grouped his own men, while the Friendlies clustered together south of the line with their backs to the village" (1944, 86).

The question of "the line," like much else, has been represented differently in a number of accounts. Lemmon's letter of September 9 stated that on the afternoon of the 7th, "in accordance with the prophesy two lines were drawn upon the ground about fifty feet apart and Yukioma took his stand half way between them. If the friendlies could push him over the line back of him he and the other unfriendlies must go; but if he and the unfriendlies could push the friendlies over the line in front of him the friendlies must leave Oraibi and go on their wanderings" (in Whiteley 2008, part 2, 997).

This may or may not be what Field Matron Miltona Keith of the Oraibi Day School was referring to in her letter of 9/16/1906.[1] Keith wrote that on September 7, "A long discussion followed between the two factions. The unfriendlies said they knew somebody had to go for it is a prophecy but each wished the other to go. Finally Yukeoma drew another line and said that which ever party was put across should go" (in Whiteley 1988a, 57; 2008, part 2, 1,004, with some variant spellings and some underlining).

Not only do we have an Anglo eyewitness to the events testifying that Yukiwma drew not one but two lines in the sand, but there is also the statement of Don Talayesva, a Hopi eyewitness, to Harold Courlander in the late 1960s or early '70s that "about three o'clock [Yukioma] made four lines on the ground and then he said . . . If you push us over the four lines we are the ones to leave" (in Yava, 149). It has also been said that Yukiwma (or someone else) drew one or two lines not in the sand but, rather, in sandstone rocks. Elizabeth Stanley, principal of the Oraibi Day School, in a letter of September 18, 1906, wrote of this, "I am told that they drew two lines on the rocks parallel to the city and agreed that the party first pushed across the lines, must go away" (in Whiteley 2008, part 2, 1,015).

Having read through all the early documents and later testimony, Whiteley writes that "in the afternoon [of the 7th] Friendly leaders, with Tawaquaptewa at the head, went out . . . and stood by a line Yukioma had drawn in the sand with his toe" (1988a, 56). It is then that the pushing match ensues with Yukiwma and the Hostiles put over this single line. As Titiev had written, "Forward and back went the opposing groups until at last Yokioma was conclusively forced well over the line, towards the north, away from the town" (1944, 86). Titiev continues, "That night the Hostiles made camp at Hotevilla, a place seven miles north of Oraibi, where there were known to be excellent springs" (86), and in time, "Hotevilla became the site of a Conservative pueblo" (87).

Yukiwma's words on that day were preserved by "a memorial of the event . . . inscribed on a flat rock" (Titiev 1944, 86) that included pictographs representing the clans of the Friendly (Tawakwaptiwa, Bear Clan) and the Hostile (Yukiwma, Fire Clan) leaders. "The legend reads, 'Well it have to be done this way now that when you pass me over this line it will be DONE'" (Titiev 1944, 86). These words in English apparently represent what Yukiwma had said in Hopi. But the memorial inscription also includes a line drawn in the rock, and the date September 8, 1906, both of which have caused some confusion. Was this the line that the opposing sides took as a significant marker and across which Yukiwma was pushed? And is the pushing match to be dated as actually occurring on September 8, 1906, or is the 8th simply the date of the memorial?

Mary-Russell Ferrell Colton, working with Edmund Nequatewa, had written that the *inscription* had been "cut into the rock by Silena, one of Youkioma's men" (2008/1936, 137, my emphasis), but that the "*line* must have been drawn by Youkioma before the day of the battle" (2008/1936, 137, my emphasis). This is surely mistaken, regardless of which day the "battle" itself took place. Don Talayesva reported Yukiwma making "a line on the rock" (116) on the day of the pushing match, which, in *Sun Chief,* he gave as the September 8 (115), a date he would repeat in the account he later gave to Harold Courlander (in Yava, 149) and also in an interview in *Southwest Crossroads,* July, 1970. September 8 is also the date given by Albert Yava (113), and Fred Kabotie said that he'd "read that the date was September 8, 1906" (4). Quite recently, that is the date for the pushing match given by Matthew Sakiestewa Gilbert (2005, 3; 2010, 51) and by some of the Hopi people he interviewed in his DVD, *Beyond the Mesas* (2007).

Mischa Titiev had many years before cited Commissioner Francis Leupp's 1906 document, "specifically" giving "September 7 as the day on which the conflict ultimately took place" (1944, 85n139), and Whiteley's chapter 20, "Immediate Reports of the Split (September 1906)," compiled from files in the National Archives, some of which I've cited above, reproduces extensive materials attesting to the fact that September 7 was indeed the date that the pushing match occurred and the Hostile faction was driven from Orayvi (2008, part 2, 995–1,016). As Whiteley (personal communication 7/1/2015) suggested, it seems almost certain that those who give the September 8 date simply have in mind the date inscribed on the rock. This would seem true of Albert Yava, who, after giving the date as the 8th (113), goes on to say, "Where that big push took place there's a mark on the rock with Yukioma's words ... and the date is engraved there too" (116), presumably the date of the Split. So, too, does Harry James, who photographed it, conflate the date on the rock with the date of the push (136). I assume that is true as well for Matthew Sakiestewa Gilbert (2005, 3; 2010, 51) and the Hopi people in *Beyond the Mesas* (2007). All of them, as I've said, speak of the Split as having taken place on the 8th.

Whiteley also makes the cogent point that from a traditional Hopi perspective now or in the past, it isn't especially important whether the events occurred on the 6th, 7th, or 8th of September (personal communication 7/1/15). Indeed, I quoted Fred Kabotie, who wrote that in Hopi "society exact wedding dates, like birthdays, are meaningless" (48), and an exact date for the pushing match might also be "meaningless." Nonetheless, in academic discourse exact dates have some meaning, so it seems useful to affirm that the Orayvi Split took place on Friday, September 7, 1906.

As for Yukiwma's words having been inscribed by "one of Youkioma's men," it needs to be recalled that "Youkioma's men" were Hostiles, opposed to the American schools. But since the inscription is in English, it can only have been inscribed by a Hopi person literate in English; if it had been done by a Hostile it would have to have been done by a Hostile who attended school (more or less like Don Talayesva). Although he made no mention of the inscription in *Sun Chief*, Talayesva would later tell Harold Courlander that "A fellow [*sic*] named Robert Silena and Charles Addington carved the words that Yukioma had said" (in Yava, 149). Along with his small photo of the memorial, not a very good one, Harry James, on p. 137 of his *Pages from Hopi History*, notes that Helen Sekaquaptewa, in Oraibi at the time, said "that the inscription was made by Robert Selena, on vacation from the school at Keams Canyon" (in James, 138). James writes, however, that it was "Poli Payestewa of Moencopi and some friends" who "went out on the flat rock and carved a short, straight line" (138) along with the rest of the inscription. In a letter of September 16, 1906, Miltona Keith had written of a man named "Pole-hon iwa" glossed by Whiteley as "[Poli Paayestiwa, Greasewood]" Clan (2008, part 2, 1,004), and in a letter of 10/25/1906, Gertrude Gates mentioned "Polihongwa, a Hopi trader from Moencopi," again glossed by Whiteley as "[Poli Paayestiwa]" (2008, part 2, 1,112). Thus there is no doubt that this man was present. No one but James, however, speaks of him as having anything to do with the inscription.

APPENDIX B:

THE NAVAJO AUTOBIOGRAPHICAL CANON

I WILL LIST THE TEXTS I BELIEVE TO CONSTITUTE THE NAVAJO AUTO-
biographical canon according to the birth dates of their subjects, the oldest
first. *Bighorse the Warrior* (1990) is the story of Gus Bighorse, born about
1846. He did not write, but told his daughter, Tianna, many stories about
his life, and her recollections of those stories, edited by Noel Bennett, make
up the text. To call the book an autobiography does, as Brumble noted,
"stretch the definition of autobiography," (1993, 144) at least a little, but
Bighorse is a fine life history nonetheless. *A Navaho Autobiography*, the story
of a man called Old Mexican—not his real name—born in 1866, was edited
by Walter Dyk and published in 1947. Dyk also published *Son of Old Man
Hat* (1938), the Indian autobiography of a man named Left-Handed, born
in 1868. It describes his life from his earliest years until his marriage at the
age of about twenty.

Left-Handed: *A Navaho Autobiography* picks up approximately where
the first autobiography ended, going on to chronicle only three years of Left-
Handed's life in a book of some 571 pages. Working from her husband's notes
after his death, Ruth Dyk published it in 1980. *Tall Woman: the Life Story
of Rose Mitchell, a Navajo Woman, c. 1874–1977*, was edited by Charlotte
Frisbie who, after some thirty years of work with Tall Woman and her family,
published the book in 2001. Together with David McAllester, Frisbie had
earlier edited *Navajo Blessingway Singer: The Autobiography of Frank Mitchell,
1881–1967* (1978), the life story of Tall Woman's husband, which I have
considered in part II. (Frank Mitchell had been born in 1881.) *The Journey
of Navajo Oshley: An Autobiography and Life History* (2000), edited by Robert
McPherson, should be noted here, after Frank Mitchell's story. That is, it
would be next in order if, as is possible, Oshley was not born until 1893; it
would precede Mitchell's story, however, if he were born as early as 1879.

Next comes *Lucky, the Navajo Singer*, based on materials Alexander and
Dorothea Leighton had recorded by 1940; these were edited and annotated

by Joyce Griffen who published the book in 1992. Lucky—not his real name—was born in about 1900. *Gregorio, the Hand Trembler*, was born about 1903, and the Leightons published his autobiography in 1949. Irene Stewart was born in 1907, and we have already looked at her *A Voice in Her Tribe* (1980). So, too, have we considered Kay Bennett's *Kaibah, Recollection of a Navajo Girlhood*. Bennett was born about 1920, and her autobiography appeared in 1964.[1]

Several other Navajo life histories of different kinds are also worth mention. In *Dezba: Woman of the Desert* (1939), Gladys Reichard wrote, as I noted, that she "used no incidents or details which are not true," although "the description of the actors, the relationships they bear to one another, and the episodes in which they appear are all fictional" (vi). Emerson Blackhorse Mitchell's *Miracle Hill*, autobiographical in some measure, is the fictional account of Broneco, a Navajo boy born in 1945. It was written for a "young adult" audience and published in 1967. John Honie's life from the age of five to sixteen is told in *Black Mountain Boy*, a collaboration between Vada Carlson, Polingaysi Qoyawayma's chronicler, and the scholar of Navajo language and culture, Gary Witherspoon. They do not give a birthdate for Honie, although I'd guess him to have been born around 1900. The book was "prepared primarily for Navaho boys and girls" (1) for the Rough Rock Demonstration School and published in 1993. No schooling is mentioned for Broneco.

Franc Johnson Newcomb published *Hosteen Klah: Navaho Medicine Man and Sand Painter* in 1964. She and her husband had established a trading post at Pesh-do-clish in 1914, and her work is the biography of a man she knew well. His story occupies the third and longest section of the book, following two chapters about members of earlier generations of his family. No date for Klah's birth is given in the book (he was, however, born in 1867), and no schooling for him is mentioned. The title of chapter 12, "Klah's Graduation Ceremony," concerns "his graduation as a medicine man"[2] (133). Lucy Bloomfield, who with her husband had bought the trading post at Toadlena, Arizona, in 1911 or 1912,[3] wrote the foreword to Newcomb's book—the Newcomb and Bloomfield families were well acquainted—in which she notes that she herself had earlier published a "book...about Chief Natana" (xi), someone she also knew well. That book, called *Natani (Navaho Chief)*, is listed as fourteen pages long in the only record of it I have found. No publisher's name is given, and the publication date appears as "196-."

In that Bloomfield says her biography appeared before Newcomb's, it would have to have been published prior to 1964. *Natani* was unavailable through Interlibrary Loan; no bookseller lists it for sale, and I have not been able to see it. A woman who was already on the Tribal Council at the time Irene Stewart ran was, as noted above, Annie Dodge Wauneka, born in 1910. She attended school at Fort Defiance and subsequently completed eighth grade at the Albuquerque Indian School. Carolyn Niethammer published a biography of Wauneka called *I'll Go and Do More: Annie Dodge Wauneka, Navajo Leader and Activist* (2001), although she had not been able to meet or work with Wauneka herself.

APPENDIX C:

APACHE BOARDING-SCHOOL AUTOBIOGRAPHIES

THE PEOPLE CALLED APACHES (THEY CALL THEMSELVES NDE, NDEH, OR Indeh, the People) were made up of four principal bands—Chiricahua, Mescalero, Lipan, and Jicarilla—each comprised of several divisions, Bedonkohe, Chihenne, Warm Springs, Mimbreno, and Nedhni among them. (These names appear in various spellings.) In 1848, at the end of the Mexican War, the United States took control of territories in what are now Arizona and New Mexico, and, as American settlers invaded the Southwest, they disrupted traditional Apache lifeways, leading to the familiar sequence of contact, conflict, and, ultimately, conquest. The Apache "wars" that took place from about the 1860s abated for a time as the Americans withdrew troops from the Southwest during the Civil War. These resumed and intensified in the 1870s and did not end until the surrender of Geronimo in 1886.

At that time a great many Apache people—women and children along with the warriors, and even the Apache scouts who had aided the government—were sent as prisoners to Fort Marion, an old Spanish fortress in St. Augustine, Florida. Many died in the humid and fetid conditions there. Along with others who had been held at Fort Pickens, in Pensacola Florida, the surviving Apaches were moved to Mount Vernon Barracks in Alabama in 1887, where they remained until 1894, when they were transferred to Fort Sill in Indian Territory. They remained prisoners at Fort Sill until 1913, when those who wished to do so were permitted to leave for the Mescalero Reservation in New Mexico. Others chose to remain in Oklahoma.

Many of the young Apaches imprisoned in Florida—and, as we will see, at least one who was not so young—went to boarding school at Carlisle, handpicked, on several occasions, by Richard Pratt himself. But we have very few accounts from these students of their People's experience in this critical period and of their own individual boarding-school experience (occasionally at schools other than Carlisle).[1] Two, Jason Betzinez and James Kaywaykla, participated in the production of book-length autobiographies that were published, respectively, in 1959 and 1970. One, Daklugie,[2] recounted his boarding-school experiences at Carlisle in some detail in interviews with Eve Ball[3] in the 1950s that she later edited and published in her book, *Indeh* (1988 [1980]). (See figure 13.) Ball's work with Apache people of that era also included interviews with Kaywaykla, said to have been the youngest Apache child to be sent to Carlisle, and which she edited to produce his autobiography, *In the Days of Victorio* (1970). But no more than two pages of that book represent his time at Carlisle.[4]

In much the same way, the Mescalero man (his father was Chiricahua) the anthropologist Morris Opler referred to as Chris said almost nothing about his experiences at the on- and off-reservation boarding schools he attended. Born about 1880, Chris and his family were sent to Florida in 1886 and then to Alabama in 1887 with the other Apache prisoners, but they were allowed to return to the Mescalero reservation in 1889, before the transfer of the Apaches to Fort Sill in 1894. On his return, Chris was "caught" by the Indian police and forced to attend the reservation boarding school for a few years. Then, when he was seventeen, he spent five years at the Albuquerque and the Santa Fe Indian schools. Opler worked with Chris in the 1930s, and in 1969 published his story, a mixture of life history and ethnography, as *Apache Odyssey: A Journey between Two Worlds.*[5] Of his boarding-school experiences, Chris offers not even a full two pages of recollections, and they are widely scattered throughout the book.

13 Daklugie, top center, with Jason Betzinez, to his left. Ramona Chihuahua, who would become Daklugie's wife is second row left, and James Kaywaykla, the youngest Carlisle Apache student is bottom right. Courtesy of the Smithsonian Institution.

Opler also worked in the 1930s with two Chiricahua men of Chris's generation, Samuel Kenoi and Dan Nicholas. Both wrote or dictated lengthy autobiographical narratives—Kenoi's is 704 typescript pages and Nicholas's is 208 pages!—and these do include representations of their boarding-school experiences at the Carlisle and Chilocco schools. But Opler published neither of these in his lifetime.[6] The typescripts are to be found among Opler's papers in the Division of Rare and Manuscript Collections at the Cornell University Library. I hope to publish the boarding-school experiences narrated in those autobiographies in the near future, but because readers of this book will not know them, I will not discuss them here.

The overlap of social crisis and boarding-school attendance of these Apaches parallels that of the Hopi autobiographers I have discussed, and of the Lakota autobiographers I will discuss in a second volume.[7] But the paucity of Apache boarding-school autobiographies makes it impossible to speak of an Apache boarding-school canon to parallel that of the Hopis or, for that matter, the Navajos.[8] Once the entirety of Kenoi's and Nicholas's autobiographies are in print, depending on their reception, it may be possible to begin to do so. But the small number of texts is why I have made this discussion of the three available accounts of Apache boarding-school experience an appendix rather than a formal "part" of this book.

I.

Near the end of a long life—he was born about 1860 and died in 1960—Jason Betzinez worked with Colonel Wilbur Nye to produce an autobiography titled *I Fought with Geronimo* (1959). A more accurate title for the book, however, might have been the one given to chapter 9, "On the Warpath with Geronimo."[9] This is only to say that while Betzinez provides detailed descriptions of battles from about 1882 forward fought by Geronimo's band in which he participated, he seems not to have fired a shot or engaged directly with opposing forces in any one of them.[10] After describing several campaigns with Geronimo, Geronimo's "Surrender" (chapter 13), and the Apaches' suffering in a chapter called "Prisoners of War" about their time in Florida, he turns to his schooling at Carlisle in chapter 16, a chapter called, "Golden Days."

"In April, 1887," it begins, when Betzinez "had been at Fort Marion for less than a year, Captain Richard Henry Pratt, Superintendent of the Carlisle Indian Industrial School, paid [the Apache prisoners] a visit. He was looking for candidates for his school" (149). Betzinez writes that Pratt chose forty-nine boys and girls and "thirteen young men," Betzinez among them. Although he is twenty-seven years old, and believes himself "too old to be a school boy" (149), he agrees to attend when Pratt encourages him to come to Carlisle despite his age. This decision, Betzinez writes more than seventy-years later, "turned out to be one of the biggest events in [his] life" (149).

From this point forward, the chapter is divided into titled sections, the first of which is called "A Great Humanitarian," Betzinez's life-long estimate of Pratt. He describes the appearance of Carlisle barracks on his arrival eight years after the opening of the school, noting its "dormitories, classrooms, shops, hospital, bakery, laundry, chapel, Y.M.C.A., printing shop, central heating plant, dining hall, and homes for the superintendent and teachers" (150). In regard to the latter, he writes that "Pratt had the wisdom to select teachers who were mature, experienced, and possessed of strong religious convictions" (150). This strongly positive assessment may indeed be accurate. Luther Standing Bear, one of the very first students to attend Carlisle in 1879, would speak of his own teacher as a "good teacher [who] had a lot of patience" (1975, 138), and even Daklugie, who would join Betzinez at Carlisle, intensely critical of the whole boarding-school enterprise as he was, also testified to having a good teacher (see below). Of course if Pratt's teachers all or mostly possessed the qualities Betzinez lists, the Carlisle staff would have far surpassed those of some other of the early boarding schools. Betzinez concludes this first section by recalling the "Great Humanitarian's" "broad shoulders . . . and military bearing," noting as well that Mrs. Pratt was a "motherly type who always had a sweet smile for us" (151).

Betzinez's next section—out of chronological order[11]—recounts the journey of his group "of sixty-two Apache 'volunteers'" (151)[12] from Fort Marion, Florida, to Carlisle, Pennsylvania. This involves train travel (which they all had earlier experienced on the trip to Fort Marion) and then a trip by steamer (a first for the group) from Charleston, South Carolina to New York City. Occasionally experiencing rough seas, the ship docks at the foot of the Brooklyn Bridge (opened only four years earlier), where the group take "horse-drawn cabs" to cross Manhattan. They next travel by "ferry across the

Hudson River to Jersey City," where they board a train for Carlisle (152). Betzinez notes that the trip from Florida to Pennsylvania took "exactly one week" (152).

When the group arrives at the school, they are first "assembled on the steps of the mess hall for a photograph."[13] (See figure 14.) Then, the boys and girls are separated "and each group was led to its respective dormitory" (152). There, Betzinez's group is "given a haircut and a bath but not as yet issued new clothing" (153). Clock time is announced by the ringing of a bell, at which point the new students look out a window and see "other students forming in ranks and being marched to dinner. Soon [they] were motioned to fall out and follow them" (153). In the dining room the new arrivals are regarded "with great curiosity," because they are "still wearing blankets"— what the photograph taken earlier would have captured—"like any camp Indians." Indeed, as Betzinez looks "today at [their] first photographs," he notes "what wild-looking creatures we were" (153). The Indians' "wildness," of course, is just what the photographs were supposed to capture.

14 Apache students on their arrival at Carlisle Indian School. Photograph by John N. Choate. Courtesy of the National Anthropological Archives, NAA INV 02089900.

The group is quickly civilized as the "school tailor shop turned out blue Army-type uniforms for the boys while the dress shop made neat dresses for the girls." Betzinez recalls that "We wore these uniforms proudly. Never before had I owned such fine-looking clothing" (153), something any number of other boarding-school students had also felt. Although he does not mention it, these finely outfitted boys and girls would before long be posed for an "after" photograph demonstrating their progress from "wild" to "civilized." (See figure 15.) Thinking back to this time more than seventy years earlier, Betzinez recalls that he was from the first determined "to be a true young man, to obey the rules, and try to please the warm-hearted man who had brought [him] there" (153). This account of an immediate and unwavering commitment to Pratt and to "civilization" as inculcated at Carlisle may well be accurate, although it just might be an example of what Franz Boas had called "the perversion of truth brought about by the play of memory with the past" (335), Boas's harsh description of Indian autobiography in general.

15 Apache Students three years after their arrival at Carlisle Indian School. Photograph by John N. Choate. Courtesy of the National Anthropological Archives, NAA INV 0209000.

Betzinez details Carlisle's routine, one consistent with those we have seen elsewhere, which, to be sure, were largely modeled on that of Carlisle. His first teacher is a "nice little lady," who names the children and instructs them in writing their names on a blackboard. His childhood name, Betzinez writes, was "Nah-delthy, which means Going-to-Run" (154). He had assumed the name "Batsinas" in 1878, when Batsinas, an old friend of his mother's, bestowed his name on the young man. Miss Low, the nice teacher, spells it "Betzinez" on the (mistaken) assumption that the name was a Spanish or Mexican name. She also gives him the name Jason, explaining that Jason "was some man who hunted the golden fleece but never found it" (154). Although the name meant nothing to him at the time, in "the intervening years," Betzinez writes, he has come to "believe that the story of Jason . . . has set a pattern for [his] life" (154). He will return to this matter at the very end of his story.

He notes the great difficulty he had learning to pronounce English and his slow progress in learning to speak it. He is persistent, however, and fortunate to have the help of teachers "who patiently went over with [him] again and again the words and phrases [he] was trying to say" (154). In time, he does well "not only in English but in [his] other subjects" (154). Although he is interested in carpentry, he is put in the blacksmith shop where he learns to weld, eventually building carriages so fine that one of his wins "a prize in the annual school exhibit" and is then "sent to the World's Fair in Chicago" (155) in 1893. Betzinez would work as a blacksmith for some thirty years.

During his long stay at Carlisle, he recalls enjoying "Saturday night sociables and other entertainment," and, in particular, "eating oysters at a little stand back of the market square" (155). He points out how unusual this was for him as a member of a tribe that "had a taboo against eating anything that lived under the water"[14] (155). He notes that "like most of the boys at the school"—and like most Indian students at other boarding schools, except that he is twenty-seven, hardly a boy—he "played baseball, basketball, football, and many other sports and games," for a time engaging, too, "in an old Indian game of shinny, a very rough sport something like hockey except that it is not played on ice" (155–56). But the "most power-ful influence on [his] life at this or at any other time was [his] introduction to the teachings of Christianity" (156). Church is compulsory on Sunday mornings, he writes, and he also "got in the habit of attending Y.M.C.A. meetings on Sunday afternoons and prayer service in the evenings"; these "changed [his] whole life" (156). Indeed, as Nye had stated in his foreword to the book, the woman Betzinez would marry "was a white missionary" (n.p.).

Although he says nothing further about classes, meals, marching, sports, and dormitory life, among other activities and practices at Carlisle, he does provide a detailed description of his first "outing" experience to a Quaker farm family named Cooper. He finds the Coopers to be "warm-hearted people, who tried numerous methods to help [him] improve [him]self" (156). He spends "three long summers" (157) with them, learning much about "agriculture ... which was useful ... in later years" (157). He decides, however, that his "education as well as [his] efforts to learn English were being retarded by being absent so long from the school" (157). This is curious in that outing to an American family was to serve, among other things, very much as an immersion in English. Nonetheless, Betzinez does indeed remain at Carlisle all the next year, "putting in more time in classwork and at the same time working in the blacksmith shop" (158) again. He also learns other vocational skills, and, in time, once more works for the Coopers, who, he says, address him as "son," "practically an adopted member of the family" (158). This makes him "proud and pleased" (158).

Betzinez recalls that although he was very busy at school, and so was "prevented from doing much courting," he had had his eye "on a young Apache girl whom [he] had known since [they] were children," now also at Carlisle. Noting that "Captain Pratt had suggested that [he] get married"— he is about thirty-two years old!—he asks the young woman out only to have her turn him down. "Though seventy years have elapsed," he writes, he is "still mad about this embarrassing outcome to [his] first effort to get a wife" (158). This section of the chapter concludes with Betzinez's last summer of farm work in 1892 (159).

The last section of the chapter begins, "After nine years attending the Carlisle Indian Industrial School, I decided that I could not progress beyond the eighth grade. I was now over thirty years of age and it was high time that I began my life work" (159). Since Betzinez had come to Carlisle in 1887, nine years later the date is 1896 and he is a full six years "over thirty years of age." This means that his narrative has completely omitted whatever may have happened during the four years from 1892 to 1896. Why might this be? On one hand, it could be because those four years were simply "more of the same," and, in general, all positive. On the other, it is possible that something in those four years may have been rather less positive (although he has not mentioned corporal punishment or other punishments, no conflict with teachers, staff, or other students, or negative experience of any kind). This is to say that Betzinez's decision to begin his "life's work" at this time is not represented as coming from a sense that it was high time to move on, or some such, but, rather, from his sense that he "*could not* progress beyond the eighth grade" (159, my emphasis). This new sense of a lack of capacity—he had described nothing but success, albeit sometimes with great effort, until this point—is confirmed when he writes, "In my discouragement I went to Captain Pratt and told him that I wanted to leave school" (159). Pratt does not approve; he says, "'Jason, I want you to stay and graduate. After that you can leave school" (159).

This causes Betzinez to leave Pratt's office "feeling rather downcast," in that his decision to leave had been made "only after much soul-searching" (159). Later, Pratt sends for him and tells him "that he had reconsidered," and that Betzinez now "had his permission to leave school and seek a job"[15] (159). Although he knows he "would be sad at first to leave Carlisle and its happy memories," he intends "to seek work in a nearby community," so that he can "easily return to Carlisle for visits if [he] became lonely or needed help." With this in mind, he "set forth with confidence and pleased antici-pation to make [his] way in the world" (159). The year is 1897.

Betzinez gets work in a steel mill for a company that will become Bethlehem Steel, and he also becomes a member of the Presbyterian Church. When he pays a visit to Carlisle not long after leaving, he finds himself sum-moned to Pratt's office where he is told that a position in the Indian Service is available in Darlington, Indian Territory. Pratt urges him to apply; he does and is accepted (160). Betzinez has mixed feelings about going west. He knows that he would be rejoining his people, but (the future-) Oklahoma is not his home; he "had never been there" (162). He goes nonetheless, and after a short time, in 1900, transfers from Darlington to Fort Sill. He remarks that the "Apache prisoners of war had been at Fort Sill for six years before [he] arrived," his mother among them (165). Shortly after his arrival, Pratt pays a visit to Fort Sill, and Betzinez, along with "Several of us former Carlisle students" (174), goes to meet his train. "When our old friend got off the train," Betzinez wrote, "his face lighted up to see us gathered there, most of us with tears in our eyes" (174). Years later, "During the first World War," Pratt would make "his last visit to Fort Sill," a visit that Betzinez also records. He and some other former Carlisle students once again go to the railway station to meet him "as anxious to see General Pratt as if he were our own father." When his train arrives and Pratt descends to the platform, Betzinez once more describes the Indians standing there "with the tears rolling down their cheeks, overcome with happiness to see their old friend" (202).

Chapter 19 is called "Working for My People," and that is surely how Betzinez saw his time at Fort Sill. As he makes clear, however, working for his people involves efforts on his part to put an end to the medicine dances which some Apaches continue to practice and to halt their gambling (181). He describes a great deal of political activity occasioned by the desire of many of the Apaches to return to their homeland, a move that Betzinez opposes. When, finally, "in the spring of 1913 . . . the Apaches were released from their status as prisoners of war and . . . a large group were transferred to the Mescalero reservation" (198) in New Mexico, he chooses to remain behind. Near the end of his story, he describes meeting and marrying the missionary, Anna Heersma; for many years of their life together, he says, he farmed and did "a little blacksmithing" (205).

The last section of the book's last chapter is called "The Golden Fleece." In it, Betzinez describes "some good fortune" (208) when the town of Lawton bought part of his farm for a water improvement project; the money this brings, along with an "oil lease on the rest of [his] land" (208), will allow him and his wife to live comfortably "for the rest of [their] days" (208). He concludes, "Unlike that earlier Jason, I have found the Golden Fleece. It is the solid gold of a grand and enduring fellowship with my many dear friends, both Indian and white, and the companionship of my beloved wife, . . . the knowledge of a life well spent and a firm faith in that sweet Message of a better life in the hereafter" (209). This one-time member of Geronimo's war parties has very much been "changed forever" by his education at boarding school.

II.

The nephew of Geronimo, the son of chief Juh,[16] a man fiercely proud of the warrior prowess and medicine power of both men, and to the end of his life contemptuous of the ways of those he calls White Eyes, the Americans, Daklugie was born about 1872. Although he served as translator for Geronimo during the latter's work on his autobiography with

S. M. Barrett, he never wrote or participated in the production of a formal autobiography of his own. This may be explained by an observation Daklugie offered to Eve Ball. He said that "S. M. Barrett... wished to write a book about my uncle. And, strangely to me, Geronimo consented. Why he wanted it done I still don't understand. It was not our way of preserving our history and traditions" (in Ball 1988, 173). Although he did not, like his uncle, want "to write a book" himself, he did, after a considerable time of watchful waiting, tell Eve Ball a great many stories about his life that appeared in her book, *Indeh: An Apache Odyssey*. I will consider what he had to say about his time at Carlisle.

First, however, a word about the title Ball chose for her book, *Indeh*. She writes that she heard the word initially from Daklugie. "Literally," she claims, "it means *The Dead*, and it is the term by which Apaches, recognizing their fate, designated themselves" (1988, xxi). Ball spent some thirty years living near and talking with Apache people, and historians like Dan Thrapp who wrote the Foreword to her book, and many admiring reviewers of her work (e.g., Donlon, Dunaway, Griffen, Satz) do not question her translation. But Ball did not know Apache, and her translation seems to me highly doubtful. As I noted at the beginning of this section, Apache people called themselves *Indeh* or *Nde* or something like that long before the time when "their fate" at the hands of the Americans might have come to seem dire. *Indeh* simply means "The People," as Navajo *Din'e* also means "The People" (Navajo and Apache are both Athabaskan languages.)

A further point. Questioned by Ball about the Ghost Dance revitalization movement, generally considered to have ended with the massacre of Big Foot's Minneconjou band of Lakotas at the end of 1890, Daklugie replied that, in fact, it never ended. The hope for the future that animated the Ghost Dance, Daklugie told Ball, was still alive: "In every reservation in the United States," he said, "it is observed at least once a year" (1988, 85). Daklugie's brother-in-law, Eugene Chihuahua, Ball writes, said that when the end time came, all the people on earth would die, but then, "after four days the Indians would be restored to life. The buffalo would return to the plains ... and the deer to the mountains" (1988, 313), much the sort of renewal envisioned by the Paiute prophet Wovoka and his Plains supporters. In view of this, it hardly follows that either Daklugie or Eugene Chihuahua would have taken hard times for Apaches as likely to be permanent, or that would they refer to their People as "the dead."[17]

After Geronimo's surrender to General Nelson Miles in September, 1886, the Apache prisoners were put on a train to Florida. The women and children would be sent to Fort Marion, in Saint Augustine, along with some of the men, while others would be detained at Fort Pickens, in Pensacola. Although Daklugie had thought his group was headed to Fort Marion, they are taken off the train at Pensacola and brought to Fort Pickens. There, he visits with his uncle, Geronimo, who gives him two important pieces of information. Geronimo first tells Daklugie that there "had been a man selecting Indian children to be taken away to a place called a school where they would be taught the evil ways of the white people." This man, "Captain Richard H. Pratt, was taking Apache children and some warriors to a place called Carlisle, Pennsylvania." Pratt, he says, wishes to take Chapo, Geronimo's son, and Geronimo "intended having [Daklugie] go also" (135). Daklugie initially refuses, but Geronimo "informed [him] that it was he who made medicine there [at Fort Pickens] and that [he] was to go to Carlisle" (135). He explained that without "this training in the ways of the White Eyes our people could never compete with them. So it was necessary that those destined for leadership prepare themselves to cope with the enemy" (136).

It is at this point that Geronimo informs Daklugie that he himself is "destined for leadership," and is "to be trained to become the leader." When Daklugie asks why Chapo has not been chosen, Geronimo replies, "Chapo is my son and I love him very much... but he does not have the qualities of leadership. Not many do." Geronimo confirms Daklugie's sense that his "father [Juh] possessed it to a great degree and, though [Geronimo himself] was never elected to the chieftainship [he] had it and men knew it" (136). After further talk about leaders and leadership, Geronimo affirms to Daklugie that "so long as the good of the tribe is hanging fire... you go to Carlisle!" (136). This powerful scene between Geronimo and Daklugie is a good illustration of some of the strengths and weaknesses of Ball's work.

An exchange like that between Geronimo and Daklugie had never before, to my knowledge, been reported, and I think it is likely that it took place when and where Daklugie said it did. Thus, on the one hand, Ball's presentation of it offers an important Apache perspective on the relationship between traditional Apache leadership and the new and largely mysterious schools. But on the other, the interview has surely been "extensively edited by the author" (xxiii), by Ball herself, as she readily acknowledged at the end of her introduction to *Indeh*. Sherry Robinson found after carefully examining

Ball's notes and manuscripts that she had a "penchant for sprucing up her [Apache] friends' speech"—"hanging fire" can only be Ball's locution—thus producing what Robinson calls "dramatized history" (xiii), something with which she found herself "uncomfortable" (xiii). Nonetheless, Robinson concluded that concerns of this sort ultimately amounted to no more than "small complaints" against Ball's procedure. She praises Ball as "the courageous and stubborn woman who earned the Apaches' trust, persuaded them to tell their side of the story, and then got that story into print" (xiv). To be sure, these "small complaints" sometime loom larger in Ball's production of *In the Days of Victorio*, which I will soon examine. And, too, any estimate of Ball's work must take into account what I have noted above, her quite extraordinary error in regard to the meaning of *indeh*.

Chapter 4 of book 2 of *Indeh* is called "Carlisle and Captain Pratt," and in it Daklugie tells of the Apache students' long and arduous train trip from Florida to Carlisle, Pennsylvania. (This is a very different route than that taken by Jason Betzinez and his party earlier.) Once again, the young Apaches are not clear about what awaits them on their arrival. Daklugie believes they "might be going to [their] death, or into slavery and degradation" (140). He is especially concerned for his fellow-passenger, Ramona Chihuahua; the two are betrothed and she would later become his wife. He has a knife and has promised to kill her rather than let her be defiled—or even eaten, a fear he has when the train becomes trapped by a heavy snowstorm and he recalls stories he has heard of the White Eyes' behavior on similar occasions. But it "did not take the ... work crew very long to enable the train to move" (141), and the party arrives "at the railway station in Harrisburg, Pennsylvania" (141) without further difficulty. They "are met by Captain Pratt, who took [them] to Carlisle." Daklugie says that "There, desperate to the extent that we did not care whether we lived or died, we were thrust into a vicious and hostile world that we both hated and feared" (141).

"Captain Pratt," Daklugie says, "was not alone. He had with him an Apache from Arizona to interpret for him. He was taller than the officer, who was a small man" (142). The interpreter is Jason Betzinez, although Daklugie, as Ball notes, "will not name the interpreter, because he was much older ... and had never been admitted by his tribe as a warrior. Even the small boys had contempt for him when they learned who he was"[18] (142). Daklugie does not describe a dining hall or a dormitory, nor does he mention a "before" photo being taken. Rather, he says, "The next day the torture began. The first thing they did was cut our hair. I had taken my knife from one of my long braids and wrapped it in my blankets, so I didn't lose it. But I lost my hair. And without it how would Ussen [the Great Spirit] recognize me when I went to the Happy Place [Heaven, more or less]?" (144). As for the Clean-Up, Daklugie says that "The bath wasn't bad. We liked it, but not what followed" (144). What followed was the order "to put on trousers." Daklugie laments: "We'd lost our hair and we'd lost our clothes; with the two we'd lost our identity as Indians. Greater punishment could hardly have been devised." There was, however, a still "greater punishment" to come. Before considering it, let's note here that while the government's mandatory de-tressing and re-dressing of young Indians was precisely intended to have them lose their "identity as Indians"—we are, after all, at Carlisle, home to the notion of killing the Indian and saving the man—Daklugie, remembering these events, remains as much an "Indian"—an Apache—as anyone could be.

The "greater punishment" in store for the young Apaches involves the Naming, something I have already noted, and Daklugie responds more strongly than many other boarding-school students. Daklugie says his group of students was "marched . . . into a room and our interpreter ordered us to line up with our backs to a wall. I went to the head of the line because that's where a chief belongs. Then a man went down it. Starting with me he began: "Asa, Benjamin, Charles, Daniel, Eli, Frank. . . ." And I became Asa Daklugie. We didn't know until later that they'd even imposed meaningless new names on us, along with other degradations. I've always hated that name. It was forced on me as though I had been an animal" (144).

Ball inserts here a short descriptive passage concerning the group being taken "to the dining room for breakfast" (144). Large boys are seated next to small boys, and Daklugie "learned that he was expected to assist his charge." The small boy is James Kaywaykla, "the youngest Apache sent to Carlisle" (144), whose brief account of his boarding-school experience I'll consider next. Daklugie himself then picks up the narrative, recalling that their "first instruction began at that table," as the interpreter tells them "the English words for tableware and food." Education "proceeded with learning to make [the] beds and hanging up [the] new clothes." "Each student had household chores to do," a problem for him in that no Apache man, he says, "wanted to do women's work." The interpreter urges them "to do everything required, like it or not" (144). The Western notion of work in general will further prove to be a matter of contention between Daklugie and Carlisle.

As time passes, not everything is an ordeal or degrading. Daklugie says that "We liked the outdoor games and contests. We liked the gymnasium, too. And the band.... Learning English wasn't too bad."[19] Then, "Before the winter was over [he] was learning to read." His teacher "was a white lady and she was very patient and kind to us. She taught us to write, too, and she was not bossy as most white ladies are. She was polite. She seemed to know without being told that I wanted desperately to be able to read and she helped me" (144). This unnamed woman's qualities would affirm Jason Betzinez's high estimate of Pratt's teaching staff. "One day," Daklugie continues, the teacher "opened a big book to show [him] Arizona, and for the first time in [his] life [he] saw a map. [He] was fascinated. When she showed [him] mountains and rivers [he] could tell her their names in [his] language. [He] knew the Spanish for some of them and a few in English. She let [him] take that geography book to the dormitory and ... [he] almost wore it out" (144–45). Ball herself concludes this chapter with a description of Daklugie's outing experience, noting his abhorrence of farm labor and his interest in raising and managing cattle, work he did not think was entirely, like farming, "beneath the dignity of a warrior" (145).

Daklugie continues his narration in chapter 5, "Life at Carlisle." Here, although he had expressed considerable excitement about reading and learning, he says that "The thing that pulled me through was the athletic training" (146). This did not, in his view, match up to his father's and Geronimo's "training routine," but it did keep him "active and fit." "In bad weather there was always the gym," where he proved to be—as he says all Indian boys did—"a good wrestler" (146). Although he himself was only "a short distance runner—five miles" (146), he notes the long-distance prowess of his fellow student, the Hopi Lewis Tewanima, who would one day be an Olympian. Tewanima, Daklugie recalls, "could start at that easy jog-trot and keep it up all day. He could outrun a horse." Most appealing about running, Daklugie says, was the fact that the runners "didn't have to wear trousers. Nobody knows how all Indian men hated those pants"—a sentiment he had earlier expressed. (Although, as we have noted, not all male Indian students felt that strongly hostile to trousers.) "The track team," he says, "wore trunks and we felt like Indians" (146).

Even if they don't match up to the Apache standards of the preceding generation, Carlisle athletics are something in which Daklugie nonetheless takes pride. "I can't say much for our academic standing," he says, but "when it came to physical achievements we had the world beat" (147). Along with Lewis Tewanima, Jim Thorpe was at Carlisle with Daklugie, as I had noted earlier, and he praises Thorpe's superiority "at almost all sports." He credits Carlisle's widely-known coach, Pop Warner, for his ability to "take a boy who had never heard of football and make a star player of him. That's what he did with Jim Thorpe"[20] (147). Daklugie, however, chose not to play football at Carlisle because it "looked silly." The only thing he "considered was whether or not a game would help [him] to survive. Football wouldn't. Leaving a place of ambush to knock your enemy down and sit on him is no way for a warrior to fight" (147). Nonetheless, he admits that he "liked to watch the games," seated in the stands with the other Carlisle boys in their uniforms, with the girls dressed "in their best clothes" (147).

"After I learned to read a little," Daklugie continues, "I just helped myself. It wasn't until I could read that I found out about my people" (147). What he "found out" comes from the newspapers of the day, which contained reports of the government's movement of the Apache prisoners. Ball herself affirms Daklugie's desire "to learn all that he could about cattle, for he was determined that the government not make farmers of the Apaches," and she repeats his opinion that any "labor . . . was stupid and unnecessary" (149). Daklugie then resumes his story, noting that "This lady taught us to use a dictionary" (150). "This lady" is the teacher he had earlier complimented for her kindness and politeness, although in the anecdote that follows, he describes her behavior as different from what it had been. "Each day," Daklugie says, "she wrote a list of words on the blackboard. We were required to learn to spell them, learn their meaning, and to write sentences in which we used them. One day I found a strange new one. It was 'ferment.' I looked for it [in the dictionary] and took the first meaning given, 'ferment, to work.' And I wrote, 'I will not ferment in the house'" (150). The teacher becomes angry and Daklugie does not know why. She does not immediately explain but only tells him that he "was to remain after the others left and write a sentence using the word a hundred times." When he asks why she is ordering him to do that, she says that it is to teach him "to use [the word] correctly." Although he doesn't mention it, the teacher must, at some point, have explained to him the correct usage of the word "ferment," for Daklugie responds, "But you have told me, and I know." Providing her with an observation about indigenous pedagogy, he continues, "Indians do not need to hear a thing but once. You are not teaching me; you are punishing me" (150). She then asks if he is "refusing to obey" her, a question to which Daklugie replies affirmatively. At that, she orders him to "Go to Captain Pratt's office.... Tell him what you have done" (150).

Daklugie recalls that he "did not go immediately," but "waited an hour or more" (150). He then provides an extraordinary account of the encounter between Pratt and himself, one, let me note, that is not to be found in Pratt's autobiography. Daklugie knocks on the door and is told to enter. He does so, upon which Pratt "closed and locked the door; then he put the key in his pocket" (150). Without a word, Pratt goes directly "to a bookcase, reached behind it, and pulled out a blacksnake [a flexible leather whip: Ball's addition]." I will let Daklugie tell the story of what happened next: "Pratt was a little man, but he might be armed [!]. I looked for a weapon but could see no sign of a concealed one. I took the whip from him and tossed it up on the bookcase. As I did so he grabbed my collar. I turned, seized his, and jerked him off his feet. I held him at arm's length and shook him a few times, then dropped him to the floor" (150). Daklugie informs Pratt that "If you think you can whip me ... you are *muy loco*. Nobody has ever struck me in all my life; and nobody ever will"—so much for the likelihood of corporal punishment for this boarding-school student! "I could break your neck with my bare hands" (150). And how does Pratt respond to this threat by a teen-aged Indian student?

First, he calls Daklugie "Asa." Pratt surely means no offense, but the use of the name makes Daklugie "again [see] red," because, as we know, it is a name he has "always hated ... forced on [him] by white people." But, strangely, as he admits, Pratt "did not get mad. Politely he asked [him] to sit down." Daklugie sits; Pratt then stands and inquires, "Why did you disobey your teacher?" The young man tells him what had happened, and, "To my surprise," Daklugie says, "he laughed." Pratt next asks whether the teacher had not been "a kind teacher." Daklugie admits "that she had up until that time," insisting—as many another bright young person from many another culture might—"that she had no right to punish [him] because [he] had done nothing to deserve it." Pratt, too, persists in his line of argument, asking, rhetorically, "Hasn't she obtained books for you, books that you needed?" And Daklugie in his: "Yes, but it was not fair for her to punish me. I did nothing wrong" (150). Pratt attempts to end the impasse with the question, "If she will admit you back to class will you be courteous as you had been before this happened?" (151). While Daklugie ponders his answer, Pratt entices him to a bit of gentlemanly banter: "You know that men must be courteous to ladies and indulge them in their whims." This only produces a figurative roll of the eyes from Daklugie, who disparagingly observes that the white men "spoil women. No wonder they are all henpecked. No wonder all white women are bossy" (151). (Although, as he had earlier noted, not this particular teacher.)

Daklugie says that he "went back and was never punished again," although he "was getting tired of the monotony, tired of being a prisoner, and tired of conforming to stupid customs imposed on [him]" (151). This gets him to thinking he might run off, and, on a berry-picking expedition, he does—only to return out of concern that Ramona—he has thought about her and exchanged furtive glances with her on several occasions—"would worry." This moves him to go back to his dormitory, where he "crawled through a window to [his] bed" (151). By this time, as he states, he had been at Carlisle for eight years, had "had no further trouble with Captain Pratt," and had even begun "to realize that some of the things he required of [the students] were beneficial." He has come to see that, to Pratt's credit, it "was his intention that all decisions be for [their] good, regardless of [their] dislike for them" (151).

Daklugie is now about twenty-two years old and he understands that Ramona wishes them to be married at Carlisle. (It would be interesting, of course, to know more about her experience at the school.) He says this is his wish as well, but he "had learned that, before taking on that responsibility in this strange and unpleasant life of another race, a man must have an occupation that would enable him to support a family. Until [he] had an income [their] wedding must be postponed" (151). It was at this time, in 1895, that "Daklugie returned to his people at Fort Sill" (162). Determined not to "ferment" either in the house or in the field, he would indeed pursue his interest in cattle-raising as means to "an income."

Later, in 1913, when the Apaches at Fort Sill were given the opportunity to go to the Mescalero reservation in New Mexico, Daklugie was not only among those wishing to do so, but, as he would tell Eve Ball, he and Eugene Chihuahua were "largely responsible for bringing [their] people here" (311), to New Mexico. He would also tell her that despite his ongoing dislike for farming, in retrospect, those who stayed in Oklahoma and "did it are better off than are the ones who came to this reservation" (311). Nonetheless, I suspect that if Daklugie had the decision to make anew, he would do just as he had done. His autobiographical recollections provide a vivid example of someone raised traditionally and forced to submit to boarding-school education, an experience that certainly changed him forever but in no way made him less fully and proudly Apache. [21]

III.

James Kaywaykla was probably the youngest of the Apaches taken north from imprisonment in Florida,[22] and, as he attests in the "Author's Preface" to his autobiography, *In the Days of Victorio: Recollections of a Warm Springs Apache* (1970), he "was a student at Carlisle Indian School in Pennsylvania" (xiv).[23] Kaywaykla's story was also written by Eve Ball, with contributions from many other Apache people. As I'd said, only two pages of the two-hundred-page autobiography offer "recollections" of those boarding-school years.

These are to be found in the book's last chapter, called "Florida." There, Kaywaykla tells of "a new menace" as "Officers and their wives went through the [prison] camp and selected over a hundred children"—the number Samuel Kenoi had reported—"to go to Pennsylvania to school" (199). Some go by train, others by sea; he is among the latter, and he finds the voyage frightening (200). "At Carlisle," he says, "we were subjected to the indignity of having our hair cut and being forced into trousers" (200). The students' old clothes "were sent to our families in Florida so that they might know that we still lived," although he does not know how "that could have convinced them" (200). He names both Jasper Kanseah and Geronimo's son, Chapo, as among the students, and says that "both were young and small" (200). "Jason, too, went," he says, referring to Jason Betzinez, "and he was a mature man." Chapo, Kaywaykla recalls, "became tubercular, and was returned to his people [in Florida] to die." He notes that "Kanseah was unhappy and not interested in school," and so "Captain Pratt let him return to his people after a few months" (200).[24] Kaywaykla affirms what Daklugie himself had said, that "Daklugie made rapid progress in school." He adds, "and I think I may say without boasting"—surely Ball's diction—"that I did" (200).

If James Kaywaykla told Eve Ball anything more about his life at Carlisle, she did not include it in the autobiography she wrote with him. He says simply, "After spending eleven years at Carlisle I rejoined my people who had been taken to Fort Sill," where they "were living on lands generously given them by their brothers, the Kiowas, Comanches, and Kiowa-Apaches" (202). He notes that through "the efforts of the younger men who had been given schooling at Carlisle (Asa Daklugie especially), the long-awaited release from bondage came" (202) in 1913. Like Betzinez, Kaywaykla chose to stay in Oklahoma rather than to relocate to the Mescalero reservation, and he says that he has "always been thankful" that he made that choice. "Those of us who settled on private land in Oklahoma encountered many difficulties," he admits, but, like Daklugie, he thinks they "are better off than those who are still in a sense prisoners, on the reservation" (202). He closes with the hope that "Before the night of oblivion closes in on [his] people" there still may be "an opening of new horizons and brighter days for the Apache people" (204). If the diction is surely that of Eve Ball, the hope for the Apache people—who most assuredly are not "the dead"— is that of James Kaywaykla.

NOTES

INTRODUCTION

1. In 1923, "at the age of eighty-five," Pratt had "dictated to his daughter" (Washburn, 323) the memoir that would become *Battlefield and Classroom*. This was available to Goodale, a great admirer of Pratt, although it was not edited and published until 1964. Ward Churchill, at the other extreme, claims that Pratt's Carlisle initiated "the genocidal impact of American Indian residential schools," using that assessment as the subtitle of his book *Kill the Indian, Save the Man* (2004). Churchill excoriates those who use the term "ethnocide"—as I will—rather than genocide, and saves his greatest contempt for those who don't even use that term. His reductive logic is that since genocide is *worse* than ethnocide, and since the boarding schools were *very bad*, not to speak of genocide is simply neocolonial apologetics. I think it is instead an attempt to be accurate. Meanwhile, I note that the Navajo poet Berenice Levchuk, who herself endured punishment at boarding school, referred to Carlisle and the boarding schools generally as "this phase of our Native American holocaust" (185). Tom Gannon, who suffered beatings at the Holy Rosary Mission School—it became the Red Cloud Indian school in 1969—notes that he had titled "a talk on [his own] Indian Boarding School experience 'A Holocaust of the Mind'" (114–15).

2. The slogan in one form or another appears in several issues of the Carlisle school's publications. Otherwise, the only place I have found it in print is in the text of a talk Pratt gave in 1892 called "The Advantages of Mingling Indians with Whites." He begins with the now-infamous remark of General Sheridan, "The only good Indian is a dead Indian" (in Prucha, 260), to which Pratt responds, "I agree with the sentiment, but only in this: that all the Indian there is in the race should be dead. Kill the Indian in him, and save the man!" (in Prucha, 261). A great many whites, however, did not wish to "mingle" with Indians, regardless of any "advantages" that

might accrue to either. This enraged Pratt, who "always eschewed racial categorization for Indians" (Fear-Segal, 3) and did not recognize the extent to which many of his fellow citizens did observe "racial categorization."

3. Joel Pfister writes that Pratt's own "formal schooling concluded when he was thirteen.... Thus he had approximately the level of education that Carlisle made available to students" (37). Robert Trennert refers to the "new school discipline of 'domestic science'" as "a modern homemaking technique, developed as a means to bring stability and scientific management to the American family" in late nineteenth-century America, "and provide skills to the increasing number of women entering the work force" (1982, 273).

4. Donal Lindsey has written that "Once at St. Augustine, Pratt removed the prisoners' shackles and staked his military commission on permitting the Indians to police themselves" (28). While it is possible to see this as a move toward producing the internalization of an oppressive order, it most certainly gave a degree of power, however circumscribed, to those who had been rendered powerless.

5. Scott Riney notes that Pratt himself had been a tinsmith prior to joining the Union Army, and showed no subsequent desire to practice the trade (1988, 226n13).

6. Hampton was established in 1868 by black and white members of the American Missionary Society to educate the freedmen. Its program for Native Americans began in 1878 and lasted (longer than Carlisle) until 1923. Ahern claims that "Beginning in 1879, the campaign for [Indian] assimilation represented an outgrowth of the antislavery reform zeal" (1985, 254), at least on the part of some of the campaigners. For more on Indian students at Hampton see Lindsey, in particular chapter 2.

7. Cf. Goffman: "On the Characteristics of Total Institutions," (1957) reprinted in his *Asylums* (1961). Asylums are "total institutions," as are, of course, prisons (cf. Michel Foucault, *Discipline and Punish*). Deena Rymhs in a recent study conflates prisons and the boarding schools, referring to them both as "carceral spaces" (83), a judgment I find not unreasonable although less than fully accurate. In the United States, although the schools were *in some measure like* prisons, they were not *just the same as* prisons. The Compulsory Indian Education Act had been passed in 1887, but by 1893, for example, the permission of parents was required before a child or young person could be sent to an off-reservation boarding school (Adams 1995a,

65), and as we will see, several young Indian people worked ingeniously to get such permission. Pratt's early experience was, indeed, with Indian prisoners, but his superintendence of them allowed more opportunities for agency than the period generally permitted to incarcerated persons. Rymhs is writing about Canada, and, in fairness, it needs to be said that the recent report of the Truth and Reconciliation Commission (see below) noted that Canadian First Nations boarding-school students, like prisoners, often had numbers, not names, and that "For many, the path from the residential school to prison was a short one" (*NY Times*, A7). The recently published *Grim Shadows: The Story of the Canton Asylum for Insane Indians* (2016) is a study of a harrowingly "total institution" whose control over those entrusted to it far exceeded that of any boarding school.

8. The Meriam Report noted "that the provisions for the care of Indian children in boarding schools are grossly inadequate," adding that "The outstanding deficiency is the diet furnished the Indian children, many of whom are below normal health" (11). This was partly because the "funding level at all federal boarding schools . . . [was] virtually frozen from the early 1900s until 1925" (Hyer, 19), although nutrition was inadequate at many of the schools prior to the 1900s and after 1925. The Navajo Frank Mitchell (see below), said of the Fort Defiance school he had attended in 1893–94, that "there was plenty to eat there, more food than I used to get at home. . . . I was willing to go to school if they were going to feed me like that" (62), and others have said much the same thing. Although nutrition was indeed poor at many of the schools, that was not always the case, nor did every Indian student find him- or herself regularly hungry.

9. Myriam Vuckovic quotes from a 1914 health report that "described how the towel system used at the school [Haskell Institute in Lawrence, Kansas] contributed to the spread of tuberculosis and trachoma" (185). Earlier, she notes, "In 1908 Haskell [had become] the target of a month-long health investigation, designed to find out why the school had such a large number of tubercular cases" (186).

10. The place was named for Thomas Keam, born in Cornwall, England, in 1842. An amateur ethnographer as well as an entrepreneur, Keam erected a number of buildings in the 1870s at the site that came to be called Keam's Canyon, Arizona, soon the seat of the Hopi federal Indian Agency and a government boarding school. Much of the literature spells the place Keams

Canyon, not Keam's Canyon, and this spelling occurs so often that it is pointless to call it "wrong." I do, however, use Keam's Canyon throughout. For more on Thomas Keam see L. Bailey, Culin, and Graves.

11. A footnote appended to this Rule states: "In some of the more advanced schools it will be practicable and advisable to have material offenses arbitrated by a school court composed of the advanced students, with school employees added to such court in very aggravated cases" (in Bremner, vol. ii, 1,356).

12. To heal the effects of these hurts in the descendants of boarding-school students is the ongoing mission of the Native American Boarding School Healing Coalition, mentioned above. The Coalition was established as "a Non-Profit corporation pursuant to the laws of the Navajo nation" and certified in June, 2012. In January of 2013, members of the Coalition attended a meeting of the Canadian Truth and Reconciliation Commission, about which more below.

13. The volume, *Respect for Life* (1974), is the "report of a conference at Harper's Ferry, West Virginia, on the traditional upbringing of American Indian children" (n.p.) and includes comments from its Native participants on how they were disciplined as children. For the most part those comments are consistent with the view expressed here, that corporal punishment was not the usual mode of discipline although it was most certainly used on occasion. See below.

14. E.g., Helen Sekaquaptewa describes a time "in the early 1930's" when "the first car came through Hotevilla." Her sons, along with some other boys, chase after it, and, when her "brother Henry saw them and told them sharply to stop . . . they didn't heed him." So "Henry took off his belt and gave each of them a few lashes." Sekaquaptewa states that "This was his privilege and duty" (233) as their maternal uncle. And Albert Yava says, "if a boy became careless about getting up on time and doing his work, his mother called on her side of the family—her clan relatives—to do something about it. They'd take you from one house to another where your relatives lived and they'd pour cold water on you" (6). Jeannette Blake, a Navajo woman born just after the turn of the twentieth century, wrote, "My father was strict with us and would whip us" (204). Other Navajos give similar accounts in Johnson's book.

15. The original petition, dated 1886, is in the National Anthropological Archives (MS 3,967). I have this information from a personal communication from Dr. Peter Whiteley (August 26, 1915).

16. My selective quotation is not meant to suggest that Ellis is an apologist for the ethnocidal practices of the boarding schools in general or of the Rainy Mountain School, his particular focus. He writes, "For most of these students, the school did not succeed in destroying their cultural identity, *which it was meant to do*" (130, my emphasis).

17. E.g., Katanski wrote of the "boarding schools as generators of a pantribal identity" (7). See also Hertzberg.

18. And yet, the complexity of these matters is at least noted in the Meriam Report in the following extraordinary passage: "The position taken . . . is that the work with and for the Indians must give consideration to the desires of the individual Indians. He who wishes to merge into the social and economic life of the prevailing civilization of this country should be given all the practicable aid and advice in making the necessary adjustments. He who wants to remain an Indian and live according to his old culture should be aided in doing so" (86). Lomawaima and McCarty cite and discuss this passage (65–66), which contains the phrase they use for the title of their study, *To Remain an Indian.*

19. As I have noted, this is not the view of Ward Churchill, or the view of the Ziibiwing Center of Anishiinabe Culture and Lifeways, established in 2004 by the Saginaw Chippewa Indian Tribe of Michigan. The Center has published "A Supplementary Curriculum Guide" titled "American Indian Boarding Schools: An Exploration of Global Ethnic and Cultural Cleansing."

20. A substantial listing of these studies is to be found in note 35 of the introduction to Trafzer, Gilbert, and Sisquoc's edited volume, *The Indian School on Magnolia Avenue* (2012), and I won't reproduce that list here. The notes and bibliography to this book should give the interested reader a good deal of material with which to pursue further study.

21. Tom, Dick, Harry, Sally, or Mary were often given to precede a student's Indian name which then became a surname assumed to derive from the student's father. On many occasions students' names were obliterated entirely and replaced by the absurd attribution of names such as Julius Caesar, Robert Burns, Betsy Ross, or William Shakespeare (an Arapaho). Renaming was a way to de-Indianize students, and to simplify matters for teachers and administrators. After the 1887 passage of the Dawes Act allotting land to individual Indians, renaming took place beyond the boarding schools to make

family relationships more apparent for the purpose of title to and inheritance of land. On this matter see Littlefield and Underhill, and more below.

22. I have recently discovered two unpublished full-length Apache autobiographies. See appendix C.

23. See *"That the People Might Live": Loss and Renewal in Native American Elegy.*

24. It is also the case that some Native writers of elegy from the nineteenth century forward did not adhere to this principle but more nearly observed elegiac manners derived from Christianity or from mainstream American culture.

25. Amelia Katanski's study, in the title of its first chapter, claims to offer "a Theory of Boarding-School Literature" (19), but I find no such theory. Katanski reads the boarding-school literature she considers for the way in which these texts "use . . . repertoires of identity and representation" to produce "narratives of Indian liberation" (215). This seems to me largely accurate but also overgeneralized.

PART I: HOPI BOARDING-SCHOOL AUTOBIOGRAPHIES

1. This is my estimate of the Hopi autobiographical canon. Whiteley had specified only two of the "better-known examples" (478), those by Talayesva and Qoyawayma. Dr. Whiteley (personal communication 5/30/15) suggested that I also consider *A Pueblo Indian Journal: 1920–1921*, with an introduction and notes by Elsie Clews Parsons. Crow-wing, the Journalist, as Parsons calls him, had attended Keam's Canyon boarding school, and composed this journal, in English, from December 19, 1920, to December 19, 1921. It is an extraordinarily detailed account of the activities, communal and ceremonial, of a First Mesa Tewa man. But Crow-wing does not say a single word about his schooling, thus eliminating it from consideration here.

Climbing Sun: The Story of a Hopi Indian Boy (1980), by Marjorie Thayer, Elizabeth Emanuel, and Anne Siberell, is the life story of the Hopi artist and craftsman Hubert Honanie, who was born on the Hopi reservation in 1917. Honanie at the age of eleven attended the Sherman Indian School in Riverside, California. But although the book is based on "conversations" with Honanie, the authors say "his story has been fictionalized for readability[!]"

and that "Many of the incidents and some of the characters have been invented" (6), leading me to exclude it from consideration.

2. See *For Those Who Come After.*

I. EDMUND NEQUATEWA'S *Born a Chief*

1. Mary-Russell Colton, who worked with Nequatewa in 1936 to produce his book, *Truth of a Hopi*, noted that Nequatewa's maternal grandfather "would take him out to the rocks and hide him" (136n40) from the Indian police or federal troops sent to bring the children of resisting families to school. As we will see, Nequatewa's paternal grandfather very much favored schooling.

2. For a fuller account see Whiteley (1988b, 106–10), and, again, briefly but definitively, Whiteley (2008, vol. 1, 4–6). The best continuous narrative account is once more Whiteley (1988a, 46–61). I draw on these and other materials for appendix A, "The Orayvi Split."

3. All three of Whiting's unpublished versions of the autobiography indicate that this incident, called "Calamity," occurred when Nequatewa was nine or ten, something one would have to guess from Seaman's account.

4. Nequatewa had been "born a chief in that his clan birthrights entailed the inheritance of a leadership role in the One Horn Society" (Ferguson 569), one of the four major priesthood societies. Also called Kwan or Agave, One Horn Society members were concerned "with the dead and supernatural protection of the village" (Whiteley 1988, 57).

5. A kachina, or *katsina* in the current spelling, is a supernatural being who dwells in the San Francisco Peaks near Flagstaff, Arizona. There are a very great many of them. They spend about half a year among the Hopis, and below I will many times note their comings and goings and the various ceremonies that involve them. But the term, as here, could also serve as a proper name.

6. For example, Parsons: "Pueblo Indians ... by 'uncle' ... mean mother's brother.... Father's brother is referred to as father" (1974, 23–24).

7. If Nequatewa was indeed born about 1880, he would be beginning school at the age of fifteen. But the exact date of his birth is uncertain. Volume 2 of the Whiting Collection includes a letter from the Superintendent

of the Department of the Interior to Alfred Whiting, dated January 9, 1962, stating that "The official Hopi Census Roll ... lists Mr. Nequatewa as having been born in 1877" (n.p.). Dr. Whiteley (personal communication 5/30/15) informed me that Nequatewa's birth date is given differently on other Hopi census rolls, something David Seaman may or may not have known. Further, in a late essay, Whiting himself wrote that "Edmund Nequatewa was born about 1885" (1971, 129). All things considered, Seaman's dating Nequatewa's birth to "around 1880" would not be far off, although, as I will note further, the way in which he handles time, dates, and chronology in the book can be confusing.

8. For example, Fred Kabotie says, "They gave us mush to eat" (12). And Helen Sekaquaptewa: "For breakfast we had oatmeal mush" (94). In Leslie White's "The Autobiography of an Acoma Indian," the narrator speaks of an initiation that took place over the course of four nights, on the third of which he says, "they gave us the *mush* to drink" (334, my emphasis). White's gloss says that "the mush" is "a mixture of corn meal and water in which are mixed the nastiest, most repugnant things they can think of" (334). Some southwestern stories mention a sweet cornmeal mixture appealing to the taste, which is also called *mush* in English, and Helen Sekaquaptewa noted that while Navajo students "didn't like the mush" at school, she and her Hopi schoolmates who were often hungry "had the mush" (95). The Mohawk Indian Institute in Brantford, Ontario, was widely referred to as the "Mush Hole," apparently for the unpalatable oatmeal that was served at breakfast and other meals as well.

9. The ostensibly Hopi words given by Qoyawayma do not translate as she states (Whiteley, personal communication, 5/30/15), perhaps a joke on her part, although one that only readers with some control of Hopi language would appreciate.

10. Charles Lummis's charges against Burton accused him not only of cruel and abusive treatment of his students but of cutting both the students' hair and that of any recalcitrant adult Hopi as a punishment. As a result of the "Moqui [older name for the Hopis] Inquiry of 1903," inspired by Lummis's articles, Indian Commissioner Jones, on September 5, 1903, wrote to Burton that "no threats and no force of any kind [should] be employed in reference to the cutting of the hair of the Indians in your charge" (in Lummis, 110). The best brief account of these matters at Hopi is once again Whiteley (1988b), pp. 91–97. Lummis's editors, Robert Easton and D. Mackenzie

Brown, mention "rusted iron shackles that had been clamped on the legs and arms of the Western Shoshones while their hair was cut by the agency barber" (122n10).

11. "A Hopi kiva is a rectangular ceremonial chamber, generally thought of as 'owned' or taken care of by a particular clan, clan segment, or clan member" (Whiteley 1988b, 61–62). It is "built underground... oriented approximately north and south," and "entered through a hatchway in the roof, by means of a stout ladder" (Titiev 1944, 103).

12. I would guess that Nequatewa had read or at least heard of *Sun Chief*, and that its title may have influenced his decision to call his own story *Born a Chief.* This would indeed seem to have been his, not his collaborator's, preference because in a letter dated June 12, 1942, very soon after taking down Nequatewa's account, Whiting wrote to Sterling Macintosh: "I am inclined to think that 'Born a Chief' sort of falls short" (volume 2, n.p.) as a title.

13. Nequatewa spells this *bahana*, a spelling widely found in the literature. More recent work (e.g., A. Geertz, Whiteley, Clemmer) uses *pahaana*, after Malotki (1978), who also contributed to the Hopi Dictionary Project's authoritative dictionary (1998). I have used some of what are now the "official" spellings, such as *pahaana* and *katsina*, but adopted Whiteley's practice of not attempting to follow any "single orthographic usage... for several reasons" (1988b, 317). For more on Hopi thought about *pahaana*, see Armin Geertz's eleven pages of "Hopi Prophecies" from 1858 to 1961 (422–32).

14. Nequatewa's grandfather says that the true *pahaana* "might be a dark bahana" (96), cultural traits here considered to be more important than skin color. Contemporary Hopi people refer to whites as *pahaanam* (plural), while in general agreement that Anglos are not "the true Pahaana" (Whiteley 1988bn8, 329; see also 270–72).

15. The outbreak was more than a "scare." Robert Trennert writes that "When the sickness passed, nearly ten percent of the Hopi tribe had died" (1992, 349).

16. A detailed description of a Hopi *katsina* initiation appears in Voth, 1901, but I will not quote from it or from most of Voth's accounts of ritual and ceremonial matters. Peter Whiteley writes that "ritual knowledge is guarded with great secrecy" (1988b, 84) by Hopi people because its dissemination "either orally to unentitled parties or... in published accounts, violates ritual sanctity and effectiveness, and may damage the spiritual health of the community" (1998, 176), and Voth published much that he should

not have. But his papers revealing Hopi "secrets" have been available for over a hundred years, and have been cited by more researchers than I can name. Nonetheless, in consultation with the editors of this series, I have adopted the following procedure. On the one hand, I will note where Voth and others have published on ritual matters that Edmund Nequatewa and, later, other Hopi autobiographers chose to mention. It just doesn't make sense to pretend that those papers don't exist. On the other, I will not quote anything from Voth or others that describes "ritual knowledge" they were not entitled to have, nor will I give specific references to these works. This is a strictly symbolic act, to be sure; anyone wishing to find the texts mentioned but not referenced will have no trouble doing so. All the same, it seemed to us better to proceed in this manner rather than to adhere to usual scholarly practice and further disseminate information that should not have been made public in the first place.

17. Eggan quotes an "informant" who (in English) notes her own "disenchantment," that she "cried and cried into [her] sheepskin that night.... hated [her] parents,... [and] was afraid to tell the others the truth for they might whip me to death" (372). Don Talayesva would note that he, too, was considerably more shaken by what he had learned than was Edmund Nequatewa.

18. Nequatewa's new name was not something he wished to keep secret. In an earlier version of the autobiography, he'd said that the man who wielded the corn and washed his hair told him that, "From now on your name is Nasingpu which means 'a snake got rid of its old skin'" (vol. 2, 224). Nequatewa's original Hopi name was Kokyanghoya, Little Spider (vol. 1, 266). Most boarding-school students—I will note some exceptions—had American names bestowed on them on their arrival at school, the topos of Naming. But such a scene does not appear in *Born a Chief*, nor do the typescripts I have examined contain an account of how Nequatewa got the name Edmund.

19. An excellent photograph of the "Phoenix Indian School Band, ca. 1895," roughly around the time Edmund Nequatewa attended the school, can be found in Archuleta, Child, and Lomawaima's *Away from Home*.

20. Two Akimel O'odham (Pima) people whose stay at the Phoenix Indian School was roughly contemporary with or just a few years after Edmund Nequatewa's have also written autobiographies. George Webb, born about 1893, attended Gila River Day School for a year and then went

on to what the anthropologist Edward Spicer, in an introduction to Webb's book, *A Pima Remembers* (1959), calls "the Indian Bureau Boarding School" (n.p.). In that the Phoenix Indian School was the only federal Indian boarding school in Arizona in 1902, the time Spicer says Webb enrolled, that must be the school he attended, and his first years at Phoenix would have overlapped with the older Nequatewa's. Webb says nothing whatever of his ten full years of boarding-school experience. Anna Moore Shaw, born in 1898, attended the Tucson Indian Mission School before enrolling at Phoenix in 1908, some four years after Nequatewa left. In *A Pima Past* (1974), she provides many details of her ten years at the Phoenix Indian School, and I will consider her further below.

21. The first telephone service in Arizona began in 1881.

22. This is Paul Wiki, from Walpi on First Mesa, as the typescripts make clear. He is described as being an "office boy" for the school, although his age is not given. Seaman represents him as a good deal more wimpy—ineffectual, whiny, at one point bursting into tears—than do the typescripts.

23. I will note for younger readers that the comedian, Bob Hope, and the singer and actor, Bing Crosby, made seven "road" films between 1940 and 1962, the first of which was *The Road to Singapore* and the last *The Road to Hong Kong*. Often spoofing popular film conventions of the time, the films were full of pratfalls, and occasions for Hope's jokes, with the action stopping every now and again so that Crosby might sing. Bud Abbott and Lou Costello were comedians of roughly the same period, beginning in radio, making films, and appearing on television. The shorter, heavier Costello was generally the fall guy and often the butt of Abbott's jokes. Their best-known routine, "Who's On First?" can be seen on YouTube, and I recommend it highly.

24. Seaman writes that the book tells of Nequatewa's life "from his birth" to "about age twenty-two, shortly after he had returned home from a forced education at the Phoenix Indian School" (xv). I would not agree that his time at Phoenix was "forced," but apart from that, because Nequatewa dates his return home "about the twenty-eighth of June, 1904" (163), and his story concludes with his marriage "Within a year" (176) after that, if Nequatewa, as Seaman had said, had been born "about 1880" (xxi), he would be nearer twenty-five than twenty-two at the end of his book. Whether he was twenty-two or twenty-five would probably not matter much to traditional Hopi

people, although from an ethnographic, historical, and literary perspective, I believe it is worth noting. The disparity between Native and settler relations to chronology will come up again.

25. Although it is not treated this way in *Born a Chief*, this is an instance of what sometimes is called "living in two worlds," a concept invoked in the subtitle of Polingaysi Qoyawayma's autobiography, *No Turning Back: A True Account of a Hopi Indian Girl's Struggle to Bridge the Gap between the World of Her People and the World of the White Man*. It also appears in the subtitle of Myriam Vuckovic's *Voices from Haskell: Indian Students Between Two Worlds, 1884–1928* (2008), and recently in the subtitle of Diana Meyers Bahr's, *Viola Martinez, California Paiute: Living in Two Worlds* (2014), as well as in a number of other publications. In almost every instance I know, neither "bridging the gap" nor "living in two worlds" is a particularly useful metaphor to conceptualize the situation to which each refers. I discuss this further in the section on Qoyawayma's life history.

26. Whiteley writes that "about fifty-two people" from the Hostile faction at Shongopavi moved to Oraibi "on 1 March 1906," and that "Many Hopis cite this influx from Second Mesa as the precipitating cause of the Oraibi split" (1988b, 105). This is something Nequatewa had mentioned in his *Truth of a Hopi*, p. 64, where he gives a very brief account of the Orayvi Split. *Born a Chief* concludes about a year before the split.

27. Cf. Whiteley: "Sootuknangw in current orthography. Variously translated as 'heart of the sky' or, my preference, 'star cumulus-cloud,' a principal deity of the above" (personal communication, 5/30/15). This deity was capable of representation: Fred Kabotie (see below) painted "Sootukwnangw" sometime between 1930 and 1935 (Seymour, 363), a painting that is reproduced on p. 301 of Seymour's volume.

28. Whiting's versions make clear that this uncle, whose name he gives as Teurema and also as Vance (vol. 1, 218), wants Nequatewa to go back to the Crane Clan house of his mother (vol. 3, 259). In large part, all the moving Nequatewa's family did earlier seems to have resulted from *an* uncle—this one perhaps—wanting his mother to go back to the Crane Clan house.

29. And yet, Nequatewa's choice of marriage as the mark of manhood is more typical of Western than of Hopi thinking. Titiev writes, "Soon after adolescence, *but usually before marriage*, a young man is expected to go through a Tribal Initiation which *marks the transition from boyhood to adulthood*" (1944, 130, my emphases). He continues, "This rite is practically

universal for the entire male population. It is known collectively as the Wuwutcim." (130). *Wuwtsim* is treated in exactly this way by Don Talayesva, and referenced by all the male Hopi autobiographers. See below.

2. ALBERT YAVA's *Big Falling Snow*

1. Edward Dozier, in *Hano: A Tewa Indian Community in Arizona*, writes that Hopi-Tewa intermarriages were forbidden "until the closing decades of the last [the nineteenth] century coincident with the establishment of the United States Government Agency at Keams Canyon, the construction of schools, and the advent of white traders" (26). This would mean that Yava's Hopi-Tewa parentage was still something of a novelty.

2. Courlander (1908–1996) is a man who should be better known to the general reader. According to the bibliography given by Nina Jaffe, he was the author of seven works of fiction—one of which, *The African*, was judged to have been plagiarized by Alex Haley, author of *Roots*, according to a 1978 court ruling; twenty-seven books on or collections of folklore from Haiti, India, the American South, Africa, and parts of Asia; two plays; and many articles. He knew and corresponded with Langston Hughes and Zora Neale Hurston, among other African American writers, and with Franz Boas and Melville Herskovits, among other anthropologists. With Moses Asch, he founded Folkways Records; thirty-three recordings produced by Courlander are in the Smithsonian Folkways Archive Collection. He first went to the American Southwest in 1968 (Jaffe, 122) and continued to visit until 1980 (Jaffe, 132). Courlander's papers at the University of Michigan include manuscripts of his *Fourth World of the Hopi* but not of *Big Falling Snow*. The catalog of a collection of his papers at the University of Southern Mississippi lists no Hopi materials.

3. Although Courlander sometimes refers to Albert Yava as "Albert," in what I have thus far quoted he refers to him—properly, I believe—as "Mr. Yava." I will have more to say about earlier editors' and amanuenses' tendency to refer to their subjects by first name alone—and to put only their own names on the spine of the book. The spine of *Big Falling Snow* has "Yava/Courlander." The spine of *Born a Chief* has "Seaman/Nequatewa."

4. In a discussion of *Soyalanu, The Winter Solstice Ceremony* that took place in December of 1911, Edward Curtis mentions a man named

"Sihtaiema, of the Cloud Clan" (128). This is surely Yava's father, whose name he gives as Sitaiema on p. 8.

5. As we will see further, the name Talayesva is a name that Chuka acquired upon his initiation into the *Wuwtsimt* society. Yava notes that when he "was initiated into the One Horn Society"—a *Wuwtsimt* initiation—"they gave [him] a ceremonial name, Eutawisa, meaning Close in the Antelopes. It was supposed to drown out [his] original name [as Talayesva "drowned out" Chuka], but people still call [him] Yava" (3). We will consider Talayesva's initiation and naming below.

6. In a review of the book, Paul Kroskrity observed that Courlander "never cites any of Dozier's major writings on this [Hopi-Tewa] group, despite their importance and availability" (98). He regards this as both a defect and a virtue insofar as Courlander's editorial work with Yava was concerned. Dozier had noted that "During the time of [his] field studies, the official Hopi interpreter was Albert Yava, a Tewa Indian" (27), and Yava surely would have met him and perhaps read some of his work. In that *Hano* appeared in 1966, two years before Yava began his collaboration with Courlander, it seems likely that Dozier's name would have come up between them.

7. In early September of 1906, Yava would either have been in Colorado picking beets during summer vacation at the Chilocco Indian School or back at the school beginning or soon to begin his second year of study. This is to say that he was not at home on First Mesa, and it is not clear when he heard about the Orayvi Split. He discusses it on pp. 111–14, but insofar as his account does not connect it to his boarding-school experiences, I cite it only when discussing other Hopi autobiographers' references to the Split.

8. Edmund Nequatewa entered the Keam's Canyon School in 1895, so that his and Yava's early years there would have overlapped, although neither mentions the other. This may be because, although the two might have been in some of the same classes, Nequatewa was about fifteen and Yava about eight, so that they would have been in different dormitories and had different friends.

9. The Phoenix Light and Fuel Company had brought electric power to the three-year-old city of Phoenix in 1884, and would have extended its service to Keam's Canyon by 1903.

10. Yava had explained that when he "was very young [he] never saw very much of [his] real father, Sitaiema.... He left [him] and [his] mother...

while [Yava] was still in the cradle" (8). Yava lived with his mother and stepfather, Peki, a "man who was well respected by everybody in the village, both for his character and the way he conducted himself" (7). Sitaiema, however, "was the headman of the One Horn fraternity," the important Kwan Society, into which Yava would eventually be initiated, and he feels fortunate that "as it turned out, [he] learned about rituals, ceremonies, and traditions from [his] father, and from [his] stepfather [he] learned how to make the land fruitful" (8).

11. This is Irving Pabanale or Standing Flower, some of whose life history was recorded and edited by Robert Black. Pabanale did not know the date of his birth and Black is confusing on this matter. He writes that Pabanale died "in 1972 at the age of ninety-one" (xii), which would make his date of birth about 1881, but also writes that he was "born around 1890" (127). Pabanale says that he went to the Polacca day school "with [his] cousin Albert Yava" (15). Yava did not attend until 1893–94, at the age of five or six, and Pabanale is not likely to have gone with him if he were only three or four. Further, since he was already employed at the Keam's Canyon School when Yava was planning to go to Chilocco about 1905, and since he had, according to Yava, already been to the Phoenix School, he must be older than Yava; thus the 1881 date could be approximately accurate for his birth. Pabanale gives an account of schooling at Polacca, Keam's Canyon, and Phoenix in a brief chapter called "The Early Years" (14–22). Nelson Oyaping, who finally signed permission for Yava to attend Chilocco, was also known as Nelson Pabanale; he is Irving's older brother.

12. Many excellent photos of the Chilocco school, both archival and recently taken by the editor, appear in Kim Brumley's book, which is well worth consulting in this regard. Unfortunately, several photos of the impressive dining hall (37–38 and passim) are captioned "Luepp Hall," although the building was named after Indian Commissioner Francis Leupp. An entire chapter is called "Luepp Hall" (104).

13. In that Dozier writes of the initiation of "a boy *or* girl [who] has reached the age of fourteen or fifteen" (61, my emphasis) as a *first* ceremonial event, it is confusing when he next writes that the "*second* important event in a girl's life occurs at the time of her first menstruation" (61, my emphasis). Assuming that the onset of menses would likely precede a girl's fourteenth or fifteenth birthday, wouldn't the puberty rite be a *first*, not a *second* important ceremonial event? Jesse Walter Fewkes had published

an account of the Winter Solstice Ceremony at Walpi (1898) and it should be noted that Yava remarked to Courlander that he couldn't give him "the details of what went on in this ceremony, but that anthropologist Fewkes has written about it, and what he tells is absolutely true" (xi). I cite Fewkes with, as it were, Albert Yava's permission.

14. Just as Curtis used the Winter Solstice Ceremony synonymously with *Soyaangw*, so, too, did he synonymously refer to the *"Wuwutsimu"* as *"the New Fire Ceremony"* (107) on First Mesa in November of 1911. He states that "The rites are not practiced at Hano, but some of its men belong to the Walpi fraternities" (107), Yava's father, it would seem, among them.

15. Cf. Whiteley, who calls the four ritual societies named by Yava "the *Aa'lt* (Two-Horn society), *Kwaakwant* (One-Horn society), *Taatawkyam* (Singers' society), and *Wuwtsimt* (usually untranslated, but roughly 'Manhood' society)" (1988b, 57). Yava's father's fraternity, the *Kwaakwant*, the "Kwan, Agave, or One Horn Society," is presumed to "enjoy some of the most intimate relations with Maasaw, the god of death" (Malotki and Lomatuway'ma 1987a, 211). Edmund Nequatewa had noted that the Kwan fraternity "is regarded with great awe by the Hopi, for it is the duty of [its] priests to look after the dead. They are in charge of the spirit on its journey from this world into Maski," the Land of the Dead. (2008/1936, 130n15). These may be Mary-Russell Colton's words rather than Nequatewa's. More on this in the discussion of Don Talayesva's story.

3. DON TALAYESVA'S *Sun Chief*

1. The autobiography White did obtain, the one he publishes here, is very brief, only eleven pages. Its subject was seventy-three in 1941 when he worked with White, and although he had been to the Albuquerque Mission School for three years, and then to Catholic School in Santa Fe for about a year, he says nothing whatever about his boarding-school experiences.

2. There is an earlier Pueblo autobiography that I suspect neither White nor Simmons knew. This is James Paytiamo's *Flaming Arrow's People, By an Acoma Indian* written by Paytiamo himself and published in New York City in 1932. Although it is dedicated to "Superintendent H. B. Pierce of Haskell Institute who was kind to me when I was far from home" (n.p.), Paytiamo

does not say anything about his Haskell education or of the schooling that probably preceded it.

3. Simmons regularly refers to Talayesva by his first name only, as does Mischa Titiev (see below). Titiev, as noted, had rented space in Talayesva's house and Talayesva says that he and Titiev—whom he calls "Misch" (323)—"became like brothers" (321). Although Simmons, later, did indeed become Talayesva's clan "brother" by adoption, he is nonetheless called "Mr. Simmons" in the text of *Sun Chief* (340). I imagine that in day-to-day interactions both Titiev and Simmons (and Fred Eggan and other whites) called Talayesva "Don"; Aberle, who says that he never met Talayesva, (preface, n.p.), also calls him "Don" throughout his lengthy analysis. I don't mean to impose a vague contemporary "political correctness" on work of an earlier time. I wholeheartedly agree that Simmons's achievement in bringing *Sun Chief* to publication is impressive, that Titiev's work on Orayvi was ground-breaking, and that the sustained attention Aberle paid to *Sun Chief* testifies to his deep appreciation of Talayesva's life story. Nonetheless, when Simmons speaks of "Don" being "taught to report on the events of the day," and his being "rewarded with praise when he included the smallest details" (5), it seems hard not to notice, from a contemporary perspective to be sure, a certain amount of infantilizing of Talayesva on Simmons's part—and, again, a determination to urge him to engage in behaviors that his culture does not approve.

In his foreword to the second edition of *Sun Chief*, Matthew Sakiestewa Gilbert raises similar issues—for example, why was Talayesva "not list[ed] as the author of his autobiography? Why was Leo Simmons's name the only one shown on the spine of the book?" (x). It's good to note that the name on the spine of the new edition is Don C. Talayesva and that Sakiestewa Gilbert's foreword refers to him as Talayesva. I'll address this matter again when discussing other boarding-school autobiographers and their editors.

4. Simmons' "Sample of Don's Composition" contains a set of "Written answers to questions" dated "3-25-[19]39," several pages titled, "The Soyal Ceremony" dated "12-17 to 21-[19]38," and "Part of a Letter" "Date 11-4-[19]41." I'll cite just the first part of "The Soyal Ceremony":

Next day December 17th starting again early in the morning we got up from our bed put on our Shoes or moccacine and we went out to the edge of the Oraibi massa toward east and say our morning prayer. then we all come back it was not so cold we don't have to put on our clothing as we go and pray in the morning. Coming back to our kiva we stay there untile breakfast time we all went out and go to our houses and took our food back to our kiva and eat (467).

Talayesva describes the Soyal ceremony in chapter VIII of *Sun Chief*. There, he gives no dates, and the details he gives here are sprinkled throughout the account—which is in standard English. Apart from the matter of style, let me note that Talayesva had remarked to Simmons that "What I do in the Soyal is secret" (6), so there is no question that Simmons pressed him for this account.

5. Aberle thanks Simmons for "the warm interest" he showed "throughout the course of [his, Aberle's] work," and on p. 28, slightly elaborates Simmons's account of how *Sun Chief* was constructed. But he makes no reference to the vast quantity of material Simmons might still have had and might have made available.

6. It was only after my trip to Yale that I recalled H. David Brumble's earlier attempt to locate "the raw data" (1988, 201n6) from which the book was produced. Brumble wrote that the "considerable effort" (1988, 201n6) on the part of Professor Frank Hole, chair of the Anthropology Department at Yale in the mid-1980s, to locate the material was unsuccessful, and that it was probably "destroyed or lost by Simmons's family after his death in 1978" (1988, 202n6).

7. This is described at length in chapter IV, "Mischief and Discipline." Talayesva notes that he took "the four blows full force," and "stood them fairly well," only to have the Whipper Kachina strike him "four more times and cut [him] to pieces," with "Blood running down over [his] body" (87). His father "had told the Katcina whipper to give [him] a double thrashing," and also had instructed his sponsor not "to protect [him]" (88). He did this to him, Talayesva says, because he "had the reputation of being the naughtiest boy in the village" (84). I'd noted earlier the focus of the First Mesa *katsinaam* on the naughtiness of the children to be whipped as acknowledged by both Edward Curtis and, later, Julian Steward. Aberle, whose study I had not read until after completing my own, also comments on this on pp. 24–25.

8. Earlier in his story Talayesva had said that he and his brother had "waged little wars with children of unfriendly families ... and we called them Hostiles" (64), implying that he and his brother were Friendlies. Again, many years later, in an account he provided to Harold Courlander in the late 1960s—Courlander includes it in his notes to *Big Falling Snow*—Talayesva speaks of "we friendly people," who "drove those hostile people from the village [Orayvi]" (in Yava, 149). But at an important point in *Sun Chief*, as I will note below, he gives the reader reason to believe that he and his family had indeed been among the Hostiles.

9. In the preceding chapter he had noted that "When the Katcinas entered the kiva without masks, I had a great surprise. They were not spirits, but human beings. I recognized nearly every one of them and felt very unhappy, because I had been told all my life that the Katcinas were gods" (88). Like Dorothy Eggan's informant, Talayesva says that he "was especially shocked and angry when I saw all my uncles, fathers, and clan brothers dancing as Katcinas" (88). Mischa Titiev, who knew Talayesva well, told Clyde Kluckhohn "of the profound effect the [initiation] ceremony had on Don's later life" (in Kluckhohn, 270), both the severity of the whipping he received and also his "disenchantment." Talayesva also remarks on the initiates being warned that "if we ever talked about this to uninitiated children we would get a thrashing even worse than the one we had received the night before," and that a long time ago "a child was whipped to death for telling the secret" (88–89). This "disenchantment" does not prevent him from honoring the *katsinam* and, as he notes, dancing as one. About midway through his story, he watches as his seven-year-old sister Mabel is "thrashed by the Katcinas." He "was sorry for her," he says, "remembering [his] own great ordeal, but [he] realized that it would do her good in the long run" (201), just as a good Hopi should.

10. *Maasaw* is a very powerful deity, or spirit. He is associated with fire, death, and the underworld, and is also considered the original lord of the Orayvi area. More on *Maasaw* below.

11. Folder 24 of Box 2, "School on the Reservation," has a bit more detail. Talayesva says, "somebody said a few words to God. I was told that his speech (Grace) went like this, 'God is gracious, Good [*sic*] is good, we thank thee for our food. Give us Lord our daily bread. Amen.' We had bread, beans, meat, cabbage, mashed potatoes, and water, but no coffee. The food was very nice" (Ms., 200).

12. Cf. Edmund Nequatewa: "Masauwu, God of the earth and guardian of the dead, is very terrible and very sacred. . . . He walks at night and carries a fiery torch" (2008/1936 130n16).

13. Albert Yava had also gone to Colorado with a group of 300 Chilocco students "to thin beets" (18), not to Rocky Ford but to nearby Lamar, Colorado.

14. But of course Edmund Nequatewa, from a Friendly family, also went to Phoenix. In two brief, recent instances of Hopi autobiography, Sakestiewa Gilbert says that his great-grandfather, Victor Sakiestewa, was among the Hopi students at Sherman with Tawakwaptiwa (2005 passim; 2006, 78), and that after returning home in 1909, he asked to return to Sherman for another term (2005, 19). Sakiestewa Gilbert also notes that his grandfather, Lloyd Gilbert, attended the Phoenix Indian School "In the mid 1940s, at the age of fifteen" (2014, 357). His grandfather's "last name was Quache (pronounced 'Kwaatsi') and not Gilbert. . . . But at some point . . . officials required" him to "get rid of his Hopi name and . . . replace it with an English name." In consultation with his siblings, he "decided to use their father's first name 'Gilbert' as their new English surname" (2014, 360).

15. Viola Martinez, an Owens Valley, California, Paiute woman who attended Sherman much later, in 1927, said that "Everything was done by the clock" (54), noting in particular that if a student was not in bed by lights out, she was sure to be punished (53).

16. In his appendix B, "Legends and Myths of the Hopi," Simmons prints two pages titled "Visits to the House of the Dead" (448–50). They begin with the experience of an unnamed "youth," and continue with a number of details that appear in Talayesva's account, and also some that are not in his account. The last paragraph in Simmons gives a brief picture of the condition of the wicked generally (e.g., not only Two-Hearts) and of the righteous that approximate descriptions of Hell and Heaven.

Albert Yava told Harold Courlander a story about a visit to Maski (99–104) that roughly parallels the narrative given by Talayesva. In *Fourth World*, Courlander had noted as "particularly intriguing about the Maski legend . . . the possibility, or probability that it had a non-Indian origin" (213). He also observed of Yava's account that "The graphic descriptions of punishments in Maski for sins committed while living, the pit of flames and the Last Judgment suggest Christian intrusions into Hopi belief . . . , despite the fact that 'Hopi traditions are generally unmarked by Christian Church influence'" (148n52). I will note another possibility of Christian "intrusion" or "influence" on Hopi story and ceremony in Helen Sekaquaptewa's *Me and Mine* below.

17. For example, Titiev: "In Hopi belief witches (*poakam*) derive power through intimate association with animals. Accordingly each witch is said to have two hearts, one human and the other that of an animal familiar" (1940, 497).

18. Box 1, Folder 8's typescript of this vision is very heavily marked up and Simmons's note appears handwritten at the bottom of msp. 214. On msp. 214, what would become pp. 133–34 of the book, "Angel" is twice crossed out and "Spirit" written in. I assume the markings are Simmons's, although it did cross my mind—I have no evidence on which to base this speculation—that some of the handwriting might have been Mischa Titiev's.

19. Talayesva's vision includes the detail that Mount Beautiful reached "like a mighty stairway to the highest point" (129). If this seems to reflect Christian influence, it should immediately be noted that as he "just touched his feet lightly on the top step," he is not met by angels or St. Peter, but, rather by a *Kwaani'ytaka*, or Kwan Warrior. On his first evening at Keam's Canyon School, when the homesick young Don Talayesva walks up the Mesa with his new friend and Hopi schoolmate, Nash, Nash tells him to look to the west. He does and "saw the top of Mount Beautiful, just beyond Oraibi" (101), which makes him long for home. Both here and in its later appearance, Mount Beautiful is very much a Hopi mountain.

20. The fullest recent materials on Maasaw and the *kwaakwant*, the "Kwan, Agave, or One Horn Society," who "enjoy some of the most intimate relations with Maasaw, the god of death," are the two 1987 volumes by Ekkehart Malotki and Michael Lomatuway'ma. My quotation is from their *Maasaw: Profile of a Hopi God* (1987a, 211). Chapter 1 of this volume, "Maasaw and the Realm of Death" (3–17), provides a great deal of interesting material, some of it bilingual, Hopi and English, and some of it from Don Talayesva.

21. In a 1937 account of a Hopi salt expedition in which Talayesva took part, Titiev notes that "Don [*sic*] began to tell his companions the story of his trip to the house of the dead, describing in advance some of the scenery along the road which he was now about to traverse for the first time, as proof of the fact that he had actually visited the region while he was 'dead'" (unconscious) (1937, 246). Titiev explains in a note that this vision took place while Talayesva had been a student at Sherman. He adds that "Such

experiences are common among the Hopi" (1937, 246). Talayesva himself had noted Chief Tawakwaptiwa's statement that the details he provided paralleled those offered by "the old people ... when they visited the House of the Dead" (129). The story of a visit to Maski narrated by Albert Yava (99–104), however, concerned a young man, as Talayesva was when he experienced his visionary journey.

22. Talayesva identifies Irene as *Maasaw* Clan at one point and Fire Clan at another. This is because although the two clans are not the same, *Masngyam* or *Masaaw* Clan and *Kookopngyam* or Fire Clan, along with a number of others, make up a phratry. Whiteley explains that "Aggregations of related Hopi clans are generally referred to by anthropologists as phratries" (1988b, 50), and Titiev had earlier stated that "Phratry lines are more clearly distinguished than clan ties" (1944, 53), so that in these regards, Talayesva might speak of Massaw Clan and Fire Clan interchangeably. Talayesva's Sun Clan, *Tawagnyam*, and the Eagle Clan, *Kwaangyam*, together also constitute a phratry. Thus Sun Clan boys and Eagle Clan boys might often marry Fire Clan girls as they might also often marry Maasaw Clan girls, aggregating the two clans as Talayesva does here.

23. I had earlier quoted Albert Yava's observation that "If a man's name is Chucka, meaning mud, you know that his father was Sand Clan, because earth and sand together cover the breast of Mother Earth" (3). Voth reports a number of names given by members of the Sand Clan (1905, 110–12) but does not include Chuka or Chucka.

24. "*Soyalangw* opens the Kachina 'season' at Oraibi. Kachinas are personated in periodic performances from December through July" (Whiteley, 1988b, 58), and Talayesva had already noted the arrival of several *katsinam*. Simmons recommends Dorsey and Voth's account of the Soyal (170), but I will not reference them in that Simmons quoted Talayesva as specifically saying, "What I do in the Soyal is secret" (6), for all that Simmons did persuade him to provide a rather full account. When Simmons told him that an account had been available "for nearly forty years," he responded, "This is awful. It makes me unhappy. That man Voth was a thief. The secrets are all exposed" (7).

25. Voth had left Orayvi in 1901, something I'll have more to say about below, and Talayesva returned from Sherman in 1909. In that his encounter with Voth here seems to be post-1909, either Voth has returned on a visit or Talayesva has displaced a memory of an earlier encounter.

4. POLINGAYSI QOYAWAYMA'S *No Turning Back*

1. Carlson also is extremely vague about chronology in *Broken Pattern: Sunlight and Shadows of Hopi History*, the title page of which lists her as author "*with* Polingaysi Qoyawayma" (my emphasis). Despite the word "history" in the title, the book is a novel, so perhaps the lack of chronological markers is acceptable. Vada Carlson was a widely published writer on a variety of Western subjects, on the one hand publishing books like *The Desert Speaks* (1956) and *High Country Canvas* (1972), and on the other, *Great Migration: Emergence of the Americas, Indicated in the Readings of Edgar Cayce* published by the mystic Cayce's Association for Research and Enlightenment in 1970. She also wrote, with Gary Witherspoon, *Black Mountain Boy* (1993), the story of the Navajo, John Honie, for a juvenile audience.

2. Qoyawayma—very differently from Albert Yava—provides no names for any one of her teachers or any of her fellow students, nor will she later, when she attends the Sherman Institute, name faculty, staff, or fellow students. Kampmeier took charge at Orayvi in 1899 and was succeeded late in 1903 by John L. Ballenger. As noted in the introduction, both were eventually dismissed from the Indian Service as unfit.

3. Helen Sekaquaptewa will note that at the Keam's Canyon School the Hopi girls were given "striped bed ticking dresses" (93) to wear. This is probably what Qoyawayma was given at Orayvi and a "ticking" dress is mentioned in passing late in the book.

4. Talayesva was only two years older than Qoyawayma, and, since he didn't attend the Orayvi Day School until he was about nine, in September of 1899 (he continued until the spring of 1901 (Aberle, 41), it's possible that some of their time there overlapped. His and Qoyawayma's attendance at the Sherman Institute in Riverside surely overlapped—they both went to California in 1906—but neither of them mentions the other. Although Qoyawayma's life story appeared more than twenty years after *Sun Chief*, she might not have read it because she had early become a strong Christian (see below), and perhaps chose to avoid its abundant sexual detail. But she surely would have known of it.

5. In a letter dated August 13, 1982, published in Jo Lindner's celebratory volume, *When I Met Polingaysi Underneath the Cottonwood Tree*, Carlson writes that some time in 1959, she "went with [Qoyawayma] to Oraibi," surely referring to this trip. Carlson says that on the way, Qoyawayma

"abruptly told [her] that she was not going to talk about herself" (in Linder, 127). Following the visit, "That evening, sitting by the big old tree in her backyard"—this is a cottonwood tree about which we will hear more—Qoyawayma nonetheless reminisces. Carlson, the following morning, "got up at sunrise and began typing the story," which she reads to Qoyawayma "at breakfast." Qoyawayma is pleased, the two collaborate further, and "In 1961, corrected, revised, retyped, we sent our 'baby' to the University Press at Albuquerque" (in Linder, 127).

6. Tawakwaptiwa, known later as Wilson Tawaquaptewa, became renowned as an artist for the *katsina* dolls he made, some few of which, so far as I can tell, are still available for purchase. He always altered one detail or another in the dolls so as not to reveal to outsiders the exact appearance of the *katsinam*. An undated photograph of Tawakwaptiwa appears in Qoyawayma's book with the caption, "Chief Tewaquaptewa, of Old Oraibi, who died in 1960 at the age of 106" (n.p.). Tawakwaptiwa did indeed die in 1960, but since he was born either in 1873 or 1875, he was not 106 at the time of his death. Qoyawayma herself in later life achieved recognition as a potter working with traditional Hopi designs.

7. In a study titled "The Adolescent Socialization of the Hopi Girl," Alice Schlegel notes the time when "the child goes to school and learns that the *bahana* (white person) world differs from the Hopi." Most Hopi students, she writes, "seem to have extracted from their school experience the knowledge useful to Hopi life" (454), although "Few have attempted to establish a permanent role in the *bahana* world or to bring *bahana* life-style into the village." "For an exception to this," she writes, "see Qoyawayma" (1973, 455).

8. Voth was working on Hopi names around this time and had noted "that comparatively few duplicate names exist in the same village" (1905, 69). Whiteley's "Hopitutungwni: Hopi Names as Literature," affirms that Hopi "names serve to individuate persons—each name is unique and confers a unique identity on the bearer" (1998, 106–7). Voth had recognized that although Hopi consultants could roughly translate any name, its actual meaning required knowing "just what the *author* [of the name] had in mind" (1905, 68, my emphasis). Hopi names, as Whiteley elaborates, "construct personal identity, cultural meaning, and interpersonal relations" (1998, 107), just what Albert Yava had said in somewhat different words. All of these meanings disappear when names such as Oliver, Albert, Max, Don, or Bessie are arbitrarily assigned.

9. Voth got this wrong. He wrote that "When the child is twenty days old it receives its first names from the grandmother, or, in case she be not living, from some aunt or other close relative *on its mother's side*" (1905, 67, my emphasis). To the contrary, Peter Whiteley, like Albert Yava, observes that "a baby's name givers are female members of its father's clan… not of its own clan" (1998, 109), which is its mother's clan. Whiteley also quotes a late-twentieth-century Hopi consultant, Herschel Talashoma: "So from my father's side, his relatives, they are my aunties. They are the ones that name you, from your father's side" (1998, 107).

10. This is an important matter. As noted in the previous section, Albert Yava reported that when he "was initiated into the One Horn Society they gave [him] a ceremonial name, Eutawisa, meaning Close in the Antelopes. It was supposed to drown out my original name [Nuvayoiyava], but people still call [him] Yava" (3).

11. In a brief introductory note to Voth's *Traditions of the Hopi*, George Dorsey wrote that "The traditions of the Hopi here presented were collected in the vernacular and without an interpreter, by Mr. H. R. Voth" (n.p.). If this is even approximately accurate it would testify to a very considerable linguistic competence on Voth's part.

12. Epp, along with his friend and ally Mrs. Gertrude Gates, was very much involved in the events of September 7, 1906. Superintendent Lemmon of the Keam's Canyon School, in letters he wrote to the commissioner of Indian affairs dated September 8, 9, 12, and 14, 1906, mentions Epp on several occasions and not favorably. E.g., Lemmon: "If I can muzzle Missionary Epp and Mrs. Gates as they ought to be muzzled we will accomplish more with the Hopis in the next sixty days than has been done in five years." This is from Lemmon's letter of September 9, p. 995 in Whiteley, 2008, vol. II. From Lemmon's letter of September 14: "Epp ought to hide himself. He has about as much judgment as a child" (Whiteley 2008, II, 1,002). There is no mention of Voth.

13. Voth lists "Civanka" as a female name given by a member of "THE BATANGA (SQUASH), CLAN." It means roughly "The One That Figures (a) Blossom" (1905, 74). To understand just how and in what way the name Civanka "figures a blossom," we would, as noted above, have to know the intentions of the name giver.

14. E.g., Kennard: "The Hopi regard life as predetermined in all important respects. All that has ever happened or will happen has been known from

the beginning" (491). Kennard mentions, however, "An example of a man who was able by his strength of will alone to obtain what he desired" (493), and his paper examines the fact that Hopi people generally believe that it is indeed the individual's will, not fate or destiny, that determines whether a sick person will get well and even when a person will die. In these regards, at least, it would seem that "fatalism" is not "a part of Hopi nature."

15. Schlegel writes that the Hopi father's attitude toward his daughter "should be one of tenderness and concern. He is not a disciplinarian; after early childhood [the daughter] is disciplined by her mother and, if necessary, her mother's brother. The father, then, is an affectionate figure, who should always support and protect his young daughter" (1973, 459–60). Mischa Titiev had earlier written that "Young daughters are usually very affectionately regarded by their fathers," while also remarking that the mother-daughter relationship "is one of the warmest bonds in the whole scheme of Hopi relationships" (1944, 20), something to recall in relation to Schlegel's specification of the mother as disciplinarian.

16. During their adolescence, Alice Schlegel writes, Hopi "Girls may get together to go to the spring for water. However, this is a somewhat dangerous activity, as the spirit of the Water Serpent, who lives in springs, may impregnate her with a snake child if she is not careful" (1973, 457). Most readers of this passage would not know that for an adolescent Hopi girl—although small, Qoyawayma is fourteen—a certain fear of water is a sexual fear. All readers will know that there is absolutely nothing of an erotic or sexual nature anywhere in the book.

17. Curtis wrote that she herself had "recorded and edited" these materials. She thanks H. R. Voth for his help, stating very clearly that "the recorder has felt obliged to hold to versions acquired through her own research among the Indians, even where such versions are more or less at variance with those kindly given by Mr. Voth" (478). A first edition of *The Indians' Book* appeared in 1907, with the first complete edition appearing in 1923. The 1968 reissue is of the complete 1923 edition.

18. Cf. Titiev: Maraw "meets in its own kiva," and is "conceptually linked with the men's Tribal Initiation ritual … the Wuwutcim" (1944, 164).

19. Apparently raw potatoes were indeed appealing to Hopi children. Helen Sekaquaptewa, who describes herself (see below) as hungry most of the time at the Keam's Canyon School, notes that when she could get it, a "raw potato … tasted good and sweet" (99).

20. Diane Notarianni writes that after H. R. Voth's arrival in 1893, "his wife, Martha, began to teach Hopi women to sew." Voth himself, she says, was aware "that Hopi men, who did most of the sewing, thought it funny that Martha Voth should teach the women to sew" (1996, 600). One might think that by the time Qoyawayma took it up at Sherman, Hopi gender relations to sewing had changed. But Helen Sekaquaptewa, six years her junior, reports that Hopi men were not only weavers (46) but also sewed their own shirts and trousers (48). Suzanne and Jake Page print photographs of Hopi men weaving sometime after 1974.

21. See also Nequatewa, "Hopi Courtship and Marriage" (1933), as well as Titiev's chapter III, "Courtship, Marriage, and Divorce" (1944, 15–29). A fascinatingly detailed account of "Hopi Marriage Rites on the Wedding Morning" is Voth's (1912). Albert Yava had given a detailed account of the "several" wedding robes given to a woman. "In the old days," he says, "the father wove all of them, but men don't have much time or inclination for weaving any more," so they may "be acquired from someone else" (104). Of these several robes, "The large white one, . . . is supposed to carry her up above the cloud when she dies" (104). He describes two other robes that would be given to a woman on the occasion of her marriage and that she would wear after death. In that "Dead people are believed to send rain in answer to the prayers of the living," one of these robes "is woven loosely to allow the rain to come through" (104).

22. Notarriani writes of "Sivenka and her husband, Qoyawayma" (606), that when "The missionaries hired Qoyawayma as a laborer[,] [h]is wife promptly converted, as did his children," although he "did not convert until old age" (607), that is, as she'd said earlier (601), not until 1925. In that Fred Qoyawayma lived to be ninety, dying in the late 1940s (Turner, 91; she also gives the date of Sevenka's death as 1951), it is probably accurate to speak of his "old age" in 1925.

23. Harold Courlander appends to Albert Yava's *Big Falling Snow* a petition drawn up by Thomas Keam from the Hopi villages "to Washington urging that the Government cease its effort to reallocate clan lands and institute private individual holdings" (165). The petition, dated March, 1894, includes the following statement: "Among us the family traces its kin from the mother, hence all its possessions are hers. The man builds the house but the woman is the owner . . . ; the man cultivates the field, but he renders its harvest into the woman's keeping. . . . A man plants the fields of his wife, and

the fields assigned to the children she bears, and informally he calls them his, although in fact they are not" (165).

24. Although, as I've said, Carlson gives very few dates in the book, here she gives two dates in a short space, 1914 and 1918. These are, of course, the dates when World War I began (although the U.S. did not enter until 1917) and ended. But there is no mention of the war. See Britten for the fullest study of *American Indians in World War I*. He notes that "Bannocks and Utes in Utah, Hopis in Arizona, Paiutes and Klamaths in Nevada and Oregon, and Shoshones from Idaho... expressed disinterest in military service" (21). Other Native men were more interested. Gerald Vizenor's extraordinary recent novel, *Blue Ravens*, is based upon the actual World War I experiences of some of his Anishinaabe (Ojibwe) ancestors.

25. A much fuller account of what I am calling *both/and* and *either/or* logics can be found in my "Trickster Tales Revisited."

26. Spicer's sadness, however, is *not* literary, for unlike Medicine, Ruoff, and myself, he finds the book to be "very competently written by Vada Carlson" (185). Spicer's sadness comes from his belief that "the influence of Mennonite missionaries" (185) prevented Qoyawayma both from "turning back" and from "going forward" (185). I have tried to show that like many boarding-school students she achieved very much the sort of identity on behalf of which she spoke, a Hopi identity, however differently Hopi.

5. HELEN SEKAQUAPTEWA'S *Me and Mine*

1. Hafen cites as the source of this information a "conversation" with Alison Sekaquaptewa Lewis (Helen Sekaquaptewa's daughter), and Kathleen Sands in 2000 (156).

2. Grace Arrington's "Biography of an Indian Latter-Day Saint Woman" mistakenly has Sekaquaptewa converting in 1951 (126). Apart from the 1984 study by Gretchen Bataille and Kathleen Sands, which I will cite, I have found very little criticism of *Me and Mine*, which has been treated, to the extent it has, by anthropologists and Mormons, groups with very different interests.

3. Kathleen Sands interviewed Helen Sekaquaptewa (personal communication from Gretchen Bataille, 11/12/2015) in Scottsdale, Arizona,

on December 20, 1979; in New Oraibi, Arizona, on June 10 and 11, 1980; and also on June 3 and September 5, 1981. She and Gretchen Bataille used information from those interviews in their 1984 book. I have tried but not succeeded in contacting Sands, so that if these interviews still exist, I have not been able to see them.

4. The 1978 interviews are described as having been conducted by "Colleen Helquist's husband and another man" (4). No one at the L. Tom Perry Collections in the Harold B. Lee Library at Brigham Young University, which holds the original manuscript of these interviews, could provide any further information as to the identities of these interviewers—who also did not understand some things. Thus, when Sekaquaptewa said that she and Udall visited the Maricopa people, the interviewers transcribed her words as "we were working in Phoenix with a Mary Copa!" (n.p.).

5. -tewa or -tiwa is an indicator of a masculine name, as, for example, Nequatewa or Tawakwaptiwa. Helen married Emory Sekaquaptewa, as we will see, both according to Hopi custom and by a Christian minister. Sekaquaptewa, whose name was Dowawisnima, "a trail marked by sand" (7), as she notes, took her husband Emory's name at their marriage. Robert Trennert is the only writer to call her "Helen Dowawisnima" during her time at school (1988, 136), which is indeed accurate.

6. Arrington's reference to the katsina initiation, "One of the traditional ceremonies" of the Hopis, calls it "something like a baptism" (124), and it may be that Sekaquaptewa picked up the comparison from Mormon friends.

7. Strictly speaking, as I'd noted above citing Titiev (1944, 94), there was no "New Oraibi" until 1911.

8. The Phoenix Light and Fuel Company had provided electricity to the Keam's Canyon School by 1893 when Albert Yava arrived, as noted earlier, and, having become the Pacific Gas and Electric Company in 1906, was probably still providing electric service to the school when Helen Sekaquaptewa arrived that same year.

9. Cf. Titiev: "During the winter of 1906, the Hotevilla settlers suffered miserably... they had not had time to build adequate shelters before cold weather came, and their food supply was pitifully low" (1944, 207). And James: "The little food which the Youkeoma group had been able to take with them from Oraibi was not sufficient to sustain them during the winter ahead... By winter Hotevila was desperate" (139).

10. A photograph of the Phoenix school's drill corps about 1915, when Sekaquaptewa was at the school, can be found in Archuleta, Child, and Lomawaima, p. 27.

11. Whatever "privileges" the Hopi girls may have received, the school nonetheless bestowed upon Shaw the rank of captain, a rank higher than Sekaquaptewa's lieutenancy.

12. I think it is this sort of relentlessly cheerful tone that caused W. David Laird to call "Mrs. Shaw's book … a disappointment," "emotionally white-washed by an overlay of religious or ethnic platitudes" (178). In her review of the book, Kay Sands writes that "On the surface, [Shaw's] story seems simplistic and naively told" (4), although she also finds in it "tenacious adherence to traditional Pima values" (4). Shaw wrote the book herself, although Bataille and Sands learned that Karen Thure, her editor at the University of Arizona Press, did a great deal of work to prepare the manuscript for publication (89ff). Although Helen Sekaquaptewa also seems to have managed well at the Phoenix School, in the 1978 interview she mentioned "having those stomach aches, I had to go about every night" (5). Bataille and Sands write that it was "cultural suppression that led Helen Sekaquaptewa to suffer from stomach cramps for months when she began to attend school" (93). They correctly note that mention of these "is totally absent in her recollections" (93), that is, in *Me and Mine*.

13. Brown arrived at the school in March of 1915 (Trennert 1988, 150) and retired in 1931 (Trennert 1988, 137). Sekaquaptewa erroneously has him retiring in 1934, but notes that after his retirement, "Nearly every summer, until his death, Mr. and Mrs. Brown came to visit us on the reservation" (139). Sekaquaptewa's relation to Brown obviously was positive, but it's also worth noting that in 1917, during the time she spent at the school, he re-introduced corporal punishment, re-opened the school jail, "and a much more rigid atmosphere descended upon the institution" (Trennert 1988, 165–66).

14. I am once more indebted to Dr. Peter Whiteley for pointing me to this, as well as for elucidating Sekaquaptewa's allusion to the Tower of Babel just below (personal communication, 12/17/15).

15. In 1978, asked by the Mormon interviewers whether "Hopi religion had prepared you to accept the church," Sekaquaptewa answered, "Yes. It is the same story that we were taught in our younger days" (3). She elaborates on p. 5 of the interview, echoing what she had reported her father having said.

6. FRED KABOTIE'S *Hopi Indian Artist*

1. He will be assigned a specific birth date when he attends the Toreva Day School, and, later in his life, some white friends, as "an excuse for a dinner party" (47), give him a birthday in September. He does not record either of those dates in his autobiography, perhaps because, as he would say later in regard to the actual date of his marriage, in Hopi "society[,] exact wedding dates, like birthdays, are meaningless" (48). In an interview with Tryntje Van Ness Seymour "*in Shungopavi in late 1985, shortly before his death*" *(*Seymour, 242, italics in original), Kabotie said that when he "needed a date of birth to get a passport in 1960, his mother and some other elders decided he must have been born 'about 1900,'... because they think [he] was about six years old when the 'hostiles' moved... to Oraibi and then Hotevilla" in 1906 (242).

2. Whiteley writes that Saalako (in current orthography) is "an elaborate Kachina ceremony performed in conjunction with *Niman*" (1988a, 162), the Home Dance. Kabotie's revival of it led to its taking place in July, 1937, "for the yearly Niman Kachina" (65). His grandfather recalled that its last performance on Second Mesa had preceded "the terrible drought and famine of the 1860s" (66).

3. While he was teaching art at Hopi High School in Orayvi, the school was visited by Polingaysi Qoyawayma, whom Kabotie refers to only as Elizabeth White. She supports the use of Hopi material in his teaching, something for which he had been criticized, as she herself had been earlier. Kabotie notes that her "English was better than [his]," and that "Even her Hopi was better" (67).

4. Some ten years later, in the 1985 interview he gave to Tryntje Seymour, he recalled the decision to go to the Santa Fe Indian School somewhat differently. There, he said that at the Toreva School, "They were fed up with me, [and] ....the principal said, 'You go to Santa Fe Indian School. That way you will go to school regularly'" (in Seymour, 243).

5. Kabotie said that "Steve, Jason, Otis, and [him]self" were the four students who went from Shungopavi. (17). Otis is Otis Polelonema, only a bit younger than Fred Kabotie; he would also become an artist. See below. A brief biography of Polelonema appears in Seymour, p. 247. I have not learned anything about Steve and Jason.

6. The "Santa Fe station" mentioned here is the Atchison, Topeka, and Santa Fe Railroad's station in Winslow, AZ. Fred Harvey was an entrepreneur who had opened a number of restaurants and Indian exhibits for travelers along the route of the Santa Fe railroad. Leah Dilworth has provided a harsh but excellent account of Harvey and his promotion of a tourism of "imperialist nostalgia" in the Southwest. The phrase quoted is from Renato Rosaldo and appears in Dilworth, p. 79. Harvey constructed a luxury hotel called La Posada in Winslow, but it did not open until 1930, much later than the time Kabotie describes here. I have not found any information about a smaller Harvey hotel in Winslow in about 1915. Much earlier, in 1883, Harvey had staffed his restaurants with all-female servers, who became known as the Harvey Girls. Judy Garland and Ray Bolger starred in the 1946 musical, *The Harvey Girls*, the first time the two had been together since the 1939 film *The Wizard of Oz*. It included the song, "On the Atchison, Topeka, and the Santa Fe," which won the Academy Award for best song. Kabotie will later speak of "the famous Watchtower at Desert View on the south rim of the Grand Canyon.... operated by the Fred Harvey Company" (48–49) for which he is asked "to do the murals in the 'Hopi Room' on the tower's second level" (49) in 1933. In later years, he would work in the Watchtower's gift shop (62–63), and in 1947, "do some murals for the Fred Harvey Company's new Painted Desert Inn near Holbrook, Arizona" (80).

7. Lamy, NM, eighteen miles south of Santa Fe, was the main railway station for the city of Santa Fe. A herdic is a carriage invented by Peter Herdic in 1881. It had side seats, a rear entrance, and a low entry point. Its capacity at about the time Fred Kabotie encountered it was eight people.

8. John Gram has found a record of the "Daily Routine for Santa Fe Indian School, 1911–2 School Year" (115), just a few years before Kabotie arrived. In that year, the first bugle woke the children at 6:15 and at 8:30 a whistle blew directing half of the students to academic training and the other half to industrial training. Breakfast time is not listed, although it would have to have been between 6:15 and 8:30. At 11:30, the first half of the school day ended and something called "Dinner" was eaten between 11:45 AM and 12:50 PM. Supper was at 4:55, and "Taps and lights out" at 9 (115). "Roll call" does not appear in Gram's table, although it surely would have been in effect in 1911–2 as it was in 1915–6 when Kabotie entered the school.

9. In the 1985 interview, Kabotie explained that his "proper Hopi name... given to him by his father's clan relatives... women and girls,... was *Naqavoy'ma*. That means, 'the sun coming up day after day.' Because [his] father belonged to the Sun clan, and the sun comes day after day" (242). But the husbands of his aunts on his father's side teased him, saying that the "name was too good" (242–43) for him, something he had also noted in the autobiography. As a joke, they gave him the name "'*Qaavotay.*' That means 'tomorrow'" (243). Seymour adds "[literally: 'made it to tomorrow']" (243). But "Kabotie," Fred Kabotie says, "that's not a good Hopi word, that's no Hopi word" (243). The meaning of his "proper Hopi name" is referenced at the very end of his story.

10. Gram quotes Petra Romero, from Jemez Pueblo, at the Santa Fe School from 1901–16, who recalled "always being hungry" and "remembered sneaking milk from the kitchen on several occasions" (138). Andrea Fragua, also from Jemez and at the school from 1919 to 1923, recalled that the food was "'very poor.'" (138). Both of these students' times at SFIS overlapped Kabotie's. A girl who was only five when she arrived at the school from San Juan Pueblo in 1915, about the same time as Fred Kabotie, was hungry enough to find the mush appealing. Sally Hyer notes that she "pointed to the mush, and one of the girls," an older girl who could speak English, explained that the little girl had said, "'She wants that'" (13). Gram observes that "Memories about the quantity and quality of the food vary among former students" (138), as was the case everywhere.

11. We know from a Santa Clara Pueblo student who was at the Santa Fe School in 1915, about the time Kabotie arrived, that Mr. Saenz's dining room duties involved more than disciplining unruly students. This student noted that Mr. Saenz, standing on a platform, would, when the students marched in, hit a triangle for them "First to stand quietly. Then he'd hit again and [the students would] say, 'God is good, God is great, we thank him for this food.... Then he'd ring the bell again and [they] sat" (Hyer, 27). Although Kabotie does not mention it, it seems that grace was indeed said before each meal.

12. The quotation begins on page 18 after which there are eight numbered pages of reproductions of Kabotie's art work, leaving the quotation to be completed on page 27.

13. Along with parsnips, root vegetables grown at the SFIS included turnips. As late as 1927, a woman from San Juan Pueblo who attended the

school remarked, "Turnips and parsnips. Oh, my gosh—I think that was their main menu. I can't stand turnips and parsnips" (in Hyer, 13).

14. Sally Hyer writes of the "carpentry teacher, a Danish immigrant," who came to the Santa Fe school in 1917 (11). She doesn't name him but this must surely be Mr. Jensen. We learn from Hyer that "his wife was the school laundress, and their son even went to classes at the school." She cites Jensen's criticism of the Indian Office's policy of buying the cheapest shoes they could for the students, shoes, he said, "with paper soles, so if we had any wet weather, they would be almost barefoot" (in Hyer, 11). Interestingly, Hyer states that "Often the recollections of staff are less positive than those of the students" (11).

15. Tryntje Seymour writes that "Polelonema studied at Santa Fe Indian School from about 1915 to 1921"—the years that Kabotie was there—"and attended Mrs. DeHuff's living-room watercolor sessions with Fred Kabotie and several other students" (247). Kabotie mentions Polelonema briefly in the 1985 interview with Seymour (243), although he is not mentioned further in the autobiography.

16. John Gram writes that "on several occasions in his diary DeHuff records playing Native American roles written by himself or by other prominent whites in Santa Fe" (216n51). I can't say whether he also performed in the school plays his wife and her colleague wrote or whether Santa Fe School students were involved in plays DeHuff or "other prominent whites" wrote.

17. Maria Montoya Martinez (1887–1980) was an internationally known potter from San Ildefonso Pueblo, some twenty miles northwest of Santa Fe. Her husband, Julian Martinez (1879–1943), himself a potter, decorated some of Maria's early works. He later became a painter, and one of his commissions was to paint murals for the Santa Fe Indian School. Maria worked with the anthropologist Alice Marriott, who wrote her biography, *Maria*. An excellent photo of Maria and Julian Martinez painting pottery in Santa Fe in 1912 appears in Babcock and Parezo, p. 222.

18. The impassioned disgust of these reformers may be conveyed by True's characterization of "the Pueblos generally as 'the Sodom and Gemorrah of the modern world'" (in Wenger, 219).

19. Wenger titles a section of her study, "Romantic Primitivism: Reenchanting the World?" (81). The question might arise, of course, as to how "cultural *modernists*" might be "romantic *primitivists*" as well, and

a very great deal has been written on this subject. Short of a fuller discussion, I'll simply quote Joel Pfister's observation that "Scholars have long recognized that two of the hallmarks of the modernisms, paradoxically, are the antimodernisms and the primitivisms" (2004, 140). A section of Leah Dilworth's study of Mary Austin (and some like-minded contemporaries) titled "Modernist Primitivism" (174–82) makes clear that the phrase is not at all oxymoronic.

20. On this phase of Lummis's career see Sherry Smith, "Charles Fletcher Lummis and the Fight for the Multicultural Southwest."

21. Wenger makes the important point that "Lummis' career revealed generally patronizing attitudes toward the Indians he wanted to help" (67), and that "Neither his opposition to coercive methods nor his praise of Hopi religion changed [his] basic view of Indians as childlike 'primitives'" (69). Similarly, K. Tsianina Lomawaima and Teresa McCarty are surely correct in concluding that John Collier replaced "federal paternalism that denigrated Native societies with a paternalism that romanticized them," for all that "Both versions of paternalism elevated federal over tribal powers" (68).

22. Kabotie told Tryntje Seymour that "At Santa Fe Indian School [he] was painting when it was against the policies of the government.... That's why Mr. DeHuff was demoted. Because they were letting me paint" (244). But, as I've noted and will note further, letting students paint was by no means the only reason DeHuff was transferred.

23. Many years later, Kabotie would also provide illustrations for *Field Mouse Goes to War* (1944), a bilingual children's book for which Albert Yava prepared the Hopi language version of a traditional tale and Edward Kennard the English. Tryntje Seymour writes that Otis "Polelonema also did illustrations with Fred Kabotie for Mrs. DeHuff's children's book, *Taytay's Tales*" (247).

24. She is Alice Talayaonema (Seymour 244), also an artist who did basket work and made silver jewelry.

25. Not only did Kabotie undergo his own Wuwtsim initiation but, as Seymour wrote, "He served four years as leader of the *Wuwtsimt* men's society" (246). There is a fine reproduction of a watercolor by Kabotie called "WUWUCHIM" and dated "circa 1928"—perhaps, thus, before his own initiation—on p. 26 of the autobiography. A smaller reproduction appears on p. 299 of Seymour's book along with detailed comments offered

by Kabotie himself, by Tryntje Seymour, and by Michael Lomatuway'ma on Wuwtsim.

26. Moe (1894–1975) was primarily associated with the John Simon Guggenheim Memorial Foundation from its founding in 1925 until his retirement as its president in 1963.

27. Kabotie does, however, include "A Niman Kachina dance photographed in 1927, before cameras were banned at our ceremonies" (75).

PART II: NAVAJO BOARDING-SCHOOL AUTOBIOGRAPHIES

1. Brumble names autobiographies by Left Handed, Frank Mitchell, and Emerson Blackhorse Mitchell as "perhaps the best known" (1993, 144). Of the three, only Frank Mitchell went to boarding school, and I mention the others in appendix B. Brumble's 1981 annotated bibliography contains references to sixty-six Navajo autobiographies, by far the most for any tribal nation. Next most numerous are those of the "Sioux" (1981, 173) for whom he lists thirty-six, and the "Eskimo" with thirty (172). Many of the Navajo titles Brumble lists are brief ethnographic texts.

2. Of many studies of these events, see, in particular, Iverson, Cheek, and Bailey (1964 and 1970). Jennifer Denetdale's *The Long Walk: The Forced Navajo Exile*, aimed at a juvenile audience, is also very informative. Of special interest is Ruth Roessel's edited collection of *Navajo Stories of the Long Walk Period*, and *Oral Histories of the Long Walk: Hweeldi Baa Hane* gathered by Lake Valley Navajo School.

7. FRANK MITCHELL'S *Navajo Blessingway Singer*

1. It was published in 1970 as *Blessingway* and contained, along with Mitchell's version, two others, by men identified as Slim Curly and River Junction Curly.

2. I have several times noted with disapproval the exclusive use of consultants' first names by anthropologists or others who worked with them. Given the long and close acquaintance of Frisbie and McAllester with Frank Mitchell and their extreme care and scrupulousness in consulting with him and his family at every point in their work together, it would be petty to

register such disapproval here. (For example, Barbara Tedlock: "The book . . . has its own importance in the history of anthropology, reflecting fully the ethical concerns of its era. It is perhaps the first book of its genre to be submitted, at the manuscript stage, to the editorial judgments of the family of its narrator" [392].) But it is difficult entirely to ignore the disparity between references by McAllester and Frisbie to "McAllester" and "Frisbie" and to Mitchell only as "Frank."

3. For example, Jay Miller: "This volume will set the standards for ethnographic biographies [sic] for some time to come" (278). Barre Toelken: "This book stands easily among the best of the 'native' autobiographies" (272). Lawrence Kelly: "Both the editors and the University of Arizona Press are to be congratulated for the superior quality of this work" (224). A second printing appeared in 2001 with the same pagination as the first edition.

4. The editors offer an endnote speculating that Mitchell's "estimates here seem to reflect the Navajo sense of time" (73), and, reflecting the Western academic sense of time, they state that he "probably was initially enrolled in 1894 when he was thirteen years old" (73n6).

5. A brief but very fine account of the life of Henry Chee Dodge (1857–1947) is David Brugge's "Henry Chee Dodge: From the Long Walk to Self-Determination."

6. Barre Toelken, in his review of *Navajo Blessingway Singer*, had written, "I find the . . . narrative so comfortably diffuse and *usefully repetitious* (making clear the import of earlier statements and actions) that I can only congratulate Frisbie and McAllester for not being more successful in their attempt to anglicize the narrative line. It came out just right" (273, my emphasis). I, too, think it "came out just right," not as the result of a failure of anglicization, but rather due to great care on the part of Frisbie and McAllester.

7. The editors write that 1904 is also the year that "Frank begins to learn some things about the Blessingway."

8. IRENE STEWART'S *A Voice in Her Tribe*

1. Shepardson was an interesting woman. She had visited Russia early in her life and on her return to the United States became an active member of the Communist Party. She also engaged in work outside the Party on behalf of racial equality. Although she had resigned from the Party in

1953, she was nonetheless called to testify before the House Un-American Activities Committee in 1957. By that time she had begun graduate work in anthropology at Stanford University, receiving her Master's degree in 1956. Possibly because she had experienced discrimination as a married, middle-aged woman, she transferred from Stanford to Berkeley, where she completed her PhD on Navajo government in 1960. Babcock and Parezo's brief account of Shepardson does not mention her political activities before studying anthropology, evidence perhaps of David Price's observation that "her past involvement in the Communist Party and her appearance before the House Committee on Un-American Activities are facts that remain largely unknown to most anthropologists" (168). For Price's account of these "facts" see his pp. 164–68.

2. Dawdy was an expert on Navajo water rights, a historian of the West, and a cataloger of American Indian painters. I have been able to find out little more about her, and nothing about her relationship to Mary Shepardson. In Shepardson's appendix, called "From My Notebooks," she writes that "Long before [she] studied anthropology, [she] used to visit Chinle [Arizona] with [her] late husband, Dr. Dwight Shepardson" (in Stewart, 81), in the 1940s, and I would guess that Shepardson met Dawdy on one of those visits.

3. Very little has been written about Stewart or *A Voice in Her Tribe*. The book is listed in Brumble's *Annotated Bibliography* (1981), and summarized in Brill de Ramirez (2007, 187–89). A brief review by the Native poet and novelist Linda Hogan appeared in 1983, and Deborah Gordon offered a tendentious and error-filled discussion in 1993. Otherwise, useful context is to be found in Charlotte Frisbie's "Traditional Navajo Women: Ethnographic and Life History Portrayals" (1982).

4. Stewart had told Shepardson that the missionary was a Mr. Black. In her appendix, Shepardson recorded Stewart's quoting Mr. Black as saying " 'Let's get rid of that *Gli Nezbah* and call you Irene.' " She says, "I liked it. I thought it was pretty but my father didn't like it. He called me *Gli Nezbah* till his death" (in Stewart, 81). We will hear more of Mr. Black.

5. Although Gladys Reichard's *Dezba: Woman of the Desert* (1939) is fiction, all its "details," Reichard claimed, "are true" (vi). (See appendix B.) Here is what it has to say on the subject of boarding-school laundries: "The laundry at the boarding-schools [*sic*] was a chamber of horrors. Every child had to put in many hours there. There grew up among Indian students a special way of referring to work in the laundry, a few words uttered in a particular

tone of voice with a subtle lift of the eyebrows, which was like the password of a secret society" (63). This and what Stewart describes exceed by a good deal Hopis' experience with boarding-school laundries, and as we will see, not all Navajo students found laundry detail so oppressive.

6. Stewart says that "We knew [Mr. Black] through uncle Lewis, who did all the interpreting for him and other Protestant missionaries" (17). The religious situation at Fort Defiance is different from what Frank Mitchell had described some twenty years earlier, in that there are now interpreters, and regardless of whether Catholics are still in the majority, there are also "Protestant missionaries" at the school.

7. The students would surely have told "Navajo stories" in Navajo. That would mean that either the stories were told out of the hearing of school staff, or this was an occasion when the requirement to speak English was suspended. Frank Mitchell, in attendance at the Fort Defiance School more than a decade earlier, had said that speaking Navajo was the norm, with, unusually, no punishment for doing so.

8. This, too, Navajos do differently. At school, Stewart says, she "learned to use patterns and go by measurements," whereas her stepmother "simply took the goods, tore it into several lengths for [her] skirt, and for the blouse she cut only where she could not tear. When she sewed them together"—by hand, in that they "did not have a sewing machine"—"they fit correctly" (18).

9. An excellent study of Kinaalda is by Charlotte Frisbie (1993 [1967]). The books on this subject by Shirley Begay et al. (1983) and Monty Roessel (1993), although written for a juvenile audience, are well worth adult attention. See also Ruth Roessel's "Navajo Mother and Child in Today's World: The Kinaalda Ceremony for Faith Roessel," the author's daughter, which provides a photographic record of some of the events making up Faith Roessel's puberty ceremony.

10. Benjamin Rader writes that from Irene Stewart's "recollection, it is not clear that Haskell even had a dress code" (440). He notes, however, that Esther Burnett Horne, a Shoshone woman who graduated from Haskell in 1929, and whose time at the school almost surely overlapped Stewart's, "provides a specific description of the school's dress requirements" (Rader, 440n27). Among these were, for girls, "a 'hickory,' a plain, short-sleeved light blue dress, while the boys all wore light blue shirts and dark pants" (440). Military uniforms, as Stewart wrote, were worn on Sundays and for special occasions. For Horne, see volume 2.

11. Clara Bow was a silent film star who transitioned to talkies successfully with her 1927 film, *It*, in which she played a shopgirl. "It" was sex appeal.

12. Mary Shepardson provides some further information about Greyeyes in her appendix. She writes that "as a boy [he] was called *Ashkii Tso*, or Big Boy. Later he was called Greyeyes." Then his sister came back from school "with the name Grace Stewart. So she named him Greyeyes Ben Stewart" (in Stewart, 82).

13. Stewart does not herself seem to have had much experience herding sheep and goats, but in recalling her father's life, she mentions that he and her stepmother had "acquired a few sheep and goats" (45). But with the "stock reduction" program of the 1930s, "it was necessary to limit the number of sheep so as to reduce erosion and grass shortage." This, she writes, "caused much confusion," and her "father ended up with [no sheep] at all" (46). I will take these matters up in the discussion of Kay Bennett's *Kaibah*, which follows.

9. KAY BENNETT'S *Kaibah*

1. Bennett told Lala Waltrip in 1981 that her birth date was "about 1924," although, Waltrip writes, "the actual date of her birth is not known because no records were kept by Navajo families at that time" (10). Maureen Reed writes that she has "seen Bennett's birth date listed as 1920, 1922, and 1924" (2005a, 318n7). Reed takes 1920 as most likely on the basis of a conversation with Bennett's stepson, Andy Bennett, and from a reading of *Kaibah*. *Kaibah* would be my source for the 1920 date. It is also the date given in Bennett's obituary in the *Los Angeles Times*, November 19, 1997, although other obituaries give different dates of birth for her.

2. In her headnote to *Kaibah*, Bennett refers to the Navajo internment at "the concentration camp at Fort Sumner" (n.p.), and, perhaps with Holocaust parallels in mind, explains her book as, in effect, an act of bearing witness. She writes: "The author believes that the history of her people would not be complete if it did not record the everyday life of a family as it was lived then," that is, "during the period from 1928 to 1935" (n.p.). In the liner notes to her LP, *Songs from the Navajo Nation* (1966), surely written by Bennett herself (she is listed as the album's producer), she describes the last song on side 1 as one that is "believed" to be "one of the songs the Navajo people sang

after being released from the concentration camp in 1868." Both of these uses of the phrase precede the publication of Lynn Bailey's *Bosque Redondo: An American Concentration Camp* in 1970. Bennett repeated the phrase, "the concentration camp at Fort Sumner" to Lala Waltrip in 1981 (13).

3. In her essay, Reed writes that "Some of the events [Bennett] depicts [in *Kaibah*] are tragic, such as when a school superintendent takes Kaibah and her siblings to school against her mother's will" (2005b, 117). This is simply not so. Reed's chapter on Bennett, in a book published the same year as that essay (2005a) corrects the error. There, Reed accurately writes that in response to the superintendent's visit to take Kaibah to school, Mother instead "arranged to send her fourteen-year-old son, Keedah, in her daughter's place" (179).

4. The paragraph concludes: "In a few days they forgot the school language and reverted to their old lives as though they had never been away" (185).

5. See also Peter Iverson's chapter, "'Our People Cried': 1923–1941."

6. Lala Waltrip wrote that "Kay sang before the public for the first time in 1951," and "In 1952, she was chosen Queen of the Flagstaff Powwow in Arizona," then, "in 1954 she represented the Navajo Tribe at the Miss Indian of [*sic*] America Beauty Contest at Sheridan, Wyoming" (12). Waltrip thought that Bennett "was highly favored among the contestants" (12), but the actual winner that year was Mary Louise Defender, Yanktanais, Sioux. The first year of the national contest was 1954, and its competitors were to have been unmarried women, ages sixteen to twenty-five. Bennett was at least thirty, more likely thirty-four. See fig. 10. Price was the name of Bennett's second husband although I do not know whether she was or was not still married to him in 1954 when she entered the contest. I discuss Bennett's political career below.

7. See Benjamin Rader for an account of how Native people used the 1926 Haskell "homecoming"—it took place in October, a few months after Irene Stewart had left the school in June—"as an opportunity to experiment with a wide range of possible identities" (431), through performance.

8. In 1952, the first "Miss Navaho Nation" was a twenty-three-year-old woman, Beulah Melvin Allen, who would go on to become a medical doctor. Marilyn Help Hood, Miss Navajo for 1977, would teach Navajo language and culture for almost thirty years. Competitors in the Miss Navajo Nation contest must speak Navajo and demonstrate competence in

such things as bread-making and butchering a sheep (this can be done by a team of competitors). Talents to be displayed include weaving, storytelling, and grinding corn.

9. MacDonald had first been elected chair of the Navajo Tribal Council in 1970 (Iverson, 246) and served in that position until 1982 when he lost to Peterson Zah. He ran again in 1986, first in a primary election with no fewer than twelve candidates, Kay Bennett among them. She received 112 votes to Zah's more than 15,000 and the more than 22,000 for MacDonald, who went on to win the general election (Iverson, 286). In 1991, MacDonald was sentenced "to fourteen years and seven months" in federal prison "for conspiracy to commit kidnapping and burglary of tribal buildings as well as for receiving kickbacks" (Iverson, 296). See MacDonald's autobiography, *The Last Warrior*, in particular pages 336–65, for his defense against these charges.

10. The first woman to be elected to the tribal council was Lily Neil in the late 1940s (Iverson, 192; Lee, 283). Annie Wauneka, a woman Irene Stewart knew well, won election in 1951 "and proceeded to serve on the council for the next thirty years" (Iverson, 199). Injured in an automobile accident, Lily Neil did not run for reelection in 1951, and Wauneka was the only woman serving on the tribal council during her long tenure (Iverson, 200; L. Lee, 283).

10. *Stories of Traditional Navajo Life and Culture*

1. Article III of the 1868 "Treaty Between the United States of America and the Navajo Tribe of Indians," the Treaty of Bosque Redondo, as I'd noted earlier, specified that the United States agrees "to be built at some point" a "school-house and chapel, so soon as a sufficient number of children can be induced to attend school" (in Wilkins, 231). Article VI stated that the Navajos "pledge themselves to compel their children, male and female, between the ages of six and sixteen years, to attend school," and that "the United States agrees that, for every thirty children between said ages who can be induced or compelled to attend school, a house shall be provided and a teacher competent to teach the elementary branches of an English education shall be furnished" (in Wilkins, 232).

2. Her transition to the subject of her early traditional Navajo training is interesting. Mrs. Bob Martin says, "As I have told you, my formal education

began in my adult years" (133). The reader may wonder at this, in that she has twice reported that she was enrolled at the Fort Lewis School at the age of ten (121, 129). But she has also told us that at the time she "became of age," she "was still at home and had a puberty ceremony" (126), as Irene Stewart, who also attended the Fort Lewis School, had not. Regardless, therefore, of her age in years, once she has had the puberty ceremony performed, she is indeed an adult. Near the end of her narrative, Mrs. Bob Martin offers the following reflection: "when I finally entered school, I had to work hard to learn; and, because I was already mature, learning was not easy" (133).

3. Thomas Clani, whose "father had to enroll [him] at the Shiprock boarding school" (243) in the fall of 1923, said, "We always were hungry; it seemed that enough food never was served at mealtime" (244), so that inadequate nutrition at Shiprock continued well beyond the conclusion of the First World War. As George P. Lee's account will show (see below), students at Shiprock were still eating poorly in the early 1950s.

4. Hanley describes no punishments at Shiprock; his account may be supplemented by Clani's slightly later one (and the still later one by George P. Lee; see below). Clani states, "When a student was naughty or did something wrong he was punished immediately. The boys' disciplinarian usually kept a strap, and he used it on the boys when they got out of hand—even just slightly. He also used such punishment as marching us back and forth in front of the boys' dorm for at least five hours on Saturday afternoons while we were supposed to be free for play, carrying signs saying, 'I am a bad boy'" (244).

5. That school is surely Hampton Institute, and it is in Virginia, not West Virginia.

6. Born in 1901, Tom Ration was "moved to the Albuquerque Indian School" in 1913. He notes that in "those days there were no high school grades. Education for Indians went only through the eighth grade," so that after two years when he "had completed the eighth grade [he] was told that [he] had graduated." This was about 1914, when "World War I had broken out" (310). A younger contemporary of Hanley's, William Cadman, "In the fall of 1928 . . . was taken to the Albuquerque Indian School" (210), where he entered the seventh grade. By this time, it is possible to stay on and graduate from the twelfth grade, and Cadman's attendance at the school would have overlapped Hanley's year there. Cadman notes the school's "military setup," its "precision drill companies . . . roll call every time we went to classes and the dining hall," and marching "in step to the captains' calls." He also saw

the girls marching and remembers "drill contests by companies" (210). What he especially recalls is his "good training in farming at the Albuquerque Indian School" (211).

7. Begay will later say, "My husband also has done his duty as a father. When a child got out of hand, he used strict punishment on him or her by using his belt to keep the son or daughter under control. I always knew it was necessary; so I never interfered by shielding them." Similar to what she herself had once said at school, she reports that her children say, "'Thank you, Dad, for the correction'" (67).

8. These are uniforms made from Holland cloth, a rough, dull-finished linen or cotton originally imported from the Netherlands.

9. The Leupp Boarding School in Arizona was named after Commissioner of Indian Affairs Francis Leupp, and was in operation from 1909 to 1942. In 1943 it became a Japanese Isolation Center for the internment of Japanese Americans.

10. Also included in Johnson's book is the narrative of Jeannette Blake, born about 1902. She had also gone to school at Tuba City, attending for nine years, from the age of six until she was fifteen. She remembers no vocational training in her time, and also that speaking Navajo was forbidden (202). The punishment for those caught speaking Navajo came on Saturdays and consisted of the girls having to put on boys' pants while the boys "were forced to put on girls' clothing" (204). Any runaways who were caught were confined in the school, "not a jail" (204), and not allowed outside for a week.

II. GEORGE P. LEE'S *Silent Courage*

1. George Bloomfield and his wife Lucy had run the Toadlena, New Mexico, Trading Post for many years from 1911 or 1912. See appendix B, where I note that Lucy Bloomfield wrote the foreword to Franc Johnson Newcomb's *Hosteen Klah*—Johnson and her husband were also the proprietors of a trading post in Navajo country—and would herself publish a brief biography of Navajo chief Natani.

2. He later confirms that it was the Bloomfields who first told him and his family "about the Book of Mormon, a volume of inspired scripture that called Indians 'the Lamanites'" (102). The LDS Church considered the Lamanites to be the ancestors of the indigenous peoples of the Americas and

possibly the world. Science has discovered no group of people who might correspond to the Lamanites.

3. Page 289 of Lee's book has a photograph captioned, "George P. Lee teaching a student to write in Navajo at the Rough Rock School," in the late 1960s. Obviously Lee had learned to do this, and, as obviously the Rough Rock School allowed him to teach it. The Rough Rock Demonstration School, now the Rough Rock Community School, was founded in 1965 and funded by the federal government but locally controlled. In 1978, pursuant to the Indian Self-Determination Act of 1975, it was permitted to contract out services formerly provided by the Bureau of Indian Affairs to whomever it chose. For an excellent account of the Rough Rock School see McCarty and Bia.

APPENDIX A: THE ORAYVI SPLIT

1. Margaret Jacobs writes that the "BIA's [Bureau of Indian Affairs's] job description for field matrons called for them to educate Indian women in the 'care of a house, keeping it clean and in order . . . adorning the home, both inside and out, with pictures, curtains, home-made rugs, flowers, grassplots, and trees.'" Ms. Keith might have taught young Hopi women to adorn the home with flowers, of which there were many in Hopi country, although there were no grassplots in their part of Arizona. A field matron was also to teach "proper observance of the Sabbath," and, in general to "lend her aid in ameliorating the condition of Indian women" (1999, 27).

APPENDIX B: THE NAVAJO AUTOBIOGRAPHICAL CANON

1. The life histories in Broderick Johnson's collection have not, in my estimation, achieved canonical status, nor has the autobiography of George P. Lee. Two more recent Navajo texts might also be included in the Navajo literary canon if not strictly the Navajo autobiographical canon. These are Laure Tohe's *No Parole Today* (1999) and Irvin Morris's *From the Glittering World: A Navajo Story* (1997). Tohe, born in 1952, has much to say about her own boarding-school experience and that of others she knows who attended the schools. Morris was born in 1958, and his book's personal narratives tell

of some of his school experiences. Tohe's book is a mix of poetry and short prose pieces, and Morris's contains versions of traditional myths and legends, passages of imagined history, and autobiographical fiction. I'll discuss both of these in volume 2 of this study, in the section called, "The Legacy of the Boarding Schools in Native American Literature."

2. Only one critic has considered Newcomb's work in any detail. Susan Brill de Ramirez, who had referenced Newcomb briefly in a 2007 publication (pp. 179–81 passim), devoted a section of her 2015 book to her (pp. 19–42). Brill de Ramirez's essential point, several times repeated, is that Newcomb's work is *good* because she knew her subject and his family well, in contrast to *bad* anthropological life-history work by people like Walter Dyk, her particular bête noire.

3. The Bloomfields would later take over the "Mancos Creek Colorado Trading Post," where George P. Lee encountered them in the late 1940s and early '50s (Lee 67ff.).

APPENDIX C: APACHE BOARDING-SCHOOL AUTOBIOGRAPHIES

1. Another Apache of this generation, Nah-deiz-az—I have found no English name for him, nor any record of him in the Carlisle archives—is said to have attended Carlisle a bit earlier, probably arriving with fifty-two Apache students in 1884 (Deloria, 99). He seems to have left the school by 1887, returning to the Southwest where he took up farming and became known as "the Carlisle Kid." In a dispute over land, he shot and killed Lieutenant Seward Mott, and was hanged on December, 27, 1889 (McKanna 1997, 117). I have found no record of his brief Carlisle experience. The little I have learned about him comes from Deloria, Pfister (2004), and McKanna (1997). The Carlisle Kid was sometimes confused with someone about his age known as the Apache Kid. Discussing the "End of [his] Service at Carlisle" in his autobiography, Richard Pratt mentions false stories being spread about some of his returned students. "One of these," he writes, "covered the alleged atrocities committed by an Arizona Apache outlaw named Kid. It was stated that Kid had been well educated at the 'Carlisle Indian University.' The facts were that Kid was an outlaw years before Carlisle was established and never attended any school" (334). Pratt says nothing about

the Carlisle Kid who had indeed attended the school. For the Apache kid, see de la Garza and McKanna (2009).

2. All the literature refers to Daklugie as Asa or Ace Daklugie, a proper name given to him when he was the first in a line of students to be named at Carlisle, and the person in charge doled out Asa, Benjamin, Charles, Daniel, and so on. Eve Ball (see note just below) quotes him more than once as saying things like, "I've always hated that name. It was forced on me as though I had been an animal" (1988, 144). Ball, however, said to be the only Anglo he trusted (more or less) and allowed to know him (more or less)—Daklugie was the principal consultant for her *Indeh: An Apache Odyssey*, in which his recollections of boarding school appear—nonetheless regularly used the "hated" name in referring to him in print. To be sure, many of his Apache contemporaries also referred to him as Asa or Esa. But in view of Daklugie's strong sense of the matter, it seemed to me best not to use the name. I call him Daklugie and treat the scene of his naming more fully below.

3. Eve Ball (1890–1984) moved to Ruidoso, New Mexico, in 1942, and lived on the edge of the Mescalero Apache Reservation. Over many years she became acquainted with several of the Apaches who passed by her home, the women first, and first among them Ramona Chihuahua Daklugie, Daklugie's wife. This acquaintance led to her acceptance by a range of Apache elders, men and women, and, eventually, even by Daklugie whose distrust and dislike of the Americans had not diminished with time.

4. At about the age of sixteen, Beshad-e, the granddaughter of the Apache leader Victorio, was sent from Florida to Carlisle, where she arrived on December 8, 1886 (Boyer, 105). Ruth Boyer imagines her as "desolate," and upset to find the Apache boys looking "strange," with their hair cut short and without their "breechcloths" (105). When she convinces a school official that she is indeed a married woman, she is returned to imprisonment in St. Augustine, Florida. We have no actual word from her of her brief experience at Carlisle, only Boyer's purely fanciful recreation of what she might have said or thought during her short time there.

5. Opler's presentation of Chris's negotiation of Apache and mainstream American culture comes close to justifying the "two worlds" metaphor of which I have been critical above.

6. In 1938, Opler published a short account of the Geronimo campaign given to him by Kenoi, but no other autobiographical material. Kenoi and Nicholas, Chiricahuas born about 1875, were very interesting and

accomplished men. Kenoi, for example, also worked with the anthropologist Harry Hoijer, narrating eight Apache Coyote stories, many more of which appear in the unpublished autobiography. Nicholas in 1939 published a paper on the important Apache puberty ceremony for girls, and mastered "the international code of phonetics" enabling him to "put the Apache language in print" (Ball, in Kaywaykla, 216), and to write Coyote stories in the language.

7. As I have shown in the first part of this book, the government's insistence that the Hopis send their children to school, though not the actual cause of the Orayvi Split (see above and appendix A), was nonetheless an important factor in this critical change in Hopi society. Apache schooling, however, came strictly as a consequence of the changes wrought by conquest.

8. Nor, for that matter, is it possible to speak of an Apache autobiographical canon apart from the boarding-school stories as it is for the Navajo. (See appendix B.) There are only *Geronimo: His Own Story*, published in 1906, and Chris's *Apache Odyssey* as the sole further examples of Apache autobiography in print, and *Apache Odyssey* has not been widely read or noted.

9. It's not clear who chose the chapter titles or the titles of sections within the chapters. I suspect that it was Nye, although it might have been the publisher, or in some cases Betzinez himself.

10. Eve Ball wrote that "Betzinez was not regarded as a fighting man by the Apaches [she] interviewed. They ridiculed the idea of his ever having done any fighting, and also the title of his book" (1988, 53n1). The jacket cover of the original 1959 edition has on it what appears to be a photograph of Geronimo, although the subject is not identified. In the acknowledgements at the conclusion of his brief foreword, Colonel Wilbur Nye, Betzinez's editor, writes that the jacket illustration is a painting "by Mr. J. Franklin Whitman, Jr. of Lebanon, Pennsylvania" (n.p.). Whitman's painting is an exact reproduction of a well-known photograph of Geronimo (it was reproduced on many picture postcards, and used on the jacket of several editions of Geronimo's own autobiography) by A. Frank Randall, probably taken on the San Carlos Reservation in 1884. In it, Geronimo, down on one knee, carries a rifle and wears a fierce expression. The inside back flap of the book's jacket does have a photo of Betzinez. It pictures the ninety-nine-year-old Apache elder at the bottom of the stairs of a TWA airplane—this was the first flight he had ever taken—shaking hands with Nye. The 1987 University of Nebraska paperback reprint uses a painting of a "Chiricahua Apache" on

horseback on the front cover. The 1987 edition reproduces the 1959 edition, so its pagination is the same.

11. Nye stated that although Betzinez had written the book on his own, he asked him to edit it "rigorously" (Foreword n .p.). Nye did this "by rearranging much of the material and by paraphrasing where necessary" (n.p.). In this particular case, it appears that Nye did not feel a chronological rearrangement was necessary.

12. Samuel Kenoi, who was also a prisoner at Fort Marion and attended Carlisle, told Morris Opler that young Apache captives were made to attend Catholic schools in Saint Augustine prior to Pratt's selection of a group of them for his school (Opler, 384). He also says that Pratt took over 100 young people to Pennsylvania, many more than Betzinez recalled (Opler, 385).

13. Carlisle was an avid user of "before" and "after" photographs of its Indian students, snapping them on first arrival in their various tribal attire and then, at some later point, in their school uniforms. These photographs were taken by John Nicholas Choate from the time of the school's opening in 1879 until Choate's death in 1902. A fuller account of the use of photography by the Carlisle school is to be found in Mauro.

14. Daklugie: "we don't eat fish; we don't eat anything that grows under water" (in Ball 1988, 127).

15. Betzinez, at age thirty-six, hardly needed Pratt's permission to leave school. Rather than "permission," he was asking Pratt for his blessing.

16. The relevant literature usually says that *Juh* is to be pronounced "Whoa" or "Ho." I believe Ho is most nearly correct and, if what Samuel Kenoi told Morris Opler is accurate, the name has no particular meaning but refers to the fact that Juh stuttered (Opler, 367).

17. It was only after writing this that I came across Claire Farrer's sharp dissent from David Dunaway's favorable review of *Indeh*, confirming my suspicions. Farrer, who does know Apache languages, wrote that Ball "grievously mistranslated *indeh*," which she calls an "idiosyncratic spelling" of "the Eastern Apachean name the people give to themselves; it is cognate with Navajo *dine*"; "it means The People," and "it most certainly does not mean 'dead'" (342).

Farrer wrote that the "book Dunaway reviewed [in 1988] carries a 1980 publication date and thus represents a reprinting of a title that should have been allowed to stay out of print" (342). While I don't agree with that harsh assessment, one may well wonder how Ball, with her thirty years of regular contact with Apache people, can have made an error of this magnitude. Ball does quote Eugene Chihuahua, brother of Daklugie's wife, Ramona, as saying, "We had long known that we were *Indeh*, the Dead . . . " (1988, 64), but this cannot be accurate.

18. Ball adds that Betzinez "and Daklugie were enemies all their lives. Daklugie regarded Betzinez as a coward, and Betzinez resented that" (142n4), as one can easily imagine he would. Betzinez would have been at Carlisle for a year at most at this time and his English cannot have been very good. This is to say that despite his best efforts, he could not have given Pratt a very accurate rendering of what the new Apache arrivals were saying.

19. Daklugie did not mention religious observances at Carlisle. Sherry Robinson, who edited Ball's papers, quotes her as having written that "Daklugie never accepted the concepts of any church" (185). Other Apache students at Carlisle did become members of one church or another, although some often returned to traditional practices. In Ball's papers, Robinson found a comment by Samuel Kenoi in which he referred to his religion as "fifty-fifty," noting that he would "pray to God direct," while he also believed "in the Indian religion" (Robinson, 185).

20. Thorpe played football and ran track at Carlisle from 1907 to 1912, taking 1909–1910 off to play professional baseball in North Carolina for $15 a week. This latter activity resulted in the Olympic medals he won in 1912 being later withdrawn, because Olympic participation was officially restricted to "amateur" athletes at the time. In 1912 he also became the intercollegiate ballroom dancing champion, although, again, Carlisle was not a college. Born in 1887, Thorpe would have been a bit older than most college men of the time.

21. Although Daklugie attended boarding school against his will, he would later choose to have his daughters educated at Carlisle. An exchange of letters between William Light, superintendent at Mescalero, and O. H. Lipps, superintendent of Carlisle in August and September of 1916, discusses Daklugie's request that Maude Daklugie, age fourteen, and her sister, Sarah, age thirteen, be allowed to enroll at the school (carlisleindian.dickinson.edu accessed 9/6/16).

22. After an attack on Lipan Apaches in 1873, American troops captured two children, a girl and a boy, about six and five years old. They lived with

various families until, "In March, 1880, the children were enrolled at the Carlisle Indian School" (Minor, 186). Known by that time as Kesetta and Jack, at Carlisle they became Kesetta Roosevelt and Jack Mather. For a fuller account of them, see Minor, and Fear-Segal (2007 and 2016). Kaywaykla, whose own date of birth is uncertain (see note below) may or may not have been younger than these two.

23. Ball writes that he "was eight or nine years old when he was sent to Carlisle" (209n3) in 1886. That would make his birth date about 1877. This may or may not be accurate. I've found census records for 1940 that give his age as sixty-six at that time, which would make his date of birth 1874 (ancestry.com/1940-census/; accessed 9/17/16). The "my heritage site" gives his birth date as 1872 (myheritage.com; accessed 9/17/16). The actual date, once more, may not matter much, although it is interesting to wonder whether the youngest Apache prisoner sent to Carlisle in 1886 was more nearly eight or nine, or instead, fourteen.

24. This is not borne out by Kanseah's student file at Carlisle, which has him attending the school from November, 1886, to November, 1895. But these files can be puzzling: the document that lists the dates of Kanseah's attendance nonetheless calls that nine-year period "five years!" (carlisleindian.dickinson.edu, accessed 9/17/16).

WORKS CITED

Aberle, David. "The Psychosocial Analysis of a Hopi Life-History." *Comparative Psychology Monographs* 21 (1951), Serial Number 101. Berkeley: University of California Press.

———. "Review of *Blessingway Singer: The Autobiography of Frank Mitchell, 1881–1967.*" *Ethnohistory* 28 (1981): 195–96.

Adams, David Wallace. "Beyond Bleakness: the Brighter Side of Boarding Schools, 1870–1940." In Trafzer, Keller, and Sisquoc, 35–64.

———. *Education for Extinction: American Indians and the Boarding School Experience, 1875–1928*. Lawrence: University of Kansas Press, 1995a.

———. "Schooling the Hopi: Federal Indian Policy Writ Small, 1887–1917." In *American Vistas: 1877 to the Present*, 7th ed., edited by Leonard Dinnerstein and Kenneth T. Jackson. New York: Oxford University Press, 1995b, 27–44 [1979].

Ahern, Wilbert. "Review of David Wallace Adams' *Education for Extinction.*" *Minnesota History* 55 (1996): 88–89.

———. "Review of Frederick Hoxie's *A Final Promise.*" *Minnesota History* 49 (1985): 254.

Arrington, Grace. "Biography of an Indian Latter-day Saint Woman." *Dialogue* 6 (1971): 124–26.

Babcock, Barbara, and Susan Parezo. *Daughters of the Desert: Women Anthropologists and the Native American Southwest, 1880–1980: An Illustrated Catalogue*. Albuquerque: University of New Mexico Press, 1988.

Bahr, Diana Meyers. *The Students of Sherman Indian School*. Norman: University of Oklahoma Press, 2014.

———, ed. *Viola Martinez, California Paiute: Living in Two Worlds*. Norman: University of Oklahoma Press, 2003.

Bailey, Flora. "Review of *Kaibah: Recollection of a Navajo Girlhood.*" *American Anthropologist* 67 (1965): 1,566–67.

Bailey, Lynn. *Bosque Redondo: An American Concentration Camp*. Pasadena, CA: Socio-Technical Books, 1970.

———. "Thomas Varker Keam, Tusayan Trader." *Arizoniana* 2 (1961): 15–19.

Ball, Eve, with Nora Henn and Lynda Sanchez. *Indeh: An Apache Odyssey*. Norman: University of Oklahoma Press, 1988 [1980].

Bataille, Gretchen. *Native American Women: A Biographical Dictionary*. New York: Garland, 1993.

Bataille, Gretchen, and Kathleen Mullen Sands. *American Indian Women Telling Their Lives*. Lincoln: University of Nebraska Press, 1984.

Begay, Myrtle. "Myrtle Begay." In Johnson, 56–72.

Begay, Shirley, Clifford Beck, Verna Clinton-Tullie, Teresa McCarty, and M. Yellowhair. *Kinaalda: A Navajo Puberty Ceremony*. Rough Rock, AZ: Rough Rock Demonstration School Press, 1983.

Bennett, Kay. *Kaibah: Recollection of a Navajo Girlhood*. Los Angeles: Westernlore Press, 1964.

———. *Kaibah*. LP. Produced by Kay Bennett, Gallup, New Mexico, 1966.

———. *Songs from the Navajo Nation by Kaibah*. LP. Produced by Kay Bennett, Gallup, New Mexico, n.d. [1970?].

Berry, Brewton. *The Education of the American Indian: A Survey of the Literature*. Washington, DC: U.S. Department of Health, Education, and Welfare Bureau of Research, 1968.

Bess, Jennifer. "More than a Food Fight: Intellectual Traditions and Cultural Continuity in Chilocco's 'Indian School Journal,' 1902–1918." *American Indian Quarterly* 37 (2013): 77–110.

Betzinez, Jason, with Wilbur S. Nye. *I Fought with Geronimo*. Lincoln: University of Nebraska Press, 1987 [1959].

Bighorse, Tiana. *Bighorse the Warrior*, edited by Noel Bennett. Tucson: University of Arizona Press, 1990.

Black, Mary. "Maidens and Mothers: An Analysis of Hopi Corn Metaphors." *Ethnology* 23 (1984): 279–88.

Blake, Jeannette. "Jeannette Blake." In Johnson, 201–5.

Blatchford, Paul. "Paul Blatchford." In Johnson, 173–81.

Bloomfield, Lucy G. *Natani (Navajo Chief)*. N.P., 196–?.

Boas, Franz. "Recent Anthropology II." *Science* (October 15, 1943): 334–37.

Bob Martin, Mrs. "Mrs. Bob Martin." In Johnson, 120–34.

Bogoutin, Howard. "Howard Bogoutin." In Johnson, 280–84.

Boyer, Ruth. *Apache Mothers and Daughters.* Norman: University of Oklahoma Press, 1992.

Bremner, Robert, ed. *Children and Youth in America: A Documentary History.* Vol. II: 1866–1932. Cambridge, MA: Harvard University Press, 1971.

Brill de Ramirez, Susan. *Native American Life-History Narratives: Colonial and Postcolonial Navajo Ethnography.* Albuquerque: University of New Mexico Press, 2007.

———. *Native American Women's Collaborative Autobiographies.* Lanham, MD: Rowman and Littlefield, 2015.

Britten, Thomas. *American Indians in World War I: At War and at Home.* Albuquerque: University of New Mexico Press, 1997.

Brugge, David. "Henry Chee Dodge: *From the Long Walk to Self-Determination.*" In *Indian Lives: Essays on Nineteenth- and Twentieth-Century Native American Leaders,* edited by L. G. Moses and Raymond Wilson. Albuquerque: University of New Mexico Press, 1985, 91–112.

Brumble, H. David. *An Annotated Bibliography of American Indian and Eskimo Autobiographies.* Lincoln: University of Nebraska Press, 1981.

———. "Review of *Bighorse the Warrior.*" *American Indian Quarterly* 17 (1993): 144–45.

Brumley, Kim. *Chilocco: Memories of a Native American Boarding School.* Fairfax, OK: Guardian Publishing, 2010.

Cadman, William. In Johnson, 206–19.

Clani, Thomas. In Johnson, 243–55.

Carlson, Vada, with Polingaysi Qoyawayma. *Broken Pattern: Sunlight and Shadows of Hopi History.* Happy Camp, CA: Naturegraph Publishers, 1985.

Carlson, Vada, and Gary Witherspoon. *Black Mountain Boy: A Story of the Boyhood of John Honie.* Chinle, AZ: Rough Rock Press, 1993.

Child, Brenda. *Boarding School Seasons: American Indian Families, 1900–1940.* Lincoln: University of Nebraska Press, 1998.

Churchill, Ward. *Kill the Indian, Save the Man: The Genocidal Impact of American Indian Residential Schools.* San Francisco: City Lights, 2004.

Clemmer, Richard. *Roads in the Sky: The Hopi Indians in a Century of Change.* Boulder, CO: Westview Press, 1995.

Cobb, Amanda. *Listening to Our Grandmothers' Stories: The Bloomfield Academy for Chickasaw Females, 1852–1949.* Lincoln: University of Nebraska Press, 2000.

Coleman, Michael. *American Indian Children at School, 1850–1930.* Jackson: University Press of Mississippi, 1993.

Courlander, Harold. *The Fourth World of the Hopi.* New York: Crown, 1971.

Culin, Stewart. "Thomas Varker Keam." *American Anthropologist* 7 (1905): 171–72.

Curtis, Edward. *The North American Indian.* Vol. xii. New York: Johnson Reprint Company, 1978 [1922].

Curtis, Natalie. *The Indians' Book: Songs and Legends of the American Indians Recorded and Edited by Natalie Curtis.* New York: Dover, 1968 [1923].

David, Gary. *The Kivas of Heaven: Ancient Hopi Starlore.* Kempton, IL: Adventures Unlimited Press, 2010.

DeHuff, Elizabeth, Fred Kabotie, and Nona Lee Penn. *Taytay's Memories.* New York: Harcourt Brace, 1924.

DeHuff, Elizabeth, Fred Kabotie, and Otis Polelonema. *Taytay's Tales.* New York: Harcourt Brace, 1922.

De la Garza, Phyllis. *The Apache Kid.* Tucson, AZ: Westernlore Press, 1995.

Deloria, Philip. *Indians in Unexpected Places.* Lawrence: University Press of Kansas, 2004.

Denetdale, Jennifer Nez. *The Long Walk: The Forced Navajo Exile.* New York: Chelsea House, 2008.

————. "Presidents and Princesses: The Navajo Nation, Gender, and the Politics of Tradition." *Wicazo Sa Review* 21 (2006): 9–28.

————. "Representing Changing Woman: A Review Essay on Navajo Women." *American Indian Culture and Research Journal* 25 (2001): 1–26.

Dilworth, Leah. *Imagining Indians in the Southwest: Persistent Visions of a Primitive Past.* Washington, DC: Smithsonian Institution Press, 1996.

Donlon, Walter. "Review of *Indeh: An Apache Odyssey.*" *Southwestern Historical Quarterly* 85 (1982): 468–70.

Dunaway, David. "Review of *Indeh: An Apache Odyssey.*" *Journal of American Folklore* 104 (1991): 411–13.

Dyk, Walter. *Old Mexican: A Navaho Autobiography.* New York: Johnson Reprint Corporation, 1964 [1947].

————. *Son of Old Man Hat: A Navaho Autobiography.* Lincoln: University of Nebraska Press, 1967 [1938].

Dyk, Walter, and Ruth Dyk. *Left Handed: A Navajo Autobiography.* New York: Columbia University Press, 1980.

Earle, Edwin. *Hopi Kachinas,* with text by Edward Kennard. 2nd rev. ed. New York: Museum of the American Indian/Heye Foundation, 1971 [1938].

Eastman, Elaine Goodale. *Pratt: The Red Man's Moses.* Norman: University of Oklahoma Press, 1935.

Eggan, Dorothy. "The General Problem of Hopi Adjustment." *American Anthropologist* 45 (1943): 357–73.

Eggan, Fred. "Review of *Me and Mine.*" *American Anthropologist* 72 (1970): 411–12.

Ellis, Clyde. *To Change Them Forever: Indian Education at the Rainy Mountain Boarding School, 1893–1926.* Norman: University of Oklahoma Press, 1996.

Farrer, Claire. "Living Names and Dead Traditions: Commentary on *Indeh* Review by Dunaway." *Journal of American Folklore* 105 (1992): 342–43.

Fear-Segal, Jacqueline. "The Lost Ones: Piecing Together the Story." In *Carlisle Indian Industrial School: Indigenous Histories, Memories, and Reclamations,* edited by Jacqueline Fear-Segal and Barbara Rose. Lincoln: University of Nebraska Press, 2016: 201–32.

————. *White Man's Club: Schools, Race, and the Struggle of Indian Acculturation.* Lincoln: University of Nebraska Press, 2007.

Ferguson, T. J. "Review: *Born a Chief: The Nineteenth-Century Boyhood of Edmund Nequaptewa.*" *The Western Historical Quarterly* 24 (1993): 569–70.

Fewkes, Jesse Walter. "The New-Fire Ceremony at Walpi." *American Anthropologist* 2 (1900): 80–138.

————. "The Winter Solstice Ceremony at Walpi." *American Anthropologist* 11 (1898): 101–15.

Foucault, Michel. *Discipline and Punish: the Birth of the Prison.* New York: Pantheon, 1977 [1975].

Frisbie, Charlotte. *Kinaalda: A Study of the Navaho Girl's Puberty Ceremony.* Salt Lake City: University of Utah Press, 1993 [1967].

————. "Traditional Navajo Women: Ethnographic and Life History Portrayals." *American Indian Quarterly* 6 (1982): 11–33.

Gannon, Tom. "Immigration as Cultural Imperialism: An Indian Boarding School Experience or the Peer Gynt Suite and the Seventh Cavalry Café." *Great Plains Quarterly* 34 (2014): 111–22.

Geertz, Armin. *The Invention of Prophecy: Continuity and Meaning in Hopi Indian Religion.* Berkeley: University of California Press, 1994.

Gill, Sam. "Disenchantment: A Religious Abduction." *Native American Religious Action: A Performance Approach to Religion.* Columbia: University of South Carolina Press, 1987, 58–75.

Gordon, Deborah. "Among Women: Gender and Ethnographic Authority in the Southwest." In *Hidden Scholars: Women Anthropologists and the Native American Southwest,* edited by Nancy Parezo. Albuquerque: University of New Mexico Press, 1993, 129–45.

Gram, John. *Education at the Edge of Empire: Negotiating Pueblo Identity in New Mexico's Indian Boarding Schools.* Seattle: University of Washington Press, 2015.

Graves, Laura. *Thomas Varker Keam: Indian Trader.* Norman: University of Oklahoma Press, 1998.

Griffen, Joyce, ed. *Lucky the Navajo Singer,* recorded by Alexander and Dorothea Leighton. Albuquerque: University of New Mexico Press, 1992.

Hafen, P. Jane. "'A Trail in the Sand': Helen Sekaquaptewa's *Me and Mine.*" *Literature and Belief* 21 (2001): 149–62.

Hamamsy, Laila Shukry. "The Role of Women in a Changing Navaho Society." *American Anthropologist* 59 (1957): 101–11.

Hanley, Max. "Max Hanley." In Johnson, 17–55.

Hertzberg, Hazel. *The Search for an American Indian Identity: Modern Pan-Indian Movements.* Syracuse, NY: Syracuse University Press, 1971.

Highway, Thomson. *The Kiss of the Fur Queen.* Norman: University of Oklahoma Press, 1998.

Hogan, Linda. "Review of *A Voice in Her Tribe.*" *American Indian Quarterly* 7 (1983): 192–93.

Hopi Dictionary-Hopiikwa lavaytutveni: A Hopi-English Dictionary of the Third Mesa Dialect with an English-Hopi Finder List and a Sketch of Hopi Grammar. By the University of Arizona. Hopi Dictionary Project. Tucson: University of Arizona Press, 1998.

Hyer, Sally. *One House, One Voice, One Heart: Native American Education at the Santa Fe Indian School.* Santa Fe: Museum of New Mexico Press, 1990.

Iverson, Peter. *Dine: A History of the Navajos.* Albuquerque: University of New Mexico Press, 2002.

———. "'Our People Cried': 1923–1941." In Iverson, 137–79.

Jacobs, Margaret. *Engendered Encounters: Feminism and Pueblo Cultures, 1879–1934.* Lincoln: University of Nebraska Press, 1999.

———. "Making Savages of Us All: White Women, Pueblo Indians, and the Controversy over Indian Dances in the 1920s." *Frontiers: A Journal of Women's Studies* 17 (1996): 178–209.

Jaffe, Nina. *A Voice for the People: The Life and Work of Harold Courlander.* New York: Henry Holt, 1997.

James, Harry. *Pages from Hopi History.* Tucson: University of Arizona Press, 1974.

Johnson, Broderick, ed. *Stories of Traditional Navajo Life and Culture: Alk'idaa' Yeek'ehgo Dine Keedahat'inee Baa Nahane': by Twenty-Two Navajo Men and Women.* Tsaile, Navajo Nation, AZ: Navajo Community College Press, 1977.

Johnson, Broderick, and Ruth Roessel. *Navajo Livestock Reduction: A National Disgrace.* Chinle, AZ: Navajo Community College Press, 1971.

Johnston, Basil. *Indian School Days.* Norman: University of Oklahoma Press, 1989.

———. "Foreword," to Sam McKegney, *Magic Weapons: Aboriginal Writers Remaking Community after Residential School.* Winnipeg: University of Manitoba Press, 2007, 3–9.

Joinson, Carla. *Grim Shadows: The Story of the Canton Asylum for Insane Indians.* Lincoln: University of Nebraska Press, 2016.

Kabotie, Fred. *Fred Kabotie: Hopi Indian Artist. An Autobiography told with Bill Belknap.* Flagstaff: Museum of Northern Arizona/Northland Press, 1977.

Kansaswood, Lee. "Lee Kansaswood." In Johnson, 273–79.

Katanski, Amelia. *Learning to Write "Indian": The Boarding School Experience and American Indian Literature.* Norman: University of Oklahoma Press, 2006.

Kaywaykla, James. *In the Days of Victorio: Recollections of a Warm Springs Apache,* edited by Eve Ball. Tucson: University of Arizona Press, 1970.

Kelly, Lawrence. "Review of *Blessingway Singer: The Autobiography of Frank Mitchell, 1881–1967.*" *Western Historical Quarterly* 10 (1979): 224–25.

Kennard, Edward. "Hopi Reactions to Death." *American Anthropologist* 39 (1937): 491–96.

Kenoi, Samuel. "Autobiography of a Chiricahua (Sam Kenoi)," edited by Morris Opler. Morris Opler Papers, #14-25-3238, Box 36, Files 2–6, 704 pages, 196?. Division of Rare and Manuscript Collections, Cornell University Library, Ithaca, NY.

Knack, Martha. "Review of *Blessingway Singer: The Autobiography of Frank Mitchell, 1881–1967.*" *American Indian Quarterly* 4 (1978): 411–13.

Kozol, Wendy. "Miss Indian America: Regulatory Gazes and the Politics of Affiliation." *Feminist Studies* 31 (2005): 64–94.

Kroskrity, Paul. "Review of Albert Yava's *Big Falling Snow: A Tewa-Hopi Indian's Life and Times and the History and Traditions of His People.*" *American Indian Quarterly* 7 (1983): 96–98.

Krupat, Arnold. *All that Remains: Varieties of Indigenous Expression.* Lincoln: University of Nebraska Press, 2009.

———. *For Those Who Come After: A Study of Native American Autobiography.* Berkeley: University of California Press, 1985.

———. *Red Matters: Native American Studies.* Philadelphia: University of Pennsylvania Press, 2002.

———. "Trickster Tales Revisited." *All that Remains,* 1–26.

———. *The Voice in the Margin: Native American Literature and the Canon.* Berkeley: University of California Press, 1989.

Laird, W. David. "Review of *A Pima Past* by Anna Moore Shaw and *Pages from Hopi History* by Harry C. James." *Arizona and the West* 17 (1975): 178–79.

Lame Deer/John Fire and Richard Erdoes. *Lame Deer: Seeker of Visions, the Life of a Sioux Medicine Man.* New York: Simon and Schuster, 1972.

Landis, Barbara. "Putting Lucy Pretty Eagle to Rest." In Trafzer, Keller, and Sisquoc, 123–30.

Lee, George P. *Silent Courage, an Indian Story: The Autobiography of George P. Lee, a Navajo.* Salt Lake City, UT: Deseret Books, 1987.

Lee, Lloyd. "Gender, Navajo Leadership, and 'Retrospective Falsification.'" *AlterNative* 8 (2012): 277–89.

Leighton, Alexander, and Dorothea Leighton. *Gregorio, the Hand-Trembler: A Psychobiological Personality Study of a Navaho Indian.* Millwood, NY: Kraus Reprint Company, 1973 [1949].

Levchuk, Berenice. "Leaving Home for Carlisle Indian School." In *Reinventing the Enemy's Language: Contemporary Native Women's Writings of North America,* edited by Joy Harjo and Gloria Bird. New York: Norton, 1997, 175–86.

Linder, Jo. *Polingaysi.* Mesa, AZ: Discount Printing, 1983.

————, ed. *When I Met Polingaysi Underneath the Cottonwood Tree.* Mesa, AZ: Discount Printing, 1983.

Lindsey, Donal. *Indians at Hampton Institute, 1877–1923.* Urbana: University of Illinois Press, 1995.

Littlefield, Daniel, and Lonnie Underhill. "Renaming the American Indian, 1890–1913." *American Studies* 12 (1971): 33–45.

Lomawaima, Hartman. "Review of *Born a Chief: the Nineteenth-Century Hopi Boyhood of Edmund Nequaptewa.*" *Journal of American History* 81 (1994): 1,330.

Lomawaima, K. Tsianina. *They Called It Prairie Light: The Story of Chilocco Indian School.* Lincoln: University of Nebraska Press, 1994.

Lomawaima, K. Tsianina, and Teresa McCarty. *To Remain an Indian: Lessons in Democracy from a Century of Native American Education.* New York: Teachers College/ Columbia University, 2006.

Lummis, Charles. *Bullying the Moqui,* edited and with an introduction by Robert Easton and Mackenzie Brown. N.P.: Prescott College Press, 1968.

Lyons, Scott. *X-Marks: Native Signatures of Assent.* Minneapolis: University of Minnesota Press, 2010.

Margolis, Eric, and Jeremy Rowe. "Images of Assimilation: Photographs of Indian Schools in Arizona." *History of Education* 33 (2004): 199–230.

Malotki, Ekkehart. *Hopi Time: A Linguistic Analysis of the Temporal Concepts of the Hopi Language.* Berlin: Mouton, 1983.

————. *The Oraibi Salt Journey to the Grand Canyon: An Ethnographic Account.* Collected, translated, and edited by Ekkehart Malotki. Berlin: VWB, 2011.

————. *Stories of Maasaw, a Hopi God.* Lincoln: University of Nebraska Press, 1987b.

Malotki, Ekkehart, and Michael Lomatuway'ma. *Maasaw: Profile of a Hopi God.* Lincoln: University of Nebraska Press, 1987a.

Marriott, Alice. *Maria, the Potter of San Ildefonso.* Norman: University of Oklahoma Press, 1948.

Mauro, Hayes Peter. *The Art of Americanization at the Carlisle Indian School.* Albuquerque: University of New Mexico Press, 2011.

McCarty, Teresa, and Fred Bia. *A Place to be Navajo: Rough Rock and the Struggle for Self-Determination in Indigenous Schooling.* Mahwah, NJ: Lawrence Erlbaum Associates, 2002.

McKanna, Clare. *Court-Martial of Apache Kid: The Renegade of Renegades.* Lubbock: Texas Tech Press, 2009.

———. *Homicide, Race, and Justice in the American West, 1880–1920.* Tucson: University of Arizona Press, 1997.

Meriam, Lewis, et al. *The Problem of Indian Administration: Report of a Survey made at the request of the Honorable Hubert Work, Secretary of the Interior, and submitted to him, February 21, 1928.* Baltimore: The Johns Hopkins Press, 1928.

Merriam. Alan. "Review of *Blessingway Singer: The Autobiography of Frank Mitchell, 1881–1967.*" *Ethnomusicology* 22 (1978): 523–26.

Miller, Jay. "Review of *Blessingway Singer: The Autobiography of Frank Mitchell, 1881–1967.*" *Anthropos* 76 (1981): 278–80.

Minor, Nancy McGown. *Turning Adversity to Advantage: A History of the Lipans of Texas and Northern Mexico, 1700–1900.* Lanham, MD: University Press of America, 2009.

Mitchell, Emerson Blackhorse. *Miracle Hill: The Story of a Navaho Boy.* Norman: University of Oklahoma Press, 1967.

Mitchell, Frank. *Navaho Blessingway Singer: The Autobiography of Frank Mitchell, 1881–1967,* edited by Charlotte Frisbie and David McAllester. Tucson: University of Arizona Press, 2003 [1978].

Mitchell, Rose, and Charlotte Frisbie. *Tall Woman: The Life Story of Rose Mitchell, a Navajo Woman, c. 1874–1977.* Albuquerque: University of New Mexico Press, 2001.

Morey, Sylvester, and Olivia Gilliam, eds. *Respect for Life: Report of a Conference at Harper's Ferry, West Virginia on the Traditional Upbringing of American Indian Children.* Garden City, NY: Waldorf Press Adelphi University, n.d. [1974].

Nequatewa, Edmund. *Born a Chief: The Nineteenth-Century Hopi Boyhood of Edmund Nequatewa*, ed. P. David Seaman. Tucson: University of Arizona Press, 1993.

———. "Dr. Fewkes and Masauwu." *Museum of Northern Arizona Notes* 11 (1938): 25–27.

———. "Hopi Courtship and Marriage." *Museum of Northern Arizona Notes* 3 (1933): 41–54.

———. "Hopi hopiwime." *Museum of Northern Arizona Notes* 3 (1931): 1–4.

———. "Truth of a Hopi and Other Clan Stories of Shungopovi," ed. Mary-Russell Colton. *Museum of Northern Arizona Bulletin* 8. Northern Arizona Society of Science and Art, Flagstaff, AZ, 1936.

———. *Truth of a Hopi: Stories Relating to the Origin, Myths and Clan Histories of the Hopi.* N.P.: Forgotten Books, 2008 [1936].

Newcomb, Franc Johnson. *Hosteen Klah: Navaho Medicine Man and Sand Painter.* Norman: University of Oklahoma Press, 1964.

Nicholas, Dan. "The Autobiography of an Apache Indian (Dan Nicholas)," edited by Morris Opler. Morris Opler Papers, #14-25-3238, Box 36, File 1, 208 pages, 196?.

Niethammer, Carolyn. *I'll Go and Do More: Annie Dodge Wauneka, Navajo Leader and Activist.* Lincoln: University of Nebraska Press, 2001.

Notarianni, Diane. "Making Mennonites: Hopi Gender Roles and Christian Transformations." *Ethnohistory* 43 (1996): 593–611.

Opler, Morris. "A Chiricahua Apache's Account of the Geronimo Campaign of 1886." *New Mexico Historical Review* 13 (1938): 360–86.

———. *Apache Odyssey: A Journey between Two Worlds.* Lincoln: University of Nebraska Press, 2002 [1969].

Ostler, Jeffrey. *The Plains Sioux and U.S. Colonialism from Lewis and Clark to Wounded Knee.* Cambridge, UK: Cambridge University Press, 2004.

Oxendine, Joseph. *American Indian Sports Heritage.* Champain, IL: Human Kinetics Books, 1988.

Pabanale, Irving. *Standing Flower: The Life of Irving Pabanale, an Arizona Tewa Indian,* edited by Robert Black. Salt Lake City: University of Utah Press, 2001.

Parsons, Elsie Clews, ed. *A Pueblo Indian Journal, 1920–1921.* Menasha, WI: American Anthropological Association, 1925.

Paytiamo, James. *Flaming Arrow's People, by an Acoma Indian*. New York: Duffield and Green, 1932.

Pfister, Joel. *Individuality Incorporated: Indians and the Multicultural Modern*. Durham, NC: Duke University Press, 2004.

———. *The Yale Indian: The Education of Henry Roe Cloud*. Durham, NC: Duke University Press, 2009.

Pratt, Richard. "The Advantages of Mingling Indians with Whites." In *Americanizing the American Indians: Writings by the "Friends of the Indian," 1880–1900*, edited by Francis Paul Prucha. Cambridge, MA: Harvard University Press, 1973, 260–71.

———. *Battlefield and Classroom: Four Decades with the American Indian, 1867–1904*, edited and with an introduction by Robert Utley. New Haven, CT: Yale University Press, 1964.

Price, David. *Threatening Anthropologists: McCarthyism and the FBI's Surveillance of Activist Anthropologists*. Durham, NC: Duke University Press, 2004.

Quoyawayma, Polingaysi (Elizabeth White). *No Turning Back: A Hopi Indian Woman's Struggle to Live in Two Worlds, as told to Vada Carlson*. Albuquerque: University of New Mexico Press, 1977 [1964].

Rader, Benjamin. "'The Greatest Drama in Indian Life': Experiments in Native American Identity and Resistance at the Haskell Institute Homecoming of 1926." *Western Historical Quarterly* 35 (2004): 429–50.

Ration, Tom. "Tom Ration." In Johnson, 299–335.

Razor, Peter. *While the Locust Slept*. Saint Paul: Minnesota Historical Society, 2001.

Reed, Maureen. "Leaving Home: Kay Bennett." *A Woman's Place: Women Writing New Mexico*. Albuquerque: University of New Mexico Press, 2005a, 171–223.

———. "Mixed Messages: Pablita Velarde, Kay Bennett, and the Changing Meaning of Anglo-Indian Intermarriage in Twentieth-Century New Mexico." *Frontiers: A Journal of Women's Studies* 26 (2005b): 101–34.

Reichard, Gladys. *Dezba: Woman of the Desert*. New York: J. J. Augustin, 1939.

Reyhner, Jon, and Jeanne Elder. *American Indian Education: A History*. Norman: University of Oklahoma Press, 2004.

Rhyms, Deena. *From the Iron House: Imprisonment in First Nations Writing.* Waterloo, Ontario: Wilfrid Laurier University Press, 2008.

Riney, Scott. *The Rapid City Indian School: 1898–1933.* Norman: University of Oklahoma Press, 1999.

Robinson, Sherry. *Apache Voices: Their Stories of Survival as told to Eve Ball.* Albuquerque: University of New Mexico Press, 2000.

Roessel, Monty. *Kinaalda: A Navajo Girl Grows Up.* Minneapolis, MN: Lerner Publications, 1993.

Roessel, Ruth. "The Kinaalda Ceremony for Faith Roessel." In R. Roessel, 83–99.

———. *Women in Navajo Society.* Rough Rock: Navajo Nation, Arizona, Navajo Resource Center Rough Rock Demonstration School, 1981.

Roessel, Ruth, and Broderick Johnson, eds. *Navajo Livestock Reduction: A National Disgrace.* Chinle, AZ: Navajo Community College Press, 1974.

Ruoff, A. Lavonne. "Review of *No Turning Back.*" *Newsletter of the Association for the Study of American Indian Literatures* 1 (1977): 22–24.

Rushforth, Scott, and Steadman Upham. *A Hopi Social History.* Austin: University of Texas Press, 1992.

Sahlins, Marshall. *How "Natives" Think: About Captain Cook, for Example.* Chicago: University of Chicago Press, 1995.

Sakiestewa Gilbert, Matthew. "A Second Wave of Hopi Migration." *History of Education Quarterly* 54 (2014): 356–61.

———. *Education Beyond the Mesas: Hopi Students at Sherman Institute, 1902–1929.* Lincoln: University of Nebraska Press, 2010.

———. "Foreword." *Sun Chief: The Autobiography of a Hopi Indian.* 2nd ed. New Haven, CT: Yale University Press, 2013.

———. " 'The Hopi Followers': Chief Tawaquaptewa and Hopi Student Advancement at Sherman Institute, 1906–1909." *Journal of American Indian Education* (2005): 1–23.

Sakiestewa Gilbert, Matthew, Allan Holzman, Stewart Koyiyumptewa, and Eric Jerstad. *Beyond the Mesas.* Santa Monica, CA: Pyramid Media, 2007. DVD.

Sands, Kay. "Review of Anna Moore Shaw. *A Pima Past* and *Pima Indian Legends.*" *Studies in American Indian Literatures* 5 (1981): 3–5.

Satz, Ronald. "Review of *Indeh: An Apache Odyssey.*" *The Oral History Review* 9 (1981): 138–40.

Schlegel, Alice. "The Adolescent Socialization of the Hopi Girl." *Ethnology* 12 (1973): 449–62.

Sekaquaptewa, Helen. *Me and Mine: The Life Story of Helen Sekaquaptewa as told to Louise Udall.* Tucson: University of Arizona Press, 1993 [1969].

———. "Interview," 1978. L. Tom Perry Special Collections, Harold B. Lee Library, Brigham Young University. MSS OH 1118.

Seymour, Tryntje Van Ness. *When the Rainbow Touches Down: The Artists and Stories Behind the Apache, Navajo, Rio Grande Pueblo and Hopi Paintings in the William and Leslie Van Ness Denman Collection.* Phoenix, AZ: The Heard Museum, 1988.

Shaw, Anna Moore. *A Pima Past.* Tucson: University of Arizona Press, 1994 [1974].

Shepardson, Mary. "The Gender Status of Navajo Women." In *Women and Power in Native North America*, edited by Laura Klein and Lilian Ackerman. Norman: University of Oklahoma Press, 1995, 159–76.

———. "The Status of Navajo Women." *American Indian Quarterly* 6 (1982): 149–69.

Shillinger, Sarah. *A Case Study of the American Indian Boarding School Movement: An Oral History of St. Joseph's Indian Industrial School.* Lewiston, NY: Edwin Mellen Press, 2008.

Simmons, Leo. "Review of *No Turning Back*." *American Anthropologist* 67 (1965): 1,567.

Smith, Andrea. *Conquest: Sexual Violence and American Indian Genocide.* Cambridge, MA: South End Press, 2005.

Smith, Sherry. "Charles Fletcher Lummis and the Fight for the Multicultural Southwest." *Re-Imagining Indians: Native Americans through Anglo Eyes, 1880–1940.* New York: Oxford, 2000, 119–44.

Sonneborn, Liz. *A to Z of Native American Women.* New York: Facts on File, 1998.

Spack, Ruth. *America's Second Tongue: American Indian Education and the Ownership of English, 1860–1900.* Lincoln: University of Nebraska Press, 2002.

Spicer, Edward. "Review of *Kaibah: Recollections of a Navajo Girlhood* and *No Turning Back*." *Journal of the Southwest* 8 (1966): 184–86.

Standing Bear, Luther. *My People, the Sioux.* Lincoln: University of Nebraska Press, 1975 [1928].

Stewart, Irene. *A Voice in Her Tribe: A Navajo Woman's Own Story*, edited by Doris Dawdy. N.P.: Ballena Press Anthropological Papers No. 17, 1980.

Szasz, Margaret. *Education and the American Indian: The Road to Self-Determination since 1928*. 3rd ed. Albuquerque: University of New Mexico Press, 1999 [1974].

———. *Indian Education in the American Colonies, 1607–1783*. Albuquerque: University of New Mexico Press, 1988.

Talayesva, Don. *Soleil Hopi*. Translated by Genevieve Mayoux, with a preface by Claude Lévi-Strauss. Paris: Plon, 1959.

———. *Sun Chief: The Autobiography of a Hopi Indian*, 2nd ed., edited by Leo Simmons. New Haven, CT: Yale University Press, 1976 [1942].

Tedlock, Barbara. "Review of *Blessingway Singer: The Autobiography of Frank Mitchell, 1881–1967*." *American Ethnologist* 7 (1980): 391–92.

Thayer, Marjorie, Elizabeth Emanuel, and Anne Siberell. *Climbing Sun: The Story of a Hopi Indian Boy*. New York: Dodd, Mead, 1980.

Titiev, Mischa. "A Hopi Salt Expedition." *American Anthropologist* XXXIX (1937): 244–58.

———. "A Hopi Visit to the Afterworld." *Papers of the Michigan Academy of Sciences, Arts, and Letters*, XXVI (1940): 495–504.

———. *Old Oraibi: A Study of the Hopi Indians of Third Mesa*. Albuquerque: University of New Mexico Press, 1992 [1944].

———. "Review of *Truth of a Hopi and Other Clan Stories of Shungopavi*." *Journal of American Folklore* 50 (1937): 415.

Toelken, Barre. "Review of *Blessingway Singer: The Autobiography of Frank Mitchell, 1881–1967*." *Western Folklore* 38 (1979): 272–74.

Trafzer, Clifford, and Jean Keller. "Unforgettable Lives and Symbolic Voices: The Sherman School Cemetery." In Trafzer, Gilbert, and Sisquoc, 159–72.

Trafzer, Clifford, Jean Keller, and Lorene Sisquoc, eds. *Boarding School Blues: Revisiting American Indian Educational Experiences*. Lincoln: University of Nebraska Press, 2006.

Trafzer, Clifford, Matthew Sakiestewa Gilbert, and Lorene Sisquoc, eds. *The Indian School on Magnolia Avenue*. Corvallis: Oregon State University Press, 2012.

Trennert, Robert. *Alternative to Extinction: Federal Indian Policy and the Beginnings of the Reservation System, 1846–51*. Philadelphia: Temple University Press, 1975.

———. "Corporal Punishment and the Politics of Indian Reform." *History of Education Quarterly* 29 (1989): 595–617.

———. "Educating Indian Girls at Non-Reservation Boarding Schools, 1878–1920." *Western Historical Quarterly* 13 (1982): 271–90.

———. *The Phoenix Indian School: Forced Assimilation in Arizona, 1891–1935*. Norman: University of Oklahoma Press, 1988.

———. "White Man's Medicine v. Hopi Tradition: The Smallpox Epidemic of 1899." *Arizona Historical Society* 33 (1992): 349–66.

Turner, Erin, ed. *Wise Women: From Pocahontas to Sarah Winnemucca, Remarkable Stories of Native American Trailblazers*. N.P.: Morris Book Publishing, 2009.

Van Winkle, Jones. "Jones Van Winkle." In Johnson, 256–65.

Voegelin, C., and F. Voegelin. "Selection in Hopi Ethics, Linguistics, and Translation." *Anthropological Linguistics* 2 (1960): 48–78.

Voth, H. R. "Hopi Marriage Rites on the Wedding Morning." The Stanley McCormick Hopi Expedition. *Publications of the Field Columbian Museum. Anthropological Series* 156 (1912): 146–49.

———. "Hopi Proper Names. The Stanley McCormick Hopi Expedition." *Publications of the Field Columbian Museum. Anthropological Series* 6 (1905): 65–69, 71–113.

———. *The Traditions of the Hopi*. Millwood, NY: Kraus Reprint, 1973 [1905].

Vuckovic, Myriam. *Voices from Haskell: Indian Students between Two Worlds, 1884–1928*. Lawrence: University Press of Kansas, 2008.

Webb, George. *A Pima Remembers*. Tucson: University of Arizona Press, 1959.

Wenger, Tisa. *We Have a Religion: The 1920s Pueblo Indian Dance Controversy*. Chapel Hill: University of North Carolina Press, 2009.

White, Leslie. "Autobiography of an Acoma Indian." *Bureau of American Ethnology Anthropological Papers*, Bulletin 32. Washington, DC: Government Printing Office, 1943, 326–27.

Whiteley, Peter. *Bacavi: Journey to Reed Springs*. N.P.: Northland Press, 1988a.

———. *Deliberate Acts: Changing Hopi Culture through the Oraibi Split*. Tucson: University of Arizona Press, 1988b.

———. "Hopitutungwni: 'Hopi Names' as Literature." *Rethinking Hopi Ethnography*, 105–24.

———. "Leslie White's Hopi Ethnography: Of Practice and In Theory." *Journal of Anthropological Research* 59 (2003): 151–81.

———. *The Orayvi Split: A Hopi Transformation. Part I: Structure and History, Part II: The Documentary Record. Anthropological Papers of the American Museum of National History*, Number 87, 2008.

———. Personal communications, 5/30/15, 8/26/15, and 12/7/15.

———. "Re-imagining Awat'ovi." In *Archaeologies of the Pueblo Revolt: Identity, Meaning, and Renewal in the Pueblo World*, edited by Robert Preucel. Albuquerque: University of New Mexico Press, 2002, 147–66.

———. *Rethinking Hopi Ethnography*. Washington, DC: Smithsonian Institution Press, 1998.

———. "Review of *Born a Chief: The Nineteenth-Century Hopi Boyhood of Edmund Nequaptewa.*" *Ethnohistory* 41 (1994): 478–80.

Whiting, Alfred. "Leaves from a Hopi Doctor's Casebook." *Bulletin of the New York Academy of Medicine* 47 (1971): 125–46.

Wilkins, David. *The Navajo Political Experience*. Lanham, MD: Rowman and Littlefield, 2003 [1999].

Womack, Craig. *Red on Red: Native American Literary Separatism*. Minneapolis: University of Minnesota Press, 1999.

Wong, Hertha. *Sending My Heart Back Across the Years: Tradition and Innovation in Native American Autobiography*. New York: Oxford, 1992.

Worcester, Donald. "Review of *Indeh: An Apache Odyssey.*" *Arizona and the West* 23 (1981): 177–78.

Wyman, Leland. *Blessingway*. Tucson: University of Arizona Press, 1975 [1970].

Yava, Albert. *Big Falling Snow: A Tewa-Hopi Indian's Life and Times and the History and Traditions of his People*, edited by Harold Courlander. Albuquerque: University of New Mexico Press, 1992 [1978].

INDEX

Note: Page numbers in italics indicate illustrations.

pan-Indian identity, xxvi–xxvii, xxx, 83–84. *See also* Indian identity
Papago Indians, 20, 144
Paquette, Peter, 180, 187–188, 190
Parezo, Susan, 322n1
Pawbinele, Irving, 37
Payestewa, Poli, 260
Paytiamo, James, 300n2
Perris Indian School, 61
Pfister, Joel, xv, 286n3, 319n19
Phoenix Indian School, 17–19, *18*, 61, 212; corporal punishment at, xxii–xxiii, 21–22, 129, 131; curriculum at, 20, 41; Denetsosie at, 240–241; jail at, 129; Mexican-Americans at, 131; military regimentation at, 19, 128–131; Nequatewa at, 18–22; Sekaquaptewa at, 117, 127–128; Trennert on, xiii–xiv, xxii
phratries, 306n22
piki (thin corn bread), 6, 99, 122, 124
Pimas, xxiii, 20, 130, 144, 191, 294n20
pneumonia, xx–xxi, 65, 181
Polacca Day School, 31–34, 108
Polaccaca, Tom, 34, 35
Polelonema, Otis, 315n5, 318n15, 319n23
pötskwani (moral law), 134
Powamu (Bean Dance), 74, 116, 161
Powamuy Society, 86
Pratt, Richard Henry, xv, *xvi*, 147, 265, 276; Betzinez on, 268, 270, 273–274; biographies on, xvi–xvii; Daklugie on, 277, 281–282; dismissal of, xix; educational level of, 286n3; memoir of, 285n1; slogans of, xvii, xxvi, 285n2

pregnancy, pre-marital, 9, 61, 125
Presbyterians, 146, 150, 155
Price, David, 322n2
Prohibition, 157
puberty (Kinaalda) ceremony, 186
public education, xiv; African Americans and, xiv; Hopi view of, xxv–xxvii, 4, 52, 81; Nequatewa on, 4, 11
Pueblo Indians, 49, 144; autobiographies of, 49, 300n2; Zia, 148, 149
Pueblo Rebellion (1680), 162

Qoyawayma, Fred, 87, 90–91, 93, 99, 102–103, 108–109; Christian views of, 90, 104; death of, 311n22; Voth and, 79, 87, 102
Qoyawayma, Polingaysi, 79–111, *105*, 192, 296n25; artwork of, 93, 308n6; Christian views of, 97–98, 106, 107, 109; cultural assimilation of, 81–84, 92–93, 98–103, 106–107, 110, 312n26; English skills of, 96, 97, 106, 109; family of, 80, 86–87, 92–93; Kabotie and, 315n3; marriage of, 87, 99, 107–108; mother of, 91–96, 99–104, 309n13, 311n22; names of, 85–88, 104; Talayesva and, 307n4; Tawakwaptiwa and, 82, 84, 92–95; teaching career of, 82, 97, 105–110; translations by, 292n9; Voth and, 86, 104
Queen, Ollie, 69–70

Rader, Benjamin, 323n10, 325n7
Rainy Mountain School, xxi, xxiv–xxvi
Randall, A. Frank, 332n10